D1499301

MAJOR POLITICAL EVENTS IN
INDO-CHINA 1945–1990

MAJOR POLITICAL EVENTS IN INDO-CHINA 1945–1990

D.J. Sagar

Facts On File
Oxford • New York

MAJOR POLITICAL EVENTS IN INDO-CHINA 1945–1990

Series editor: Thomas S. Arms
Copyright © 1991 by D.J. Sagar

Facts On File, Inc.   *or*   Facts On File Limited
460 Park Avenue South   Collins Street
New York NY 10016   Oxford OX4 1XJ
USA   UK

Library of Congress Cataloging-in-Publication Data
Sagar, Darren.
   Major political events in Indo-China, 1945–90 / Darren Sagar.
      p.   cm.
   Includes bibliographical references and index.
   ISBN 0-8160-2308-5
   1. Indochina—Politics and government—1945– —Chronology.
I. Title.
DS550.S34   1991
959.05'02'02—dc20   91–23682

A British CIP catalogue record for this book is available from
the British Library

Facts On File books are available at special discounts when
purchased in bulk quantities for businesses, associations,
institutions or sales promotions. Please contact the
Special Sales Department of our Oxford office on 0865
728399 or our New York office on 212/683–2244 (dial
800/322–8755 except in NY, AK or HI).

Jacket design by Richard Garratt
Typeset by Selectmove Ltd, London
Manufactured by the Maple-Vail Book Manufacturing Group

Printed in the United States of America

10 9 8 7 6 5 4 3 2 1

This book is printed on acid-free paper.

C O N T E N T S

FOREWORD

'It's a proud day for Americans,' President George Bush triumphantly proclaimed in the wake of the electrifying victory over Iraq, 'and by God, we've kicked the Vietnam syndrome once and for all.' Paradoxically, one of the reasons for that victory is that the American military had never developed a 'Vietnam syndrome'. Instead it had devoted itself to an intense study of what went wrong there – how a nation whose military was never defeated on the battlefield nevertheless ended up losing the war.

The lessons drawn from that unfortunate experience – the importance of public opinion, of war-fighting doctrine, of command and control, of setting clear-cut and attainable objectives – led to sweeping changes within the US military. The victory in the Gulf was literally forged from the defeat in Vietnam.

It is an introspection that still continues. In October 1990, for example, a major symposium on the Vietnam War was held at the US Air Force Academy in Colorado, drawing scholars from across the United States. And at West Point and Annapolis and at the military's war colleges and staff colleges the study of the Vietnam War is a mandatory part of the curriculum.

The introspection is not limited to the United States. At the same time as the conference at Colorado Springs was under way, Vietnamese Foreign Minister Nguyen Co Thach was in Washington, DC, seeking better ties with the United States. In Vietnam's case it was a matter of winning the war but losing the peace. Forty years of Communism, Thach said, had turned his nation into a 'charity house', and complained that reliance on Marxism-Leninism had been 'our greatest mistake during these past forty years' because such a state-dominated economy 'couldn't work'.

Such dissatisfaction is widespread. Dr Duong Quynh Hoa, one of the founders of the National Liberation Front, told CBS News reporter Morley Safer that she was 'thoroughly disillusioned' with what she called 'the second-rate people who had taken over'. Former Viet Cong Colonel Pham Xuan An said bitterly that 'All that talk about "liberation" twenty, thirty, forty years ago, all the plotting, and all the bodies, produced this, this impoverished, broken-down country led by a gang of cruel and paternalistic half-educated theorists.

In Southeast Asia, truths are not always what they seem. That's why this book is so important, for it puts events there in their historical context. Long before the United States existed, and long before the birth of Marx, Lenin, Ho Chi Minh or Pol Pot, the Khmers and the Vietnamese were at each other's throats.

'It is difficult to understand the conflict in Indo-China, and in particular the ongoing war in Cambodia,' the introduction states, 'without reference to the region's troubled history.' In its brief overview beginning with the first settlements in the first and second centuries and continuing through the colonial era, the two Indo-China wars to developments in the 1990s, this work provides not only that reference but much more as well.

A detailed chronology beginning in 1945, a biographical section on the principal actors, appendices, a glossary and a complete index and bibliography combine to make this a particularly useful reference work.

The potential 'Vietnam syndrome' may be licked, but the need to understand

Indo-China and its continuing influence on the world remains. This is especially true of the post-Vietnam War generation. 'Students have made it clear to me,' said junior high school teacher Bill McCloud in his opening remarks to the Air Force Academy Symposium, 'that they see [the Vietnam War] as a war no one wants to talk about. They seem to be saying that they know the war is the skeleton in America's family closet, and they think they are now old enough to be let in on the secret.'

A good place to begin is *Major Political Events in Indo-China 1945–1990.*

COLONEL HARRY G. SUMMERS, JNR

(A combat veteran of the Korean and Vietnam wars, Colonel Summers is the author of the award-winning *On Strategy: A Critical Analysis of the Vietnam War,* the *Vietnam War Almanac,* and is the editor of *Vietnam magazine.*)

INTRODUCTION

Despite the massive political, economic and social changes which have taken place in Asia over the last 45 years, war in Indo-China has endured. As the countdown for the twenty-first century – the 'Pacific Century' – begins, most of the countries of Southeast Asia are positioning themselves to take maximum economic advantage; Indo-China, meanwhile, is 11 years into its third war. Countless lives have been lost during the decades of conflict nourished by the global competition for influence in Asia waged by the major powers and inflamed by local antagonisms.

This new book attempts to set down a clear and concise chronological account of the significant events which have taken place in Indo-China since the end of World War II. Inevitably, the Second Indo-China War (the Vietnam War) is given prominent coverage; it was, after all, the longest revolutionary effort in modern times and one of the watersheds of twentieth-century history. However, the chronology also provides an account of internal political affairs in the three Indo-Chinese states, covering Communist Party developments, elections, major government changes and many other events and issues.

Indo-China

Indo-China is a confusing term. It denotes the convergence of Indian and Chinese cultural currents in mainland Southeast Asia, so that in a purely geographical sense Indo-China might comprise Burma, peninsular Malaysia, Singapore, Thailand, Cambodia, Laos and Vietnam. A major danger with the term is that it tends to obscure the fact that these countries have strongly-marked national cultural identities and are not simply appendages of the two great Asian civilizations. In the nineteenth century the French procured the term 'Indo-China' for their Southeast Asian colonies in Cambodia, Laos and Vietnam. As a political entity, the French Indo-Chinese Union ceased to exist after 1954, but the term 'Indo-China' has remained in common usage to describe the three countries.

Shaped like two rice sacks hanging from a pole, Indo-China is bordered to the north by China and Burma, to the west by Thailand and to the south and east by the South China Sea. Geographically, the region is dominated by the Mekong River which enters northwestern Laos and flows through Cambodia before emptying into the South China Sea through southern Vietnam. Laos is a long, narrow, land-locked country, sparsely populated by ethnic Lao and members of tribal groups such as the Hmong. Vietnam, a country of mountains, coastal plains and deltas, occupies the eastern part of Indo-China. The deltas of the Red River in the north and the Mekong in the south produce most of the country's rice. Cambodia lies to the south of Laos and to the west of Vietnam. It is a small country and its main topographical feature is the Tonle Sap ('the Great Lake'), a large inland sea surrounded by a broad plain. During the rainy season the overflow from the Mekong runs back up the connecting river to the Tonle Sap, reversing its course, and causing the lake to expand to several times its dry season size. As the water level of the Mekong falls, the process is reversed.

As a result of this annual phenomenon, the Tonle Sap is one of the world's richest sources of fresh-water fish.

A Brief History

It is difficult to understand the conflict in Indo-China, and in particular the ongoing war in Cambodia, without reference to the region's troubled history. What appear to be modern regional antagonisms invariably have deep and ancient roots. The first Indo-Chinese states were the Khmer and Cham kingdoms established in the first and second century in the lower Mekong regions of modern Cambodia and the southernmost parts of Vietnam. These states, and their successors, were heavily influenced by Indian culture and religion. In the ninth century a Khmer prince, Jayavarman II, established what is conventionally known as the Angkor empire, with its capital to the north of the Tonle Sap. Angkor reached its apogee under the rule of Suryavarman II, the patron of the remarkable temple complex of Angkor Wat, who consolidated Khmer rule over much of modern Cambodia, Thailand and Laos, while successfully taking his armies east into the kingdom of Champa and south to the Malay peninsula. Meanwhile, in the tenth century, a Vietnamese state (Dai Viet, based around the northern Red River delta) had finally attained an independence, of sorts, from China after a millennium of Han domination. The Vietnamese state was fundamentally different from its southern 'Indianized' counterparts. Chinese domination had left its mark so that the political and philosophical substructure of the Vietnamese state was heavily grounded in Chinese Confucianist ideology. Vietnam adopted the hierarchical system of Mandarin bureaucracy, which included a programme of civil-service examinations. This encouraged the development of a highly effective political system based on bureaucratic authority, rather than the traditional, feudal authority exercised by the *devarajas* (God-Kings) of the 'Indianized' states.

Suryavarman's expansive external ambitions seriously weakened the Angkor empire and during the twelfth century the resurgent Chams liberated the Champa kingdom from Khmer domination. In the fifteenth century Angkor finally fell to the Thai kingdom of Ayutthaya; the diminishing Khmer kingdom was re-established at Phnom Penh, the site of the current capital. The Lao, meanwhile, trace their ancestry back to the great southward migration of Tai people from southern China to lands on the periphery of the Angkor empire. In the mid-fourteenth century Fa Ngum, a Lao prince raised at Angkor, brought together a number of scattered Lao principalities into the powerful kingdom of Lan Xang ('a million elephants'), with its capital at Luang Prabang. The expansion of the Vietnamese state, prompted largely by population pressures in the Red River delta, occurred in several stages. Between the eleventh and fifteenth centuries the Vietnamese battled against the Chams, finally defeating them in the late fifteenth century. In the seventeenth century the Vietnamese drove further south, eventually capturing the Khmer-controlled Mekong River delta (known to the Khmers as Kampuchea Krom). Vietnam's move into the Mekong delta meant that Cambodia was effectively trapped between two powerful competing states (Vietnam and Thailand), each of which claimed progressively more and more Khmer land. So started Cambodia's long experience as a 'buffer state'. Vietnam's occupation of the Mekong delta had been slowed by a serious internal division which took the form of a long civil war between the royal households in Hanoi and Hue. By the nineteenth century the Hue Court had triumphed and it ruled over a united Vietnamese state; however, the period of unification was short-lived and was ended by the entry of the French in strength in the 1850s.

European contact with Indo-China began in the sixteenth century with the arrival of Portuguese adventurers and missionaries in Vietnam. French Catholic missionaries arrived in the seventeenth century and at the same time the French, Dutch, Portuguese and English all established trading centres. They all failed dismally, and only the French continued with their efforts, spurred on by the prospect of trade with China and English advances elsewhere in Southeast Asia. The persecution of French missionaries in Vietnam provided France with the pretext for armed intervention against the Vietnamese rulers, and in 1859 French troops captured Saigon. Eight years later France had completely conquered the whole of southern Vietnam, which became the French colony of Cochin-China. After a new war in 1883 France secured Hanoi and the following year they took over Annam (central Vietnam) and Tongkin (northern Vietnam) as protectorates. French rule over Cambodia evolved out of the European power's involvement in neighbouring Vietnam. Conquests in Cochin-China during the 1850s induced the French to expand northwesterly in order to secure the Mekong against potential aggressors, principally the Thais and the British. Therefore, in 1863 King Norodom was pressured into accepting a protectorate status for his kingdom. In 1884 Norodom was forced, literally at gunpoint, into signing an agreement transforming Cambodia into a full French colony. The Lao state was seriously weakened in the eighteenth century by warfare among rival princes, and, as in the case of Cambodia, both Vietnam and Thailand made large-scale territorial acquisitions. During the early nineteenth century pressure from Vietnam and Thailand on a divided and weak Laos increased, and the situation worsened in the 1870s when Chinese bandits started moving into the north in great numbers. France, meanwhile, having secured Vietnam, started to show an interest in Laos in the 1880s. Eventually, in 1893, the Thais ceded to the French all Lao territory to the east of the Mekong and by 1907, French control had been extended to include Sayaboury and parts of Champassak to the west of the river. Once in control, the French paid little attention to Laos: it was enough that the country acted as a buffer between Thailand and France's valuable holdings in Vietnam.

French rule in Vietnam was extremely authoritarian, much more so than British control of Burma or India. The French aimed primarily to develop a modern export centre in Vietnam based on rice and rubber. The impact of the money-making efforts of the French colonialists on the land system was incalculable, but needless to say the peasantry, who composed the vast majority of the population, were exploited mercilessly and were frequently displaced. The French did improve the infrastructure and built a number of high-level educational institutions, but these changes were of little benefit to most Vietnamese. Limited guerrilla resistance to French domination continued until the early twentieth century under the leadership of members of the imperial family and the mandarin class. Many underground nationalist organizations were founded in the 1920s, the main one being the Vietnamese Quoc Dan Dang (VNQDD), which modelled itself on Chiang Kai-shek's Kuomintang. In 1930 Ho Chi Minh succeeded in reconciling the small, disparate Communist groups in Vietnam and established the Indo-Chinese Communist Party (ICP). That year the VNQDD led a nationalist uprising in Tongkin which fuelled a peasant revolt under Communist leadership. Both rebellions were brutally repressed by the

French and the VNQDD was decimated. During the early 1930s thousands of ICP supporters and leaders were imprisoned by the French, although many were released during the late 1930s when the left-wing Popular Front governed France and her colonies. For many ICP members imprisonment was a crucial educational experience where they taught each other socialist theory and planned for the future. At the outbreak of World War II the ICP was by far the strongest anti-colonial movement in Vietnam.

Soon after the French took control in Cambodia in the 1860s, anti-colonial and anti-monarchical revolts started to erupt. Achar Sva and Achar Leak, both Buddhist monks, led unsuccessful rebellions in the mid-1860s and a decade later Si Votha, the king's half brother, led a revolt which was put down by the French army. Further rebellions broke out after Cambodia was transformed into a full French colony in the mid-1880s. However, unlike Vietnam, which underwent a period of social and political upheaval in the 1920s and 1930s, Cambodia remained a relatively calm backwater. The fact that the Khmer monarchy condoned French rule effectively ensured that the countryside remained peaceful. The Khmer peasantry laboured under terrible conditions, but they lived in awe of the king and, at this stage, would not rise against him. The ICP operated some cells in Cambodia during the 1930s, but ethnic Khmer involvement was extremely limited. However, during the late 1930s a moderate nationalist movement finally emerged in Cambodia. Led by Son Ngoc Thanh, members of the group (the predecessors of the Khmer Issaraks) travelled around the country's monasteries and temples discreetly disseminating anti-French propaganda.

As in Cambodia, the survival of the Lao royal family in Luang Prabang under French colonial rule contributed greatly towards the country's relative political stability. Initially, the French had planned to develop Laos rapidly, but the scheme faltered, largely because of the reluctance of the ethnic Lao to work within the colonial economic system. The French tried to compensate by bringing in large numbers of Vietnamese to work in trade and the bureaucracy. However, in the end the French did very little to develop Laos' resources and the greatest part of their efforts appeared to go into opium production in the northwest, the area known today as the Golden Triangle. The ethnic Lao accepted French rule with little overt concern and the main opposition came from the tribespeople of the northern and southern highlands. The Bolovens Plateau in southern Laos was a particular centre of anti-French activity. However, in the towns and cities apathy reigned and there was very little interest in nationalism or Marxism. Attempts by the ICP to recruit Lao members during the 1930s were largely fruitless.

The First Indo-China War

Japan occupied Indo-China in 1940, but decided to leave the French (pro-Vichy) colonial administration intact. The French acquiesced to Japanese demands to convert Indo-Chinese rice lands to produce industrial agricultural materials needed for the war effort: the result was a serious food shortage, particularly in northern Vietnam. Ho Chi Minh, meanwhile, had established the Viet Minh in China in 1941 as an alliance of Communist and nationalist organizations. Viet Minh units carried on a guerrilla resistance to the Japanese, with some assistance from the US military authorities, particularly the Office of Strategic Services (OSS), the precursor of the Central Intelligence Agency (CIA). At this time Ho, spurred on by the 1941 Atlantic Charter in which US President Roosevelt and

British Prime Minister Winston Churchill appeared to pledge self-government to the colonies, was apparently convinced that Washington would support full Vietnamese independence after the war.

The declining fortunes of the Axis Powers during 1944 fostered insecurity among the Japanese, and in March 1945 they suddenly interned the French in Indo-China and established puppet regimes in Cambodia, Vietnam and Laos. However, after the Japanese surrender in August 1945 the Viet Minh took control of Hanoi and Saigon, Vietnam's two main cities. Bao Dai, the malleable play-boy emperor of Annam and head of the 'puppet' government, quickly abdicated, and in early September the Democratic Republic of Vietnam (DRV) was established with Ho Chi Minh as president and the northern city of Hanoi as its capital. Under the terms of the Potsdam Agreement concluded by Roosevelt, Churchill and Stalin towards the end of World War II, Vietnam was temporarily divided into two zones, the north to be occupied by Chinese Kuomintang troops and the south by British forces. The Chinese, a massive ragged bunch intent on plundering as much of northern Vietnam as they possibly could, offered de facto recognition to Ho's government. The British, however, had secretly agreed to help the French to reoccupy their Indo-Chinese colonies and they proceeded to rearm French Legionnaires interred by the Japanese and allowed them to launch a coup in September against the Viet Minh authorities in Saigon. From this point onwards the French and the Viet Minh slid into war; full-scale fighting broke out in the North in late 1946, forcing Ho and his government to move out of Hanoi into the northern hills.

The US had no clear Indo-China policy at this stage. During 1945 Ho had written a series of letters to Roosevelt's successor, Truman, asking him to press for Vietnam to be accorded the same status as the Philippines for a period of tutelage pending independence. Truman failed to reply to Ho's letters. In 1947 the 'Truman Doctrine' was enunciated, calling for the containment of international Communism and asserting Washington's support of free peoples resisting domination by 'armed minorities' or external pressure. Nevertheless, the Truman administration was deeply critical of what Secretary of State General George Marshal called France's 'dangerously outmoded colonial outlook' in Indo-China. Truman, whilst supporting efforts to impede left-wing takeovers in Greece and Turkey, went on to reject French requests for arms and for planes and ships to transport French troops to Indo-China. This policy of equivocation was not abandoned until 1949 and the catalyst was the Communist revolution in China. The 'loss' of China was a staggering blow to the Truman administration's avowed policy of containment and the shock-waves reverberated in Washington throughout the 1950s and into the 1960s. Mao Zedong's success eventually spawned the 'domino theory' which, as formulated by the National Security Council in 1954, predicted that 'the loss of any single country' in Southeast Asia would ultimately lead to Communist control of Southeast Asia and then of India and Japan and would eventually endanger European security. In late 1949 Truman approved a National Security Council study which recommended that the US should help to meet 'threats of Communist aggression' by 'providing political, economic and military assistance where clearly needed' and that 'particular attention should be given to the problem of Indo-China'. A few months later the US recognized the Bao Dai regime, established by the French in Saigon in 1949 as an alternative to Ho's government. Shortly afterwards the US announced that it would provide economic and military aid to the French in Indo-China.

On the ground the First Indo-China War began as a succession of modest engagements between small Viet Minh units and French troops backed by hastily-created 'national' Indo-Chinese armies. In 1950 the Viet Minh forces, led by former history teacher Vo Nguyen Giap, raised the tempo. Having built up the Viet Minh ranks and logistical support units, Giap led his men into a series of main-force engagements in the north. In the south and centre, however, the war carried on as a series of guerrilla or small-force actions. Apart from his great skill as a military tactician, Giap's brilliance as a commander lay in his grasp of the central importance of political struggle as a major component of revolutionary warfare. He recognized that the masses, once fully mobilized, would constitute the ultimate weapon. Under Giap's direction the political struggle (*dau tranh*) encompassed a vast range of economic, psychological and ideological weapons aimed at strengthening the resolve of friendly civilians and troops whilst converting their enemy counterparts. In this way, Giap worked, successfully, to undermine the French position in Indo-China at every level. Ultimately, the French never really had a chance to win in Indo-China because they lacked the support of the Vietnamese people. One element of the Viet Minh's *dau tranh* was to prepare people for a long drawn out war. For the French, this was unacceptable; the public were simply not prepared to accept a protracted conflict, and so the military were pressurized by the politicians to inflict a quick and decisive defeat on the Viet Minh. With Giap conducting a classic guerrilla war until the early 1950s, the French generals found it impossible to engage the Viet Minh in the large-scale battles they required. It is interesting to note that when Giap finally decided to confront the French in main-force engagements in the early 1950s, the Viet Minh suffered some serious set-backs. However, Giap never allowed the French to take full advantage and, as domestic pressure increased in Paris, the military continued in their search for the one, elusive big confrontation. When the French finally had their way, they did so under Giap's terms and were roundly drubbed at Dien Bien Phu in 1954. With the battle raging at Dien Bien Phu the Eisenhower administration in Washington gave serious consideration to intervening militarily (perhaps with a series of tactical nuclear strikes on Vietnam and China) on behalf of the French. It appears that British reluctance to enter the fray alongside the US acted to halt Washington's entry into Indo-China at this stage. The French defeat at Dien Bien Phu destroyed the French will to remain in Indo-China. Nevertheless, in the south, the French managed to leave behind them the rickety framework of an anti-Viet Minh administration that could, given the necessary determination, be built upon and strengthened. The Geneva conference on Indo-China, which opened immediately after Dien Bien Phu in May 1954, provided some stability to the southern political framework. The Geneva Agreements temporarily divided Vietnam into two zones, the North being controlled by Ho Chi Minh's government and the South by the Bao Dai regime, but provided that the country should be reunited following the holding of nation-wide general elections in 1956. For the Viet Minh, Geneva was a lesson in big power politics. The Viet Minh representative, Pham Van Dong, was shocked that the Soviet Union and China were prepared to pressure him into accepting a divided Vietnam in order to decrease the risks of their involvement in a wider conflict.

The Geneva conference was also convened to consider the situation in Laos and Cambodia. There was, however, a sharp contrast between events in Vietnam during the post-World War II period and events in the two other Indo-Chinese states. After the Japanese surrender in 1945, the king of Laos, Sisavang Vong, had moved quickly to reaffirm France's protectorate role. The king's action provoked a group of nationalist princes (Souphanouvong and his half brothers Phetsarath and Souvanna Phouma) to rebel and proclaim a Free Lao (Lao Issara) Government. The French, supported by right-wing elements of the traditional Lao elite, had little trouble in regaining control of the country in 1946. The Lao Issara soon divided into a left-wing pro-Viet Minh faction, and a more traditional, conservative faction. The former group, led by 'Red Prince' Souphanouvong formed the Pathet Lao group in 1950. The conservative faction rallied to the king, and Souvanna Phouma formed a Royal Lao Government in Vientiane in 1951, two years before the French granted Laos independence. The Pathet Lao quickly developed very close links with the Viet Minh, an inevitable development given the importance of northeastern Laos to Giap's overall military strategy. But, although it was pro-Communist and pro-Vietnamese, the Pathet Lao was first and foremost a force for Lao nationalism and charges by some commentators that it was little more than a Viet Minh sub-division are exaggerated. Unlike Vietnam, Laos emerged intact from the Geneva conference although the Pathet Lao were granted temporary 'regroupment areas' in the northeastern provinces of Phong Saly and Sam Neua.

Cambodia, bordering on the relatively peaceful southern and central regions of Vietnam, did not play a major part in the First Indo-Chinese War. Viet Minh units operated in the east of the country, but not to the extent that they did in northeastern Laos. Consequently, the links between the Viet Minh and the indigenous Khmer Issarak nationalist guerrillas were not as close as the Viet Minh's links with the Pathet Lao. The Khmer Issarak were a disparate, if increasingly effective, bunch, strongly divided into leftists and rightists and pro- and anti-Viet Minh units. The Issaraks favouring links with the Viet Minh, led by Son Ngoc Minh, formed a small Communist Party in the early 1950s, after Ho Chi Minh's ICP had agreed to dissolve itself into three national parties for Vietnam, Cambodia and Laos (although a separate Lao party was not formed until the mid-1950s). Meanwhile, in the early 1950s another revolutionary trend was developing among Cambodian students studying in Paris, who had formed a Marxist Circle. Several members of this group, including Ieng Sary (the group's leader) and his friend Saloth Sar (Pol Pot), returned to Cambodia in 1953. Mainstream Cambodian politics during the period of the First Indo-China War were dominated by the young King Norodom Sihanouk. The Vichy French authorities had placed the 18-year-old Sihanouk on the Cambodian throne in 1941, apparently in the expectation that the prince's inexperience would allow him to be easily manipulated. A few weeks after the Japanese surrender in 1945 Sihanouk, like Sisavang Vong in Laos and Bao Dai in Vietnam, was pressured into proclaiming his country's 'independence'. The French returned to take control of Cambodia in late 1945, which they did with ease. A few minor concessions towards Cambodian independence were introduced, such as the abolition of its protectorate status and its introduction into the French Union as an 'autonomous state'. In 1947 a Constitution was introduced which permitted popular political activity. However, political stability was elusive and by 1950 Khmer Issarak rebels controlled large areas of the countryside. Sihanouk abolished the country's National Assembly and declared martial law in early 1953 before embarking on a 'Royal Crusade for Independence'. The French, facing an increasingly stiff military test in Vietnam and Laos and concerned about the possible drift away from the conservative throne to the Viet Minh-associated wing of the Issarak, conceded Cambodia's independence in November 1953. The 1954 Geneva conference was a triumph for Sihanouk, with his royal government being accorded international recognition as the sole legitimate authority within Cambodia.

The Second Indo-China War

Of the parties attending the Geneva conference, the US was the most hostile to the final outcome. In particular, Washington considered the restrictions placed on the introduction of US forces into Vietnam by the conference to be a disaster. US intent to pursue an aggressive policy in support of the Saigon regime became evident even before the conference had finished when the Eisenhower administration approved the dispatch to South Vietnam of a team of US agents, headed by Colonel Edward Lansdale, to conduct clandestine operations against the North. Lansdale's operations were small scale and had little serious effect on the North. However, Lansdale's introduction into the southern internal political system did have major ramifications. The colonel's overt support for the southern premier, Ngo Dinh Diem, firmed up Washington's wavering patronage for Diem. When Diem ousted Bao Dai in 1955, ostensibly through a referendum that was so obviously rigged that US officials were deeply embarrassed, and established himself as a virtual dictator in Saigon, he did so with full US support. Diem opposed absolutely the Geneva provision to hold all-Vietnam elections in 1956 despite, or more likely because of, pressure from the North to go ahead with the polling. The North was convinced, probably correctly, that the level of support for the Viet Minh in the South was great enough to ensure a victory for the Communist Party in the event of an election. The US certainly condoned Diem's refusal to go ahead with the elections, although Washington has always denied that it pushed Diem to pursue such a policy.

Why did the Second Indo-China War, the Vietnam War, start? The official view adopted by Saigon and Washington, namely that the conflict was imposed on the South by northern aggression, does not stand up to close scrutiny. It seems more likely that the roots of the southern rebellion lie in Diem's oppressive and authoritarian policies and the endemic corruption within Saigon's ruling circles. Even before he had formally ousted Bao Dai in 1955, Diem had launched a draconian anti-Communist witch-hunt which resulted in as many as 100,000 people being locked up in detention centres. Only a small percentage of those detained were actual Viet Minh (a maximum of 10,000 Viet Minh cadres had remained in the South after Geneva), so that the remainder were a collection of potential trouble-makers from various groups. On one level Diem's policies succeeded in striking a serious blow to the genuine Viet Minh 'stay-behind cadres'. But his failure to ensure proper discrimination went some way towards ensuring popular support for a revolt. The US and South Vietnamese charges of North Vietnamese aggression must have been particularly galling for the southern cadres, most of whom were appalled at the very lack of northern support for armed struggle. Following Geneva, the North's primary concern had been to build an effective economic base. With substantial Chinese and Soviet help, the Communist Party initiated an ambitious industrialization programme. Early in 1957 southerner Le Duan had been a lone voice urging his politburo colleagues of the necessity to support armed struggle against Diem. The views of northerners such as Truong Chinh held sway, with their emphasis on 'political struggle' in the South. It was not until early 1959, when Diem intensified his system of repression, that the politburo agreed to support limited armed resistance in the South, to go hand-in-hand with the continued political struggle. Infiltration from the North began (usually along the 'Ho Chi Minh Trail' running through Laos), although until 1964 the infiltrators were almost all southerners who had travelled to the North after Geneva.

Early in 1960 the southern guerrillas launched a major wave of assassinations and ambushes aimed at officials of the Saigon regime. The guerrilla tactics seriously diminished the authority of the Diem regime in many rural areas. In late 1960 the National Liberation Front (NLF) was formed to lead the southern struggle. The NLF was much more than the Communist Party front it is sometimes portrayed as, although the party undoubtedly had great influence on the organization. The strength of the NLF, derogatively dubbed the Viet Cong by Saigon and Washington, lay in its ability to foster a close relationship with the southern peasantry. This allowed guerrilla fighters to mingle with the villagers during the day, and then carry out operations in the evening. So, during the first few years of the 1960s the war was a classic guerrilla struggle, with small NLF units operating against relatively soft targets, and being hounded in turn by poorly-trained and poorly-motivated South Vietnamese army (ARVN) troops.

As the scale of the southern rebellion increased in the early 1960s the attitude of the US government towards the conflict altered. In May 1961 the recently-elected US president, John Kennedy, approved a programme of unconventional warfare against North Vietnam and Pathet Lao forces in Laos along with the dispatch of small numbers of special forces (Green Berets) troops to South Vietnam. However, for Kennedy, the principal foreign policy problem during his first months in office was Laos rather than Vietnam. In the aftermath of the Geneva conference the Pathet Lao had boycotted elections held in 1955. Subsequent negotiations between Souvanna Phouma and his half brother and Pathet Lao leader, Souphanouvong, resulted in the formation, in late 1957, of a broad-based coalition government. The coalition soon collapsed in favour of a staunchly anti-Communist regime after the US withdrew all aid to Laos. By December 1960 the country was divided, with a 'neutralist', regime led by Souvanna Phouma based in the Plain of Jars and a US-backed 'rightist' regime in Vientiane under the control of 'strongman' General Phoumi Nosavan. The Pathet Lao, often fighting alongside North Vietnamese troops, took advantage of the confusion to extend the areas under their control. By early 1961 General Phoumi's forces were suffering defeat at the hands of the Pathet Lao and neutralist forces. Kennedy, who had inherited Eisenhower's commitment to back the Lao right, came under internal pressure to intervene on Phoumi's behalf, and show the level of US commitment to its anti-Communist clients in Asia. Coming so soon after a US-sponsored invasion of Cuba by anti-Castro exiles was defeated at the Bay of Pigs, Kennedy decided against taking a stand in Laos and sought a political compromise instead. However, another attempt to establish a coalition regime in Laos in 1962 collapsed within months and the fighting between the right and left intensified. President Kennedy's decision to refrain from taking military action in Laos meant that he became more or less compelled to show strength in Vietnam as his only available means of reassuring the US' Asian allies and proving to Moscow that the US would not stand by and allow its dominoes to fall. So, in late 1961, after long and detailed discussions in Washington, Kennedy approved the commitment of US units 'of modest size' for the 'direct support' of ARVN's efforts. The number of US troops in South Vietnam rose from under 1,000 in late 1961 to over 16,000 at the time of Kennedy's assassination in November 1963. The number killed or injured in combat also rose, from under 20 in 1961 to almost 500 in 1963. However, most US effort during this period was aimed at improving ARVN's performance.

During 1962 official US assessments of the progress of the war were extremely optimistic, to the extent that in the middle of the year Defence Secretary Robert McNamara ordered planning to begin for a total pull-out of US forces. But, during 1963 the political situation in South Vietnam deteriorated so profoundly that all planning for a pull-out had to be shelved. A conflict pitting the Catholic Diem and his entourage (including his increasingly powerful brother, Ngo Dinh Nhu) against the savagely persecuted Buddhist community turned large sections of the population against the government. Despite pressure from the US to make concessions to the Buddhists, Diem and Nhu acted to suppress all demonstrations and arrested large numbers of monks and nuns. Diem's brutality and his inability to control his brother led the Kennedy administration to conclude that his continuation as president could only be detrimental in the fight against the NLF. The US encouraged senior ARVN officers to topple Diem and in November 1963 he and his brother were deposed and shot. A prolonged period of political instability followed with 12 changes of government occurring before the establishment of a military regime in February 1965 under General Nguyen Van Thieu and Air Vice-Marshal Nguyen Cao Ky.

US involvement in Indo-China entered a new phase in 1964 under the command of Kennedy's successor, Lyndon Johnson. The Johnson years came to be known as the years of escalation. Early in 1964 the president approved a programme of clandestine military operations against North Vietnam, known as Operation Plan 34A. The operations went far beyond the boy-scout tricks employed by Lansdale in the 1950s and included commando raids and naval bombardment of coastal installations. Another aspect of the operation was the launching of air operations over the 'Ho Chi Minh Trail' in Laos; the trail meanwhile was being improved and expanded. In August, the US Congress passed the Tongkin Gulf Resolution which authorized Johnson to 'repel any armed attack against the forces of the United States and to prevent further aggression'. The resolution was passed after North Vietnamese patrol boats had allegedly attacked US vessels patrolling in the Gulf of Tongkin. After the attack, the US launched reprisal air raids on North Vietnamese naval bases. Unbeknown to the people of the US the attacks on the warships were the direct result of previous US and South Vietnamese assaults on North Vietnamese targets under the clandestine Plan 34A programme. The resolution, which was approved with virtually no domestic criticism, served as the legal basis for Johnson's escalation of what became in effect an undeclared war against North Vietnam.

The southern insurgency flourished during 1964, with battalion-strength NLF units attacking their demoralized ARVN counterparts. A number of provincial capitals were seized and temporarily held, whilst US intelligence reports towards the end of the year indicated that NVA regiments had entered, or were about to enter, the fray. A major NLF attack on US troops at the Bien Hoa air base north of Saigon in November prompted Johnson to organize a working group to draw up options for direct action against North Vietnam; in December the US began systematic bombing of the 'Ho Chi Minh Trail'. At the same time pressure was put on the Saigon government to introduce reforms to undermine the increasingly powerful NLF. It was a fruitless task; General Khanh, Saigon's strongman at the time, responded to the US pressure by rounding up his opponents. In these circumstances the US abandoned attempts to force through political reforms in Saigon and decided to proceed with a northern bombing campaign. By this stage the protection of the South Vietnamese people was hardly the issue; the principal US concern was to avoid a humiliating defeat which would damage Washington's reputation as a guarantor. In March 1965 the Rolling Thunder bombing campaign against North Vietnam started and continued with occasional breaks, until late 1968; during the same month US ground combat troops were introduced into South Vietnam for the first time. The bombing campaign was an attempt to soften up the Hanoi government and force it to accept a negotiated settlement which would be favourable to the US. It soon became obvious that the attacks were not having the desired effect, but the US could not halt Rolling Thunder because to have done so would have been seen as a sign of weakness.

As the Vietnam War started in earnest in 1965, the roots of the US' future humiliation were already exposed. Despite endless optimistic briefings by US officials, the situation in the South was critical. Because the NLF had a substantial rural support base it was often impossible to distinguish enemy fighters from peasants. The US-sponsored 'Pacification' programme aimed at eliminating guerrilla contact with villages and hamlets was a heavy-handed failure which probably increased support for the NLF. Those southern peasants who did not actually support the NLF certainly had very little faith in the bickering military cliques vying for power, and illicit riches, in Saigon. In the cities, Buddhist and student pressure for a negotiated settlement and the establishment of a neutralist regime was increasing and in the armed forces defeatism was rife. Meanwhile, the war on the ground was settling into a routine which inevitably favoured the NLF and the NVA. The two sides in the conflict were operating under entirely different rules of engagement. For the ARVN and US forces the war was localized in that soldiers were forbidden from pursuing the enemy into Laos, Cambodia or across the Demilitarized Zone (DMZ) into North Vietnam. Yet, the NLF and the NVA had sanctuaries and logistics bases in all of these areas. In order to have had a chance of winning the ground battle the US/ARVN force would have had to widen the war to take in the whole of Indo-China. However, if the war had been broadened it would have led to a much greater confrontation, possibly involving China and the Soviet Union.

One theory commonly propounded on the Vietnam War holds that the US military were hampered by US politicians wary of taking hard unpalatable decisions, and that if the generals had been given a free hand then the outcome of the conflict would have been entirely different. However, the response of the US generals to the conflict suggests that they, along with most of the politicians, consistently underrated the ability of the NLF and the NVA and consistently overrated the advantages of their own superior military hardware. During the early stages of the war, General Westmoreland, the US commander in Vietnam, had no clear idea of how many troops he required, which explains his 'strategy' of asking for increased deployments periodically. Every time Westmoreland received more troops, it was still never enough because Hanoi, and the NLF, were always able to mobilize fresh forces quickly. Divisions within the Johnson administration over the conduct of the war were evident at the onset of escalation. The first main administration dissenter was Under Secretary of State George

Ball who advocated seeking a compromise settlement through a multi-national conference as early as June 1965. By early 1966 the obvious ineffectiveness of Rolling Thunder and the US military's mounting demands for increased troop levels created increasing doubts among other senior officials. By late 1966 the 'doves' had gained their biggest convert, Defence Secretary Robert McNamara, who was pressing for an end to Rolling Thunder and also opposed General Westmoreland's requests for more troops.

The 1968 Tet offensive was the single most important event in the Vietnam War. During the Tet (lunar new year) holiday in early 1968 the NLF launched a massive offensive in the South, attacking Saigon, Hue and many other towns and military installations. The NLF aimed to deliver a crippling blow to General Nguyen Van Thieu's Saigon regime by engendering a mass uprising and decimating the southern army. In the event the NLF failed in its military aims, suffering such staggering losses that the front never fully recovered and as a consequence became increasingly dependent on North Vietnamese soldiers. Nevertheless, on a political level the offensive was a major success, effectively forcing the Johnson administration to reconsider its Vietnam policy. The offensive caught President Johnson completely unawares and his shock was particularly severe because he had discounted negative appraisals of US policy put forward by his administration's 'doves' and had relied instead on General Westmoreland's optimistic assessments of the conflict. Johnson was not alone in being shocked by images on television of US Marines battling with NLF guerrillas in the US embassy compound in Saigon; the US public were deeply depressed by what appeared to be a radical turnaround in the fortunes of the NLF. For months before Tet US spokespersons had been issuing highly optimistic public statements about the situation in Vietnam, implying that the Communist forces were in terminal decline. But, the public reasoned, if the NLF had been as weak as Westmoreland and others had told them, then they certainly could not have launched such a significant and audacious offensive, regardless of its final outcome. In the aftermath of the offensive Westmoreland pushed for a major increase in US troop numbers in Vietnam, insisting that Tet had been a great US victory and that with the necessary number of soldiers the weakened Communists could now be beaten. Johnson came under great pressure from senior figures within, and outside, his administration to refuse the general's request. A key opponent of further escalation was Clark Clifford, who had replaced McNamara as defence secretary shortly after Tet. Public pressure on Johnson also began to mount as speculation grew that he was seriously considering further escalation. For instance, in mid-March Senator Eugene McCarthy, campaigning on an anti-war platform, was only narrowly defeated by Johnson in the Democratic presidential primary in New Hampshire. Eventually, Johnson consulted with a group of his most senior advisers (the so-called 'wise men') who recommended that he halt Rolling Thunder and begin working towards a negotiated settlement. Johnson had little choice but to take their advice, so in late March he announced that only an extra 13,500 troops would be sent to Vietnam (as opposed to the 200,000 requested by Westmoreland) and he also announced a partial cessation of the Rolling Thunder raids. The partial bombing halt opened the way for talks between Washington and Hanoi which eventually got under way in Paris in mid-1968. In October Johnson ordered a complete halt to the Rolling Thunder aerial assault on the North, claiming that an 'understanding' had been reached at the Paris talks. Nevertheless, the US bombers continued to operate south of the seventeenth parallel dividing North and South Vietnam, and air attacks over Laos were greatly intensified.

Johnson, who had the air of a defeated man about him after the Tet debacle, was replaced as president by Richard Nixon in early 1969 and the Vietnam War entered a new phase. Nixon and his powerful national security adviser, Henry Kissinger, decided to push ahead with the policies Johnson had been forced to accept towards the end of his presidency. The term 'Vietnamization' (a programme supposedly to build up the strength of the ARVN) was coined to disguise what was in effect a policy of withdrawal. The policy was activated in mid-1969 when Nixon announced details of the first US troop pull-out. At the time of the announcement, General Creighton Abrams, Westmoreland's successor, had over half-a-million Americans under his control in Vietnam. Nixon ensured that 'Vietnamization' was accompanied by enlarged peace talks in which representatives from the Saigon regime and the NLF (which was reconstituted in mid-1969 as the Provisional Revolutionary Government of South Vietnam – PRG) were included. Meanwhile, in early 1970 more substantive negotiations opened in secret between Kissinger and a leading power in the Hanoi regime, Le Duc Tho.

Paradoxically, US disengagement from Vietnam led to an intensification and a widening of the conflict. In March 1969, for instance, Nixon approved a series of limited, secret bombing raids against NVA and NLF sanctuaries in eastern Cambodia. At the time of the raids the Nixon administration claimed to be scrupulously respecting Cambodian neutrality. As with Rolling Thunder, once the bombing had started it acquired its own momentum and it stretched on, secretly, for 14 months, killing untold numbers of Cambodian civilians without seriously disrupting the enemy sanctuaries. Throughout the 1960s, Cambodia, like Laos, was a sideshow to the greater conflict under way in Vietnam. Of the Indo-Chinese leaders, Norodom Sihanouk had gained the most from the Geneva conference and he used this success as a base from which to gain control of the country's internal political machinery. Once firmly in charge he set about navigating a path through the Vietnam War, adopting the pursuit of neutrality as the key to his nation's survival. He possessed a quirky diplomatic style which sometimes verged on genius and for the early part of the war he managed to keep Cambodia out of the main arena of battle. With the onset of escalation under Johnson he decided to cut away from the US and enter into closer relations with China and North Vietnam. NVA and NLF forces were allowed to establish sanctuaries in Cambodia's eastern provinces. The bases became of vital strategic importance to the Vietnamese revolutionary struggle after the decimation of the NLF during the 1968 Tet offensive. In return for allowing the establishment of the sanctuaries, Beijing and Hanoi agreed to pressure the internal Khmer Communists (the Khmers Rouges) to refrain from launching their own internal rebellion. The Khmers Rouges, already fiercely independent from the Vietnamese Communists, refused to go along with the deal for very long and in early 1968 they launched their own Tet, taking control of large chunks of the western Cambodian countryside. The uprising placed added pressure on Sihanouk who was already troubled by Cambodia's serious economic problems. His control over the levers of power weakened whilst the pro-US right wing, led by Lon Nol, increased in strength. Eventually, in March 1970, Lon Nol, with the help of Sihanouk's cousin, Sirik Matak, successfully moved against the prince and established a new right-wing regime. Sihanouk, meanwhile, ever the pragmatist, moved to Beijing where he established a united front with his former enemies, the Khmers Rouges. The Lon Nol-Sirik Matak coup shattered the illusion of Cambodian neutrality and allowed the full force of the Vietnam War to shift west. The conflict literally shifted west in April and May 1970 when Nixon ordered a massive US/ARVN force into Cambodia. The troops were sent into Cambodia to destroy the main NLF/NVA bases, the very same bases which the US had been secretly pounding from the air since early 1969. The invasion possibly neutralized a number of sanctuaries and some equipment was captured, but for the most part the operation was a failure. The NVA/NLF units simply avoided confrontation, shifting deeper into the Cambodian interior. Meanwhile, the brutality of the invading forces towards the Khmer civilians caught up in the assault only served to swell the Khmer Rouge ranks. In the US the invasion caused a vast outcry of protest during which four students were shot dead by the National Guard in Ohio.

In early 1971 ARVN forces moved into Laos in an attempt to cut the 'Ho Chi Minh Trail'. US forces had been prohibited by Congress from entering Laos or Cambodia after the 1970 push into Khmer territory, so US troops were restricted to supplying air, artillery and logistical support. Unlike the Cambodian adventure, the NVA stood their ground in Laos and a major battle ensued, with both sides suffering heavy casualties. ARVN units were eventually forced to retreat in disarray after failing to cut any of the supply lines. The invasion of Laos by South Vietnam was an indication of just how central Laos had become to the Vietnamese conflict. The US had started to carry out clandestine bombing missions into Laos in 1964 in an attempt to sever supply lines. The raids had also been carried out in an attempt to tie down the Pathet Lao and NVA forces in northern Laos, thereby preserving Souvanna Phouma's pro-Western 'neutralist' regime in Vientiane. The bombing reached saturation levels in the late 1960s, forcing the Pathet Lao leadership to live underground in limestone caves in northeastern Laos. The bombing was low profile and relentless; more tonnage of bombs were dropped on Laos during the 1960s than were dropped by US aircraft during the whole of World War II. Not once was the 'Ho Chi Minh Trail' rendered non-operational. As always, the effect on the civilian population was immense and tragic, with perhaps a quarter of the country's population being uprooted by the US B-52 bombers.

In late 1971 the US again started to carry out bombing raids over North Vietnam, claiming that the attacks were necessary to protect US servicemen (i.e. pilots flying alongside the bombers in reconnaissance aircraft). Further air attacks were launched in March 1972 after NVA troops, with minimal NLF support, pushed over the DMZ in a large-scale operation against ARVN troops and a US force reduced to under 100,000. ARVN, with the help of major US air support, managed to halt the NVA, but only at the expense of diverting men from NLF strongholds, thereby allowing the southern revolutionaries to regain some of their lost strength. By late 1972 the Kissinger-Le Duc Tho negotiations were reaching a critical phase with an agreement of sorts almost in place. In what appeared to be a final act of vengeance, the US launched a last, massive bombing raid on Hanoi and Haiphong over Christmas, killing large numbers of civilians. Early the next year the Paris Agreements were finally signed by the US, the PRG and the North and South Vietnamese governments. Despite the length and legalistic complexity of the agreements, they altered very little and simply provided for the US to withdraw all their remaining troops and take home their

POWs. Nevertheless, Nixon proclaimed that the agreements provided for 'peace with honour', a sentiment not shared by the South Vietnamese leader Nguyen Van Thieu who regarded the settlement as a brutal betrayal. Both Nixon and Thieu knew that 'Vietnamization' had been a fraud, a conceptual cloak that allowed the US out of the Vietnamese quagmire. On the ground 'Vietnamization' had done very little to improve the morale or fighting ability of the southern soldiers, who were now expected to fight on alone against an enemy which had defeated the army of the most powerful country in the world. The final irony of the 'Vietnamization' programme was that it served to unite the Saigon and Hanoi regimes on at least one issue – complete distrust of the US.

For the US the Paris Agreements meant that the war was finally over, save for a final round of bombing over Cambodia. An undeclared war, it had nevertheless been the longest ever fought by US troops and the first in which they had been conspicuously defeated. Over 50,000 Americans died in the fighting (compared with over 1 million Vietnamese) and many more still shoulder enormous psychological scars, as do thousands more Vietnamese, Lao and Cambodian civilians and soldiers. The war had a profound effect on US politics and society. During the 1960s the war was a major divisive issue which served to radicalize a large section of society, mainly young people, but also including many other groups and individuals. Politically, the war placed great pressures on the constitutional system of checks and balances. As the 1971 *Pentagon Papers* showed, all the post-World War II administrations had used a high level of deception in the pursuance of goals in Indo-China. Under Nixon the level of deception reached fresh heights with the secret bombing of Cambodia. The roots of the US public's strong reaction to Watergate rested in part in the distrust of government which had been generated by Nixon and Kissinger's conduct of the war. The US defeat in Vietnam had a major impact on foreign policy, so that both Presidents Ford and Carter were deeply reluctant to embroil themselves in another Vietnam (Angola, Iran or Afghanistan?). An activist foreign policy only re-emerged under Reagan in the 1980s, and this after Vietnam had been officially 're-evaluated' as a just war, badly managed.

As might have been expected, soon after the Paris Agreements were signed ending US involvement in Vietnam, a parallel agreement was signed in Laos, imposing a cease-fire and providing for a Pathet Lao-Royal Lao government coalition. After 14 months of negotiations, during which the Pathet Lao consolidated their position, the third, and final, Lao coalition was established. Souphanouvong returned to Vientiane from the Pathet Lao's northeastern base to set about forging a future for Laos alongside his half brother, Souvanna Phouma. In Cambodia, meanwhile, the signing of the Vietnamese and Lao agreements had little effect on the raging civil war. The Khmers Rouges rejected attempts to organize peace talks with Lon Nol, insisting instead that the fight would continue. The Khmers Rouges had greatly extended their control over Cambodia during 1972 so that they controlled some 80 per cent of the area of the country and half the population. Their decision not to take the Lao path of victory by negotiation motivated the US to embark on one last major bombing spree before departing from Indo-China. Between February and August 1973 US B-52s dropped over a quarter-of-a-million tons of bombs over the country. The assault ended, and with it US operations in Indo-China, in mid-August, after Congress blocked the use of funds to continue the air war. The bombing most likely prevented the Khmers Rouges from taking control of Cambodia during 1973, but it also served to further brutalize the young Cambodian revolutionaries. Is it any wonder that the Cambodians who took control of the country in 1975 had a ruthless and paranoid attitude towards potential enemies given the horrors they had suffered at the hands of the 'civilized' world?

For the Vietnamese, the Paris Agreements had little effect on the war. Although all the various parties signed a cease-fire, fighting did not halt for even one day. During 1973 the NVA and NLF troops kept low and it was the ARVN units that were the more aggressive force. From mid-1974, however, the NVA adopted an increasingly offensive strategy, encouraged in part by the collapse of the Nixon administration over the Watergate scandal. However, Hanoi completely underestimated the level of decay within the ARVN ranks so that when the NVA launched a major offensive in early 1975, ARVN's virtual collapse took them by surprise. The North Vietnamese had been planning to capture Saigon in late 1976 or early 1977, but by March 1975 the southern defences had collapsed and the city was there for the taking. In late April the NVA tanks rolled into Saigon, and the US and their richer South Vietnamese supporters made an ignominious retreat. Although it was not officially reunified until 1976, the whole of Vietnam was, as of 30 April 1975, under the effective control of the Communist Party of Vietnam (CPV). A fortnight earlier, the Khmers Rouges had carried out its final victorious assault on Phnom Penh; by the time Saigon was liberated, Phnom Penh had been emptied, the people having been herded into the countryside to work the land. In the wake of the Communist victories in Vietnam and Cambodia, the Pathet Lao gradually, and peacefully, gained total control of the coalition administration. A Communist regime was formally established in Vientiane in December 1975.

The Third Indo-China War

The sight of victorious Communist forces marching through the avenues of Saigon and Phnom Penh in early 1975 raised expectations in the West of peace in Indo-China after three decades of war. This perception ignored the fact that the conquering forces represented two nations on the verge of war, utterly divided ideologically and historically.

During the 1960s Hanoi's influence within the Cambodian Communist movement waned as older Viet Minh-trained cadres were replaced by younger radical Communists rooted in the Paris Marxist Circle group of the early 1950s. This group included Saloth Sar (Pol Pot), Ieng Sary, Son Sen, Nuon Chea, Koy Thoun and the two sisters, Khieu Thirith (Sary's wife) and Khieu Ponnary (Sar's wife). By 1965 Cambodia had begun to play a vital part in the Vietnam War, with North Vietnamese and NLF fighters using the eastern provinces as a launching pad for attacks against the ARVN and US forces. In 1967, however, the Cambodian Communists (dubbed Khmers Rouges by Prince Sihanouk) launched a purely Khmer uprising against the Phnom Penh government, in opposition to North Vietnam's wishes. Hanoi appealed to the Khmers Rouges to suspend their war against Sihanouk (who, at this stage, was turning a blind eye to the NVA/NLF sanctuaries in eastern Cambodia) for the good of the wider Indo-Chinese struggle. It was a directive which bred deep resentment amongst the Khmers Rouges and served to intensify simmering ultra-nationalist, anti-Vietnamese tendencies within the movement. After Sihanouk's deposition in 1970 a large group of older Khmer Communists returned to Cambodia from exile in Vietnam; they were progressively liquidated by the Khmer Rouge. At the same time NVA and

NLF troops operating in the eastern Cambodian sanctuaries began to be treated with increasing suspicion by the Khmer Rouge commanders, and attacks were occasionally launched against them. Border clashes, instigated almost entirely by Cambodia, began immediately after the fall of Phnom Penh and Saigon in April 1975. As the secretive Khmer Rouge leadership churned out ever-more aggressive and racist anti-Vietnamese propaganda, they openly expounded their expansionist designs, reflecting on the glories of the Angkor epoch and promising to 'liberate' the ethnic Khmers of Vietnam's Mekong delta region. In late 1977 the border situation deteriorated seriously after Khmer Rouge troops invaded the Vietnamese province of Nay Ninh, massacring hundreds of civilians, and provoking the first major Vietnamese counteroffensive. By mid-1978 Pol Pot had managed to purge all of his potentially pro-Vietnamese opponents, dispelling any hopes in Hanoi that their 'western problem' might be solved by an internal uprising. Not surprisingly, during this period relations between Vietnam and Pol Pot's patrons in Beijing deteriorated sharply. The Soviet Union responded by adopting a strongly pro-Vietnamese stance, accusing China of full responsibility for the conflict.

The seriousness of the crisis along the Cambodian-Vietnamese border during the mid- to late-1970s went largely unrecognized in the West, as did the internal situation in Cambodia. Once they had taken power in 1975 the Khmer Rouge government severed the country's links with the outside world (with the exception of their patrons in Beijing) and then embarked with gruesome relish on a pre-planned economic and social experiment, based, to a large extent, on the Chinese 'Great Leap Forward' of the late 1950s. The Khmer Rouge leadership estimated that the vast majority of urban dwellers were unproductive and that their labour served only the elite. Hence, they advocated that they should be set to work in productive sectors of the economy, particularly agriculture. Once in control the policy was put into effect: the cities were emptied and the urban populace were placed in agricultural co-operatives to work the land. Conditions in the co-operatives varied widely, but the most primitive ones were reserved for the evacuees; 'base' people (i.e. peasants who had lived under Khmer Rouge control before 1975) were often allowed to cultivate private plots of land and keep livestock. Traditional Khmer family life was not permitted in the co-operatives and education tended to be solely political. The Khmer Rouge experiment failed badly and many hundreds of thousands of people died from brutal treatment, starvation and disease. Much of the brutality stemmed from an internal power struggle that was under way for most of the Khmer Rouge period of rule. The leadership was deeply divided, and it was not until 1978 that Pol Pot and Ieng Sary's ultra-nationalist faction attained full control of the revolution. In the process, military commanders allied with this faction liquidated almost all opposing elements within the ruling elite. Opponents were invariably accused of harbouring pro-Vietnamese sentiments. Villages and communes under the control of Pol Pot's opponents, most notably in the east of the country, were subjected to the most ferocious purges.

By mid-1978 all pro-Vietnamese internal opposition to Pol Pot had been extinguished and Hanoi, reluctantly, started to draw up invasion plans. After first organizing anti-Pol Pot refugees from eastern Cambodia into a United Front, crack Vietnamese troops swept into Cambodia in late December 1978. Pol Pot's forces put up little resistance and were quickly driven towards the Thai border. A People's Republic of Kampuchea (PRK) was quickly proclaimed by members of the United Front and other (Hanoi-based) Khmer exiles. Vietnam's invasion of Cambodia was attacked by China (who launched a brief, bungled raid of their own into northern Vietnam) and the US who both continued to support Pol Pot from his base on the Thai border. Despite these attacks from Beijing and Washington there is strong evidence that the Vietnamese invasion was a legitimate act of self-defence and that Vietnam had previously responded to the brutal Khmer Rouge border assaults with remarkable restraint. As for the PRK government's reliance on Vietnamese support for its survival, the level of dependence was similar to that achieved by Lon Nol with relation to the US, and the Khmer Rouge regime with relation to China. Nevertheless, pressure from China, the US and Association of Southeast Asian Nations (ASEAN) ensured that Pol Pot's regime retained its UN seat. However, international unease over Pol Pot's dreadful human-rights record led the West to try to camouflage the Khmers Rouges within a coalition. So, in 1982 Prince Sihanouk and Son Sann were both pushed reluctantly into joining the Khmers Rouges in the Coalition Government of Democratic Kampuchea (CGDK). On the ground the crack, battle-hardened Vietnamese forces overwhelmed the rebel forces and during the 1984–5 dry season CGDK guerrillas based along the Thai border were easily routed. By this time, the PRK regime, with the help of Vietnam and the Soviet Union, had firmly established itself in Phnom Penh. Negotiations between the PRK and the CGDK made little headway until the late 1980s when improved Sino-Soviet relations allowed substantive negotiations to take place.

Vietnam withdrew the last of its troops from Cambodia in September 1989, a move long sought by the West; the Khmers Rouges responded by launching a heavy and prolonged offensive. Increased activity on the battlefield during 1990 was accompanied by heightened diplomatic activity.

In July, 15 years after the end of the Vietnam War, US President George Bush initiated a dialogue with Vietnam over Cambodia. It was not a dialogue entered into through choice: Bush was pushed into it by a Congress made nervous over reports coming out of Cambodia suggesting that the Khmer Rouge forces, supported by the US and the West, were on the verge of a military victory. If, the US reasoning went, Pol Pot's men took Phnom Penh and carried on where they left off in 1978 then the US would be deeply implicated in a fresh Asian holocaust.

A month after the US volte-face on Indo-China, the five permanent members of the UN Security Council announced that they had finally worked out a 'framework document' for a solution to the Cambodian civil war. The plan called for the establishment of an all-faction Supreme National Council (SNC) to occupy Cambodia's UN seat. The SNC would turn over most of its powers to the UN until a new Cambodian government was elected. The CGDK and the Phnom Penh government met in Jakarta in September and approved the UN 'framework document'. However, shortly afterwards the first meeting of the newly-formed SNC (comprising six members of the Phnom Penh government and six CGDK members) broke up in disarray after the members had failed to reach agreement on any issue. The SNC convened again in December, but little progress was made towards a final agreement. Meanwhile, the attention of the UN Security Council had shifted away from Cambodia to the escalating conflict in the Middle East. On the ground, the diplomatic manoeuvring had little impact, with both sides continuing to battle throughout 1990 in order to gain ground ahead of the inevitable cease-fire.

C H R O N O L O G Y

1 9 4 5

9 March The Japanese move to disarm the French in Indo-China, ending French rule formally. Japanese forces carried out what amounted to a successful coup d'etat against the French authorities in Indo-China. French colonial administrators and troops were quickly interned, with only a few isolated French garrisons holding out against the Japanese forces.

The newly-installed Vichy regime in France, under pressure from Berlin, had signed agreements with the Japanese in 1940 and 1941 which had allowed the French to maintain a presence in Indo-China. Effectively, the agreements placed the whole of Indo-China under Japanese military control, but the French were permitted to retain formal sovereignty and they continued to manage local administration and security functions. The collusion allowed both Tokyo and Paris to benefit from the continued exploitation of the region's natural resources, and also permitted collaboration in the suppression of the burgeoning Vietnamese nationalist movement. The collapse of the Vichy government in August 1944 prompted the Japanese to investigate the possibility of seizing full and formal control of Indo-China. At the time, the Vichy governor-general of Indo-China, Admiral Jean Decoux, had convinced Tokyo of his ability to stop Gaullist sentiments taking root amongst the French in Indo-China. However, by the beginning of 1945 it became obvious to the Japanese that Gaullist influence was spreading through the French ranks, and further driven by fears of an impending Allied invasion (the US had taken Manila in February) they made their move in March.

A few days after the Japanese coup the leadership of the Indo-Chinese Communist Party (ICP) issued a set of instructions for members to deal with the 'new situation' (the ICP had been formed in 1930 by Ho Chi Minh (see biographies) and in May 1941 it became the dominant component of the nationalist Vietnamese Independence League – Viet Nam Doc Lap Dong Minh Hoi, or Viet Minh as it became known). Members were instructed to concentrate on the 'Japanese fascists' as the 'main, immediate and sole enemy of the Indochinese peoples'; those French that were conducting resistance had, as a result of the coup, become new allies. The instructions also called for the mobilization of the people to welcome and fight alongside the Allied forces.

11 March Emperor Bao Dai proclaims an 'independent Annam'. Two days after overthrowing the French, the Japanese made their first tentative move towards winning a measure of Vietnamese support for their action. Bao Dai, the emperor of Annam (see biographies), was instructed by the Japanese to renounce Annam's protectorate treaty with France (signed in 1884) and establish an 'independent' government. It was an extremely limited sort of independence set within the strict confines of Japanese Greater East Asia. Tokyo retained control of defence, internal security, foreign affairs and communications; initially it did not even encompass the two other sections of Vietnam, Cochin-China or Tongkin (the former came under the control of a Japanese governor, the latter

1

a resident-superior). Bao Dai's declaration was rejected by the Viet Minh, whose guerrilla units stepped up their attacks on the Japanese forces; by July the Viet Minh controlled six provinces north of the Red River and in the major cities political agitation – spurred by a terrible famine which had beset the north – gained momentum.

13 March Cambodian 'independence' is declared. As in Vietnam and Laos, the Japanese moved against the French in Cambodia on 9 March; four days later the Japanese pressured the Cambodian monarch, Norodom Sihanouk (see biographies), to abrogate his country's existing treaties with the French and declare independence. Sihanouk subsequently formed a new government, composed in the main of members of the pro-French elite. The only minister with genuine nationalist credentials was Foreign Minister Son Ngoc Thanh who arrived in Phnom Penh to take up his post in late May after three years of exile in Tokyo. Thanh, leader of Cambodia's small nationalist movement during the 1930s, had, with the alleged support of some Japanese officers, launched an unsuccessful coup against the French in 1942.

24 March The Free French government outline their future plans for Indo-China. Some two weeks after the Japanese coup, the provisional French government issued a declaration on the status of post-war Indo-China, which clearly established that de Gaulle's aim was effectively one of recolonization. The plan envisaged the creation of an Indo-Chinese Federation (comprising Annam, Tongkin, Cambodia, Cochin-China and Laos) to sit within the 'French Union' (Union Francaise). Although each of the five territories would have its own administration and elected assembly, ultimate power would rest with a French governor-general. Issues of foreign relations and defence would be settled in Paris.

8 April The Japanese press King Sisavang Vong into declaring Laos' 'independence'. As in neighbouring Cambodia and Vietnam, the Japanese moved against the French authorities in Laos on 9 March. In Vientiane, the country's administrative capital, the French put up little resistance, but further north some French forces defiantly stood their ground and it took the Japanese three weeks to reach Luang Prabang, the royal capital. In Luang Prabang, the crown prince, Savang Vatthana, had issued a call for a mass uprising soon after hearing of the March coup in Vientiane. So, when the Japanese entered Luang Prabang, Savang was quickly dispatched to Saigon. King Sisavang Vong responded to Japanese pressure and, on 8 April, he repudiated all ties with France and declared Laos' independence.

12 April US President Roosevelt dies, prompting a review of US policy towards Indo-China. Upon Roosevelt's death US policy towards Indo-China was irresolute in the extreme. Throughout the war, Roosevelt had criticized French colonial policy in the region, and had advocated in its place a form of international trusteeship arrangement. His anti-colonial outlook (illustrated in the so-called 'Atlantic Charter' of 1941 in which both he and Churchill pledged 'to see sovereign rights and self-government restored to those who have been forcibly deprived of them') had encouraged Ho Chi Minh to count Washington as a potential ally in its anti-French struggle. Ho's positive feelings about the US were further shaped by the fact that the Viet Minh and the US

Office of Strategic Services (OSS, the forerunner of the Central Intelligence Agency – CIA) had worked closely together on anti-Japanese operations in Indo-China. Roosevelt's convictions on colonialism were not shared by the US State Department; not surprisingly, the European section in particular favoured French restoration in Indo-China. Roosevelt's successor as president, Harry S. Truman, did not possess his predecessor's enthusiasm for the trusteeship policy. Within days of Roosevelt's death the State Department's European division was openly recommending that the US government should not oppose the restoration of Indo-China to France, a strategy that was eventually confirmed in August when de Gaulle visited Washington. Meanwhile, from October 1945 until the following February, Ho wrote a stream of letters to Truman formally requesting US and UN intervention against the French; none of the letters were answered.

2 August The Potsdam conference ends after Britain and the US have reached an agreement on Indo-China. At the conference, US President Truman (Eisenhower's replacement) and British Prime Minister Clement Attlee (who replaced Churchill as prime minister towards the end of the conference) reached an agreement that provided for the division of Indo-China at the sixteenth parallel once the Japanese had been defeated. The decision envisaged that Chinese troops would occupy the northern half of Indo-China and British forces the remainder.

9 August Supporters of Son Ngoc Thanh launch a 'palace coup' in Cambodia. With the Japanese surrender imminent, a small group of supporters of Foreign Minister Son Ngoc Thanh stormed the royal palace in Phnom Penh and effectively forced Sihanouk to appoint Thanh as prime minister. Thanh appointed a new cabinet and set about trying to establish a genuinely independent Cambodia. He also strove to improve relations with Vietnam, and in early September, his government recognized the Democratic Republic of Vietnam (DRV), recently proclaimed in Hanoi by Ho Chi Minh.

12 August The Viet Minh issues a call for a general insurrection. Japan's offer to surrender on 11 August prompted the Viet Minh to call for the insurrection to seize power in Vietnam. The people responded to the call with breathtaking speed and enthusiasm, initiating what came to be known as the 'August Revolution'. The eagerness of the people to respond to the Viet Minh call was prompted partly by the effects of a terrible famine which had recently stricken Tongkin as a result of an earlier Franco-Japanese decision to convert paddy fields into industrial crop belts. Within days of the call millions of people had taken to the streets of Hanoi, Hue and Saigon and control of the cities quickly shifted from the hands of the vanquished Japanese into those of small Viet Minh committees. Eventually on 25 August, after massive demonstrations in Hue, Bao Dai formally abdicated.

1 September In Vientiane, Prince Phetsarath reaffirms King Sisavang's independence proclamation. Following the Japanese surrender in mid-August, Prince Phetsarath, the powerful viceroy and premier, decided that the French, having been removed from power by Japan, had no right to resume their control of Laos. Therefore he contacted the king in Luang Prabang and officially reaffirmed the monarch's April declaration of independence. The king, however, responded by rallying to the French and on 17 September he sent a telegram to Phetsarath informing him that the French Treaty of Protectorate was still valid.

2 September Ho Chi Minh declares the independence of the DRV. The Viet Minh leadership (effectively the ICP standing committee) gathered in Hanoi in late August and announced the formation of a 15-member provisional government, headed by Ho Chi Minh. On behalf of the government, Ho proclaimed the independence of the DRV at a mass meeting in Hanoi. Ho began the declaration with quotes from the American Declaration of Independence and the French Declaration on the Rights of Man. He ended with a prophetic warning, stating that the Vietnamese people would 'mobilize all their spiritual and material forces and . . . sacrifice their lives and property in order to safeguard their right of Liberty and Independence'.

13 September British and Chinese troops start arriving in Vietnam with the ostensible aim of disarming the vanquished Japanese forces. As agreed at the Potsdam conference, some 1,800 British and Indian forces, under the command of General Douglas Gracey, arrived in Saigon on 13 September to disarm the Japanese forces (privately, however, an understanding had been reached between Britain and France that the British forces would assist the French in regaining control of Indo-China). Saigon was in a chaotic state with the Viet Minh's control of the city under challenge from rival Vietnamese groups. After just over a week in Saigon General Gracey proclaimed martial law and at the same time freed a number of French troops who had been interned by the Japanese. The French POWs, many of them Foreign Legionnaires, proceeded to launch what amounted to a coup d'etat against the Viet Minh authorities on 22 September. The Viet Minh called a general strike on 24 September and the city erupted into violence, with the French, British and Indian troops even enlisting the support of the defeated Japanese forces. Eventually, on 3 October French reinforcements, under the command of General Jacques-Philippe Leclerc (see biographies), arrived in Saigon. Leclerc's forces quickly gained control of Saigon and then took the offensive throughout the south (Cochin-China).

Meanwhile, under the Potsdam agreement, Chiang Kai-shek's Chinese nationalist forces had been entrusted with the task of disarming the Japanese in northern Indo-China. The first of a massive 180,000-strong Chinese force, under the command of General Lu Han, arrived in northern Vietnam on September 16. The Chinese spent a great deal of their time looting, but showed little desire to act against Ho on behalf of the French.

26 September The first US soldier dies in Vietnam. Lieutenant-Colonel Peter Dewey, leader of a seven-party OSS mission to Saigon, was killed in a Viet Minh ambush in late September. Dewey, a relative of Governor Dewey of New York, was the first of nearly 60,000 Americans to die in Vietnam over the next 30 years.

12 October Prince Phetsarath forms a Free Laos Government in Vientiane. After rallying to the French in September, King Sisavang announced the dismissal of Phetsarath as viceroy and premier on 10 October. Two days later, Phetsarath responded by announcing the formation of a Lao Issara or Free Laos Government, with attendant provisional constitution and provisional National Assembly. The government was headed by the former governor of

Vientiane province, Phaya Khammao, and also included Phetsarath's brother, Souvanna Phouma (see biographies). Meanwhile, in early November, Phetsarath and Souvanna's younger half brother, Prince Souphanouvong (see biographies), returned to Vientiane from a trip to Hanoi where he had held talks with Ho Chi Minh and other leaders of the newly formed DRV. Once in Vientiane, Souphanouvong was also drafted into the Lao Issara government, as defence minister and commander-in-chief of the armed forces.

15 October The French resume control in Cambodia. Unlike in neighbouring Vietnam, the French managed to re-establish their authority in Cambodia with ease. British forces entered Phnom Penh in early October, and on 15 October Prime Minister Thanh was bundled out of Cambodia into forced exile in Saigon, and later France. Some of his supporters fled into Vietnam, where they joined Viet Minh units. A few weeks after the resumption of French control Sihanouk issued a declaration affirming the loyalty of himself and his people to France and welcoming French plans for the creation of an Indo-Chinese Federation within the French Union.

31 October Admiral d'Argenlieu is appointed as the new French high commissioner to Indo-China. De Gaulle appointed Admiral Georges Thierry d'Argenlieu (see biographies) to replace Admiral Decoux, and he arrived to take up his post in late October. The appointment of d'Argenlieu, a staunch advocate of a full French return to Indo-China, was an indication of de Gaulle's strong determination to reimpose French rule (see Appendix 1 for French diplomatic representation in Indo-China, 1940–54).

11 November Ho Chi Minh dissolves the ICP. The ICP, founded in 1930, was formally dissolved into an Association of Marxist Studies. The ICP as such was never reinstigated, with separate Vietnamese, Lao and Cambodian Communist parties emerging in the early 1950s. There is little doubt that the disbanding of the ICP was a largely cosmetic exercise, and that the party continued to function and thrive. A number of explanations have been offered for the move: some commentators have claimed that the extraordinary success of the united-front strategy adopted during the August Revolution persuaded Ho that he had to extend the policy he had initiated with the formation of the Viet Minh, other commentators claim that Ho had other reasons to camouflage his Communism, including his continuing efforts to gain US support and as a method of appeasing the Chinese nationalist forces currently occupying northern Vietnam.

1 9 4 6

4 January A Franco-Cambodian agreement is signed in Phnom Penh transferring limited autonomy to Cambodia. Under the agreement, Cambodia was no longer designated a protectorate, but rather an autonomous unit of the Indo-Chinese Federation and French Union. Although services of purely Cambodian internal interest (e.g. police, public works and health) were to be administered solely by Cambodians, services of federal interest (e.g. finance, foreign affairs) were to be administered by a French high commissioner. In addition, the Cambodian cabinet was 'obliged' to consult with French advisers 'in certain cases'.

28 February A Franco-Chinese treaty is signed providing for the withdrawal of all Chinese forces from northern Indo-China (including the Democratic Republic of Vietnam – DRV) by late March. In return, the French agreed to abandon its extraterritorial rights in China, including their concessions at Shanghai, Tientsin, Canton and Hankow. Meanwhile, British control of Indo-China south of the sixteenth parallel officially ended on 4 March when responsibility reverted to the French.

6 March A Franco-Viet Minh agreement is signed in Hanoi, under which the DRV is recognized as a 'free state' within the French Union. The signing of the Franco-Chinese agreement on the withdrawal of Chinese forces from northern Indo-China in late February increased pressure on Ho Chi Minh to reach some sort of accommodation with the French. The February agreement meant that a full-scale conflict between the Viet Minh and France was looming, with the French forces stationed south of the sixteenth parallel soon to be arriving in the north. However, Ho's most urgent fear concerned Chiang Kai-shek who he believed might attempt to impose a pro-Kuomintang regime in Hanoi before his troops departed from Vietnam. Therefore, Ho needed some form of agreement with the French to ensure the removal of the Chinese. Discussions between Ho and Jean Sainteny, de Gaulle's special emissary, had been under way since late 1945. On 6 March the two signed a Preliminary Convention, the basis of which had been proposed by Ho in mid-February.
    Under the terms of the convention, Paris recognized the DRV as a 'free state which has its own government, its parliament, its army and its finances, and is a part of the Indochinese Federation and of the French Union'. On the question of the reunification of the three parts of Vietnam, the French government pledged itself 'to confirm the decisions reached by the populations consulted by means of a referendum'. For its part, the DRV government declared itself ready to receive, 'in a peaceful manner', a 15,000-strong French army force. Both agreed to enter immediately into 'friendly and frank' negotiations on the future status of Indo-China.

19 April Franco-Vietnamese negotiations open at Dalat. The conference, called in accordance with the Preliminary Convention, ended on 11 May without agreement being reached on any substantive issues. The essential point at issue was whether the DRV government was a government of the whole of Vietnam, or only of Tongkin. However, the hardline French high commissioner, Admiral Thierry d'Argenlieu, made sure that the discussion centred on minor financial and cultural matters.

24 April French forces eventually enter Vientiane after a brave stand by Lao Issara fighters. From late 1945 onwards, the French reoccupation forces made steady advances against poorly-armed Lao Issara guerrillas. In March 1946 Souphanouvong and a small Lao Issara band made a brave stand at Thathek, a town situated just east of the Mekong in the southern province of Khammouane. The French managed to take Thathek on 21 March, and Souphanouvong fled, injured, across the Mekong into Thailand. A month later French troops entered

6

Vientiane and Prince Phetsarath and the Lao Issara government were forced to join Souphanouvong in Thailand, where they were provided with offices and support by the government of Pridi Phanomyang. In May Luang Prabang came under French control and by September France was again in command of all the Lao provinces.

1 June France recognizes the Republic of Cochin-China as an independent state within the French Union. In a show of contempt for the Franco-Vietnamese Preliminary Convention, Admiral d'Argenlieu announced the formation of what amounted to a separate puppet regime in Saigon to counterbalance Ho's Hanoi government. D'Argenlieu's announcement that France had recognized the Republic of Cochin-China as an independent state of the Indo-Chinese Federation within the French Union came the day after Ho Chi Minh had left Hanoi for Paris for negotiations with the French government. The new 'government' of Cochin-China was headed by President Nguyen Van Thinh, who subsequently hanged himself in November and was replaced by Van Hoach.

9 July The Fontainebleau conference on Vietnam begins but talks break down after two months. The Franco-Vietnamese conference opened in Fontainebleau, near Paris, with the two delegations led by Pham Van Dong (see biographies) and Max Andre, a member of the Paris municipal council. As with the previous discussions at Dalat, little progress was made on the central issues of independence and Cochin-China. The Vietnamese side withdrew from the discussions on 1 August after Admiral d'Argenlieu had convened a separate conference in Dalat attended by representatives from Cambodia, Laos, Cochin-China and non-Viet Minh Vietnamese to discuss the future of Indo-China.

27 August The French government provides Laos with limited autonomy, as in the case of Cambodia in January. As a member of the Indo-Chinese Federation, Laos enjoyed little real autonomy, with France retaining political, military and economic control. The provision of limited autonomy was opposed by the Lao Issara, and Souphanouvong, aided by Viet Minh advisers, conducted a guerrilla campaign against the French throughout late 1946. The guerrillas succeeded in partly disrupting the election of a 44-member Constituent Assembly in mid-December.

1 September Elections to a Cambodian Constituent Assembly result in a victory for moderate nationalists. A 67-member Constituent Assembly was elected in early September to deliberate on and approve a draft constitution drawn up by a Franco-Cambodian committee. The moderate, nationalist Democratic Party, led by its founder Prince Sisowath Youtevong, took 50 of the 67 seats, with another 14 going to the pro-monarchist Liberal Party and the remainder to independents.

14 September France and the DRV sign a *modus vivendi* in Paris. After the breakdown of the Fontainebleau talks in August, Ho Chi Minh remained in Paris where he signed the interim understanding or *modus vivendi* with the French colonial minister, Marius Moutet. The understanding, which did little to resolve the Cochin-China issue, afforded France a number of economic and cultural concessions in return for a measure of political freedom for pro-Viet Minh elements in the south. Ho returned to Vietnam in October and implored his compatriots to 'display a generous policy' towards the French in order to allow them to 'hear the voice of reason'.

23 November French warships bombard Haiphong and the First Indo-China War begins in earnest. Despite Ho Chi Minh's call for tolerance towards the French (which culminated in the issuing of a nation-wide cease-fire in late October), relations between the two sides on the ground in the north had deteriorated sharply by the end of the year with skirmishes frequently erupting. One such skirmish broke out in Haiphong on 20 November after DRV soldiers abducted a group of French border patrolmen during a dispute over harbour controls. Admiral d'Argenlieu and other hardliners recognized that the incident afforded the French forces an opportunity to demonstrate the full force of the French military might to the DRV military. After receiving Prime Minister Georges Bidault's approval, d'Argenlieu informed like-minded officers to prepare for an attack on Haiphong. DRV military leaders in Haiphong were informed on 23 November that they had two hours to withdraw all their men from the city. After the two hours had passed the French launched a massive naval and aerial bombardment on the city, killing up to 6,000 civilians.

19 December The DRV government issues a call for armed resistance and withdraws from Hanoi. Following the French assault on Haiphong, tension in the north increased dramatically. On 18 December French troops occupied a number of DRV ministry buildings in Hanoi and on the next day France demanded that DRV troops in the capital lay down their weapons. Instead, General Giap, the DRV defence minister and commander-in-chief (see biographies), responded by ordering sabotage attacks on Hanoi's power plants; at the same time Ho Chi Minh and other DRV leaders fled the capital and established bases in the surrounding countryside. During the evening of 19 December an order by General Giap was broadcast calling on soldiers and militia throughout the country to 'stand up in unison, dash into battle, destroy the invaders and save the country.'

---

1 9 4 7

19 January Thailand officially restores to Laos territory annexed in 1941. The Thai government restored the land on the west bank of the Mekong in order to obtain membership of the UN. The appropriation of Sayaboury province and part of Champassak province by the Thais had been supported by the Japanese who were eager to encourage the collusion of the anti-Chinese and anti-Western regime of Phibun Songkhram in Bangkok.

19 February After weeks of serious fighting the French retake control of Hanoi. The city had been a battleground since the Viet Minh had launched their offensive in December. On 14 February French troops, with strong air support, attacked the Viet Minh forces in the city with the aim of relieving the besieged garrison. The French encountered serious opposition and were forced to fight a gruelling street-by-street battle and victory was assured only through the use of tanks and aircraft.

5 March Emile Bollaert, a civilian, replaces Admiral d'Argenlieu as French high commissioner for Indo-China. D'Argenlieu had been sacked in February by the new French premier, Paul Ramadier, who had replaced his fellow Socialist Leon Blum. The appointment of Bollaert, a civilian, signalled the intention of the new government to work towards a political solution to the Vietnamese problem. However, in March Ramadier's position was weakened when the Communists resigned from the coalition government, thereby strengthening the hand of the Christian Democrats who tended to favour a d'Argenlieu-style military solution.

11 May A new Constitution is promulgated in Laos. King Sisavang Vong promulgated the new Constitution, a month after its adoption by the country's Constituent Assembly. The Constitution declared Laos to be an independent state within the French Union and provided for a single-chamber system of government with deputies elected at four-yearly intervals. It also provided for the appointment of a Royal Council, nominated jointly by the assembly and the king, to advise the monarch and act as a cabinet.

12 May French envoy Paul Mus meets with Ho Chi Minh in an unsuccessful attempt to arrange a settlement. Professor Paul Mus, a distinguished French orientalist and an adviser to High Commissioner Bollaert, met with Ho Chi Minh in Viet Minh-controlled territory north of Hanoi. Bollaert arranged the meeting in response to appeals by Ho and the Democratic Republic of Vietnam (DRV) foreign minister, Hoang Minh Giam, for a cease-fire and a peaceful settlement. At the meeting Mus presented Ho with what amounted to a set of conditions for a Viet Minh surrender, including the laying down of arms and munitions. Ho rejected all the conditions set down by Mus, declaring that they constituted a derogation of Vietnam's sovereignty and were tantamount to surrender.

15 July King Sihanouk approves Cambodia's first Constitution. The Democrat-dominated Cambodian Constituent Assembly elected in September 1946 spent the first half of 1947 debating and revising a draft Constitution. Through Democrat pressure, the document provided for a powerful National Assembly similar to that of the Fourth French Republic. After approving the Constitution, the Constituent Assembly was dissolved and fresh elections were held in December for a new National Assembly. The Democrats, although shocked by the mysterious death of their leader Prince Sisowath Youtevong in July, nevertheless retained control of the new assembly winning 54 seats against 21 for the Liberals. A new party contesting the elections was Lon Nol's right-wing Khmer Renovation which failed to win any seats.

31 July Ho Chi Minh forms a new DRV government which includes a number of nationalist moderates. In a move designed to appeal to French and Vietnamese moderates Ho reshuffled the DRV cabinet in late July. In the new cabinet, Communists were confined to only the key posts, with moderate nationalists filling most of the portfolios. An interesting appointment was that of former Emperor Bao Dai as supreme adviser to the government. At the time Bao Dai was living in Hong Kong, and was being courted by the French who had made moves to entice him back to the Vietnamese throne. He had refused, insisting that France must first acknowledge Vietnamese independence.

10 September Emile Bollaert outlines French terms for a final settlement in Indo-China. In the speech, delivered in Hanoi, he explained that the terms had to be accepted or rejected as a whole. In his speech Bollaert proposed what at best could be described as a heavily circumscribed form of independence, which he must have known would be unacceptable to Ho Chi Minh. According to the plan France would retain military and diplomatic leadership of Indo-China, and the unity of Tongkin, Annam and Cochin-China would be left to the decision of the peoples concerned, although France would prevent the victimization of those elements which had co-operated with the French. Inevitably, the proposals were rejected by the DRV government as being far too limited.

28 September General Nguyen Van Xuan, a hardline opponent of the Viet Minh, is appointed premier of Cochin-China. Dr Van Hoach resigned as premier of the government of Cochin-China in late September and was replaced by Brigadier-General Nguyen Van Xuan, hitherto vice-premier and defence minister. Brigadier-General Xuan was a naturalized French citizen who spoke little Vietnamese, but he was vehemently opposed to the Viet Minh and to Vietnamese unity. Soon after coming to power, Xuan proposed the establishment of a Federal State of Vietnam (comprising Annam, Tongkin and Cochin-China) within a United States of Indo-China, with each state closely allied to France by treaties of mutual assistance.

7 October French forces launch their first major assault on the Viet Minh headquarters, and Giap and Ho only narrowly escape. A month before the offensive was launched, the commander of the French forces, General Jean Etienne Valluy, had confidently predicted that the Viet Minh would be easily defeated by the end of the year. Operation Lea was aimed at capturing the Viet Minh political and military headquarters at Bac Kan, north of Hanoi. The Viet Minh were surprised by the attack and Ho and Giap only just avoided capture. However, after their near success, the operation deteriorated; Giap's forces rallied and, after two weeks of combat, inflicted a punishing defeat on Valluy's troops. Two other offensives were launched in late 1947; the first, carried out by French forces south of Bac Kan, succeeded in capturing a large amount of Viet Minh supplies; in the second offensive, the French used indigenous mountain tribesmen to great effect against Viet Minh units in the Fan Si Pan mountain range, between the Red and Black Rivers.

6 December Bao Dai and Emile Bollaert meet for talks. In early September Bao Dai, formally an adviser to the DRV government, met with a group of anti-Viet Minh Vietnamese nationalists in Hong Kong who entrusted him to enter into negotiations with the French. Ho Chi Minh denounced Bao Dai's intention to open a dialogue with France as a 'perfidious manoeuvre' instigated by 'French colonists' and designed to divide the Vietnamese people. Eventually, Bao Dai met for talks with High Commissioner Bollaert aboard a French cruiser in the Bay of Along, north of Haiphong.

1 9 4 8

1 February A Khmer 'Issarak' committee is formed in western Cambodia. The first Khmer nationalist Issarak ('freedom') group had been formed in 1940, but, along with other similar groups, it made little progress in the fight for Cambodian independence. By the mid-1940s the Khmer independence movement was highly fractionalized, although the various ideological strands often co-operated militarily. The large Issarak group formed in Battambang, provided the movement with a measure of unity and stability. Unlike other smaller Issarak groups in other parts of the country (such as Son Ngoc Minh's southwestern group), the Khmer People's Liberation Committee (KPLC) was not wholly pro-Viet Minh, although half of its leaders did favour a Vietnamese style path to independence. The KPLC's 800-strong military force was led by Dap Chhuon, who subsequently made his mark as a noted rightist.

1 March Viet Minh guerrilla forces launch a severe attack on a French convoy on the Saigon to Dalat road in Cochin-China. Some 60 French soldiers died in the attack, including Colonel de Sarigne, commander of the Foreign Legion in Indo-China. Two days later another convoy was attacked whilst travelling from Saigon to Sadec (about 68 miles (110 kilometres) southwest of Saigon), resulting in the death of some 25 French and Cochin-Chinese soldiers.

The March attacks in Cochin-China took place at the start of a quiet year, militarily, in Vietnam. The military situation remained in a deadlock, with the French controlling urban areas throughout the country and the Viet Minh the countryside; however, the further north the French travelled, the more tenuous their hold on the towns became. General Giap used the lull in large-combat operations to carry out a reorganization of the Viet Minh, transforming it from a collection of guerrilla units to a conventional fighting force. Viet Minh troops were retrained, both politically and militarily and vital logistical support was built up.

25 March Prince Boun Oum, a pro-French aristocrat, is appointed prime minister of Laos. He replaced Prince Souvanareth on the final day of the Lao National Assembly's first session. Boun Oum, heir to the throne of the obsolete kingdom of Champassak, was conspicuously pro-French, having organized anti-Japanese resistance in support of France in the aftermath of the March 1945 coup.

20 May The premier of Cochin-China, Brigadier-General Nguyen Van Xuan, is 'elected' as president of a Provisional Central Government of Vietnam. French plans towards establishing a 'national' government in Vietnam as a counterweight to the DRV took a major step forward with the election. Bao Dai, who at this stage remained wary about resuming his imperial duties, apparently sent his written approval of General Xuan forming such a government. France officially recognized the central government on 23 May in an exchange of letters between Xuan and High Commissioner Bollaert.

Xuan was elected in Saigon by 40 'representative personalities of the leading spiritual and political sections' of Tongkin, Annam and Cochin-China. After his election, Xuan announced that a new 22-member central government would be formed, comprising nine ministers from Cochin-China, seven from Tongkin and six from Annam. In a speech delivered after the election, General Xuan said that he would 'endeavour to harmonize gradually the regional administrations of North, Central and South Vietnam'. He also said that he was currently investigating the terms of an armistice, but that it was 'out of the question' to conclude a peace agreement with the Viet Minh.

5 June The Bay of Along Treaty is signed affording the central Vietnam government 'independence' within the French Union. At a meeting on board a French cruiser in the Bay of Along, High Commissioner Bollaert, Bao Dai and General Xuan signed a formal treaty laying down the relations between France and the Provisional Central Government of Vietnam. Under the terms of the agreement, France recognized Vietnamese independence within the French Union (i.e. Paris would retain control of Vietnamese military, financial and foreign affairs). France also recognized the right of Vietnam 'to bring about freely its unity'. After the signing of the agreement, Bao Dai, who had always been a reluctant signatory, left Vietnam declaring that he would not return as emperor until true independence had been achieved. Ho Chi Minh responded to the treaty by issuing a statement to the effect that General Xuan would be tried as a traitor and that the Viet Minh would continue their war against the French as the 'only means to achieve our independence'.

27 September The US State Department issues its first full-length policy statement on Indo-China. According to the State Department paper, the immediate objective of US policy in Indo-China was to assist in a solution to the present impasse which would be mutually satisfactory to the French and the Vietnamese peoples, would result in the termination of the present hostilities and would be within the framework of US security. However, the paper concluded that there was no easy solution to the present impasse; the department supported neither a French military reconquest nor a complete withdrawal. Reconquest would delay indefinitely the attainment of US objectives, as Washington would 'share inevitably in the hatred engendered by an attempted military reconquest and the denial of aspirations for self-government'. Withdrawal, on the other hand, would be 'equally unfortunate as in all likelihood Indo-China would then be taken over by the militant Communist group'. 'At best', the paper went on, 'there might follow a transition period, marked by chaos and terroristic activities, creating a political vacuum into which the Chinese inevitably would be drawn or would push'. The State Department concluded that it would, therefore, support the French in every way possible in the establishment of a truly nationalist government in Indo-China.

20 October Leon Pignon is appointed as the new French High Commissioner for Indo-China replacing the disillusioned Emile Bollaert. Leon Pignon had served in various administrative posts in Indo-China during the 1940s. According to reports in the French press, Bollaert had resigned the post in disappointment at events in Indo-China since the signing of the Treaty of the Bay of Along, especially at the progress and conduct of the Xuan regime.

1 9 4 9

8 March The Elysee Agreement is signed by Bao Dai and the French government making Vietnam an Associated State within the French Union. Negotiations between Bao Dai and the French government culminated in the signing of the treaty which guaranteed the independence of a unified Vietnam. Up until the last moment Bao Dai had insisted that he had no intention of returning to Indo-China until the French government gave effect to its promises of Vietnamese unity.

Under the terms of the agreement, signed by Bao Dai and French President Vincent Auriol in the Elysee in Paris, Vietnam was guaranteed: independence within the French Union; recognition of the unity of the three Vietnamese territories; administrative, judicial and financial autonomy; the right to have its own army, although with French instructors; the right to receive foreign diplomatic representatives (accredited to both the head of state and the president of the French Union) and to send its own diplomats to China, Thailand and the Vatican; the right to send 19 representatives to the assembly of the French Union. France, meanwhile, was guaranteed: strategic military bases in Vietnam; the right of free passage for its troops; co-ordination of the French and Vietnamese armies by a liaison committee, which in time of war would become a general staff with a French head; and safeguards for French cultural and economic rights.

By the end of 1949 the French National Assembly had not yet ratified the Elysee Agreement (nor the similar agreements signed with Laos and Cambodia). However, the agreement came into force after a formal exchange of letters between Bao Dai and High Commissioner Pignon in Saigon on 14 June. The two signed a series of conventions on 30 December implementing the agreement and providing for the transfer of the French government's administrative powers to the Vietnamese government.

4 June President Auriol of France signs a bill providing for Cochin-China's union with Vietnam. Moves to integrate Cochin-China into a 'unified' Vietnamese framework began immediately after the signing of the Elysee Agreement. A Cochin-Chinese Territorial Assembly was elected on 10 April to replace the colony's non-elected Consultative Council; two weeks later the assembly voted in favour of the abrogation of Cochin-China's separate status and for union with a Bao Dai-led Vietnam. The bill was ratified by the French National Assembly on 3 June and signed by President Auriol the next day. The Cochin-China government formally surrendered its powers to Bao Dai on 23 June.

30 June Bao Dai finally forms a unified Vietnamese government. Bao Dai returned to Vietnam in late April after three years in exile and two months later he formed the first 'unified' Vietnamese government, with himself as chief-of-state and prime minister. Brigadier-General Xuan, president of the Provisional Central Government since May 1948, was appointed vice premier and minister of defence and interior. Journalist Nguyen Phan Long, like Xuan Cochin-Chinese, was appointed as foreign minister. The only northerner in the cabinet was Vung Oc Tran, a secretary of state for the interior. An ordinance signed by Bao Dai on 1 July stated that a 45-member National Consultative Assembly would be appointed by Bao Dai to assist the government until elections were held.

19 July A Franco-Lao treaty is signed making Laos an 'independent' Associated State within the French Union. French President Vincent Auriol and Lao King Sisavang Vong signed the treaty in Paris. Under the terms of the agreement, the Lao government was afforded a greater say in the country's foreign, military and economic affairs. Laos sent three representatives to the assembly of the French Union.

27 July A new French military commander-in-chief is appointed in Indo-China. General Roger Blaizet, who had replaced General Valluy as French commander-in-chief in Indo-China in 1948, was himself replaced by General Marcel Carpentier. The new commander arrived in Vietnam with no experience of the Far East and he immediately handed effective control of operations to General Marcel Allessandri, an old Indo-China hand. General Allessandri, wary of Valluy's disastrous set-piece tactics, launched the first of a long line of 'pacification' initiatives in Vietnam. Slowly and carefully he gained control of piece after piece of the Tongkin delta's vital rice grounds, with the aim of starving and generally demoralizing Giap's troops. The tactics partly succeeded: the Viet Minh's rice supplies were drastically reduced and Giap was apparently tempted to embark on what would have proved a disastrous premature offensive. However, Allessandri's tactics failed ultimately through a lack of troop numbers and because of the Viet Minh's superb propaganda network. As the French 'pacified' one area and moved on to the next, the Viet Minh simply stole back into the inadequately defended villages, where they tended to be warmly welcomed by the largely supportive peasant population.

18 September Under pressure from France, Sihanouk dissolves the troublesome Cambodian National Assembly. Although by far the most popular party in Cambodia, Democrat support for the increasingly troublesome Khmer Issaraks brought them into conflict with Sihanouk and the French during the late 1940s. Eventually Sihanouk moved to curtail Democrat influence by dissolving the National Assembly and postponing *sine die* elections due to be held in November. Sihanouk formed a new government, responsible only to himself, of right-wing Democrats led by Yem Sambaur.

Nevertheless, political stability remained elusive and at least six cabinets were formed during the two-year period following the assembly's dissolution. Dap Chhuon, the most powerful of the Issarak leaders, surrendered to the government shortly after the dissolution and, in return, he was left free to control a large section of northern Cambodia. Meanwhile, other pro-Viet Minh Issarak bands continued to harass the government and by the end of the year they claimed to control over 400 villages in some 10 provinces.

1 October Mao Zedong proclaims the People's Republic of China (PRC). Mao's momentous defeat of Chiang Kai-shek's nationalist forces and the establishment of the Communist People's Republic of China had a major effect on the conflict in Indo-China. It boosted the morale of Ho and the Viet Minh who were no longer subjected to enemy encirclement, but shared a border with an awesome ally. It opened up the possibility of increased weapon supplies and placed further pressure on France to hold onto her border posts at all costs. For the US, the 'fall of China' was a tremendous shock which, more than any other event, served to firm up what until October had been at best an ambivalent Indo-China policy. With containment of Communism at the very top of the agenda, concerns over the intricacies of French policy in Vietnam simply became of secondary importance.

24 October Divisions within the Lao nationalist movement finally lead to the dissolution of the Lao Issara government-in-exile. The Franco-Lao treaty of July served to accelerate the inevitable collapse of the Bangkok-based Lao Issara government. Before the treaty was signed the exiled government was already seriously divided with a majority faction opposed to Souphanouvong's pro-Viet Minh stance. The dispute led Souphanouvong to resign his government portfolios in March and five months later he formed a separate Lao Liberation Committee and set off with his supporters for the Viet Minh headquarters in northwestern Vietnam. At the same time, most of the other Issara leaders, including Souphanouvong's half brother, Souvanna Phouma, rallied to the new Associated State in Vientiane and in October the exiled government was formally dissolved.

8 November A Franco-Cambodian treaty is signed at the Elysee making Cambodia an 'independent' Associated State within the French Union. The treaty was the third of a series of similar agreements defining the status of the Indo-Chinese territories within the French Union, having been preceded by agreements between France and Vietnam and France and Laos. Cambodia subsequently sent five representatives to the assembly of the French Union.

---

1 9 5 0

5 January Bao Dai resigns the premiership of the Saigon government and is eventually replaced two months later by Tran Van Huu. Bao Dai resigned the premiership in order to devote himself exclusively to his duties as chief-of-state. Two weeks later Nguyen Phan Long, hitherto minister of foreign affairs, formed a new government. The Long government collapsed in late April, partly as a result of an outbreak of serious rioting in Saigon in March during a visit by two US Navy destroyers. Tran Van Huu, the governor of southern Vietnam, replaced Long as prime minister, although increasing political power rested in the hands of Bao Dai's security chief, Nguyen Van Tam.

18 January China establishes diplomatic relations with the Democratic Republic of Vietnam (DRV) and two weeks later the Soviet Union follows suit. Zhou Enlai, the Chinese premier and foreign minister, announced his country's recognition of the DRV on 18 January. The Soviet Union announced recognition on 31 January and the Czechs, Poles, Romanians and Hungarians quickly followed suit. The Chinese and Soviet move came after Ho Chi Minh had issued an appeal on 14 January for countries to open diplomatic relations with the DRV. Ho had issued his appeal in response to the impending ratification of the Elysee Agreements by the French National Assembly, which he presumed, would lead to Western recognition of the Bao Dai regime. France and the US responded strongly to the Soviet decision to recognize the DRV. On 31 January the US State Department declared that Ho had 'a long record under various aliases as a Moscow agent' and that 'the fact of his recognition should destroy any illusion of Ho Chi Minh as a purely Nationalist leader, and place him in his true colours as an agent of world Communism'.

29 January France ratifies the March 1949 Elysee Agreements granting Associate State status to the Indo-Chinese nations. The French National Assembly approved the ratification of the Elysee Agreements with Vietnam, Laos and Cambodia by 401 votes to 193. The bills were ratified only after a heated two-day debate in which the measures were opposed by Communist deputies who argued that the agreements provided for what amounted to a disguised form of colonialism. The agreements, which had been signed in 1949 in March, July and November respectively, granted each country independence as an Associated State within the French Union.

7 February The US announces its recognition of the Saigon-based Bao Dai regime. The US made its announcement a week after the Soviet Union had declared its recognition of the DRV. The US also announced its recognition of the royal regimes in Cambodia and Laos. Following the announcement, the US established an embassy in Saigon, headed by Donald Heath. The move to recognize officially the Saigon government had been opposed by some senior State Department officials who had questioned Bao Dai's leadership potential. The British government (which had also proffered recognition on 7 February) had originally argued that de facto rather than de jure recognition would serve to induce the French to consider granting more far-reaching independence to the Indo-Chinese states.

19 April The pro-Vietnamese Unified Issarak Front (UIF) is formed in Cambodia at the end of a three-day congress. The formation of the UIF, which was led by the Indo-Chinese Communist Party (ICP) member Son Ngoc Minh, constituted the most important move to date towards the creation of a unified, pro-Vietnamese revolutionary movement in Cambodia. In mid-June, Minh, in the name of the UIF's central committee, declared Cambodia's independence, claiming to control over 30 per cent of the country's territory. Meanwhile, in 1950, another revolutionary current was developing among Khmer students in Paris (including Ieng Sary, Saloth Sar – Pol Pot – (see biographies) and Son Sen) who had formed a Marxist Circle.

8 May The US announces that it will provide economic and military aid to the French in Indo-China. Dean Acheson, the US secretary of state, announced that Washington had agreed to provide military and economic aid beginning with a grant of $10 million (by the year end, a total of $150 million had been provided). Acheson's announcement came after talks in Paris with the French foreign minister, Robert Schuman.

The US State Department had created a working group in January to investigate the possibility of funding the French effort in Indo-China. The group had supported the distribution of aid to the individual Indo-Chinese governments, an option subsequently rejected by the French who insisted that the aid was delivered into their hands. The French formally requested the aid in mid-February, and in early March Acheson has recommended allocation to President Truman; in his memorandum, Acheson claimed that 'the choice confronting the US is to support the legal governments in Indo-China or to face the extension of Communism over the remainder of the continental area of Southeast Asia and possibly westward'. The first shipment of US military equipment to the French took place in late June, about a month before Truman actually signed the bill authorizing the delivery. The outbreak of the Korean War on 26 June had led Acheson to urge an acceleration of the delivery process. Formal military aid conventions between the US, France and the Associated States were signed in Saigon in late December.

29 June A conference on the Indo-Chinese economy opens in Pau, France. The conference was designed to arrange the transfer of certain administrative and economic services from French to Indo-Chinese control. The conference closed on 27 November with draft conventions having been signed on a number of things, including: the creation of a central Indo-Chinese bank; the transfer of the control of foreign trade from France to the Associated States; the transfer of customs services to the Associated States; and the transfer of the administration of Saigon port to the Bao Dai government.

13 August A pro-Viet Minh Lao resistance movement, the Pathet Lao, is created. Souphanouvong, who had left Thailand prior to the dissolution of the exiled Lao Issara government, arrived in the Viet Minh heartlands of northwestern Vietnam in late 1949, where he consulted with Ho and other leaders. He returned to northeastern Laos and in mid-August he presided over a congress at which the pro-Viet Minh Lao resistance government was formed. The government, and the Lao Communist movement in general, came to be known as the Pathet Lao, literally 'Land of the Lao'. Souphanouvong was appointed as premier and foreign minister in the government, Kaysone Phomvihane (see biographies) was defence minister, Nouhak Phoumsavan finance minister and Phoumi Vongvichit interior minister. In line with Ho's united-front strategy, a broad-based Free Lao Front (Neo Lao Issara) was formed, with a 19-member central committee. A 12-point manifesto was issued which stated the front's aim to drive out the French and establish a coalition government in Vientiane.

16 September General Giap's Viet Minh forces launch their first major offensive of the First Indo-Chinese War. It was directed against French positions in the Chinese border region. The offensive opened at Dong Khe, a French post situated about 100 miles (160 kilometres) north of Hanoi on Route 4 between Cao Bang and Lang Son, and after 60 hours of fighting the post fell. Cao Bang itself was evacuated on 3 October, its garrison and civilians travelling south through mountainous jungle and encountering little resistance; a French column originally from Lang Son which had been sent to meet the Cao Bang force and cover its retreat was, however, continually harassed by the Viet Minh. The two forces eventually made contact on 7 October, but were trapped by Viet Minh forces in a gorge near Dong Khe, most of the French being captured or killed. After this disaster the French posts crumbled: That Khe was abandoned on 11 October and a week later Lang Son, the main French stronghold in the border region, was abandoned. The final border post at Lao Cai was evacuated in early November. Of the 10,000-strong French force stationed in the border regions prior to Giap's offensive, only 4,000 survived.

10 October Brigadier-General Francis Brink, the commander of the 35-man US Military Assistance Advisory Group (MAAG) arrives in Saigon. President Truman had ordered the dispatch of the MAAG to Vietnam soon after the outbreak of the Korean War in June. The group's official task was to supervise the use of US military equipment, but not surprisingly their know-how was deeply resented by the French forces in Vietnam.

14 December The French war hero General de Lattre de Tassigny is appointed French high commissioner and commander-in-chief in Indo-China. After the French disaster in the Sino-Vietnamese border region, personnel changes were inevitable. Both Commander Carpentier and High Commissioner Pignon were sacked and replaced, in mid-December, by one man, General Jean de Lattre de Tassigny (see biographies). As a military leader General de Lattre was held in the same esteem in France as Patton in the US and Montgomery in Britain. He had served as commander of the French First Army during War II and subsequently as commander-in-chief of the Western Union Land Forces.

1 9 5 1

13 January General Giap launches his 'general counteroffensive' which ultimately fails to dent the French 'de Lattre line'. General Giap, emboldened by his successes against the French in late 1950, launched the counteroffensive in order to capture the valuable rice lands of the Red River valley in the Tongkin delta. Giap launched his first attack on 13 January, dispatching 20,000 troops against French positions at Vinh Yen, some 31 miles (50 kilometres) northwest of Hanoi. At first it appeared that the French would collapse as they had done in the northern border lands in October 1950. However, General de Lattre quickly took personal charge of Vinh Yen's defence: he brought in troop reinforcements and deployed napalm-laden fighter-bombers against the Viet Minh positions. By 17 January, Giap, having suffered massive casualties, was forced to pull his remaining men back from Vinh Yen after suffering the first major defeat of his career. After Giap's withdrawal, de Lattre constructed a new defensive line (the 'de Lattre line') around French-controlled territory in the delta.

Urged on by Chinese advisers, General Giap launched a second attempt to penetrate the delta on 24 March with an attack on Mao Khe, some 25 miles (40 kilometres) northwest of Haiphong. As in the attack on Vinh Yen, the initial stages of the offensive went Giap's way but after two days the French responded with a massive naval bombardment carried out by a number of destroyers which had travelled up the Da Bac River. Giap withdrew his forces on 28 March, after losing 3,000 men. A final attempt was launched by Giap in late May, when he deployed three battalions against French forces dug in along the Day River, southwest of Hanoi. The offensive, launched three weeks into the wet season, took de Lattre by surprise. However, the Viet Minh were slowed by the rain and mud and they came up against some stiff opposition from local Catholic militia groups. Eventually, Giap was again forced to begin withdrawing on 10 June and eight days later his third and final attempt to pierce the 'de Lattre line' ended.

29 January French Premier Rene Pleven arrives in the US for talks with Truman on Indo-China. The US delegation to the talks included a large number of officials who would go on to play a major part in US Indo-China policy, including the secretary of state, Dean Acheson, the assistant secretary of state for Far Eastern affairs, Dean Rusk, Truman's foreign affairs adviser, Averell Harriman, the chairman of the Joint Chiefs-of-Staff, General Omar Bradley, and the US ambassador to Paris, David Bruce. During the talks Pleven attempted, unsuccessfully, to persuade Truman to agree to more formal co-ordination on Indo-China by the Western nations; Truman specifically rejected a proposal for the creation of a joint Franco-British-US consultative body on Southeast Asia. Pleven also lobbied, again unsuccessfully, for the provision of US economic assistance for the indigenous national armies of the Associated States. However, Truman did agree to increase US military aid to France and the Indo-Chinese states. It was also agreed that the US would assist in the evacuation of French forces in the event of a Chinese attack on Indo-China.

8 February The second congress of the Indo-Chinese Communist Party (ICP) opens in Vietnam. The congress was held in Viet Minh-controlled territory in February and March. Although the party had formally been dissolved by Ho Chi Minh in late 1945, it had nevertheless continued to lead the revolution covertly. At the congress, a decision was taken to dissolve the ICP into three separate national Communist parties for Vietnam, Laos and Cambodia. The decision was opposed by some Vietnamese cadres who were apprehensive about delegating too much autonomy to Lao and Cambodian Communists. However, the only new party created formally at the congress was the Dang Lao Dong Viet Nam (Vietnamese Workers' Party or Lao Dong Party). Ho Chi Minh was elected chair of the new party and Truong Chinh general secretary (see biographies). Lao Communists did not form a separate party until the mid-1950s and the Lao ICP members, such as Kaysone Phomvihane and Nouhak Phoumsavan, probably transferred membership to the Lao Dong Party. In Cambodia the evidence suggests that a separate party, or at least the essential basis of a party, was formed by Son Ngoc Minh and others during the months following the ICP congress. Some commentators claim that an organization was created in June, others that it was in September. Other Khmer sources indicate that only a provisional central committee was established in 1951 and that the party's inaugural congress was not actually held until 1960.

18 February Tran Van Huu fails in his attempt to broaden the base of the Saigon government. In mid-January Bao Dai requested his prime minister, Tran Van Huu, to enter into negotiations with a wide variety of groups with a view to forming a more broad-based government. Most of the groups approached by Huu, including Roman Catholic, Cao Daist and Hoa Hao Buddhist groups, refused his offer to enter the government. In mid-February he managed to form a new government, with participation of the northern Vietnamese right-wing Dai Viet Party. Unfortunately for Huu, the two Dai Viet ministers (Nguyen Huu Tri and Phan Huy Quat, defence and education respectively) resigned at the first cabinet meeting of 21 February in protest at the premier's refusal to grant additional portfolios to their party.

14 June Details of a Cao Daist mutiny are released. Colonel Trinh Minh Tay, the Cao Daist chief-of-staff, had led a 1,600-strong group of his men from Tay Ninh into Cambodia, declaring his opposition to both the Bao Dai and Democratic Republic of Vietnam (DRV) regimes. The mutiny was widely attributed to Cao Daist discontent with the policies of the Bao Dai government and to disagreements between Colonel Tay and General Tran Quang Vinh, the Cao Daist commander-in-chief. The Cao Daist rebels went on to carry out a number of political assassinations, including that of General Chanson, French commissioner in southern Vietnam in late July, and a bombing campaign in Saigon in January 1952. (See Appendix 2 for details of the three 'sects', Cao Dai, Hoa Hao and Binh-Xuyen.)

11 August The Democrats win another large victory in Cambodian elections. After a two-year suspension of the National Assembly, fresh general elections were held in Cambodia in August. As in the previous elections, the Democrats won a large majority, gaining 55 seats compared to 17 by the Liberals. Other parties which gained representation included right-wing groups such as the 'Khmer Renovation' led by Lon Nol (see biographies) and former Issarak leader Dap Chhuon's 'Victorious North-East'. In fact, the disparate right performed very well, polling over 100,000 votes nation-wide, compared with under 150,000 for the Democrats. However, a new Democratic cabinet was formed under the leadership of Huy Kanthoul. Following their victory, the Democrats came under increasing pressure from the right-wing parties over their alleged Issarak sympathies. Such criticism increased following the return to Phnom Penh in late October of Son Ngoc Thanh, the nationalist leader who had been exiled to France in 1945.

14 November The French forces capture the Viet Minh town of Hoa Binh, situated outside of the 'de Lattre line', some 31 miles (50 kilometres) southwest of Hanoi. De Lattre, who was suffering from cancer and was unofficially replaced as commander-in-chief by General Raoul Salan a week after the capture of Hoa Binh, had launched the attack in an attempt to persuade the French and US governments that the war against the Viet Minh was winnable and worthy of financing.

21 November Souvanna Phouma is appointed prime minister of Laos. Prince Souvanna Phouma, the former Lao Issara leader and half brother of Pathet Lao leader Souphanouvong, replaced Phoui Sananikone who had held the post from February 1950 to October 1951.

1 9 5 2

11 January General de Lattre dies in Paris and is replaced as commander-in-chief by Raoul Salan. General de Lattre had been forced to leave Indo-China in late 1951 after he was diagnosed as suffering from cancer. His death was a great blow to the French as he had done so much during his brief term as high commissioner and commander-in-chief to restore the morale of the troops. Salan, his successor as commander-in-chief, had previously served as de

Lattre's chief-of-staff, while Letourneau, his successor as high commissioner, was minister for the Associated States, a post he retained in conjunction with the commissionership.

22 February After holding Hoa Binh for some three months, the French commander-in-chief, General Raoul Salan, is finally forced to order a withdrawal of his forces. The town, which lay outside of the so-called 'de Lattre line', had been under French control since November 1951 when Salan's predecessor General de Lattre launched an offensive. General Giap had responded to the French offensive in early December, launching a series of 'human wave' assaults on French positions along the Black River, north of Hoa Binh. By mid-January, Giap had managed to close the river and also the road leading out of the town. With some difficulty, the French managed to reopen the road in late January, by which time it was obvious to Salan that the Viet Minh had dealt a telling blow to de Lattre's ambitious plans to shift from a defensive to an attacking strategy. Hence, plans were devised to pull the French forces back towards Hanoi, within the safe confines of the 'de Lattre line'.

8 March Bao Dai appoints a Vietnamese officer to head the national army. The new chief-of-staff was General Nguyen Van Hinh, son of future Premier Nguyen Van Tam. The appointment meant that the army was for the first time, at least nominally, under the direct control of a Vietnamese rather than a French officer.

2 June Bao Dai dismisses Tran Van Huu and appoints Saigon 'strongman' Nguyen Van Tam as his new prime minister. Nguyen Van Tam had long been the principal source of power in the Bao Dai regime. Tam formed a new cabinet on 25 June, many of whose members had served under Huu. According to a private report by the US consul in Hanoi, the new cabinet was composed of 'opportunists, nonentities, extreme reactionaries, assassins, hirelings, and, finally, men of faded mental power' (Karnow, Stanley, *Vietnam: A History*, London 1984, p. 180). The new prime minister also announced details of a new political and security programme, which included plans to increase the Vietnamese army from its present strength of four divisions to six divisions by the end of 1952, and to hold elections to a Vietnamese legislature. In what was described as a move towards democratic government, a Provisional National Council, a consultative body of 21 members nominated by Bao Dai, convened in Saigon in early September.

10 June Official figures of French military expenditure in Indo-China are published in *Le Monde* showing an increase in spending from 3,200 million francs in 1945 to an estimated 435,000 million francs in 1952. (See Appendix 3.)

15 June Sihanouk dismisses the Democrat government in Cambodia. In early June leaflets were distributed in Phnom Penh, signed by the right-wing Issarak 'warlord' Dap Chhuon, calling upon King Sihanouk to dismiss the Democrat government. In response, the Democrats rounded up a number of rightists for questioning, provoking an opposition outcry. In these circumstances, Sihanouk dismissed the government and unsuccessfully beseeched the assembly (in which the Democrats had a large majority) to allow him to assume personal leadership of the country, guaranteeing full independence by 1955. Instead, Sihanouk formed a new government with himself as prime minister.

11 October The Viet Minh launch their highly successful Black River campaign. General Giap launched the offensive with the aim of seizing a string of French posts along the Fan Si Pan mountain range, between the Black and Red Rivers. The offensive opened on 11 October when three Viet Minh assault divisions moved south across the Black River. The first major battle erupted at the French garrison of Nghia Lo on 18 October; the post fell quickly after a heavy bombardment and fierce hand-to-hand fighting. As many as 700 French troops died at Nghia Lo and the collapse of the garrison opened up the whole of the French ridge-line, so that by mid-November Giap's men had crossed the Black River and were pushing towards the Lao border. General Salan had countered Giap's offensive in late October, launching Operation Lorraine aimed at drawing the Viet Minh away from the Black River by threatening their northern supply bases. Giap called Salan's bluff by refusing to redeploy and allowing the French to advance northward. The French pushed as far north as Phu Yen Binh (some 50 miles (80 kilometres) north of the 'de Lattre line'), which they reached on 14 November, capturing some Viet Minh supplies on the way. However, the French were so overstretched that it was impossible for them to launch any meaningful attack on the major logistical centres, and after reaching Phu Yen Binh they turned back, having failed in their attempt to draw Giap away from the Black River. Viet Minh radio announced on 4 December that a 'People's Government' had been formed in the recently occupied areas around the Black River. (See Appendix 4 for details of the opposing forces as of late 1952.)

17 October A plot is uncovered by police to assassinate the US ambassador to Saigon, Donald Heath. Details of the plot were revealed to the police by a captured Viet Minh supporter. The police subsequently raided the headquarters of the 'Assassination Committee', killing the ringleader, Nguyen Ban Thu, who, they claimed, had resisted arrest. Documents found on Thu's body included a plan of Heath's Saigon villa.

4 November Eisenhower is elected president of the US. General Dwight D. Eisenhower defeated Adlai Stevenson, and 10 weeks later he was sworn in as the country's first Republican president for 20 years. Eisenhower's new administration included John Foster Dulles as secretary of state and Charles Wilson as defence secretary.

19 December The French high commissioner for Indo-China defends the government's policy in the region during a National Assembly debate. Jean Letourneau, high commissioner for Indo-China and minister for the Associated States reaffirmed his refusal to enter into negotiations with the Viet Minh. He gave a positive assessment of the military situation throughout Indo-China, claiming that even in the Viet Minh heartlands, the French had managed to hold the vital centres and roads. Socialist and Communist deputies criticized the government's policies, and called for talks to be held between the Viet Minh and the Bao Dai regime.

1 9 5 3

13 January Sihanouk finally dissolves the Democrat-led Cambodian National Assembly and effectively takes personal control over the country. King Sihanouk finally moved against the Democrat-led National Assembly thereby aligning himself with Lon Nol and the Cambodian right. In mid-1952 the assembly had refused Sihanouk's request to be granted increased powers which, he claimed, would help him improve national security and press for greater independence. In January he pressed the assembly to declare a state of emergency to counter the increasing Issarak threat, and again the assembly refused his request. In response, he dissolved the assembly and issued a decree declaring that 'the nation was in danger' and providing the government with a long list of draconian powers to meet the threat. Nine Democratic members of the assembly were subsequently arrested under the decree and in an interview with *Le Monde* on 16 January Sihanouk described the assembly as 'a refuge of treason' and alleged that a number of Democrats had links with the Viet Minh. At the end of the month Sihanouk appointed a new government headed by Pen Nouth, which quickly established a compliant Consultative National Council to replace the assembly.

25 January The Bao Dai regime holds local elections in the 'pacified areas' of Vietnam. Voting was confined to under 2,000 towns and villages out of a total of about 20,000 and the electorate numbered less than a million out of a total population of 22 million. The Viet Minh had called on its supporters in the 'pacified areas' to cross out the names of the candidates and substitute that of Ho Chi Minh, but according to government figures only 5 per cent of the papers were spoilt. The government also claimed to have swept the board in southern Vietnam, although it conceded that in the pacified north it had suffered at the hands of the right-wing Dai Viet and the left-wing Thong Nhat.

9 February Prince Sihanouk begins his 'Royal Crusade for Cambodian Independence'. Internal opposition to Sihanouk's dissolution of the National Assembly in January roused the monarch into launching the 'crusade' in an effort to disarm his critics. The 'crusade' began when Sihanouk arrived in France to press his demands for full independence. He had little luck in Paris and so in April he flew to a number of Western capitals where he warned leaders that the Issarak rebellion in Cambodia was being fanned by French reluctance to grant full independence. In June Sihanouk placed himself in internal exile in Siem Reap and threatened not to return to Phnom Penh until independence had been achieved.

9 April For the first time Viet Minh forces advance deep into Laos. General Giap ordered three Viet Minh divisions into Laos in April and, with some assistance from Pathet Lao units they quickly penetrated deep into the northern part of the country, threatening even the royal capital of Luang Prabang. Giap avoided any major clashes with French units, which for the most part were stationed on the Plain of Jars, and in May, after the early arrival of the monsoon, he ordered an unexpected withdrawal. Nevertheless, the incursion produced a number of positive results for the Viet Minh. Giap gained control of some 19,000 square miles (50,000 square kilometres) of Lao territory, including the town of

Sam Neua, where Souphanouvong was encouraged to establish his Pathet Lao government. At the same time the invasion strengthened the Viet Minh's grip on the west bank of the Black River and improved communication links with China.

8 May General Henri Navarre (see biographies) replaces General Salan as French commander-in-chief in Indo-China and quickly sets to work devising a plan to defeat the Viet Minh. Other command appointments in Indo-China included Air General Pierre-Louis Bodet as Navarre's deputy and General Rene Cogny as commander of Franco-Vietnamese land forces in northern Vietnam. The new commander-in-chief quickly devised what became known as the 'Navarre plan', which was approved in July by the new French government headed by Joseph Laniel; the US had reservations about the plan, but in September they agreed to provide an extra $385 million in military assistance to help finance it. Under the plan, the French would remain on the defensive in northern Vietnam during the 1953–4 campaign season; major set-piece battles with the Viet Minh would be avoided. In order to stop Giap carrying out a major northern offensive, French forces would initiate a series of small spoiling attacks throughout the country. Meanwhile, the French would deploy some of their European land, air and naval units in Vietnam, at the same time accelerating the training of the indigenous Indo-Chinese national armies, with the eventual aim of seeking a major confrontation with Giap during the 1954–5 season. Once the Viet Minh were defeated during a big set-piece battle, the plan stated, France would be able to settle the war honourably.

3 July The French government announces its intention to bring about complete independence for the Associated States. The French prime minister, Joseph Laniel, announced his government's intention to 'complete the independence and sovereignty of the Associated States' within the French Union and proposed the opening of discussions on the points at issue in the economic, financial, judicial, military and political fields. On the same day, the appointment of Maurice Dejean, French ambassador to Japan, as commissioner-general for Indo-China was announced from Paris.

Laniel's declaration was warmly welcomed in Saigon and Vientiane, but met with a cooler reception in Phnom Penh. In an official statement on behalf of his government the Cambodian ambassador in Washington, Nong Kimny, said on 11 July that although Laniel's announcement 'constituted a real step forward', the Cambodian position was 'somewhat special' and therefore the proposal 'did not quite meet the aspirations of the Cambodian people' who desired 'an unequivocal declaration of independence'.

12 October 'Nationalist groups' convene in Saigon where they attack Bao Dai's pro-French outlook. Bao Dai and his premier, Nguyen Van Tam, visited France in August and September for talks on the implementation of the French declaration of 3 July. A number of nationalist groups used Bao Dai and Tam's absence to intensify their attacks on the government's policies, which they criticized as being too pro-French. On 6 September a number of Cao Dai, Hoa Hao, Binh Xuyen and Roman Catholic leaders congregated in Saigon for a 'conference of national unity and peace'; a manifesto issued at the end of the meeting declared that 'Vietnam remains the only country of Southeast Asia where patriots continue to be oppressed and where the people are still waiting to take a direct part in the conduct of affairs.' Another 'nationalist' congress was held in Saigon from 12 to 17 October, at which 200 representatives adopted a strongly-worded resolution demanding complete independence for Vietnam. The resolutions adopted by the Saigon congress aroused great resentment in France despite attempts by Bao Dai and Nguyen Van Tam to play down their significance.

22 October Laos is granted full independence as a member of the French Union. Following French Prime Minister Joseph Laniel's 3 July declaration, talks opened in Paris between Lao and French delegations on 15 October. A week later King Sisavang Vong and President Auriol signed a Treaty of Amity and Association between Laos and France, under the terms of which France recognized Laos as a fully independent and sovereign state within the French Union.

9 November Sihanouk proclaims Cambodian independence. In late August King Sihanouk, who was living in internal exile in western Cambodia, organized a large military show of strength in Battambang in a further effort to persuade France to grant full independence. The French, facing an increasingly stern military test in Vietnam, and concerned about the possible drift away from the conservative throne to the Cambodian left, eventually decided to enter into serious negotiations which resulted in the signing of a military agreement in mid-October providing for the transfer to Sihanouk of the territorial command of the whole country, with France retaining operational control east of the Mekong (i.e. along the Vietnamese border lands). The transfer was completed on 7 November and two days later Sihanouk, who had returned to Phnom Penh the previous day, formally declared full independence at a parade of withdrawing French troops.

20 November French paratroopers take the strategic territory around Dien Bien Phu, in northwestern Vietnam. In late October General Giap pushed the 316th Viet Minh Division towards the Lao border, indicating that he was about to cross the border again. In response, General Navarre decided to establish a fortified airhead in the Dien Bien Phu valley from where he expected to be able to defend northern Laos. Situated near the border with Laos, some 174 miles (280 kilometres) northwest of Hanoi, Dien Bien Phu had been occupied by the Viet Minh since late 1952. Crack French paratroopers dropped into the valley on 20 November and they quickly secured the airstrip and began digging in. Reinforcements followed and with Dien Bien Phu apparently secure, the French carried on with implementation of the 'Navarre plan', in particular the diversionary attacks aimed at upsetting Giap's plans for a major offensive. Navarre's underestimation of the Viet Minh's strength and determination meant that he never seriously considered the possibility that Dien Bien Phu itself might be the stage for Giap's major offensive. Navarre believed that the Viet Minh would find it impossible to deploy the necessary men and equipment in the hills surrounding the valley. So that even when it did become obvious that the Viet Minh were planning an assault on the valley, Navarre badly miscalculated the size and strength of Giap's forces and therefore failed to reinforce the garrison with anything like the correct numbers.

Giap *had* chosen Dien Bien Phu as the set-piece battle in which he aimed to inflict a killing blow to the French. After the French paratroopers had landed in November he began building up his forces in the hills around the valley. In what was probably one of the most outstanding logistical manoeuvres in the history of warfare Giap arranged for massive amounts of Soviet and Chinese artillery and ammunition to be carried into the hills by peasant porters operating on foot or, extraordinary as it might seem, bicycle.

28 November Ho Chi Minh announces that he is prepared to enter into peace talks with France. In an interview with the Swedish newspaper *Expressen* in late November, Ho Chi Minh said that his government would be prepared to enter into peace talks with France 'provided that the French government ends its war of aggression in Vietnam'. 'The basis for such an armistice,' he said, 'is that the French government should show sincere respect for the genuine independence of Vietnam.' Ho went on to say that French independence, like Vietnamese independence, was 'gravely threatened' by US imperialism.

By linking together France and Vietnam against the US Ho was clearly playing on the rising anti-war feeling amongst the French public, a mood that was increasingly reflected in the National Assembly. The Eisenhower administration was disturbed by this shift in French opinion; for Secretary of State Dulles Franco-Viet Minh negotiations were tantamount to the start of the collapse of containment as a workable doctrine. Nevertheless, despite the US attitude, the momentum during 1953 was definitely towards negotiation. Not only was the French appetite for the war waning, but the atmosphere on the international stage was generally more conciliatory. The death of Stalin in March had allowed a Soviet government to preach 'peaceful co-existence'. Similarly, the Korean armistice in July had increased pressure on the warring sides in Indo-China to arrange a peaceful settlement.

1 December Ho Chi Minh addresses the Democratic Republic of Vietnam (DRV) National Assembly. The DRV National Assembly convened in late 1953 for the first time since the start of the resistance war. The main pieces of legislation placed before the deputies, and subsequently approved by them, concerned the vital issue of land reform. In his report to the assembly on 1 December, Ho Chi Minh claimed that peasants accounted for almost 90 per cent of the population, but owned only 30 per cent of the arable land. Hence, the goal set for land reform was to 'wipe out the feudal system of land ownership, distribute land to the tillers, liberate the productive forces in the countryside'. The 'guiding principle for land distribution' would be to allot land in priority to those who have been tilling it.

Measures to bring about land reform had been laid down in mid-1949, but implementation had been haphazard, and in many cases corrupt. In many ways the 1953 assembly session simply reiterated many of the 1949 measures, but fresh emphasis was placed on improving the implementation mechanism. It was agreed that party central committee cadres would be dispatched to villages to facilitate the formation of Peasant Associations and press for the full implementation of the law. The new rigorous approach to land reform had arisen out of the party's realization that peasants would have to be provided with material incentives if they were to be expected to support fully the Viet Minh's military effort. Nevertheless, the initiation of what amounted to a radical agrarian revolution in the midst of a full-scale resistance war was by any standards a brave venture that reflected the certainty of the Communist Party general secretary, Truong Chinh, and others that land reform, and its attendant mobilization of the masses, was the only sure method of ensuring military victory.

17 December Nguyen Van Tam resigns as premier of South Vietnam. During early December Nguyen Van Tam attempted to persuade Bao Dai to adopt a new government programme which would include: (i) the inclusion of 'nationalist' representatives in the cabinet; (ii) the election of a National Assembly; and (iii) eventual negotiations with the Viet Minh. Bao Dai rejected the programme, and Tam resigned. Prince Buu Loc, the Vietnamese high commissioner in Paris, was appointed by Bao Dai as the new premier on the same day.

1 9 5 4

13 March The decisive battle of the First Indo-Chinese War begins at Dien Bien Phu; after two months of brutal fighting the French are defeated and the war comes to a close. By early March General Giap had managed to position some 49,000 troops in the high ground overlooking the French entrenchments in the Dien Bien Phu valley. His forces were equipped with a phenomenal amount of military hardware, dragged into the hills by hordes of peasants, including a range of howitzers and mortars, anti-aircraft guns and Katyusha six-tube rocket launchers. Despite the advantage of air surveillance, the French were largely ignorant of the full extent of the Viet Minh build-up in the hills. The French had under 11,000 soldiers in the valley, including battle-hardened German Legionnaires and North African and T'ai troops, and they were woefully underarmed, although they did have a number of light tanks. The valley had been converted into nine fortified strongpoints; 'Gabrielle' in the north, 'Anne-Marie' in the northwest and 'Beatrice' in the northeast; 'Isabelle' in the south; and an inner ring of 'Huguette', 'Claudine', 'Dominique', 'Elaine' and 'Francoise'.

On the eve of the battle Giap issued a prophetic appeal to his men: 'the victorious Dien Bien Phu campaign,' he said, 'will have a resounding influence both within and outside the country'. Giap struck at the northern posts first, employing heavy artillery assaults and prolonged infantry advances. 'Beatrice' fell on the first night, 'Gabrielle' on 15 March and 'Anne-Marie' on 17 March. For General Navarre, and his commander at Dien Bien Phu, Colonel Christian de Castries, the start of the battle was a complete disaster. They had lost three of their most heavily defended positions and with them some 1,600 of their best fighters. After the fall of 'Anne-Marie' there was a two-week lull in the fighting, during which the French made frequent, but largely unsuccessful, attempts to resupply the valley from the air. On 30 March the Viet Minh launched the second phase of their offensive, quickly pushing to within a mile (1.5 kilometres) of the main compound bunker, before being beaten back. Desperate fighting continued for 24 hours, with some positions changing hands six times. Colonel Castries appealed urgently for airborne reinforcements, which never arrived, the airfield having been rendered unuseable by the Viet Minh artillery barrages. By late April the French position was hopeless, with their ammunition running low and facing a solid Viet Minh line less than three-quarters of a mile (1 kilometre) away. Giap launched his third, and final, major assault on 1 May. Unlike the previous two it was carried out without artillery preparation, the Viet Minh simply launching wave after wave of assaults. After seven days of heavy, brutal hand-to-hand fighting, Giap's troops overran the French command bunker, taking the remaining French forces as prisoners. Minutes before the Viet Minh stormed his compound General Castries sent a telephone message to General Cogny: 'the situation is extremely grave,' it went, 'Confused fighting everywhere. I feel the end is near. But we will fight to the end. We will destroy our guns and all our radio material. I am blowing up all our installations. The munitions dump is exploding already. *Adieu, mon general. Vive la France!*'

The French debacle at Dien Bien Phu meant that for the first time the US faced the prospect of direct military intervention in Indo-China. In late March the French chief-of-staff, General Paul Ely, had visited Washington in what proved to be a successful attempt to procure additional US aircraft for Indo-China. During his visit General Ely met with Admiral Arthur Radford, the chair of the joint chiefs-of-staff, who apparently proposed that US B-29 bombers stationed at Clark Air Force Base in the Philippines would launch a massive strike, possibly with nuclear weapons, at Giap's forces massing around Dien Bien Phu. General Ely was impressed with the offer, but when Radford showed the plan, Operation Vulture, around Washington he failed to receive the necessary backing. Congressional leaders, including Lyndon Johnson (see biographies), in particular opposed a unilateral US action and pressed instead for a coalition of European and Asian nations to take some form of military action. In April Eisenhower and Secretary of State Dulles attempted to bring together such a coalition for a united action, aimed principally at deterring Chinese intervention. The Asian nations expressed enthusiasm for the move, but Britain refused to countenance any intervention until after the forthcoming Geneva conference on Korea and Indo-China. The French too opposed an internationalization of the war, and continued to press the US for one major bombing raid to relieve their forces at Dien Bien Phu. Finally, at the end of April the Eisenhower administration formally decided to refrain from any military action until the outcome of Geneva was known.

8 May Immediately following the fall of Dien Bien Phu the world powers convene in Geneva to discuss Indo-China. The convening of an international conference on Indo-China and Korea had been agreed at a meeting of the foreign ministers of Britain, France, the Soviet Union and the US in Berlin in February. The Korean session had opened in Geneva's Palais de Nations on 26 April but the talks quickly stalled. (See Appendix 5 for heads of delegations attending the Geneva conference.)

Little progress was made in May and early June in the search for a cease-fire and a political settlement. At the start of the session Pham Van Dong, the North Vietnamese foreign minister, attempted, unsuccessfully, to gain representation at the conference for the two 'resistance governments' in Laos and Cambodia. He also proposed a cease-fire in Indo-China, to be followed by a 'regroupment' of French forces, a withdrawal of all 'foreign forces' (including the Viet Minh) from the Associated States and free national elections to be held under local supervision. The French foreign minister, Georges Bidault, made no proposals on a political settlement to accompany a cease-fire, but called for regular forces in Indo-China to be assembled, under international supervision, in 'zones of concentration'.

1 June Edward Landsdale arrives in Saigon, heralding an increasing US interest in Vietman. Even before the French defeat at Dien Bien Phu placed US military involvement in Indo-China at the top of the government's foreign policy agenda, the Eisenhower administration had already formulated plans to send a Saigon Military Mission (SMM) team to initiate secret operations against the Viet Minh. Colonel Edward Lansdale (see biographies), a Central Intelligence Agency (CIA) man who had made his reputation helping to suppress the 'Huk' rebellion in the Philippines, arrived in South Vietnam with a brief 'to undertake paramilitary operations against the enemy and to wage political-psychological warfare'. After Geneva, the mission was modified to 'prepare the means for undertaking paramilitary operations in Communist areas rather than wage unconventional warfare'. Lansdale was joined in early July by Major Lucien Conein, a paramilitary specialist who was assigned to the US Military Assistance Advisory Group (MAAG) for cover; 10 more US officers were seconded to the SMM before mid-August and they in turn recruited a number of Vietnamese. The sort of tasks Lansdale and the SMM carried out during 1954–5 included providing security for Diem, spreading anti-Viet Minh propaganda and launching minor sabotage operations (for example, the team ruined the engines of a number of Hanoi buses in an attempt to undermine the Viet Minh administration of the city).

4 June A treaty providing for Vietnamese independence is finally initialled in Paris. The treaty providing for Vietnam's independence within the French Union was initialled by Buu Loc and Joseph Laniel, the Vietnamese and French premiers, midway through the Geneva conference. (The treaty was initialled, but never formally signed nor ratified by either government.) The Laniel government had announced its intention to complete the process of independence in Indo-China in mid-1953 and later that year treaties had been signed with Laos and Cambodia.

16 June Bao Dai appoints the increasingly powerful Ngo Dinh Diem (see biographies) prime minister of South Vietnam. Prince Buu Loc, the prime minister of the Saigon regime, had resigned in mid-June. A devout Catholic with nationalist credentials and fervent anti-Communist views, Diem's appointment, according to some commentators, resulted from his association with a powerful 'Vietnam lobby' in the US, whose members included John Kennedy and Mike Mansfield. Diem took over the reins of a country which was descending into a state of anarchy. The government's authority was confined to parts of Saigon and a few other large towns, the greater part of the country being controlled by the Cao Daists, Hoa Hao and Binh Xuyen, or by the Viet Minh. Bao Dai's prestige and authority, which had never been high, was extremely low and was greatly weakened by the fact that he resided for most of the time in France.

17 June Pierre Mendes-France, the new French premier, pledges to resign if a peaceful agreement on Indo-China is not reached by 20 July. A month into the Geneva conference the French National Assembly voted Premier Joseph Laniel out of office and invited the Radical Party deputy, Pierre Mendes-France (see biographies), to form a government. Mendes-France, who had been publicly opposed to the French involvement in Indo-China for years, was confirmed as the premier on 17 June. Mendes-France declared his intention to resign if he had not obtained a cease-fire in Indo-China by 20 July, in his first speech to the assembly. Following the appointment of Mendes-France the principal negotiations on Indo-China took place outside of the confines of the conference.

On 23 June for instance, Chinese Premier Zhou Enlai met with the new French premier in Switzerland where the former raised the possibility of temporarily partitioning Vietnam as a means of separating the warring parties. Zhou also made it known that China opposed a Viet Minh presence in Laos and Cambodia. Mendes-France agreed to partition, but Pham Van Dong made it known that he opposed the idea. The US remained aloof, utterly opposed to any concessions to the Chinese, but wary of being blamed for the collapse of the peace talks.

20 July A general armistice in Indo-China is reached at the Geneva conference. The agreement was reached only hours before the time-limit which Mendes-France had set himself. The next day separate cease-fire agreements were signed in respect of Vietnam, Laos and Cambodia (a cease-fire came into effect throughout North Vietnam on 27 July). The conference ended on 21 July with the publication of a series of declarations (see Appendices 6, 7, 8). An eight-nation declaration 'on the problem of restoring peace in Indo-China', was tacitly adopted, but not signed, by all the attending nations except the US. The US issued a unilateral declaration in which it stated that it would refrain from threat or the use of force to disturb the cease-fire agreements and would view any renewal of aggression with grave concern. The South Vietnamese foreign minister, Tran Van Do, also issued a declaration which set forth his government's objections to the cease-fire agreement. Do claimed the agreement abandoned territories to the Viet Minh which were 'essential for the defence of Vietnam against further Communist expansionism'. At the same time separate declarations were issued by the French, Lao and Cambodian governments. (See Appendices 6, 7 and 8 for texts of Final Declaration, Unilateral US Declaration, and Lao Declaration.)

During July China and the Soviet Union had both exerted pressure on Pham Van Dong to accept a period of partition, prior to national elections, as the only realistic means of removing the French and (the primary concern for the Chinese) blocking the entry into Indo-China of the US. As Mendes-France's deadline approached, the threat of the talks breaking loomed as arguments raged over the precise latitude of the demarcation line and the timing of national reunification elections. At the eleventh hour the Soviets finally managed to persuade Dong to agree to a division at the seventeenth parallel and a two-year span before elections. The elections would be held with the aim of establishing a unified government and they would be supervised by an International Control Commission (ICC) comprising Indian, Polish and Canadian representatives. Viet Minh and French forces would regroup in North and South Vietnam, respectively, within 300 days. Viet Minh forces would withdraw from Cambodia and Laos. The Laotian delegation, led by Foreign Minister Phoui Sananikone, accepted the designation of the northeastern provinces of Phong Saly and Sam Neua as Pathet Lao regroupment areas. These areas would be integrated into Laos after elections to be held in 1955. Unlike the revolutionaries in Vietnam and Laos, the Cambodian Communists and Issaraks were not allotted regroupment areas, leading to subsequent accusations among Khmer Communists that they had been betrayed at Geneva by Hanoi or Beijing. The Cambodian delegation did agree to institute a free and open political system (based on the 1947 Constitution), which would be demonstrated through the holding of internationally supervised elections in 1955.

20 August The US National Security Council's (NSC's) first post-Geneva policy document is approved, indicating Eisenhower's intention to support fully the Saigon regime. The NSC's first post-Geneva policy document entitled 'Review of US Policy in the Far East' was approved by President Eisenhower on 20 August. The document viewed Geneva as a loss of prestige for the US in Asia and as a major success for 'the Communists' which, it was claimed, had gained 'an advance salient in Vietnam' and had increased their 'military and political prestige in Asia'. Under a section entitled 'courses of action', the document proposed, amongst other things: (i) negotiating a Southeast Asian security treaty with friendly European and Asian countries; (ii) if requested, carrying out 'covert and overt support' for any 'legitimate local government which requires assistance to defeat local Communist subversion'; (iii) working with France 'only insofar as necessary' to assist the Indo-Chinese nations militarily and economically and, where, possible, dealing directly with Saigon, Vientiane and Phnom Penh.

8 September The Southeast Asia Treaty Organization (SEATO) is signed in Manilla. The weakened position of the US in post-Geneva Asia spurred the Eisenhower administration into pushing ahead with its collective defence plans which had been rejected by the French and British at the time of Dien Bien Phu. The creation of a collective defence treaty in Asia had long been a goal of Secretary of State Dulles who believed that such a cloak would be a great help in his battle to confine Communism to the Eurasian land mass. The Southeast Asian Collective Defence Treaty and Protocol was signed in the Philippines in September by the governments of Australia, France, New Zealand, Pakistan, the Philippines, Thailand, Britain and the US. The treaty agreed on the establishment of SEATO, which established its headquarters in Bangkok in early 1955 after the treaty had been ratified.

The key article of the treaty (article 4) stated that 'each party recognizes that aggression by means of armed attack in the treaty area against any of the parties, or against any state or territory which the parties by unanimous agreement may hereafter designate, would endanger its own peace and safety, and agrees that it will, in that event, act to meet the common danger in accordance with its constitutional processes'. A protocol on Indo-China designated the states of Laos, Cambodia and 'the free territory under the jurisdiction of the State of Vietnam' as parties to the treaty in respect of article 4.

1 October President Eisenhower writes to Saigon Premier Ngo Dinh Diem formally pledging US support for his government. In the letter Eisenhower said that the US government had been 'exploring ways and means to permit our aid to Vietnam to be more effective'. Towards this end he said he was instructing the US ambassador in Saigon 'to examine with you . . . how an intelligent program of American aid given directly to your government can serve to assist Vietnam in its present hour of trial, provided that your government is prepared to give assurances as to the standards of performance it would be able to maintain in the event such aid were supplied'.

19 October A cabinet crisis forces Souvanna Phouma to relinquish the premiership in Laos. He had held the post since later 1951. Souvanna was replaced in November by Kathay Don Sasorith, leader of the National Progressive Party and a former finance minister. Souvanna had resigned as a result of a cabinet crisis precipitated by the assassination of the defence minister, Kou Voravong, by 'nationalist Laotians' in mid-September.

19 November The deadline is reached for foreign troop withdrawals from Laos. In accordance with the terms of the Geneva Agreements, all Viet Minh, and all but 5,000 French troops, were evacuated from Laos by 19 November. At the same time, the Pathet Lao forces were withdrawn to the northeastern provinces of Sam Neua and Phong Saly pending a political settlement. Earlier in November, the Franco-Lao land forces command had been officially dissolved, its powers having been transferred to the Royal Lao Army.

1 9 5 5

4 February The Hanoi government issues the first of a series of conciliatory statements on North-South relations. In early February, the North Vietnamese Council of Ministers issued a statement on 'the question of restoring normal relations between North and South Vietnam on either side of the provisional military demarcation line'. The statement said that, in conformity with the spirit of the Geneva Agreement, the North was prepared to grant facilities to people in both zones to encourage economic, cultural and social exchanges. The statement said that the northern authorities hoped that the Saigon authorities would 'agree to the restoration of normal relations . . . with a view to bringing about solutions favourable for the entire people'. Although the Diem government did not respond to the initiative, the North issued another proposal in early June. Pham Van Dong, Hanoi's foreign minister, announced that his government wanted to open consultations with the South in preparation for the July 1956 elections. At the same time, Dong assured the Saigon regime that the North desired free elections in which 'all political parties, organisations and individuals' would be able to take part.

2 March In a surprise move Prince Sihanouk abdicates the Cambodian throne in favour of his father, Norodom Suramarit. In his proclamation Sihanouk claimed he had stepped down from the throne 'in order to live . . . among my people a life as humble as that of my subjects'. In actual fact, Sihanouk's abdication was not quite as selfless as he implied and was largely motivated by his desire to avoid constitutional constraints on his political activities.

At Geneva, Cambodia had committed itself to holding free elections under the terms of the 1947 Constitution. Many of the provisions of the Constitution had been undermined by Sihanouk during the early 1950s, but in its unadulterated form the charter severely restricted the political role of the monarch and provided for a strong legislature. In the post-Geneva atmosphere it seemed that free elections would result in a victory for the leftist forces Sihanouk had so ably undermined during his 'Royal Crusade for Independence'. Ironically, Sihanouk's success at Geneva in keeping the country intact had left the revolutionary opposition with little option but to withdraw to North Vietnam or enter the political process. Son Ngoc Minh and a group of his supporters opted for the former option and withdrew to Hanoi. However, another group of Minh's associates, led by Keo Meas and Non Suon, returned to Phnom Penh where they created the Pracheachon (Citizens') Party. At the same time supporters of Son Ngoc Thanh founded a party and a more radical version of the Democrats emerged, many of its leading figures drawn from the Paris Marxist Circle. The resurgence of the left ahead of internationally supervised elections frightened the Cambodian right, led by Lon Nol and Dap Chhuon, into settling their difference and forming a coalition in late 1954. However, this rightist coalition broke up in February 1955, with most of its membership joining the Sangkum Reastr Niyum (Popular Socialist Community), which had been formed that month by Sihanouk as the vehicle to take him into the political arena proper.

4 March The powerful Vietnamese 'sects' form a United Front. During the first months of 1955 Diem faced a major political crisis as he attempted to demonstrate his authority to the powerful sects. On 4 March the Cao Dai, Hoa Hao and Binh Xuyen had formed a 'United Front of Nationalist Forces'. The front's manifesto demanded the formation of a strong 'government of national unity', a demand which it reiterated in a 21 March ultimatum presented to Diem, accusing the premier of totalitarianism and nepotism. The crisis was partly eased in late March and early April when Colonel Lansdale, the US Saigon Military Mission (SMM) chief, paid out an enormous amount of Central Intelligence Agency (CIA) money to Cao Dai and Hoa Hao generals to get them to rally to Diem. At the same time Lansdale, who was meeting with Diem on a daily basis, helped the beleaguered premier draw up plans to inflict a military defeat on the Binh Xuyen, who Diem had refused to deal with. Skirmishing between Binh Xuyen and Diem's forces broke out in Saigon in late March.

22 March A Lao People's Party (LPP), the forerunner of the Communist Lao People's Revolutionary Party (LPRP), is formed. Some 25 delegates attended the inaugural congress of the LPP in northeastern Laos in March. The LPRP went on to rule the country following the Pathet Lao victory in 1975. At the congress, the delegates elected Kaysone Phomvihane as the party secretary-general. There had not been a Communist Party in Laos since the disbanding of the Indo-Chinese Communist Party (ICP) in 1951, although leading Lao Communists had held membership of the Vietnamese Lao Dong Party.

18 April The Bandung conference opens and is attended by leaders from all three Indo-Chinese countries. The Asian–African conference was held in Bandung, Indonesia, between 18 and 24 April. The conference, which had been organized by the five 'Colombo powers' (Indonesia, India, Burma, Pakistan and Ceylon) was attended by representatives from 29 countries, including Pham Van Dong from North Vietnam, Nguyen Van Thoai from South Vietnam, Prince Sihanouk from Cambodia and Kathay Don Sasorith from Laos. At the conference a series of meetings took place between the North Vietnamese, Laotian, Cambodian and Chinese delegations. Pham Van Dong and Kathay Don Sasorith signed an agreement on 23 April whereby the latter affirmed Laos's adherence to the 'five principles' of co-existence, and Pham Van Dong gave an assurance that Hanoi had no designs on the Pathet Lao-controlled provinces of Sam Neua and Phong Saly. Similar assurances of non-interference were given by Dong to Cambodia and by Chinese Premier Zhou Enlai to both Laos and Cambodia.

28 April Diem launches an assault on the Binh Xuyen forces at the start of his ultimately successful effort to crush the influence of the 'sects'. Although Colonel Lansdale gave the full weight of his support to Diem during the sect crisis, other Americans in Saigon were less enamoured of the premier. General J. Lawton Collins, President Eisenhower's personal representative in Saigon, was convinced that Diem was doomed. Collins was supported in his assessment by the French, whose disapproval of Diem was at least partly motivated by their sponsorship of the Binh Xuyen. General Collins returned to Washington in late April to brief Secretary of State Dulles on the Saigon situation, and Dulles eventually agreed that Diem would have to go. However, while this decision was being taken in Washington, events were moving quickly in Saigon. On 28 April Binh Xuyen units launched an attack on government troops in Saigon, and Diem, urged on by Lansdale, ordered a large counteroffensive. After a short but bloody pitched battle Binh Xuyen were pushed out of Saigon into the marshy grounds south and west of the city. As the battle raged, Diem faced a fresh threat from Paris, where Bao Dai announced that he had dismissed Diem as chief of the armed forces. However, after his suppression of the Binh Xuyen, Washington, urged by Lansdale, had immediately reversed its policy and offered Diem its full support; this support, along with the support of most of the officer corps, gave Diem the security to ignore Bao Dai's announcement and to begin planning for the emperor's deposition.

16 May Cambodia signs a military aid agreement with the US. The agreement, signed in Phnom Penh, served to unnerve the left. The International Control Commission (ICC) subsequently investigated certain clauses of the agreement, which, it was suggested, did not conform with the Geneva Agreements. In reply, the government assured the commission that the agreement did not constitute an alliance, nor did it cede military bases, but was merely a continuation of the assistance previously given by France. The commission accepted these assurances.

18 May The 300-day period for the evacuation of civilian Vietnamese refugees set down under the Geneva accord ends. However, South Vietnam successfully petitioned the ICC for the period to be extended and a new deadline of 20 July was set. By this date a massive flow of refugees had crossed the seventeenth parallel, the majority travelling from North to South. As many as 900,000 northerners journeyed South, over 80 per cent of whom were Catholics. The US organized a large naval task force, dubbed 'Passage to Freedom', to transport the refugees. The flood of refugees, which had been encouraged by propaganda originating from Lansdale's SMM unit, brought the number of Catholics in the South to over a million and they provided Diem, himself a Catholic, with a vital support base. No statistics were published of the total number of refugees leaving South for North Vietnam, but estimates suggest the number was under 5,000. However, some 150,000 Viet Minh troops were evacuated from the South on Polish and Soviet ships, the final withdrawal taking place on 3 May. The evacuation of French Union forces from North Vietnam was completed 10 days later, when the French garrison left Haiphong.

19 July North Vietnam again contacts the South on the election issue. Ho Chi Minh and Pham Van Dong wrote to Bao Dai and Ngo Dinh Diem asking the southern leaders to appoint their representatives to a Consultative Conference to discuss the holding of elections. Under the terms of the Geneva Agreements such a conference was due to convene by 20 July 1955. The southern regime made no official response to the letter, but instead ordered 20 July (the anniversary of the conclusion of the Geneva Agreements) to be observed as a 'day of national shame'. On the day armed mobs took to the streets of Saigon, picking out for attack the offices and personnel of the ICC. Diem described the riots as 'striking proof of the determination of the Vietnamese people to fight Communism'. A week after the riots, US, French and British diplomats in Saigon handed identical notes to Diem urging him to open discussions with the North. However, according to some commentators, the US was probably advising Diem against holding the nation-wide elections, although the *Pentagon Papers* contend that Diem's opposition to the pre-election consultation was at his own initiative. Nevertheless, the Eisenhower administration was certainly apprehensive about the possibility that elections might be held, as can be gauged from a National Security Council study completed in mid-May. This study claimed that the 'Communists' would hold certain advantages in all Vietnam elections, namely 'Communist popular appeal derived from long identification with the struggle for independence,' and 'the continuing difficulties of the Free Vietnam Government in consolidating its political control in its own zone and moving ahead with programs of popular appeal'. The South Vietnamese government issued a statement on the election issue on 9 August. The government reiterated that it did not consider itself bound in any respect by the Geneva Agreements and made it clear that it would never enter into negotiations with the North as long as the Communist regime remained in power.

11 September General elections in Cambodia result in a massive victory for Sihanouk's newly-formed Sangkum. The Sangkum's victory followed an election campaign characterized by serious harassment of the opposition. The elections had originally been due to be held in April, but Sihanouk had managed to have them postponed in order to give the newly-formed Sangkum more time for electioneering. Although a number of reports came out of Cambodia alleging that people had been intimidated into voting for the Sangkum, the ICC certified the election as 'correct'. According to the official results, the Sangkum won all 91 assembly seats and gained 82 per cent of the vote, with the Democrats gaining 12 per cent and Pracheachon 4 per cent. At a press conference after the elections, Sihanouk said he was 'slightly embarrassed' by his 'too complete victory' but affirmed that the results were genuine. 'If I had falsified the elections,' he said, 'I would never have had the effrontery to give us all the seats'. The new assembly offered Sihanouk the premiership on 25 September, and after a period of deliberation, he accepted it for a three-month period.

20 September Pham Van Dong is elected as the North Vietnamese premier by the National Assembly. Dong, who retained his Foreign Ministry portfolio, replaced Ho Chi Minh who had previously combined the post with the presidency. At the same time Defence Minister Vo Nguyen Giap and Interior Minister Pham Ke Toai were both elected as vice premiers.

26 October Bao Dai is officially deposed and the Republic of Vietnam is proclaimed with Diem as president. Diem, assisted by Lansdale, sought to consolidate finally his power by holding a referendum on whether Bao Dai, who remained in France, should be deposed as chief-of-state. The referendum, held on 23 October, was a corrupt affair which resulted in a 98 per cent majority against Bao Dai. Three days later the former emperor was officially deposed and South Vietnam was officially proclaimed a Republic with Diem as its president. Diem also retained the posts of premier and defence minister and assumed that of supreme commander of the armed forces. The new Republic was quickly recognized by the US and other Western countries.

25 December Elections to a 39-member National Assembly take place in government-controlled areas of Laos. The Pathet Lao had refused to contest the elections, so voting did not take place in Sam Neua or Phong Saly provinces. The results were as follows: National Progressive Party (led by Kathay Don Sasorith) 21, Independent Party (led by Phoui Sananikone) 8, Democrats 3, National Union Party 2, and Independents 5.

Elections had originally been scheduled to take place in late August, but they had been postponed as a result of an impasse in negotiations between the Vientiane regime and the Pathet Lao. The talks, which had been under way since September 1954, were aimed at reaching a political settlement which would allow the full integration of the two Pathet Lao provinces into the rest of Laos. Intermittent negotiations were held throughout 1955, but the chances of a quick settlement diminished after an outbreak of fighting in Sam Neua in July and August.

---

1 9 5 6

6 January The Pathet Lao leadership creates a political front organization. Leading figures from the Pathet Lao and from the recently-formed Lao People's Party (LPP) convened in secret in northeastern Laos in early January. On 6 January the delegates announced the formation of a broad political front organization, the Neo Lao Hak Sat (Lao Patriotic Front – LPF), with Souphanouvong at the head of a 40-member central committee.

11 January President Diem issues an ordinance providing a legal basis for the arrest of anyone threatening national security. Even before he had formally deposed Bao Dai in October 1955, Ngo Dinh Diem had launched a vicious anti-Communist campaign in the South in direct contravention of the Geneva Agreements. In early 1956 he provided himself with a legal basis to widen the scope of the campaign to include political opponents of any hue, so that by the end of the year as many as 50,000 people had been imprisoned and an unknown number executed. The legal basis for Diem's actions was 'ordinance no 6' issued by him in January. Under the broad terms of the ordinance any individual who was considered 'dangerous to national defence and common security' could be confined by executive order in one of a number of newly-created political re-education camps.

13 February Prince Sihanouk begins a nine-day stay in China. In Beijing the prince signed a Sino-Cambodian declaration of friendship which reaffirmed

Cambodia's policy of neutrality. At the same time Sihanouk accepted a Chinese aid package, the first given by Beijing to a non-Communist country. Following his Chinese visit, Sihanouk went to the Soviet Union and Czechoslovakia in mid-1956, where he also received economic aid packages. Sihanouk defended his actions by claiming that Cambodian neutrality required that the country receive assistance equally from Communist and Western countries.

4 March A Constituent Assembly is elected in South Vietnam. The South Vietnamese government announced in late January that general elections for a 123-member Constituent Assembly would be held in March. During the campaign harsh government treatment of its political opponents meant that most of the opposition parties boycotted the election. Voting passed off peacefully in the urban areas, but in the countryside a number of polling stations were attacked. The results of the election showed that a large majority of the assembly would support the government, with four pro-government parties (National Revolution Movement, Citizens' Rally, Workers' Party and the Conquest of Liberty Party) gaining 101 seats. The only two opposition parties to contest the election, the Social Democrats and the Dai Viet, gained three seats. The assembly set about drafting a new Constitution in mid-March.

21 March A new government is formed in Laos by Souvanna Phouma. The new National Assembly elected in December 1955 convened for the first time on 13 February and the following day the prime minister, Kathay Don Sasorith, resigned to clear the way for the formation of a new government. Both Kathay Don Sasorith and Prince Souvanna Phouma made efforts to form a new government, the latter eventually succeeding. With the appointment of Souvanna as premier again after a 16-month interval, the atmosphere for fresh negotiations with the Pathet Lao improved markedly.

30 March Prince Sihanouk resigns the Cambodian premiership. Sihanouk had been appointed to his second term as premier at the start of the month; he was replaced by Khim Tit. The prince claimed that he had resigned largely because of foreign criticism of his February visit to China. The visit had provoked a deterioration in Cambodia's relations with neighbouring South Vietnam, with both countries closing their borders in late March. Sihanouk also alleged that he had been placed under some pressure by the US as a result of the visit and also because of an earlier decision whereby he had refused an invitation for Cambodia to formally join the Southeast Asia Treaty Organization (SEATO). However, by not capitulating to US pressure, Sihanouk improved his standing among the Cambodian urban left, large elements of which he had previously alienated at the time of the 1955 elections. As a consequence of this the left-wing Pracheachon Party even offered to enter into coalition with the prince's Sangkum at a Sangkum congress held in Phnom Penh on 21/22 April. The congress had been called to rally support for Sihanouk's neutralist policies.

10 April Talks open between the two co-chairs, Britain and the Soviet Union, of the Geneva conference. The negotiations opened in London and were aimed at examining the problems relating to the fulfilment of the Geneva Agreements, particularly the provision for the holding of nation-wide elections in Vietnam in mid-1956. The two delegations were led by Andrei Gromyko, the Soviet foreign minister, and Lord Reading, the British minister of state at the Foreign Office. The meeting had been called partly in an attempt to assuage the Chinese, who were publicly pressing for a reconvening of the Geneva conference to ensure the full implementation of the agreement.

The London meeting ended on 8 May and in their report Gromyko and Reading invited both Saigon and Hanoi to transmit to them as soon as possible their 'views' about the time required for the opening of consultations on the organization of nation-wide elections. In return for the inclusion of this specific request in the report, the Soviet delegation refrained from pressing for a full reconvening of the Geneva conference. The North Vietnamese premier, Pham Van Dong, responded on 11 May by sending a letter to the South Vietnamese government in which he reiterated Hanoi's position that it was ready to attend a Consultative Conference on the elections issue. Two weeks later the South responded with a statement which reiterated its refusal to recognize the Geneva Agreements. The government in the South, it claimed, supported free elections, but 'the absence of liberties in North Vietnam makes impracticable at the moment any approach to the problem of electoral and pre-electoral operations'. Pham Van Dong subsequently issued notes to the British and Soviet Foreign Ministries in July and August, asking them to urge Saigon to choose a date for a conference and suggesting that if Diem refused then a new Geneva conference should be held.

28 April The French high command in South Vietnam is formally dissolved. General Pierre Jacquot, the French commander-in-chief in Indo-China, sailed from Saigon on 28 April and with his departure the French high command in Indo-China ceased to exist. The dissolution of the French high command meant that the formal responsibility for the training of the South Vietnamese army (ARVN) passed to the US Military Assistance Advisory Group (MAAG).

7 July A new Constitution is officially promulgated in South Vietnam. A new South Vietnamese Constitution, which had been unanimously approved by the Constituent Assembly elected in March, was officially promulgated in early July. The Constitution provided for a formal separation of powers between the executive, headed by the president, the Legislative Assembly and the Judiciary. It was agreed that the Constituent Assembly should serve as the first legislature. Legislation could be sponsored by the president and the assembly, although the former could veto laws passed by the latter; a three-quarters majority of the assembly might override the presidential veto. Ironically, given the ongoing crackdown on all of Diem's opponents, the Constitution guaranteed freedom of speech, of the press and of assembly; however, the president had the right to suspend these rights by proclaiming a state of emergency.

21 July The Geneva deadline passes for the holding of nation-wide elections in Vietnam, without any progress having been made towards a political settlement. Despite this lack of progress, the Lao Dong Party continued to reiterate its support for a policy of peaceful political struggle in the South. However, south of the seventeenth parallel, any form of political struggle had become increasingly precarious in the atmosphere of repression created by Diem. After the passage of the July deadline many southern Communists began pressing for a change in the party line to incorporate armed resistance. The party remained adamant that armed struggle in the South would have negative consequences. However, a number of Communists and Viet Minh veterans initiated terrorist campaigns of their own, targeting local Diemist officials for assassination and kidnap. The campaign increased in intensity over the following months so that during 1958 there were almost 200 assassinations in the South.

5 August A preliminary peace settlement is signed in Laos. After the formation of the Souvanna government in March there was a noticeable decline in tension between the Vientiane forces and their Pathet Lao counterparts in the northeast. The improvement in the security situation eased the way for peace negotiations to begin, and on 1 August Souvanna and the Pathet Lao leader Souphanouvong met for talks in Vientiane. Despite serious opposition to any sort of compromise with the Pathet Lao from the US and the Lao right, the two leaders signed a preliminary agreement after less than a week of discussion. The agreement provided for a cessation of hostilities, the integration of the Pathet Lao-controlled areas of the northeast into the rest of the country, the integration of the Pathet Lao into the Vientiane army, civil service administration and government and the holding of nation-wide elections in which the LPF would be permitted to compete.

2 November It is announced that Truong Chinh has been dismissed as party secretary general in North Vietnam after criticism of the land-reform programme. During 1955 the North Vietnamese land-reform programme entered a particularly radical phase. Throughout the countryside People's Special Agricultural Reform Tribunals were established to identify and punish landlords. Central pressure on the tribunals to produce results meant that many innocent peasants were tried and imprisoned or executed on the weight of flimsy evidence. In all, as many as 15,000 people were executed during 1955–6 and a further 20,000 were imprisoned. By mid-1956 criticism of the tribunals was mounting, provoking a serious debate in the party leadership. Eventually, on 7 August Ho Chi Minh issued a 'letter to the peasants' which criticized the implementation of the land-reform policy. In his letter, Ho said that people who had been wrongly classified as 'landowners' and 'rich peasants' would be reclassified and that special consideration would henceforth be shown to landowners who had been sympathetic to the revolution. After this the party central committee embarked on a marathon 40-day session to discuss the future of the land-reform programme. Some of the results of the party session were reported on Hanoi radio on 2 November. A number of reforms, under the title of a 'democratization' programme, were announced including the abolition of the tribunals, the improvement of living conditions through 'a more reasonable wage system' and greater freedom of movement and expression. The report stated that these reforms had been made necessary by 'grave mistakes' in the enforcement of the agrarian reform laws. It was also announced that the three leading officials responsible for the programme had been dismissed, among them Truong Chinh, from his post as Lao Dong Party secretary-general; Chinh retained his politburo post.

31 December Further progress is made in the Lao peace process. Following the signing of the August preliminary agreements by Souvanna and Souphanouvong, discussions continued between the two sides in an attempt to arrange the implementation of all the provisions. On the final day of the year the two leaders signed another agreement. The agreement, which was largely on timing, provided for the integration into Laos of the Pathet Lao provinces of Sam Neua and Phong Saly and the formation of a coalition government to take place prior to nation-wide elections.

1 9 5 7

12 January The fourth congress of Prince Sihanouk's ruling Sangkum ends in Phnom Penh after officially adopting neutrality as its foreign policy. Speaking to a crowd of some 15,000 supporters, Sihanouk said that a neutral Cambodia had made an important contribution toward the co-existence of the two major world blocs. He recalled his visits to countries with diametrically opposed political systems and the friendships established with them and noted that these countries all respected the independence and neutrality of Cambodia. The prince also formally invited the International Control Commission (ICC), the body established to supervise and implement the 1954 Geneva Agreements, to stay on in Cambodia and help guard the country's neutrality.

30 January The ICC criticizes South Vietnam for its failure to co-operate in the implementation of the Geneva accords. In its sixth interim report released in January, and covering the period December 1955 to July 1956, the ICC complained of non-cooperation by the Saigon regime in its work. According to the report neither zones had offered full protection and assistance to the ICC, but the major part of its difficulties had arisen in the South. The difficulties experienced by the ICC concerned either cases 'where the Commission's activities are being hindered' or cases 'where one of the parties refuses to put into effect the recommendation of the Commission'.

7 April Prince Sihanouk forms a new government in Cambodia. The internal political situation in Cambodia was highly unstable during the mid-1950s; a total of eight cabinets were formed in the period between January 1956 and July 1957. Prince Norodom Sihanouk formed his fourth government in early April in which he held the posts of premier and minister of foreign affairs, interior and planning. The prince replaced San Yun, who had resigned as prime minister in late March after the National Assembly had censured his government's economic policy. The censure vote was motivated by rising prices and growing unemployment. After some two months as premier, the prince resigned, ostensibly on grounds of ill-health. He permitted a new government to be formed in late July, headed by Sim Var.

6 May The South Vietnamese president, Ngo Dinh Diem, arrives in the US at the start of a 14-day visit, for talks with President Eisenhower and other top officials of the US administration. Diem addressed a joint session of Congress on 9 May in which he thanked the US for both moral and material aid given to his country. He told Congress that the peoples of Asia craved rapid economic development and were eager to reduce their economic dependency. In a joint communique issued the next day, Diem and Eisenhower attacked the governments of China and North Vietnam. The two stated that China's refusal to 'subscribe to the standards of conduct of civilized nations constituted a threat to the safety of all free nations of Asia', as did the North's 'build-up of Communist military forces'. Both agreed that the Southeast Asia Treaty Organization (SEATO) played a vital role shielding the region from Communist aggression and Eisenhower assured Diem of the willingness of the US to 'continue to offer effective assistance within the [US] constitutional processes'.

30 May Prince Souvanna resigns as prime minister of Laos after criticism of recent negotiations with the Pathet Lao. Negotiations between Souvanna Phouma's government and the Pathet Lao on the implementation of the December 1956 agreement reached deadlock in March. One of the main reasons for the breakdown of the talks was Souvanna's outright rejection of Pathet Lao demands that Laos should accept a $70-million aid package from China to counter the substantial US aid programme. On 29 May the National Assembly passed a vote of no confidence in Souvanna's government after an intense debate during which the prince's conduct of the negotiations came under heavy criticism. Opposition to Souvanna's handling of the negotiations had been organized by his right-wing deputy, Kathay Don Sasorith. Souvanna resigned on 30 May and in early June King Sisavang Vong invited Kathay Don Sasorith to try to form a new government.

8 June The North Vietnamese premier, Pham Van Dong, sends a note to the British and Soviet foreign ministers (the two co-chairs of the Geneva conference) attacking southern (and US) plans to sabotage the Geneva Agreements. Dong claimed that the US had some 2,000 military advisers in the South, over 1,700 more than permitted by the agreements. However, two days later General Samuel Williams, the commander of the US Military Assistance Advisory Group (MAAG) in Saigon, denied that the number of US advisers in the South exceeded the 243 limit. General Williams claimed that the North had an army of some 300,000 with a large number of Chinese advisers.

18 July The North Vietnamese premier, Pham Van Dong, calls for North–South discussions on nation-wide elections and reunification, in a letter to President Diem. North Vietnam renewed its demands for the South to implement the terms of the 1954 Geneva Agreements after Dong also proposed that postal services be opened up between the two zones as a first step towards reunification. The Saigon regime replied to Dong's letter in a government communique issued on 26 July which stated that the existence of a Communist political system north of the seventeenth parallel constituted a fundamental obstacle to reunification. Nevertheless, in September, the North made a further gesture proposing the holding of a conference to consider the re-establishment and development of North–South economic relations.

9 August Prince Souvanna Phouma forms a new government and embarks on fresh negotiations with the Pathet Lao, but only after a 70-day cabinet crisis during which at least two unsuccessful attempts were made to create new cabinets. He soon outlined his government's new policies which were considerably more accommodating towards the Pathet Lao than those adopted before the 70-day crisis. Souvanna offered to include the Pathet Lao in government, to incorporate their forces into a national army and to allow candidates from their political wing (the Lao Patriotic Front – LPF) to compete in elections. On the basis of these policies, Souvanna entered into a new round of talks with his half brother and Pathet Lao leader, Souphanouvong.

23 October An agreement is signed in Vientiane between the Royal Government and the Pathet Lao. A comprehensive political and military agreement was eventually signed in Vientiane by Souvanna Phouma and Souphanouvong. The agreement was approved by the National Assembly on 2 November and provided for the following: (i) an immediate halt to hostilities; (ii) the integration of Pathet Lao forces into the Royal Lao Army; (iii) the integration of Pathet Lao civil servants into the national administrative system: (iv) recognition of the LPF as a legal political party; (v) the granting of equal civil rights for all Lao citizens; (vi) the formation of a new government of national union, with Pathet Lao participation; (vii) the pursuance of a neutral foreign policy; and (viii) the restoration of Vientiane's authority over the Pathet Lao heartlands in the northeast.

15 November The UN secretary-general, Dag Hammarskjold, announces details of a 20-year development plan for the Mekong River basin. It was to be carried out in co-operation between the governments of South Vietnam, Laos, Cambodia and Thailand, and with UN assistance. The 2,587 mile-(4,160 kilometre-) long Mekong River had its source in the mountains of Tibet, flowed through northern Laos, forming the border between Laos and Thailand for some 500 miles (800 kilometres) and then flowed through Cambodia and South Vietnam to enter the South China Sea near Saigon. The long-term plan involved the construction of hydro-electric stations, irrigation systems, flood-control works and land-reclamation projects. The first stage consisted of a three-year programme of preparatory work; the US, Japanese, Indian and French governments had all expressed their willingness to give financial and technical assistance (the cost of the first stage was an estimate $3 million per year). In December General Raymond Wheeler, who had previously been entrusted by the UN with the task of clearing the Suez Canal, arrived in Saigon for discussions on the project with the governments concerned and the UN Economic Commission for Asia and the Far East (ECAFE).

18 November A coalition government is eventually formed in Laos. The National Assembly passed a vote of confidence in the new 16-member coalition government in Vientiane. The cabinet, headed by Prince Souvanna, included two Pathet Lao representatives: Souphanouvong as minister of planning, reconstruction and urbanization, and Phoumi Vongvichit as minister of religion and fine arts. On the same day, the Pathet Lao formally tranferred Sam Neua and Phong Saly provinces to the control of the new government. A Vientiane governor was appointed in Sam Neua, with a Pathet Lao deputy and a Pathet Lao governor in Phong Saly, with a Vientiane deputy.

1 9 5 8

7 February Ho Chi Minh gives details of the North's reunification proposals. President Ho Chi Minh paid a 10-day visit to India in February for talks with the Indian prime minister, Jawaharlal Nehru. It was in an address to the Indian Council of World Affairs that Ho advocated North–South discussions in preparation for the holding of internationally supervised national elections. Once a single assembly had been elected, Ho said, it should choose a national coalition government; the two Vietnamese armies should be gradually merged. Pending reunification, he stated, 'the parties and people's organisations which support peace, unity, independence and democracy must be granted legal status; normal economic, cultural and social relations established; and free communication between the two zones guaranteed'.

5 March Pathet Lao forces are formally integrated into the Lao army, reports the International Control Commission (ICC). The Pathet Lao had put forward 1,500 of their best men for integration, and a further 4,300 had apparently been demobilized. A total of 1,500 had been established as an upper limit because of budgetary restraints; with their formal incorporation, the army was about 25,000 strong.

7 March North Vietnamese Premier Pham Van Dong calls for troop reductions and the establishment of North–South trade relations in a letter to President Diem. Dong requested an 'early meeting of the competent authorities' to discuss 'the question of bilateral reduction of armed forces and find ways and means to promote trade exchanges between the two zones'. The implementation of these measures, Dong claimed, would 'create favourable conditions for a rapprochement and mutual understanding between the two sides, thus paving the way for the consultative conference and free general elections with a view to reunifying the country'. The letter strongly criticized 'the American policy of intervention . . . in Vietnam and in Southeast Asia'. In Saigon, the northern offer was described as 'phoney' and a 'propaganda trick' and was officially rejected by the government in a statement released in late April. The statement declared that negotiations could only be held with the North once the authorities in Hanoi had met a number of conditions, including renouncing 'methods of terrorism and sabotage' and establishing 'democratic liberties similar to those existing in the South'. Premier Dong sent another letter to Diem in December, repeating his proposals for mutual force reductions and economic exchanges and calling for free movement between the two zones and an end to hostile propaganda.

23 March Prince Sihanouk's Sangkum wins a massive victory in Cambodian elections to the National Assembly. Alone amongst the opposition, Pracheachon fielded five candidates, four of whom withdrew at the last minute; the remaining aspirant, Keo Meas, courageously contested a Phnom Penh seat, but received less than 400 votes. Sihanouk personally selected all Sangkum candidates, one for each of the country's 62 constituencies. Among the candidates were a few young, left-wing intellectuals and after the election Sihanouk embarked on a fresh experiment, bringing a number of these intellectuals into the government. Hou Yuon, Hu Nim and Chau Sau were all given cabinet posts, although they remained outweighed by members of the 'old guard' right.

4 May The Pathet Lao perform well in 'supplementary' elections in Laos held in line with the Vientiane Agreement of November 1957. Under the terms of the agreement the Pathet Lao, in the guise of the Lao Patriotic Front (LPF), were to be permitted to compete for 20 seats, thereby increasing the assembly's size to 59 (in addition, a contest was also held to replace a member who had recently died). The LPF campaign concentrated on the issue of governmental corruption, especially in relation to the burgeoning US aid programme. The US, meanwhile, attempted to thwart the LPF campaign by launching Operation Booster Shot, a crash village-aid programme (see Appendix 9 for details of US aid to Laos during the 1950s). The programme had little political impact, with the LPF winning nine of the 21 seats; Souphanouvong received more votes than any other candidate in the country. Another four seats were won by the left-wing neutralist Santiphab (Peace) Party, led by Quinim Pholsena. The pro-government coalition, the National Liberty Front (NLF), gained only eight seats, with the right-wing components suffering a number of serious defeats.

25 June Cambodia releases details of a serious border violation by South Vietnamese troops. In a broadcast the Cambodian premier, Sim Var, claimed that several regiments of the South Vietnamese army (ARVN) had recently penetrated some 9 miles (15 kilometres) into the northeastern province of Stung Treng. The forces apparently pulled back a few days later. However, at the time of the invasion the US ambassador to Cambodia, Carl Strom, had cautioned Sihanouk against repelling the Vietnamese troops and had threatened him with the cancellation of US aid if Khmer troops forced the issue. According to US National Security Council documents in the *Pentagon Papers*, such incursions were designed to provoke Sihanouk into adopting a more pro-US stance. The action conspicuously failed to do this, and according to some commentators, the prince's irritation at the incursion motivated the Central Intelligence Agency (CIA) to begin preparations for his deposition.

24 July It is announced in Phnom Penh that Cambodia has established diplomatic relations with the People's Republic of China. Prince Sihanouk stressed that the move would not effect Cambodia's policy of neutrality. The move appeared to be part of an attempt by Sihanouk to increase pressure on North Vietnam, through China, to accept Cambodian neutrality.

18 August Phoui Sananikone replaces Souvanna Phouma as prime minister of Laos. The US, already distrustful of Souvanna Phouma's efforts to forge a meaningful coalition with the left, were deeply shocked by the LPF's electoral success in May. Washington responded by effectively suspending monthly aid payments to Vientiane and at the same time they encouraged a group of 'Young Turks' in the army and the civil service to form an anti-Communist Committee for Defence of National Interests (CDNI). The committee, created in June, quickly capitalized on the financial crisis engendered by the suspension of US aid and in late July Souvanna was more or less forced to resign as Prime minister. Attempts by Souvanna to form a new coalition were frustrated by the CDNI and so in mid-August Phoui Sananikone, the staunchly right-wing foreign minister, formed a new government. Phoui dropped the LPF ministers, Souphanouvong and Phoumi Vongvichit, from the cabinet and installed in their place CDNI members.

1 9 5 9

14 January The Lao National Assembly grants Prime Minister Phoui Sananikone emergency powers. The right-wing prime minister appealed to the National Assembly on 12 January to grant him emergency powers for 12 months. He claimed, falsely according to many commentators, that he required the new powers because of the recent entry of North Vietnamese troops into Lao territory. The assembly approved Phoui's request on 14 January and 10 days later he formed a new cabinet, which included for the first time a number of army officers, amongst them Colonel Phoumi Nosavan. Like the other army cabinet members Phoumi was closely associated with the Committee for the Defence of National Interests (CDNI) which already had cabinet representation. The granting of emergency powers to Phoui, and the government reshuffle, effectively denied Lao Patriotic Front (LPF) deputies any further meaningful political role in Vientiane, and some fled the city.

21 January The first details of an anti-government conspiracy in Cambodia are released. According to the reports, the coup attempt had been led by Sam Sary, the former prime minister, and Dap Chhuon, the powerful right-wing 'warlord' and governor of Siem Reap province. After the plot had been uncovered, apparently by Chinese and French diplomats, Sary escaped to Thailand where he joined veteran Issarak leader Son Ngoc Thanh; Chhuon, however, was killed whilst trying to reach the Thai border. In an interview with the *Observer* newspaper on 22 February, Prince Sihanouk implicated South Vietnamese, Thai and, more obliquely, US diplomats in the coup attempt.

6 May Legislation is passed in Saigon creating special military courts. The increasingly repressive anti-opposition measures introduced by the Diem regime since the mid-1950s culminated in May with the passage of Law 10/59. The legislation provided newly-created military courts with the authority to sentence to death 'whoever commits or attempts to commit . . . crimes with the aims of sabotage, or of infringing upon the security of the state' as well as 'whoever belongs to an organisation designed to help prepare or to perpetrate [these] crimes'. The courts also had jurisdiction over crimes of espionage and treason and economic crimes and it was impossible to appeal against their decision.

11 May Tension increases in Laos after Phoui Sananikone's government orders the immediate 'integration' of Pathet Lao battalions. The Vientiane government ordered the two Pathet Lao battalions stationed near Luang Prabang and Xieng Khouang to 'integrate' immediately into the Royal Lao Army (RLA). According to a report by the International Control Commission (ICC), 'integration' had been completed formally in early 1958. The Chinese government denounced the government move as being 'tantamount to launching openly a civil war in Laos'. RLA units surrounded both battalions on 14 May and ordered them to surrender their arms; the First Battalion, based outside Luang Prabang, complied on 17 May, but the Second Battalion managed to escape their RLA watchers and headed towards the Vietnamese border. In Vientiane, deputies, including Souphanouvong, were placed under house arrest following the escape of the Second Battalion.

14 May The Lao Dong central committee approves the use of armed force in southern Vietnam. The committee, holding its fifteenth plenum, approved the use of armed force in southern Vietnam, but only in support of the political struggle and not for the purpose of militarily defeating the Diem regime. The resolution had been approved by the politburo in January, after which a number of 'infiltration groups', composed in the main of southerners who had fled North in 1954, were created. The adoption of so-called 'Resolution 15' with its support, however half-hearted, for armed struggle in the South, represented the culmination of a major political victory for the party faction, led by Le Duan and Le Duc Tho (see biographies), which had been lobbying for such a move for some time. Another party faction, led by Truong Chinch and General Giap, believed that the strengthening of the northern economy was a greater priority than reunification.

8 July Two US servicemen are killed in South Vietnam, The two men were killed by a bomb at Bien Hoa airbase; they were the first US soldiers to die during the post-Geneva phase of the Indo-China conflict. The attack was an indication of the increasing confidence of the southern guerrillas, as was the massive escalation in their assassination programme during the latter half of 1959. In late September, guerrillas launched their first attack on a large South Vietnamese army (ARVN) unit, killing 12 soldiers and capturing a large haul of weapons.

4 August The Vientiane government declares a state of emergency in a number of Lao provinces after outbreaks of fighting. Fresh fighting broke out in Laos in mid-July when guerrilla units, possibly composed of members of the Pathet Lao Second Battalion, attacked a number of isolated RLA outposts in Sam Neua province. The flare-up allowed the Vientiane government to arrest Souphanouvong and seven other LPF deputies in late July; the eight were placed in detention on suspicion of plotting against the security of the state. The government proclaimed a state of emergency in Sam Neua and Phong Saly, and also in the south-central provinces of Xieng Khouang, Thakhek and Savannakhet. On the same day, a note was dispatched to the UN alleging North Vietnamese involvement in the fighting, a claim vociferously denied by Hanoi, Moscow and Beijing, all of which alleged that the crisis had been engineered in Washington. The US, of course, denied any involvement but on 26 August Washington announced that it had authorized an emergency military aid package for the Phoui government.

The RLA Commander-in-chief, General Ouan Rattikone, visited Sam Neua in early September. General Ouan issued a grave report of the security situation in the province and on 5 September the government extended the state of emergency to cover the the whole country. On the previous day the government had sent another note to the UN accusing Hanoi of 'flagrant aggression' against Laos and requesting the UN to dispatch an 'emergency force' to northeastern Laos. The UN Security Council agreed to send a four-member sub-committee to compile a report on the situation, a move which appeared to calm the situation.

30 August President Diem responds to US pressure and holds general elections in South Vietnam. All but two of the 123 National Assembly seats were won by parties or independent candidates supporting Diem, which was hardly surprising given the level of intimidation and vote-rigging which accompanied the election. The two opposition members returned were not even allowed to take their place in the assembly after they were both found guilty of electoral malpractice.

31 August The Cambodian king escapes an assassination attempt. King Norodom Suramarit and Queen Sisowath Rossanak narrowly escaped death when a bomb exploded in the Royal Palace in Phnom Penh. At least two people were killed by the bomb which was hidden in a lacquer box supposedly containing a gift for the queen. Government sources claimed that the assassination attempt had been carried out by Khmer emigres, aided by 'a foreign organisation specialising in murder and subversion'.

29 October King Sisavang Vong of Laos dies at the age of 74. He had ascended to the Luang Prabang throne in 1905 and at the time of his death his reign was the longest of any monarch in the twentieth century. The crown prince, Savang Vatthana, the king's eldest son, succeeded to the throne on the death of his father and was formally proclaimed monarch on 4 November.

31 December The army, effectively led by General Phoumi Nosavan, takes over control of Vientiane from the Phoui government. In early December the Phoui government announced that general elections, due to be held before the end of the year, would be postponed until April 1960 and that the life of the National Assembly would be similarly prorogued. The CDNI and the army took issue with Phoui's decision, claiming that the country should be governed by a provisional cabinet appointed by the monarch until fresh elections could be held. Phoui responded by sacking all the CDNI ministers on 15 December, a move approved by the National Assembly a week later. Troop movements were reported on the streets of Vientiane on 22 December and three days later Phoui submitted his resignation, apparently in the belief that the assembly would retain its mandate until the April elections. King Savang Vatthana announced on 31 December that he had accepted Phoui's resignation, and soon afterwards the army took up key positions in Vientiane; a communique issued by General Phoumi Nosavan stated the army had 'taken charge of the situation' and that the National Assembly, which they claimed had been sitting in violation of the Constitution since 25 December, had been dissolved.

1 9 6 0

7 January The Lao military allow King Savang Vatthana to appoint a new interior government headed by 'elder statesman' Kou Abhay. This ended army rule in Laos, imposed by General Phoumi Nosavan and the Committee for the Defence of National Interests (CDNI) in late December. The army's decision to allow the king to appoint a fresh government came after intervention from Western diplomats had convinced General Phoumi that a military regime in Vientiane was, at this point, unacceptable. Instead, General Phoumi was brought into the new government as defence minister. In his first policy statement as premier, Kou Abhay announced his intention to hold general elections as soon as possible.

3 April King Norodom Suramarit of Cambodia dies at the age of 65. Norodom Suramarit had become king of Cambodia in 1955, when his son, Prince Norodom Sihanouk, abdicated in order to assume the premiership. After the king's death, the National Assembly established a Council of Regency to exercise the royal prerogatives until a new monarch was chosen (the Cambodian throne not being hereditary). Prince Sihanouk refused to accept the crown, and on 13 April he resigned as prime minister; Pho Proeung, a candidate put forward by the prince, was appointed as the new premier.

24 April General elections are held in Laos and result in an overwhelming victory for the right. The government, reportedly funded and advised by the Central Intelligence Agency (CIA), blatantly rigged the elections and all 59 National Assembly seats contested were won by right-wing candidates, the majority by the CDNI- and army-backed Democratic Party for Social Progress (Paxasangkhom). The Lao Patriotic Front (LPF) had been firmly discouraged from taking part in the election by new electoral rules introduced by the government prior to polling.

Kou Abhay's caretaker government, appointed in January, resigned after the elections and was replaced on 2 June by a new rightist-dominated government headed by Tiao Somsanith. General Phoumi retained the defence portfolio and was widely regarded as the most powerful member of the new government.

30 April A group of Saigon notables petition President Diem to liberalize his regime. Insurrectionary activity against the increasingly repressive Diem regime escalated dramatically from the end of 1959 onwards, most notably in the Mekong delta region. By spring, discontent with the government had spread beyond the confines of the delta and had reached political and military circles in the capital. Early in 1960 a 'Committee for Progress and Liberty' had been formed by a group of former ministers, intellectuals and professionals, with the aim of encouraging Diem to adopt a more liberal stance. Towards this end, the committee sent a petition to Diem in late April accusing the government of utilizing what amounted to 'Communist dictatorial methods' of coercion against any of its opponents. The committee also charged that the government was paralysed by nepotism and corruption. The majority of those who signed the petition were subsequently arrested.

24 May Pathet Lao leader Souphanouvong escapes from a police camp outside Vientiane where he has been held in detention for 10 months. With him were 15 other Pathet Lao members (including Phoumi Vongvichit, Nouhak Phoumsavan and Phoune Sipaseuth) who had been in detention since July 1959. The escapees, accompanied by their former guards, made their way on foot to the Pathet Lao strongholds, eventually arriving in Sam Neua in November 1960.

5 June Sihanouk's neutralist policies are approved by national referendum and the prince is appointed chief-of-state. The National Assembly had called the referendum in October 1959 in view of an intensification of both right- and left-wing opposition activity. Sihanouk had made it clear that if the vote went against neutralism, then he would be fully prepared to go into exile. In the event, the official figures showed that over 2 million votes were cast for the prince against less than 300 votes for the Communists and the Khmer Serei.

After the vote, Sihanouk initially refused to take on any new official position because of the unresolved problem of the succession following the king's death in April (after which the prince had resigned as premier). However, on 20 June Sihanouk accepted the post of chief-of-state; on the same day, he told the National Assembly that his mother, Queen Kossamak, would henceforth symbolize the Cambodian throne.

8 August Captain Kong Le, a 26-year-old unknown Lao soldier, leading the Royal Lao Army's Second Parachute Battalion, seizes control of Vientiane in a bloodless coup d'etat and establishes a new neutral government. The paratroopers made their move whilst General Phoumi and most other government members were in Luang Prabang attending funeral rites for the late King Sisavang Vong. After seizing control of the city, Kong Le set up a 'Revolutionary Committee' and announced that it had assumed 'the task of maintaining the neutrality of Laos' and of consolidating 'nation, religion, throne and constitution'. He would end the government's US-backed military campaign against the Pathet Lao, and denounced all circumstances 'of brother having to fight brother'. He also expressed his intention to 'clean up' corrupt elements within the armed forces and the National Assembly. Kong Le's speeches, simple, honest and naive, were greeted with great enthusiasm by the people of Vientiane who took to the streets in support of his paratroopers.

Soon after taking control of Vientiane, Kong Le invited former Prime Minister Souvanna Phouma to form a new government. Souvanna insisted that Kong Le respect constitutional procedures and so the National Assembly (two-thirds of whose members had remained in Vientiane) was convened on 13 August and a vote of no-confidence in Tiao Somsanith's government (most of whose members were awaiting developments in Luang Prabang) was passed; four days later the assembly approved a new cabinet headed by Souvanna and consisting of men who had not held any posts under Somsanith. Souvanna pledged to restore internal peace in the country and pursue a genuinely neutral foreign policy. Kong Le announced that his 'Revolutionary Committee' had handed over all administrative powers to Souvanna's government, although the captain subsequently made it clear that he intended to monitor developments closely until a neutralist policy was actually in operation. Meanwhile, as the formation of the new Souvanna government was under way, General Phoumi had travelled from Luang Prabang to the southern town of Savannakhet where, along with 21 cabinet and National Assembly members, he established a rightist 'counter-coup committee'. The Pathet Lao, on the other hand, announced in a broadcast in mid-August that they fully supported Kong Le's action and pledged full support to his policy of neutrality and national reconciliation.

29 August In an apparent mood of compromise, a new coalition government is formed in Laos; the agreement soon collapses and clashes between neutralists and rightists break out. A period of tense uncertainty followed the mid-August formation of the new Souvanna Phouma neutralist government in Vientiane, with the threat of war between Captain Kong Le's pro-Souvanna forces and General Phoumi Nosavan's 'counter-coup' forces looming. Souvanna, however, was fully determined to press ahead with his pledge to re-establish peace in Laos, and towards this end he opened negotiations with General Phoumi. After a number of meetings, both sides announced in late August that an agreement had been reached on the formation of a new coalition cabinet, to be headed by Souvanna, but also including General Phoumi as deputy premier and four other rightists from the Somsanith regime toppled in the 8 August coup. The new government was due to be sworn in on 2 September in Vientiane, but General Phoumi and a number of his colleagues simply never turned up for the ceremony, remaining instead in Savannakhet, the southern base of the rightists' 'counter-coup' committee. According to some commentators, the general had been strongly advised to remain in Savannakhet by his US backers. A period of stalemate followed until 10 September when General Phoumi announced the formation of a 'Revolutionary Committee' (effectively a second government) in Savannakhet, headed by Prince Boun Oum. Just over a week later, the Phoumist Committee announced that it was preparing to 'liberate' Vientiane; on the same day, the Pathet Lao leadership called on its troops to refrain from attacking neutralist (i.e. Souvanna Phouma/Kong Le) forces and concentrate their efforts on General Phoumi's forces. The next day (20 September) the first open clashes between neutralist and rightist forces were reported to have broken out near Paksane. The battle-lines were drawn much more clearly in October when Souvanna's government opened negotiations with the Pathet Lao, invited the Soviet Union to place an ambassador in Vientiane, and accepted an offer from Moscow for economic assistance. The US, meanwhile, had been caught completely unawares by the August coup and the subsequent unravelling of events with the end result that, by late October, Washington was supplying the cash to pay Kong Le's troops, and at the same time providing arms for General Phoumi's forces.

5 September The third congress of the Communist Party of Vietnam (CPV) opens. The Vietnamese Workers' Party (VWP or Lao Dong Party, the name by which the party had been known since its re-emergence in 1951) approved a programme of armed insurrection in the South to be organized by a National United Front organization. This was the first time that Hanoi had publicly announced its support for the insurgency currently under way in the rural South. The third congress represented a victory for the policies of Le Duan and other party members who had long stressed the inevitability of armed struggle in the South. Until 1959, the party had followed Truong Chinh in emphasizing the primary importance of the northern economic base and in assuming that peaceful political action in the South would speed Diem's inevitable collapse. However, as Diem's methods became increasingly repressive in the late 1950s, so Le Duan's arguments for military action in the South began to gain support and by early 1959 the party had agreed to approve the use of armed force, whilst still expressing its wariness of a full-scale conflict. Pressure on the party to provide a firm lead increased in March 1960 when a group of former southern Viet Minh issued a declaration expressing frustration and impatience with the North's hesitancy.

30 September Cambodian Communists hold a secret congress in Phnom Penh railway station at which members of the Pol Pot faction are elected to leading positions. Although it was only attended by some 20 members, it marked a turning point in the history of Cambodian Communism. The congress was held despite an intimidatory atmosphere in Phnom Penh following a recent government crackdown on the left when newspapers had been closed and prominent leftists, including Khieu Samphan (see biographies), detained and beaten. The meeting elected Tou Samouth as party general secretary, Nuon Chea as his deputy and Saloth Sar (Pol Pot) as the third-ranking politburo member. Other members of the future Pol Pot faction of the Khmer Rouge leadership, including Ieng Sary, were elected to the central committee.

The Pol Pot faction maintain that the September meeting was in fact the inaugural congress of the Communist Party of Kampuchea (CPK), thereby reducing the (Viet Minh-supported) Communist organization of the 1950s to non-party status. The current Phnom Penh regime, however, hold that the meeting was the party's second congress, at which it was renamed the Workers' Party of Kampuchea.

11 November An unsuccessful coup is launched against President Diem by disgruntled South Vietnamese army (ARVN) officers. Opposition to the Diem regime within the ARVN surfaced when a group of officers, led by Colonel Nguyen Chanh Thi and Lieutenant-Colonel Vuong Van Dong, attempted to carry out a coup d'etat in Saigon with the aim of establishing 'true democracy and liberty' in the South. The coup was badly organized and had little chance of success and after 48 hours loyalist troops had suppressed the revolt. According to official statements, over 300 people were killed and wounded, including 45 rebel parachutists. Colonel Thi and Lieutenant-Colonel Dong both escaped to Cambodia and in mid-1963 a number of soldiers and civilians arrested for their involvement in the coup were tried and sentenced to prison terms of up to 18 years.

17 November In Laos an agreement is reached between Souvanna's government and the Pathet Lao providing for a cease-fire and the creation of a coalition government. To seal the agreement, Souvanna flew to Sam Neua to meet with Souphanouvong, his half brother and the Pathet Lao leader. Meanwhile, General Phoumi Nosavan's rightist forces, fortified by US and Thai military supplies, were storming towards Vientiane. On 11 November, Luang Prabang, the royal capital, came under the general's control when the commander of the city's garrison mutinied and at the end of the month his forces opened a general offensive against Souvanna and Kong Le. As the rightist forces closed in on the capital, panic spread and on 9 December Souvanna and a number of his ministers fled to Cambodia. The next day, Quinim Pholsena, the neutralist information minister and Kong Le's 'political adviser', travelled to Hanoi, where he arranged a formal alliance between Kong Le's forces and the Pathet Lao in return for Soviet arms. Soviet weaponry, and a number of North Vietnamese advisers, started to be flown into the Lao capital on 11 December.

13 December General Phoumi's rightist forces launch a successful offensive against Kong Le's neutralist troops in Vientiane. After three days of heavy fighting Kong Le's troops were forced out of the city. They headed north and after regrouping they joined with the Pathet Lao in launching a successful offensive on the Plain of Jars. In Vientiane, yet another cabinet was formed on 25 December. Although the new government was nominally headed by Prince Boun Oum, real power rested in the Defence Ministry once again headed by General Phoumi.

20 December The National Liberation Front (NLF–Viet Cong) is established in South Vietnam. Southern dissidents from various organizations gathered to establish formally a National Liberation Front of South Vietnam. Although the establishment of the front had been approved by the CPV at its third congress held in September, it would be totally misleading to regard the NLF as nothing more than a northern Communist front. Of course, the core of the NLF was composed of members of the southern party branch, but the very reason for adopting a front strategy was in order to attract the social and political elements not already aligned with the anti-Diem movement. So, during the months preceding the NLF's formation intense efforts were made to attract members from as many sources as possible, including the sects, banned political parties and the intelligentsia. The 10-point programme issued by the anonymous front leadership was direct in its opposition to Diem and in its anti-Americanism, but adopted a more moderate tone in other areas, calling, for instance, for 'gradual' and 'peaceful' reunification to be brought about through 'negotiations and discussions'. (See Appendix 10 for the NLF's 10-point programme.)

1 9 6 1

10 March Talks take place in Phnom Penh between the rival Lao governments of Prince Souvanna Phouma and General Phoumi Nosavan, but fighting continues. Two separate governments had existed in Laos since late 1960. General Phoumi's right-wing military government in Vientiane was formally headed by Prince Boun Oum na Champassak and was recognized by the West and armed by the US. Prince Souvanna's neutralist government was based in Xieng Khouang (on the Plain of Jars) and was supported by Captain Kong Le's neutralist forces and the Pathet Lao who both received considerable amounts of weaponry from Soviet airdrops; Souvanna's government was recognized by North Vietnam, China, the Soviet Union and India amongst others.

Immediately after the Phnom Penh meeting, an optimistic joint statement was issued offering hope for an agreement. However, after a few days, the initial assertions of optimism gave way to harsher statements which more accurately reflected the hostility on the ground. According to some commentators the shift was inevitable because China, North Vietnam and the Pathet Lao had all indicated to Souvanna their opposition to a compromise with Phoumi. As if to reinforce their opposition, the Pathet Lao – aided by Kong Le's neutralist forces and North Vietnamese troops – achieved some major battlefield success against the rightist forces in late March and April. On Route 13 (the road between Vientiane and Luang Prabang) Pathet Lao troops – supplied continuously by Soviet airdrops – advanced to within 50 miles (80 kilometres) of the capital.

9 April South Vietnamese President Diem and Vice-President Nguyen Ngoc Tho are re-elected for another term. They defeated opposition tickets led by Nguyen Dinh Quat and Ho Nhat Tan. Diem and Tho received about 85 per cent of votes cast, although both opposition candidates claimed that their supporters had been subjected to serious intimidation. Diem was inaugurated in late April and a month later he appointed a new cabinet, which included (for the first time) three so-called 'super-ministers' to co-ordinate security, economic and social matters.

20 April President Kennedy appoints an 'interdepartmental task force' on Vietnam which recommends, amongst other things, the commencement of a campaign of unconventional warfare against North Vietnam. US President Kennedy appointed the 'interdepartmental task force' the day after the collapse of the Bay of Pigs invasion of Cuba, to devise a programme of action to 'prevent communist domination of [Vietnam]'. The task force was headed by Roswell L. Gilpatric, the deputy secretary of defence, and also included representatives from the State Department, the President's Office, the Central Intelligence Agency (CIA) (including Edward Lansdale) and from the Joint Chiefs-of-Staff. Amongst the other task-force recommendations secretly approved by Kennedy on 11 May were: the deployment of a 400-strong special forces contingent and a 100-man increase in the existing Military Assistance Advisory Group (MAAG); and the initiation of discussions between the US (Saigon) ambassador, Frederick Nolting, and President Diem 'regarding the possibility of a defensive security alliance despite the inconsistency of such action with the [1954] Geneva accords'. In fact, the secret dispatch of the special forces troops also directly contravened the Geneva accords, which had stipulated a 685-man limit on the US MAAG in Saigon.

24 April Britain and the Soviet Union appeal for a cease-fire in Laos and call for the convening of an international conference to deal with the crisis. After weeks of complex diplomatic manoeuvring, interspersed with bouts of brinkmanship from the various combatants and their patrons, the joint chairs of the 1954 Geneva conference on Indo-China (Britain and the Soviet Union) issued a statement which effectively gave notice to the warring factions that the major powers were unwilling to allow the crisis to escalate into a more threatening conflict. The British-Soviet statement appealed for a cease-fire, requested India to revive the International Control Commission (ICC) and summoned an international conference on Laos to convene in Geneva.

The civil war in Laos preoccupied President Kennedy during his first months in the White House, exactly in the way that outgoing President Eisenhower had warned him it would do. On the one hand, the poor military performance of the US' client (General Phoumi) acted as an incitement to some form of direct US action, yet, on the other hand, the level of Soviet intervention on behalf of the Pathet Lao demanded restraint. In late April, after the British-Soviet statement had been issued, but before a cease-fire had come into effect, Kennedy came under increasing pressure within the National Security Council to take a stand in Laos, or face a later conflict elsewhere in Southeast Asia. Kennedy resisted the Lao option, and in early May the crisis calmed.

3 May A de facto cease-fire comes into effect in Laos. Although neutralist, rightist and Pathet Lao commanders issued the cease-fire orders on 3 May, it was not until 5 May that representatives of the two warring sides met for talks. Members of the Indian-led ICC landed in Vientiane on 8 May, and in its first report issued three days later it stated that it had 'arrived at the unanimous conclusion that a general and obvious discontinuance of hostilities had taken place'. Delegates from the rival governments and the Pathet Lao met at Ban Namone, some 31 miles (50 kilometres) north of the Lik River, and signed statements ratifying the cease-fire and undertaking to issue new orders to their forces to observe it on all fronts.

11 May US Vice-President Johnson arrives in Saigon for talks with President Diem. Johnson stayed in Saigon until 13 May, during a trip which also took him to the Philippines, Taiwan, Thailand, India and Pakistan. During his time in Saigon, Johnson met with President Diem, whom he subsequently described to Kennedy as 'a complex figure . . . remote from the people [and] surrounded by persons less admirable and capable than he'. An agreement for increased US military and economic assistance for South Vietnam was made public in a joint communique issued in Saigon by Johnson and Diem. Upon his return to Washington in late May, Johnson's recommendation to President Kennedy was for 'a clear-cut and strong program of action' to militarily and economically bolster Diem's regime. The involvement of US combat troops, he stated, was 'not required' and 'not desirable'. Americans, he went on, possibly failed to 'appreciate fully the subtlety that recently-colonial peoples would not look with favour upon governments which invited or accepted the return this soon of Western troops'.

16 May The 14-power Geneva conference reopens to discuss Laos. (See Appendix 11 for list of delegations attending conference). The conference was boycotted by the Lao rightists until late June in opposition to the presence of the Pathet Lao. During the first sessions progress was minimal, and the deadlock became worse after the Pathet Lao forces, in contravention of the cease-fire, captured Padong (south of the Plain of Jars) from rightist forces on 7 June. Progress improved after the meeting of the 'three Lao Princes' in Zurich in late June, and on 22 August the conference approved a draft declaration on Lao neutrality; an additional clause to this declaration was subsequently adopted in December along with a formula outlining in detail the mandate of the ICC (a major stumbling block during earlier discussions) and a timetable for the withdrawal of foreign forces.

19 June The 'three Lao Princes' open negotiations in Zurich on the formation of a provisional coalition government. The 'three Lao Princes', Souvanna Phouma, Souphanouvong and Boun Oum na Champassak, announced, three days after the talks had begun, that an agreement had been reached on the formation of a provisional government of national union. The three met again in Laos in early October to try to formulate the exact composition of the proposed government, but an agreement was not reached. In early December, Britain and the Soviet Union sent a joint message to the princes expressing concern over the delay in the formation of a government. After receiving the message, the three held yet another round of talks in Xieng Khouang but, by the end of the year, negotiations had effectively broken down, giving rise to fears of a renewal of full-scale civil war.

19 September The National Liberation Front (NLF) launches a major assault on Phuoc Thanh province. In a dramatic display of increasing military prowess and confidence, two NLF battalions, estimated at least 600 strong, attacked and overran Phuoc Vinh, the capital of Phuoc Thanh province, some 56 miles (90 kilometres) northeast of Saigon. The NLF held the town for a full day and, before being driven out by government troops, they publicly beheaded the provincial governor.

18 October The Taylor mission arrives in Saigon to determine whether US troops should be sent to Vietnam. President Kennedy dispatched his military adviser, General (retired) Maxwell Taylor, to South Vietnam to 'discuss . . . ways in which we can perhaps better assist . . . Vietnam in meeting . . . [the] threat to its independence'. As if to emphasize the reality of such a threat, President Diem imposed a state of emergency throughout South Vietnam on the day of Taylor's arrival in Saigon. The emergency decree, imposed not only as a result of the increased NLF activity but also because of severe flooding in southern rice-producing areas, empowered Diem to suspend constitutional processes and take any action necessary for national security.

Following his trip to South Vietnam, Taylor recommended to President Kennedy in early November that the US send a 6,000- to 8,000-strong military task force to South Vietnam. He suggested that they be dispatched as a flood-relief team, but that their primary task would be to raise national morale in the South and prove to other Asian countries US intent 'to resist a Communist take-over'.

The deterioration of the security situation in the South during the summer and autumn had increased the pressure on Kennedy to approve direct US military intervention. At the time of Vice-President Johnson's visit to Saigon in May, Diem had reportedly reacted coolly to the notion of US ground troops being stationed in South Vietnam. However, in July, Diem had written to Kennedy asking for financing for a major expansion of the South Vietnamese army (ARVN) and urging a build-up of 'selected elements of the American armed forces'. Kennedy agreed to finance a further 30,000 South Vietnamese soldiers, but made no decision on increasing the numbers of US military advisers. In late September, Diem met with Ambassador Nolting and formally requested a bilateral defence treaty with the US, apparently out of concern over the possibility of mass Communist infiltration from Laos. Two weeks later, Saigon Defence Minister Nguyen Dinh Thuan met with Nolting and specifically requested the introduction of US and Chinese nationalist combat units, the former to be introduced as 'combat-trainer units'. Thuan told Nolting that he would want the US troops stationed just below the seventeenth parallel to prevent attacks in the area and free ARVN units to operate further south. Meanwhile, pressure in Washington for some form of intervention was also mounting – a Joint Chiefs-of-Staff plan suggested direct Southeast Asia Treaty Organization (SEATO) intervention in Laos; Walt Rostow (see biographies) talked of a SEATO presence along Vietnam's western border with Laos; other plans specifically mentioned a direct US force in the South. It was in an attempt to procure a coherent intervention option that Kennedy dispatched General Taylor to Saigon in mid-October.

22 November Kennedy rules in favour of 'support troops' rather than 'combat troops' for South Vietnam. The first reaction to General Taylor's recommendation came from Secretary of State Dean Rusk (see biographies) who questioned the usefulness of the introduction of US troops if such a measure were not accompanied by political reforms in South Vietnam. However, Defence Secretary McNamara (see biographies) and the Joint Chiefs-of-Staff both indicated their support for Taylor's proposals, although McNamara warned that the impending military struggle might be prolonged and if so would eventually require over 200,000 US soldiers. However, McNamara's initial support for Taylor waned and, in mid-November, he and Rusk issued a memorandum to Kennedy which cautioned against the introduction of large organized units 'with actual or potential military missions'; instead they proposed that 'units of modest size required for the direct support of [the] South Vietnamese military effort' be introduced as quickly as possible. The adoption of such a cautious approach, they argued, would reduce the chances of hostilities resuming in Laos. The Rusk-McNamara recommendation was accepted by Kennedy and was formally embodied in a national security action programme on 22 November.

14 December The build-up of US support troops in South Vietnam is formally announced with a public exchange of letters between Kennedy and Diem. Three days earlier, the US aircraft carrier *Core* had arrived in Saigon with 33 H-21C helicopters and 400 air and ground crewmen to operate them for the ARVN. The *New York Times* of 20 December reported that uniformed US troops and specialists were operating in battle areas with South Vietnamese forces and although not in combat, were authorized to fire back if fired on.

1 9 6 2

19 January False hopes of an agreement on the formation of a Lao coalition government are raised in Geneva. After further talks in Geneva with Prince Boun Oum na Champassak (nominal leader of the rightist government in Vientiane), Prince Souvanna Phouma (leader of the neutralist government based on the Plain of Jars) announced that a general agreement had finally been reached on the formation of a government of national union. Souvanna's announcement came after appeals from the ongoing Geneva conference and also after the US government had increased its pressure on the rightists to adopt a more conciliatory attitude. However, on 21 January the rightist 'strongman', General Phoumi Nosavan, announced that he could not approve of the agreement because it would place the Defence and Interior Ministries under neutralist control. In an attempt to bring further pressure on Phoumi to agree to the formation of a coalition, the US State Department announced in mid-February that it was suspending payments of its monthly subsidy (a sum which varied between $3 million and $4 million) to the Boun Oum government.

8 February A new US military command is formed in Vietnam. The greatly strengthened US military presence in Vietnam necessitated a more substantial command operation, and in February the Defence Department announced that a new unit, the US Military Assistance Command, Vietnam (MACV), had been created to co-ordinate all US military support for the Diem government. The new unit was to be commanded by General Paul D. Harkins, hitherto army deputy commander-in-chief in the Pacific, and would complement, and supervise, the existing Military Assistance Advisory Group (MAAG). On the day before the formation of the MACV two US Army air-support units totalling 300 men had arrived in Saigon, raising the number of US military personal in Vietnam to 4,000.

16 February The first National Liberation Front (NLF) congress opens at a secret location in South Vietnam and the organization's leadership and constituent political components are revealed (see Appendix 12). The congress elected Nguyen Huu Tho as NLF president. Tho, a prominent Saigon lawyer, had been active in the anti-French movement and had been arrested by Diem in the mid-1950s. He had apparently escaped from prison in later 1961. Nguyen Van Hien was elected as secretary-general, and of the five vice-presidents, Superior Bonze Son Vong, Phung Van Cung, Huynh Tan Phat, Ydut Ramago and Vo Chi Cong, only the latter was a representative of the Communist People's Republican Party (PRP).

24 February China issues a protest against US intervention in Vietnam. In late February, the Chinese Foreign Ministry issued a statement which said that the US was involved in an 'undeclared war' in South Vietnam and that this action was not only a 'direct threat' to North Vietnam but also placed in jeopardy 'the security of China and the peace of Asia'.

27 February South Vietnamese fighter-bombers launch an attack on President Diem. Two fighter-bombers of the South Vietnamese air force attacked the presidential palace in Saigon in the early morning of 27 February. President Diem and his entourage escaped unhurt; the only person known to have been killed was a US technician who plummeted to his death from the roof of a nearby building while watching the assault. Following the attack, both pilots headed west; one was captured just outside Saigon after his plane succumbed to ground fire and crashed, and the other was arrested after crash-landing in Cambodia.

17 March The Soviet Union issues a statement on US involvement in Vietnam. The Soviet Union sent a diplomatic note to all the participants in the 1954 Geneva conference which asserted that US military personnel and equipment had been introduced into South Vietnam in violation of the Geneva Agreement. The Soviets called for the discontinuation of the delivery of war materials by the US and the immediate evacuation of all US military personnel. Britain (as joint chair with the Soviets of the 1954 conference) issued a reply to the Soviet note in mid-April which claimed that the subversive activities of the North Vietnamese authorities were the major cause of the 'present troubles in South Vietnam'.

22 March The 'strategic hamlets' initiative is launched in South Vietnam. South Vietnam's first major counteroffensive against the NLF was launched in Binh Duong province, north of Saigon. The principal strategy of the campaign, dubbed Operation Sunrise, was largely based on the system of 'strategic hamlets', which was intended to sever the NLF from the peasantry. Under Operation Sunrise, peasants were shifted from isolated villages into fortified settlements which were later organized into self-defence units. The policy had been briefly adopted in 1960, but was revived and expanded in 1962 upon the recommendation of a British advisory mission headed by veteran counter-insurgency expert Sir Robert Thompson. With US financial backing, and the support of President Diem's brother and adviser Ngo Dinh Nhu, the strategy was adopted as the government's main response to the problem of rural pacification. Initially, the 'strategic hamlets' programme was viewed as a great success, by both the US and the South Vietnamese. However, it soon became obvious that the strategy was failing to produce the desired results and was in fact strengthening peasant resentment against Diem and increasing support for the NLF. By early 1964 about half of the hamlets had been abandoned by their defence units, and of the remainder many had been penetrated by the NLF.

9 May Pathet Lao fighters capture General Phoumi Nosavan's garrison at Nam Tha. Small-scale fighting had broken out around Nam Tha, the capital of the northwestern province of Houa Khong, in January as the Pathet Lao, with North Vietnamese Army (NVA) support, began strengthening its presence around the town's rightist garrison. Despite US warnings not to respond to the build-up, General Phoumi poured reinforcements into Nam Tha in March and early April, increasing the strength of the garrison to 5,000 men. Fighting broke out around Nam Tha in mid-April and the garrison itself fell on 9 May after a concerted mortar barrage. The rightists made virtually no attempt to resist, and simply withdrew in panic, the majority travelling south to the Mekong and crossing the river into Thailand. Pathet Lao forces pursued the rightists for part of the way, thereby practically completing the occupation of most of northwest Laos. The fall of Nam Tha and the flight of the rightists across the Mekong prompted President Kennedy to order US and air ground units to take up positions in northeast Thailand.

2 June An International Control Commission (ICC) report issued by the Canadian and Indian members, accuses both North and South Vietnam of violating the 1954 Geneva Agreement.

North Vietnamese violations: the report claimed that evidence demonstrated that 'armed and unarmed personnel, arms, munitions, and other supplies have been sent from the zone in the North to the zone in the South with the object of supporting, organising, and carrying out hostile activities, including armed attacks, directed against the armed forces and administration of the zone in the South'. In addition, the report alleged that the North Vietnamese Army had 'allowed the zone in the North to be used for inciting, encouraging and supporting hostile activities in the zone in the South, aimed at the overthrow of the Administration in the South'.

South Vietnamese violations: South Vietnam, the report claimed, had violated Articles 16 and 17 of the Geneva Agreement by receiving increased military aid from the US. The report went on to state that 'though there may not be any formal military alliance between [the US and South Vietnam], the establishment of a US Military Assistance Command in South Vietnam, as well as the introduction of a large number of US military personnel beyond the stated strength of the MAAG (Military Assistance Advisory Group), amounts to a factual military alliance, which is prohibited under Article 19 of the Geneva Agreement'.

10 June General elections take place in Cambodia and result in another victory for Sihanouk's Sangkum. In the election all 77 candidates of Prince Sihanouk's Sangkum were returned unopposed. In the months before the elections, the prince, motivated by rightist pressure, had ordered the arrest of almost the entire leadership of the left-wing Pracheachon Party, and as a result no opposition group had offered a challenge to the Sangkum. However, after the election, Sihanouk incorporated a number of members of the Sangkum's left-wing faction into his new cabinet, including Khieu Samphan, Hou Yuon and Hu Nim.

12 June The 'three Lao Princes' sign a formal agreement on the formation of a government of national union. Following the rout of its forces in May, the rightist government had little choice but to agree to a further round of talks on the formation of a coalition government. Boun Oum, Souvanna and Souphanouvong met on the Plain of Jars between 7 and 12 June, at the end of which the three princes signed the agreement. The new government, formed in Vientiane on 23 June, consisted of seven neutralists and four representatives each of the rightists, the Pathet Lao and the so-called right-wing neutralists. The principal members of the coalition government were: (neutralists) Souvanna Phouma, prime minister and defence, Quinim Pholsena, foreign affairs; (Pathet Lao) Souphanouvong, deputy premier and economy and planning, and Phoumi Vongvichit, information, propaganda and tourism; and (rightists) General Phoumi Nosavan, deputy premier and finance.

20 July Pol Pot becomes acting Communist Party of Kampuchea (CPK) general secretary. Tou Samouth, the previous general secretary of the CPK was kidnapped from his house in Phnom Penh in mid-July; he was never seen again, and was assumed to have been assassinated shortly after his abduction. According to a number of commentators Pol Pot and his supporters were directly responsible for Tamouth's disappearance.

23 July The Geneva accords on Laos are signed. The Geneva conference on Laos had opened in May 1961, and concluded when the foreign ministers of the attendant nations signed two agreements, the first a declaration on the neutrality of Laos and the second a protocol to the declaration. In the declaration, the 13 attendant nations agreed to respect the neutrality of Laos and to withdraw all foreign military personnel.

7 October The deadline for the withdrawal of foreign forces from Laos is reached, but accusations are levelled that NVA and Chinese nationalist forces remain in the country. According to a report by the ICC in late October, 666 US troops, 403 Filipino civilian technicians and 40 North Vietnamese had left the country via the official withdrawal points by 7 October. Soon after the deadline, complaints were issued to the ICC alleging the continued presence of foreign troops. The US claimed that thousands of North Vietnamese forces remained in northern Laos; the Pathet Lao, meanwhile, claimed that Chinese nationalist forces remained stationed along the east bank of the Mekong.

18 December Senator Mansfield issues the first pessimistic report on US involvement in Vietnam. After visiting South Vietnam in early December as a personal representative of President Kennedy, Senator Mike Mansfield became the first major US official to deliver a bleak assessment of US involvement in Vietnam. In his report to the president delivered on 18 December, Mansfield warned that US policy in Vietnam was 'predicated on the assumption that existing internal problems in South Vietnam will remain about the same'. However, Mansfield noted, the possibilities of the conflict escalating were very real and this could easily lead to a 'truly massive commitment of American military personnel and other resources – in short going to war fully ourselves against the guerrillas – and the establishment of some form of neocolonial rule on South Vietnam'.

1 9 6 3

2 January The National Liberation Front (NLF) win a major military victory in early January when a small number of guerrillas defeat a far larger number of South Vietnamese troops during a battle in the Plain of Reeds. As many as 1,500 soldiers of the South Vietnamese army's (ARVN's) seventh Division, accompanied by US advisers (including Lieutenant-Colonel John Paul Vann), launched an attack on about 350 members of the NLF's 514th Battalion at Ap Bac on 2 January. The US advisers organized the assault with the intention of demonstrating to the NLF the superiority of the ARVN troops, who went into the battle apparently convinced of the invincibility of US training, airsupport and state-of-the-art weaponry. In the event, the ensuing two-day battle went extremely badly for the US and the South Vietnamese. The NLF guerrillas not only survived the assault with very few casualties, but inflicted about 80 deaths on the ARVN forces, as well as killing three US advisers and destroying five helicopters. The most worrying aspect of the defeat for the US advisers had been the obvious lack of fighting spirit and battlefield discipline amongst the ARVN troops, many of whom had simply refused to obey their superiors' orders.

20/21 February Pol Pot is confirmed as Cambodian Communist Party leader. The Communist Party of Kampuchea (CPK) held its third congress at a secret location in Phnom Penh on 20/21 February. The main purpose of the congress was to confirm Saloth Sar (Pol Pot) in his post as party general secretary (a position he had held in an acting capacity since mid-1962). The membership of the new politburo and central committee also confirmed the dominant position within the party of Saloth Sar's supporters and the weakening of the position of the older, Viet Minh-trained revolutionaries.

8 March Following the outbreak of serious rioting in Siem Reap and Kompong Cham in February, Prince Sihanouk responds to calls from Lon Nol and the right for a crackdown on the left by publishing a list of Cambodia's leading 'subversives'. The list included leftists cabinet ministers Khieu Samphan and Hou Yuon and CPK leaders Saloth Sar and Ieng Sary. The latter two left their teaching jobs in Phnom Penh in May and disappeared into the forests of Kompong Cham. At first, Samphan and Yuon remained in the cabinet despite constant right-wing attacks on the policies they were pursuing. However, in early July both resigned from the cabinet and the left's attempts to bring about peaceful internal reform effectively ended.

31 March Fighting breaks out between rival neutralist units on the Plain of Jars. A brawl between rival neutralist forces in Xieng Khouang in late March led to full-scale fighting on the Plain of Jars. A split within the neutralist camp had become evident during late 1962. A left-wing faction led by Colonel Deuane Siphaseuth (and supported by Foreign Minister Quinim Pholsena) accused Kong Le's right-wing forces (supported by Souvanna Phouma) of a pro-US bias. The tension between the two factions increased markedly on 12 February when Kong Le's chief-of-staff, Colonel Ketsana Vongsavong, was assassinated. On 1 April, after the outbreak of fighting on the Plain of Jars, Foreign Minister Quinim was shot dead in Vientiane by a soldier who had served under Colonel Ketsana. After April, the neutralists effectively ceased to exist as a unified force, with the 'right-wing neutralists' entering into a de facto alliance with General Phoumi's Royal Lao Army and Colonel Deuane's 'left-wing neutralists' fighting alongside the Pathet Lao and the North Vietnamese.

8 April Souphanouvong leaves Vientiane amidst an outbreak of fresh fighting in the city. The outbreak of hostilities between the neutralists and the assassination of Quinim prompted Souphanouvong, the Pathet Lao leader and a member of the coalition cabinet, to leave Vientiane for the relative safety of Pathet Lao-controlled Khang Khay. He was followed on 19 April by Phoumi Vongvichit, the other Pathet Lao minister and although both of their portfolios were held vacant they remained in northern Laos.

8 May Buddhist demonstrations against Diem break out in Hue. Large numbers of South Vietnamese Buddhists took to the streets during 1963 in demonstrations against the Diem regime. At the outset the unrest was essentially religious in character, but it quickly took on political overtones and soon came to represent the Buddhist majority's deep resentment at Diem's discrimination in favour of his fellow Catholics and of the generally oppressive character of his rule. Under Diem, Buddhists had been ousted from key positions in all the major power centres, including the government, the armed forces and the civil service.

The first clashes broke out in Hue on 8 May, when South Vietnamese soldiers and police shot dead nine Buddhist demonstrators and injured 20 others. The dead and injured had been amongst a large crowd protesting against a government order that outlawed the display of Buddhist flags and the staging of parades to commemorate the birthday of Gautama Buddha (8 May). Buddhist leaders met with Diem in Saigon on 15 May and submitted a list of modest demands, including an equal legal status for Buddhism and Catholicism. Diem, under pressure from his brother, Ngo Dinh Nhu, and his brother's wife (who together had gained almost a complete ascendency over the president), refused to offer any major concessions and in early June the army and police again resorted to violence in order to suppress further protests in Hue.

11 June Thich Quang Duc, a 73-year-old Buddhist monk, burns himself to death in a public square in Saigon in protest at the government's refusal to meet the demands of Buddhist demonstrators. Thich Duc's act of self-immolation was part of a long tradition of Buddhist protest suicides and it provided the protest movement with a new credibility. During the years to follow many more monks and nuns burned themselves to death but it was photographs of Thich Duc's self-immolation which provided one of the most potent images of the Vietnam War. Five days after the suicide, a compromise agreement was signed by the government and Buddhist leaders, but within hours further Buddhist demonstrations had broken out in Saigon.

21 August Martial law is proclaimed in South Vietnam and Nhu's forces launch a series of co-ordinated assaults on southern Buddhist centres. The Diem government launched a blistering attack on the Buddhist protest movement on 21 August when Vietnamese special forces troops raided Buddhist pagodas in Saigon, Hue, Quang Tri, Quang Nam and Nha Trang, arresting up to 1,400 people, mostly monks. The worst clashes occurred at the Tu Dam pagoda in Hue, where some 30 monks and nuns were killed during running street battles with the troops. The Central Intelligence Agency (CIA)-trained special forces were controlled by Ngo Dinh Nhu, and it was not clear whether Nhu's brother, the president, knew of the anti-Buddhist raids in advance. Initially, it was thought that the regular army had carried out the raids, particularly as President Diem had proclaimed a 'state of siege' throughout the country early on 21 August which had, amongst other things, provided the army with widespread powers of search and arrest.

Reaction to the raids was intense. In Saigon, (Buddhist) Foreign Minister Vu Van Mau resigned his post, shaved his head and embarked on a pilgrimage to India. In Washington, the US State Department denounced the raids as a reversal of an earlier promise made by Diem to the US to forge a reconciliation with the Buddhist community.

2 September President Kennedy publicly criticizes Diem's treatment of the Buddhist community. In a television interview in early September, US President Kennedy, himself a Roman Catholic, declared that South Vietnam's repressive actions against the Buddhists 'were very unwise'. He confirmed that the US would continue to assist the Saigon regime in its war with the NLF, but added 'I don't think that the war can be won unless the people support the effort, and . . . in the last two months, the [South Vietnamese] government has gotten out of touch with the people.' Only 'changes in policy and perhaps with personnel' could enable Diem's regime to regain the people's support, Kennedy said.

Kennedy's allusion to possible 'personnel changes' in Saigon reflected the growing belief in Washington that Diem's rule was turning into a complete disaster and that both he and his brother would have to go. Shortly after Nhu's special forces had raided the country's Buddhist pagodas in mid-August, Henry Cabot Lodge, the newly-appointed US ambassador to Saigon, had made contact with restless army officers. Lodge duly reported the contacts to the US State Department and a controversial reply drafted by George Ball (acting as secretary of state in Dean Rusk's absence) on 24 August effectively provided US authorization for the plotting of an anti-Diem coup to begin.

2 October President Kennedy approves economic sanctions against Diem. US President Kennedy approved a series of recommendations from his defence secretary, Robert McNamara, in early October including the freezing of certain loans and subsidies to South Vietnam in an attempt 'to impress upon Diem our disapproval of his political programme'. Three days later, a CIA officer in Saigon met with General Duong Van Minh (see biographies), who requested to be told the US government's position on a possible change of regime in South Vietnam in the near future. Replies from Washington over the next few days indicated that the US would not thwart a coup attempt; requests were made to General Minh to keep the US government informed of developments so that it might judge correctly the prospects of success.

12 November The Diem regime is overthrown in a bloody coup. High-ranking ARVN officers launched a coup against President Diem on 1 November. The leaders of the coup were identified as General Duong Van Minh (military adviser to Diem), General Ton That Dinh (military governor of Saigon) and

General Tran Von Dong (the armed forces chief). The rebels quickly crushed all resistance except at the presidential palace itself, where Diem and Nhu held out with the support of loyal special forces units. Nhu must have been particularly aggrieved at the assault on the palace, because in late October General Minh had successfully lured him into what turned out to be a false coup plot against General Dong and General Dinh. Before fleeing the palace via a secret tunnel, Diem contacted US Ambassador Lodge who informed the president that the coup leaders were offering him and his brother safe conduct out of the country. However, Diem and Nhu escaped to Cholon (Saigon's Chinatown) early in the morning of 2 November where they were captured by rebel forces and shot to death inside an armoured vehicle travelling to military headquarters in Saigon. On 4 November a civilian-military government headed by ex-Vice-President Nguyen Ngoc Tho, assumed office. The new government pledged that it would not become a military dictatorship, asserting that 'the best weapon to fight communism is democracy and liberty'. The new government was recognized by the US on 7 November. According to the *Pentagon Papers* immediate recognition was delayed in order to reduce the appearance of US complicity in the coup.

19 November Prince Sihanouk renounces US aid for Cambodia. Cambodia's relations with the US deteriorated sharply when Prince Sihanouk renounced US economic and military aid, after alleging that Washington was actively supporting right-wing rebels operating from Thailand and South Vietnam. US funding for Cambodia was replaced by increased aid from the Soviet Union and China, with which Phnom Penh's relations became correspondingly closer. Sihanouk's announcement came a matter of days after the prince had indicated a radical turn to the left in the country's economic policy; new measures included the replacement of all import-export firms by 'state buying and selling offices' and the nationalization of all banking business.

22 November Lyndon Johnson assumes the US presidency after Kennedy is assassinated. Less than a month after President Diem was ignominiously shot in Saigon, US President Kennedy was assassinated in Dallas. In Johnson's first policy document on Vietnam, issued four days after being sworn into office, he sanctioned a programme of increased covert operations against North Vietnam thereby indicating that he was not intending to implement a major revision of the Kennedy administration's overall strategy.

1 9 6 4

30 January General Nguyen Khanh seizes power in South Vietnam. The Military Revolutionary Council (MRC) which had ruled South Vietnam since Diem's overthrow in November 1963 was itself ousted by dissident military officers led by General Khanh. General Khanh announced that the coup had been carried out to frustrate a plot by General Minh and other members of the deposed junta to impose a neutralist policy on South Vietnam with French support (France had established diplomatic relations with China on 27 January and on the day after Khanh's coup President de Gaulle had proposed that the West enter into negotiations with Beijing with the aim of achieving a 'neutrality agreement' for the Southeast Asian states). General Minh was initially placed under arrest by the coup leaders but he was subsequently released to serve the new regime as an adviser. In early February, General Khanh appointed himself prime minister at the head of a new government which included General Tran Thien Khiem as defence minister and Phan Huy Quat as foreign minister. Shortly after Khanh's accession to power the National Liberation Front (NLF) called for negotiations to end hostilities; the new regime rejected the offer, and over the following months Khanh and his supporters issued a series of statements in support of a more aggressive policy towards Hanoi.

1 February The US launch a new programme of covert military operations against North Vietnam in an attempt to coerce Hanoi into ordering a halt to guerrilla operations in South Vietnam and Laos. The programme, code-named Operation Plan 34A, was drawn up by the Central Intelligence Agency (CIA) and Military Assistance Command, Vietnam (MACV) in Saigon, presented to Secretary of Defence McNamara in December 1963 and was subsequently approved by President Johnson. The programme differed from previous covert operations in that it was controlled by the US military in Saigon, and not by the CIA. According to disclosures in the *Pentagon Papers* the operations were divided into two major segments: (i) included commando raids on the North Vietnamese infrastructure, kidnapping of North Vietnamese citizens and flights over the North by spy planes; (ii) included the bombing of North Vietnamese and Pathet Lao troops in Laos by US and Thai pilots flying in planes marked with Royal Lao Air Force markings.

5 March US Defence Secretary Robert McNamara starts an eight-day fact-finding visit to South Vietnam. In his report to President Johnson on his return McNamara stated that the security situation in the South had 'unquestionably been growing worse, at least since September'. He recommended that planning be initiated for two new military programmes, the first ('retaliatory actions') would include provisions for South Vietnamese air raids on North Vietnam 'on a tit-for-tat basis' in response to NLF guerrilla attacks, the second ('graduated overt military pressure') would go beyond reacting on a tit-for-tat basis, and would include (disguised) US air assaults on North Vietnamese military and industrial targets.

According to McNamara, the greatest weakness of the present situation was the 'uncertain viability of the Khanh government'. He estimated that the NLF controlled about 40 per cent of the South Vietnamese countryside; that desertion rates within the South Vietnamese army (ARVN) were 'high and increasing'; that security within the strategic hamlets was 'poor and falling'; that there were 'some signs of frustration within the US contingent'; and that North Vietnamese support for the NLF was increasing. Despite such a negative appraisal of the situation, McNamara, asserted that the 'military tools and concepts' of the South Vietnamese/US effort were 'generally sound and adequate' and that 'substantial reductions in the numbers of US military training personnel should be possible before the end of 1965'.

6 April The second Lao Patriotic Front (LPF) congress opens. The second congress of the LPF, the political wing of the Pathet Lao, was held in Sam Neua province from 6 to 11 April. The congress adopted a new 10-point political programme and elected a 63-member central committee. Elections to the LPF's leading organs were also held: Souphanouvong was elected LPF chair; Kaysone Phomvihane, Phay Dang and Sithone Komadam were elected vice-chairs; Phoumi Vongvichit was elected secretary-general; Nouhak Phoumsavan, Khamtay Siphandon, Phoune Sipaseuth, Sisomphou, Nhia Veu and Kham Moun were elected to the standing committee.

19 April A group of Lao generals launch an unsuccessful coup attempt. On 17 April the Lao premier, Souvanna Phouma, made an effort to re-form the collapsed coalition government by organizing talks on the Plain of Jars between himself, rightist 'strongman' General Phoumi Nosavan and Pathet Lao leader Souphanouvong. At first the talks went well, with all three leaders agreeing to transfer the coalition government away from Vientiane to Luang Prabang, the country's royal capital situated just west of the Plain of Jars. However, a disagreement soon arose over details, prompting Souvanna to announce his intention to resign on 18 April. Souvanna's threat prompted a group of young rightist generals to launch a coup attempt in Vientiane the next day. The rebels, led by General Khouprasith Abhay (commander of the Vientiane military region) and General Siho Lanphouthacoul (commander of the military police), apparently acted in part to prevent General Phoumi from taking the soon-to-be-vacant premiership (General Phoumi's reputation within the army had also been seriously eroded by his corrupt handling of Finance Ministry affairs). The coup was partly foiled by foreign intervention, in that the Soviet, US, British and French ambassadors in Vientiane all condemned the action. However, the coup was successful in that Souvanna was obliged to increase non-Phoumist, right-wing representation in the cabinet; moves were also made in the aftermath of the coup attempt to integrate the neutralist and rightist forces, a move that was condemned by the Pathet Lao.

17 May Kong Le's neutralist forces are defeated by the Pathet Lao on the Plain of Jars. On 16 May Pathet Lao forces supported by Colonel Deuane Siphaseuth's 'left-wing neutralists' attacked Kong Le's neutralist base at Muong Phanh on the Plain of Jars. Kong Le was routed and forced to evacuate his command post; a large number of his troops defected to the Pathet Lao. The US responded to the fall of Muong Phanh by increasing its air operations over Pathet Lao-controlled areas of Laos. These operations, involving US pilots flying T-28 fighters marked with Lao air force colours, had been under way since early 1964 as part of a general covert operation aimed at destabilizing North Vietnam. In early June the US launched low-altitude reconnaissance missions over Laos; the flights were accompanied by US fighter jets which frequently bombed and strafed Pathet Lao and North Vietnamese Army (NVA) areas in response to alleged attacks on the reconnaissance planes. In mid-October US fighters launched their first bombing raids on NLF/NVA infiltration routes and facilities in the Laos panhandle (the so-called 'Ho Chi Minh Trail' – see Appendix 13) after gaining the permission of Premier Souvanna Phouma.

19 May The UN Security Council convenes to discuss Cambodian complaints over alleged 'acts of aggression' by US and South Vietnamese forces. In mid-May the Cambodian government requested a meeting of the UN Security Council to consider 'repeated acts of aggression by US-South Vietnamese forces against the territory and civilian population of Cambodia'. Cambodia's relations with South Vietnam had deteriorated rapidly during 1963 as a result of the incursions and accusations by Saigon that Prince Sihanouk was allowing NLF and NVA troops to establish bases in eastern Cambodia. Eventually, in late August, diplomatic relations were broken off by Cambodia.

At the meeting, the Cambodian delegation claimed that US and South Vietnamese forces had violated Cambodian territory over 260 times in 1963 and the early months of 1964. The delegation from Saigon admitted that South Vietnamese forces had entered Cambodia, but maintained that they had done so only because NLF guerrillas and NVA troops had sanctuaries there and because the frontier had never clearly been defined. The US denied that American advisers had crossed into Cambodia, except inadvertently on one occasion in March, and claimed that any border problems that did exist were directly related to the fact that North Vietnamese troops were using Cambodian territory as 'a passageway, source of supply, and sanctuary from counter-attack by the forces of South Vietnam', an accusation firmly denied by the Cambodian delegation. The Soviet delegation repeated an earlier call by Prince Sihanouk for the convening of a Lao-style international conference to guarantee Cambodian neutrality. However, the US rejected the suggestion of a new Geneva conference. The Security Council meeting ended on 28 May with the unanimous approval of a resolution which, amongst other things, dispatched a UN mission to the Cambodian-South Vietnamese border. The mission subsequently issued a report recommending that UN observers be sent to the Cambodian side of the frontier, an option rejected by both Cambodia and South Vietnam.

20 June General William C. Westmoreland (see biographies) is appointed head of US MACV. He succeeded General Paul Harkins as commander, US Military Assistance Command, Vietnam (COMUSMACV), whose deputy he had been. Three days later, Henry Cabot Lodge resigned as US ambassador to South Vietnam and was replaced by General Maxwell Taylor, hitherto chairman of the Joint Chiefs-of-Staff.

19 July General Khanh launches a 'march north' campaign at a massive public rally held in Saigon to mark the tenth anniversary of the 1954 Geneva accords. A few days later Air Vice-Marshal Nguyen Cao Ky (see biographies), the flamboyant air force commander, told journalists that the South was fully prepared to launch an air attack on the North. The call for an extension of the war to the North by Khanh and Ky was probably partly motivated by the recent nomination of hardliner Barry Goldwater as the Republican Party's presidential candidate. After meeting with Khanh, US Ambassador Taylor telegrammed Secretary of State Dean Rusk on 25 July and proposed that the US express a willingness to begin joint contingency planning with Saigon on a possible assault on the North. This, Taylor claimed, would 'provide an outlet for the martial head of steam now dangerously compressed but would force the generals to look at the hard facts of life which lie behind the neon lights of the "March North" slogans'.

31 July South Vietnamese commandos raid North Vietnamese islands off Vinh. South Vietnamese naval commandos carried out the amphibious raid on two islands off the North Vietnamese port of Vinh as part of the US-directed '34-A' covert operations which had been under way since early 1964. At the same time, the two islands (Hon Me and Hon Nieu) were bombarded by South Vietnamese warships. Hanoi reacted immediately by sending a telegram to the International Control Commission (ICC) complaining of 'an extremely serious violation of the 1954 Geneva agreements' by the US and the Saigon regime.

2–4 August North Vietnamese patrol boats attack two destroyers operating in the Gulf of Tongkin. On 2 August North Vietnamese torpedo-boats attacked the US destroyer *Maddox* which was sailing in the Gulf of Tongkin some 28 miles (45 kilometres) off the North Vietnamese coast. Two of the attacking vessels were driven off by US planes from a nearby carrier and one was sunk; no casualties or damage were sustained by the *Maddox*, which, it was subsequently revealed, had been carrying out electronic surveillance along the North Vietnamese and Chinese coast. On 3 August the Joint Chiefs-of-Staff ordered a second destroyer, the *C. Turner Joy*, to join the *Maddox* in the Gulf and for them both to resume surveillance operations in order to 'assert [the] right of the freedom of the seas'. Later that evening, South Vietnamese commandos carried out two more '34-A' clandestine assaults on the North Vietnamese mainland. About 24 hours later North Vietnamese torpedo boats launched what the US Defence Department described as a 'deliberate attack' on the *Maddox* and on the *C. Turner Joy*, both operating over 62 miles (100 kilometres) from shore. The department said that the destroyers, assisted by carrier-based planes, repelled the attackers and apparently sank two North Vietnamese boats in a three-hour clash. In a statement issued on 5 August North Vietnam accused the US of 'fabricating' the Gulf of Tongkin incident to conceal its 'illegal acts' in Southeast Asia.

5 August US aircraft launch strikes on North Vietnam. In retaliation for the alleged attack on its warships, the US responded by launching bombing attacks on the North Vietnamese torpedo-boat bases along the coast and at an oil-storage depot at Vinh.

7 August US Congress approves the Gulf of Tongkin resolution conferring widespread powers on President Johnson to act in Southeast Asia. Soon after the US had launched the reprisal attack on North Vietnam, President Johnson submitted to Congress a resolution which permitted in advance the president taking 'all necessary measures to repel any armed attack against the forces of the US' (see Appendix 14). It also authorized the president to 'take all necessary steps, including the use of armed force' to assist South Vietnam or any other member or protocol state of the Southeast Asia Treaty Organization (SEATO). Congress approved the resolution on 7 August, the House by 416 to 0, the Senate by 88 to 2 (the two dissenting votes against were cast by Wayne Morse and Ernest Gruening, Democratic senators for Oregon and Alaska respectively). The North contended that the resolution was unconstitutional as 'a predated declaration of war power'.

16 August General Khanh assumes the South Vietnamese presidency. The top military leaders in South Vietnam (i.e. the MRC) approved a new 'National Charter' in mid-August which provided for a presidential system of government. Once approved, the MRC quickly elected Premier Khanh, as president; General Minh, the nominal chief-of-state since the January coup, was dismissed. The new 'National Charter' increased Khanh's powers to an almost dictatorial level and aroused widespread opposition, especially among students and the Buddhist community. Violent demonstrations against General Khanh erupted in Saigon and other cities and towns only days after his assumption of the presidency. The unrest was heightened by communal clashes between Catholics and Buddhists and many of the demonstrations had noticeable anti-US undertones.

25 August General Khanh resigns the South Vietnamese presidency and resumes the premiership. The anti-government riots which had broken out in mid-August increased in intensity and forced General Khanh to resign the presidency and annul the 10-day-old 'National Charter'; he also pledged to dissolve the MRC once a new chief-of-state had been chosen. The council convened the next day in riot-torn Saigon, but failed to reach an agreement on a new chief-of-state. Instead, the council agreed to dissolve itself and transfer power to a Provisional Leadership Committee composed of General Khanh, General Minh and the defence minister, General Tran Thien Khiem. On 29 August it was announced that Nguyen Xuan Oanh, a former deputy premier, had been appointed as acting prime minister while General Khanh travelled to Dalat, ostensibly for rest and medical treatment. Meanwhile, students and Buddhists stepped up their nation-wide demonstrations and many cities, including Saigon, descended into virtual anarchy in late August. The political crisis seriously worried the US who were fearful that the Saigon military's indecision would spur on the demonstrators and could conceivably lead to the creation of a neutralist regime in the South. So, in early September General Khanh returned to Saigon and resumed the premiership, at the same time announcing plans to introduce democratic civilian rule within two months. General Minh was reinstated as chief-of-state, whilst other military members of the government were dismissed.

13 September A group of right-wing and Catholic officers attempt to overthrow General Khanh's Saigon regime. The coup leaders were General Lam Van Phat, who had recently been dismissed as interior minister, and General Duong Van Duc, who was due to be relieved as army commander in the Mekong delta. The uprising, staged in Saigon, collapsed under a government display of military force led by Air Vice-Marshal Ky. General Khanh's regime continued to be plagued by internal unrest during the remainder of September. Nevertheless, on 26 September Khanh formed a 17-member civilian High National Council to prepare for the installation of a civilian government.

27 September Prince Sihanouk arrives in Beijing at the start of a nine-day visit. A joint statement issued at the end of Prince Sihanouk's visit to Beijing included a Chinese commitment to offer Cambodia 'all-out support' in the event of foreign aggression. During his visit Sihanouk accepted substantial military and economic aid, including light and heavy arms for 22,000 soldiers.

1 November The NLF launch their first major attack on a US military facility. During the early morning of 1 November NLF guerrillas launched a mortar attack at the US air base at Bien Hoa, only 12 miles (20 kilometres) north of Saigon. The attack killed four Americans and two South Vietnamese and destroyed five US jet bombers. The guerrillas all fled without loss and six hours after the raid another mortar attack was carried out on a military base 6 miles (10 kilometres) north of Saigon, killing one US officer. (See Appendix 15 for details of 1964 casualty figures in Vietnam and Appendix 16 for strength of forces in action at the end of the year.)

Following the attack on Bien Hoa, President Johnson came under increasing pressure to launch retaliatory strikes on North Vietnam. With only two days to go before the US presidential election, Johnson (who, during his campaign, had attempted to portray himself as a moderate against his escalation-minded opponent Barry Goldwater) rejected calls from the Joint Chiefs-of-Staff and Ambassador Taylor to bomb the North. Instead, he appointed an interagency working group under assistant Secretary of State William Bundy to draw up a number of options for action against North Vietnam.

4 November A civilian government is established in South Vietnam. The High National Council created in late September carried out a series of measures during October that led to the eventual establishment of the civilian government in South Vietnam. On 20 October a provisional constitution was promulgated providing for a chief-of-state, a prime minister, a cabinet and a legislative assembly. The council elected its chairman, Phan Khac Suu ('an octogenarian who advertized his obsolescence by dressing in a black mandarin gown' – Karnow, Stanley, *Vietnam: A History*, London 1984 p. 381) as chief-of-state on 24 October. Suu was sworn in two days later and he accepted General Khanh's resignation as premier. On 4 November Tran Van Huong, a former mayor of Saigon, was sworn in as the new premier at the head of a new 17-member civilian cabinet. General Khanh was appointed as commander-in-chief of the armed forces.

1 December President Johnson approves a limited bombing programme against North Vietnam. The recommendations of the Bundy group (formed by Johnson in the aftermath of the Bien Hoa attack) all included provisions for the bombing of the North. The option eventually adopted by Johnson in early December called, in the first instance, for reprisal air strikes and an intensification of covert operations against the North. The future expansion of the bombing programme to include military and industrial targets was, the president stressed, dependent upon the ability of the Saigon regime to achieve some sort of political stability.

19 December General Khanh once again seizes control in Saigon. The appointment of the new civilian government did little to assuage the Buddhist opposition who assailed Premier Huong for appointing a cabinet full of Diemist technicians and civil servants rather than politicians. Fresh street protests broke out and on 26 November the government declared martial law. According to some commentators, General Khanh interpreted Huong's declaration of martial law as a power-play by General Minh (who had recently returned to Vietnam from a long foreign tour). Despite US warnings not to respond, Khanh established a pact with a group of 'young Turk' officers (including Air Vice-Marshal Ky, General Nguyen Chanh Thi and General Nguyen Van Thieu – see biographies) and on 19 December they seized virtual control of the government. General Minh and other officers were detained and the civilian High National Council abolished; the ineffectual Huong, however, was allowed to remain as premier. The overthrow of the Huong government brought General Khanh and his 'young Turk' co-conspirators into direct conflict with the US, and in particular with Ambassador General Maxwell Taylor who warned that Washington might have to reconsider its close alliance with Saigon unless civilian rule was restored.

1 9 6 5

27 January Much to the irritation of the US, General Khanh removes Premier Huong's civilian government in Saigon. General Khanh's effective ouster of the Huong civilian government in December caused a crisis in Washington's relations with Saigon. Alarmingly, for the US, Khanh's increasingly public altercations with Ambassador Taylor appeared to endear him to the Buddhist leadership. In early January, the Buddhist leaders renewed their agitation against the Huong cabinet. The unrest increased after 9 January when it was announced in Saigon that a compromise agreement had been reached by the military, the government and the US, under which Huong would retain his position as head of government. On 20 January, the prime minister increased the military's presence in his cabinet, granting portfolios to four officers including Air Vice-Marshal Ky and General Nguyen Van Thieu. At the same time two ministers who had faced sharp criticism from the Buddhists were removed from the cabinet. Nevertheless, the unrest increased and the demonstrations took on an increasingly anti-US tone. Eventually, on 27 January, General Khanh and the Armed Forces Council carried out a new coup in Saigon. Premier Huong formally resigned the next day and Khanh was given all powers deemed necessary to establish a stable government. Nguyen Xuan Oanh, hitherto deputy premier, was appointed by Khanh as acting premier. The US State Department announced on 28 January that endorsement of the new regime would be withheld until the structure of the new government was clarified.

31 January Laos' rightist 'strongman', Phoumi Nosavan, flees Laos after an outbreak of serious intra-rightist fighting. He fled to Thailand in early February after the uprising by some of his supporters in the army was quelled by rival units. The unrest within the military broke out in early January, when Souvanna Phouma carried out a reorganization of the High Command of the Royal Lao Army, a move which effectively weakened General Phoumi's already diminishing power base. A military force led by some of General Phoumi's supporters seized Vientiane radio station on 31 January in an apparent coup attempt. Over the next few days, serious fighting erupted in Vientiane as rival rightist units battled for supremacy. The fighting forced large numbers of civilians to cross the Mekong into Thailand and at least 60 civilians were killed in the fighting. After fleeing from Laos in early February, General Phoumi was removed from the cabinet and was charged, in absentia, with rebellion and embezzlement of public funds.

7 February President Johnson orders a raid on North Vietnam. US fighters and fighter-bombers raided targets in North Vietnam as a reprisal for a National Liberation Front (NLF) attack earlier the same day on a US airfield at Pleiku in the central highlands. A barracks was blown up in the attack, killing eight Americans and wounding over 120 others. The US reprisal attack was aimed at targets in and around Dong Ho (50 miles (80 kilometres) north of the seventeenth parallel), a town which, the White House claimed, had been 'actively used by Hanoi for training and infiltration of Viet Cong personnel into South Vietnam'. The next day South Vietnamese fighter-bombers attacked the Van Linh area of North Vietnam (just north of the Demilitarized Zone – DMZ) and on 12 February

US and South Vietnamese planes carried out further attacks on the North as a reprisal for an attack on a US Army billet in Qui Nonh the previous day in which 23 Americans had died.

North Vietnam claimed that the raids constituted 'a new act of aggression of extreme gravity' and condemnatory statements were issued also by China and the Soviet Union. The Indian and French governments called for the Geneva conference to be immediately reconvened in an effort to lessen the danger of a full-scale war breaking out in Vietnam. Meanwhile, anti-US demonstrations were staged throughout the world, including Moscow, Beijing, Shanghai, Budapest, London, Sofia, Jakarta and Caracas. In the US itself the great majority of Congress members expressed their support for the attacks; those who voiced their disapproval included Senators Morse, Church and McGovern.

13 February President Johnson approves a 'program of measured and limited air action' against North Vietnam which was called Operation Rolling Thunder. The programme had been outlined to the President on 7 February in a memorandum from McGeorge Bundy, his special assistant for national security affairs. In his document Bundy had called for the 'development and execution of a policy of sustained reprisal against North Vietnam – a policy in which air and naval action against the North is justified by and related to the whole Viet Cong campaign of violence and terror in the South'.

The first attack of Operation Rolling Thunder took place on 2 March, when over 160 US and South Vietnamese aircraft bombed an ammunition depot at Xom Bang (10 miles (16 kilometres) north of the seventeenth parallel) and the Quang Khe naval base (over 62 miles (100 kilometres) north of the seventeenth parallel). From 19 March onwards air raids on North Vietnam became increasingly frequent, and were directed at targets increasingly further north.

21 February General Khanh is deposed as South Vietnam's 'strongman' by his military colleagues. General Khanh and the Armed Forces Council took the first step towards establishing a stable, civilian-based government on 16 February when Dr Phan Huy Quat was appointed premier at the head of a new 21-member cabinet. Quat, a figure acceptable to the increasingly powerful Buddhist leadership, had been chosen at the expense of at least two candidates favoured by Ambassador Taylor. Three days after Dr Quat's appointment dissident military officers failed in an attempt to overthrow General Khanh. The coup was instigated by three influential right-wing, Catholic officers, including Colonel Pham Ngoc Thao, who had recently served as a press attache in the South Vietnamese embassy in Washington. Although the coup attempt failed, it succeeded in seriously weakening General Khanh's position, to the evident delight of the US. The Armed Forces Council met in Bien Hoa on 21 February and dismissed Khanh as council chairman and armed forces commander; he was replaced in the former post by General Thieu and in the latter by General Tran Van Minh.

27 February The US State Department issues a white paper alleging North Vietnamese aggression in South Vietnam. The paper aimed to demonstrate that the NLF revolt was not a 'spontaneous and local rebellion against the established government' but a long-term 'war of aggression' waged by North Vietnam. Amongst other things, the white paper alleged that 'the hard core' of the Communist forces attacking South Vietnam were men trained in North Vietnam. They were ordered into the South and remained under the military discipline of the military command in Hanoi. Since 1959, the report suggested, nearly 20,000 NLF officers, soldiers and technicians had entered South Vietnam. The Hanoi government was now assigning native North Vietnamese in increasing numbers to join the NLF.

8 March US combat troops arrive in South Vietnam. Two US Marine battalions, comprising some 3,500 men, landed in Danang on 8 March, the first group of US combat troops (as opposed to 'advisers') to arrive in Vietnam. Secretary of State Rusk had announced the previous day that the marines were being sent to defend the air base at Danang and not to fight against NLF guerrillas. However, on 1 April President Johnson approved a 'change of mission for all Marine Battalions deployed to Vietnam to permit their more active use'. At the same time he gave General Westmoreland two more marine battalions as well as 18,000–20,000 logistical support troops. The momentous decision to shift the role of US combat troops to the offensive was not publicly released until 8 June when a State Department spokesman accidentally revealed that General Westmoreland had been authorized to commit his ground forces to routine, direct combat. US troops participated in their first major operation on 28 June when some 3,000 US 173rd Airborne Division troops teamed up with South Vietnamese forces for an assault on an NLF stronghold some 22 miles (35 kilometres) northeast of Saigon. The operation proved largely fruitless and was called off after three days.

7 April President Johnson announces that the US government is prepared to enter into 'unconditional discussions' on Vietnam in a speech at Johns Hopkins University in Baltimore. Johnson also proposed to inaugurate a massive aid programme for Southeast Asia, including North Vietnam, and invited other industrialized countries, including the Soviet Union, to co-operate.

The talks, Johnson said, could be 'discussion or negotiation with the governments concerned; in large groups or in small ones; in the reaffirmation of old agreements or their strengthening with new ones'. The 'essentials' of any final settlement were 'an independent South Vietnam, securely guaranteed and able to shape its own relationships to all others, free from outside interference, tied to no alliance, a military base for no other country'. He also warned the leaders of North Vietnam that he had recently ordered the bombing attacks over their land to convince them of a simple fact: 'we will not be defeated. We will not grow tired. We will not withdraw, either openly or under the cloak of a meaningless agreement'.

After the president's speech Johnson's aides told reporters that the US' readiness for 'unconditional discussions' included a willingness to hold talks with North Vietnam and China but not the NLF.

8 April North Vietnam issues a four-point peace formula. The North Vietnamese premier, Pham Van Dong, put forward the formula for a peace settlement in a speech to the National Assembly on the day after President Johnson's offer of 'unconditional discussions'. The plan proposed: (i) the withdrawal of all US forces and military personnel from South Vietnam and a cessation of 'all encroachments' on North Vietnamese territory in accordance with the Geneva

Agreements; (ii) pending the peaceful reunification of Vietnam, the two zones must refrain from joining any military alliance or permitting the establishment of foreign military bases; (iii) South Vietnam's 'internal affairs' must be settled by the South Vietnamese people themselves, in accordance with the NLF programme and without any foreign interference; and (iv) Vietnam's reunification must be settled by the Vietnamese people in both zones, without any foreign interference. (See Appendix 17 for details of other major 1965 peace manoeuvres.)

26 April US Defence Secretary Robert McNamara claims that North Vietnamese regulars are operating in the South. He announced that North Vietnamese infiltration of arms and personnel into South Vietnam had recently increased despite US air raids on supply routes. According to McNamara it had recently been established that a battalion of the NVA's 325th Division was operating in Kontum province, in the north central highlands. In mid-June McNamara announced that there were indications that eight other NVA battalions were operating in the central highlands; he estimated the NLF force at 65,000 regular combat and combat-support troops and as many as 100,000 'part-time guerrillas'.

2 June The first Australian troops arrive in Vietnam. The first detachment of Australian troops to be sent to fight alongside US forces in Vietnam arrived in Saigon. The Australian prime minister, Sir Robert Menzies, had announced in late April that an infantry battalion of some 800 soldiers would be made available to the Saigon government. (See Appendix 18 for details of Allied involvement in Vietnam.)

19 June A new military-dominated cabinet headed by Air Vice-Marshal Nguyen Cao Ky is formed in Saigon. The deposition of General Khanh in February weakened Premier Quat's position with regard to the military leadership, now dominated by 'young Turks' such as Thieu and Ky. However, initial opposition to Quat came most powerfully from conservative Catholics who charged that his cabinet was preparing to enter into a neutralist settlement with the NLF. The stability of the government was seriously shaken with the discovery on 20 May of an alleged right-wing military plot to overthrow Quat. As in the case of General Khanh, the plot failed, but nevertheless served to undermine Quat's position vis-a-vis the 'young Turks'. So, on 12 June Quat resigned and four days later a 10-member military junta (the Committee for the Direction of the State, or 'Directory'), headed by General Thieu took control. The new cabinet, headed by Air Vice-Marshal Ky, was sworn in on 19 June.

8 July Henry Cabot Lodge is reappointed US ambassador to South Vietnam. General Maxwell Taylor resigned as US ambassador to Saigon in July after serving in the post for just over a year. His replacement, Henry Cabot Lodge, had previously served in the same post from 1963 to 1964.

18 July Elections take place to a new Lao National Assembly. The National Assembly in Vientiane was elected by neutralist/rightist-controlled areas of Laos. Under a new electoral law passed before the election, only some 20,000 people were entitled to vote, the majority of whom were members of the armed forces, civil service and other professions. Inevitably, the elections were boycotted by the

Lao Patriotic Front (LPF) and the new assembly was dominated by the right and particularly by members of Sisouk Na Champassak's Youth Movement. The new assembly convened in mid-August and in early September Souvanna Phouma appointed a new cabinet; the four Pathet Lao portfolios remained vacant.

28 July President Johnson increases the US fighting force in Vietnam. In a nation-wide broadcast delivered in late July, President Johnson announced that he had ordered US forces in Vietnam to be increased from 75,000 to 125,000 men almost immediately. Additional forces would be sent as requested, he said, and this would make it necessary to raise the monthly draft call from 17,000 to 35,000 men a month and to intensify voluntary recruiting. It was announced in early August that over 27,000 men would be conscripted in September and over 33,000 the following month – the largest number called up since the Korean War.

In early June General Westmoreland had implored the president to increase the US troop strength in Vietnam to 44 battalions. This, the general claimed, would allow him to take the offensive against the NLF. His request was apparently prompted by the poor showing of the South Vietnamese forces in battles with the NLF in May. Westmoreland's concern over the inability of the South Vietnamese forces to deal adequately with a swiftly deteriorating security situation was shared by many other senior figures who also called for increased troop deployment. Perhaps the sole dissenting figure at this time was the state under secretary, George Ball, who, in a 1 July memorandum to Johnson, warned against escalation (which he claimed would lead to 'national humiliation') and called for a negotiated settlement of the war.

31 August President Johnson makes 'draft-card burning' illegal. A law was signed by President Johnson which made 'draft-card burning' an offence punishable by five years' imprisonment. The public burning of draft cards had become a widespread form of anti-war protest during 1965. The first American tried under the new law was David Miller, a Catholic pacifist who publicly burned his draft card on 15 October and was subsequently sentenced to 30 months' imprisonment in 1967.

15/16 October The first anti-war demonstrations are held in the US. The first major demonstrations against US involvement in Vietnam were held in New York, Berkeley and some 40 other cities in mid-October. The demonstrations were organized in the main by students, but another march held in Washington in late November was initiated by prominent authors, artists and civil-rights activists. Also in November the US anti-war movement gained its first martyr when Norman Morrison burned himself to death outside the Pentagon in Washington.

14 November What is perhaps the first major conventional battle of the war starts in the Ia Drang Valley, some 6 miles (10 kilometres) west of Pleime and 5 miles (8 kilometres) from the Cambodian border. The battle was an extension of a heavy engagement under way since mid-October around the US special forces camp at Pleime. The First Battalion of the Seventh Cavalry (the same division that had perished at Little Big Horn under General Custer) was helicoptered into the midst of a suspected North Vietnamese Army (NVA) base area in the Ia Drang Valley on 14 November. At least three NVA battalions responded to the challenge the following day and a brutal, close-quarter battle broke out. However, US artillery, fighter-bombers and B-52s pummelled the NVA positions forcing them to retreat. Before the retreat, a cavalry battalion was ambushed on 17 November and suffered heavily in hand-to-hand fighting, one company being almost wiped out. A US military spokesman in Saigon reported in late November that almost 1,200 NVA troops had been killed in the Ia Drang Valley, against 240 US troops. The conflict in the valley, and in other parts of the central highlands, during October and November accounted for a record number of casualties on all sides.

15 December US planes bomb Haiphong, their first raid on a major northern industrial target. The aircraft apparently destroyed a North Vietnamese thermal power station at Uong Bi, which was situated some 12 miles (20 kilometres) north of Haiphong. Defence Secretary McNamara said that the attack on the plant, which had been the primary source of power for the Hanoi-Haiphong industrial area, was 'representative of the type of attacks we . . . will continue to carry out'. McNamara also claimed that the raid was 'appropriate to the increased terrorist activity in Vietnam'.

28 December The US government issues its '14 points' statement and opens a so-called 'peace offensive'. As 1965 drew to a close, the US launched a so-called 'peace offensive'. The offensive was launched with the publication of a list of 14 points which the Johnson administration had previously made public and which, it was claimed, demonstrated the US' eagerness to end the war immediately through unconditional negotiations. At the same time, Johnson dispatched a number of high-ranking representatives to over 30 countries to illuminate the US position on Vietnam (see Appendix 19). The 'peace offensive' also coincided with a reduction in hostilities, the US having ordered a halt to its northern bombing programme on 25 December (an earlier six-day bombing pause had been ordered in May). In a statement issued in early January, the North Vietnamese Foreign Ministry denounced the US 'peace offensive' as a large-scale deception.

The 14 points were as follows: (i) 'The US accepts the 1954 and 1962 Geneva Accords as a good enough basis for negotiations'; (ii) 'It would welcome a conference on Southeast Asia'; (iii) 'It is ready for unconditional negotiations'; (iv) 'It is also ready, if Hanoi so prefers, for informal unconditional discussions'; (v) 'A cease-fire could be the first order of business at a peace conference, or be preliminary to such a conference'; (vi) 'It is willing to discuss the North Vietnam four-point programme'; (vii) 'It wants no military bases in Southeast Asia'; (viii) 'It does not want a continuing military presence in South Vietnam'; (ix) 'Free elections will be supported'; (x) 'The reunification of the two Vietnams can be decided by the free decision of their peoples'; (xi) 'Southeast Asian countries can be non-aligned or neutral: the US wants no new allies'; (xii) 'It is prepared to contribute $1,000 million to a regional development program in which North Vietnam could take part'; (xiii) 'The Viet Cong [NLF] would have no difficulty in having their views represented at a conference after hostilities have ceased'; (xiv) 'The bombing would be stopped if it is stated what would happen next'.

1 9 6 6

31 January After a 37-day pause the US resume air strikes against North Vietnam. The first attack was aimed at targets around Dong Hoi, Vinh and Thanh Hoa. A US military communique claimed that bridges, roads, ferry points, supply depots and a truck convoy had been hit. In a broadcast announcing the resumption of the air war, President Johnson stated that there had been 'no readiness to talk – no readiness for peace' in North Vietnam. However, he also stated that the resumption of the bombing did 'not mean the end of our own pursuit of peace'.

7/8 February Top US and South Vietnamese leaders meet in Honolulu for talks on South Vietnam's political and economic development and on the progress of the war. The South Vietnamese delegation included 'Directory' leaders General Nguyen Van Thieu and Air Vice-Marshal Nguyen Cao Ky and a number of ministers. The US side included President Johnson, Dean Rusk, Robert McNamara, Henry Cabot Lodge, General Westmoreland, Averell Harriman, McGeorge Bundy and General Earle Wheeler. At the end of the talks a 'Declaration of Honolulu' was issued which set out the aims of the two governments. Amongst the aims propounded by the Saigon regime were: 'defeat of the Viet Cong and those illegally fighting with them'; the 'eradication of social justice among our people'; and the formulation of 'a democratic Constitution in the months ahead'. The US declaration stated that Washington sought no bases or colonial presence in Vietnam, nor did it seek to impose an alliance or alignment. Instead it offered its 'full support to the purpose of free elections proclaimed by the Government of South Vietnam and to the principle of open arms and amnesty for all who turn from terror toward peace and rural construction'. The US pledged to give 'special support' to the South Vietnamese people 'to build even while they fight'.

10 March The dismissal of a leading South Vietnamese general prompts serious Buddhist unrest. Emboldened by the guarantees of US support he had received at Honolulu, Air Vice-Marshal Ky moved to consolidate his power in early March by removing General Nguyen Chanh Thi, a powerful rival, from his military command. General Thi was dismissed from his command of I Corps, comprising the five northernmost provinces of South Vietnam. Thi had succeeded in building up a substantial power base around Hue where he had the support of Buddhist Nationalist elements. Two days after Thi's dismissal Buddhist-led demonstrations against the Ky-Thieu junta erupted in Hue and Danang. The demonstrations, which soon spread to Saigon and other cities, were the start of an extended campaign of protest which served to weaken Ky's position. The most important political force in the agitation was the United Buddhist Church, and especially its Institute for the Propagation of Dharma (Vien Hoa Dao). The Institute's main political leaders were the moderate Thich Tam Chau and the militant Thich Tri Quang assisted by Thich Thien Minh and Thich Ho Giac. Under pressure from the demonstrators Air Vice-Marshal Ky announced on 25 March that a Constitution would be in place within two months and that a general election would be held before the end of the year. Ky's announcement failed to deter the unrest, and by late March Catholic leaders in the northern provinces had begun to voice their criticism of the ruling junta and its US backers.

The unrest, which had spread to open rebellion in many areas of the north by early April, aroused fears in Washington that the Ky-Thieu junta might fall and be replaced by a neutralist Buddhist-led regime which would be prepared to enter into coalition with the National Liberation Front (NLF). This fear prompted the US to move to help the junta and on 5 April South Vietnamese army (ARVN) Marines were flown, by US pilots, into Danang to restore order. In the event, fighting in the city was averted after Ky and Buddhist leaders met in Saigon later that day and appeared to arrive at some form of compromise agreement. However, after a few days fresh demonstrations and strikes erupted and these continued until 14 April when the junta announced details of a conciliatory political package which included: elections to a Constituent Assembly within four months; the assembly to be empowered to turn itself into an interim legislative organ; the resignation of the junta after the elections; an agreement by the junta not to use force in Danang and Hue. With the presentation of this package, the Buddhist leadership called off the demonstrations and unrest.

12 April US B-52 aircraft from the US Strategic Air Command base in Guam bomb North Vietnam for the first time. The B-52, which had been designed as a strategic nuclear bomber in the late 1950s, subsequently became the principal delivery vehicle for conventional bombs in Vietnam. By the early 1970s, television coverage of the bombing meant that the B-52 became one of the most graphic symbols of the war in Vietnam.

28 April Senator Fulbright delivers his 'arrogance of power' speech. William Fulbright, a Democrat senator from Arkansas and chairman of the Senate Foreign Relations Committee, rose to prominence during 1966 as one of Washington's leading 'doves' on Vietnam, along with others such as Senators Frank Church of Idaho and George McGovern of South Dakota. In a speech delivered on 28 April in New York, Fulbright claimed that 'America is showing some signs of that fatal presumption, that overextension of power, which brought ruin to ancient Athens, to Napoleonic France and to Nazi Germany'. 'Gradually but unmistakably' Fulbright went on 'America is succumbing to that arrogance of power which has afflicted, weakened and in some cases destroyed great nations in the past'. Congress had become politically and psychologically a 'war Congress,' he said, and 'the President simply cannot think about implementing the great society at home while he is supervising bombing missions over North Vietnam'.

President Johnson replied to Fulbright on 11 May in an address at Princeton University. Attacking Fulbright's assertion without mentioning him by name, Johnson urged 'responsible' intellectuals, 'in the language of the current generation, to "cool it" – to bring what my generation called "not heat but light" to public affairs'. 'The exercise of public affairs in this century,' Johnson went on 'has meant for all of us in the US not arrogance but agony'.

15 May The Saigon junta moves against Buddhist demonstrators in Danang. Premier Ky started revoking elements of the 14 April agreement with the Buddhist nationalists in early May. On 7 May, for instance, he announced that the junta would not be prepared to resign after elections, but would remain in power for a further 12 months. A week later, with US support, Ky moved troops into Danang, and after some heavy fighting the city was brought under the control of the junta on 23 May. While the fight to take Danang raged, Ky denounced the Buddhist militant leader Thich Tri Quang as a 'Communist' and hinted that elections would be postponed until 'security and order' had been created throughout the country. Some of the troops in Danang moved to Hue on 7 June and 12 days later the last area of the city under rebel control was taken. Finally, on 15 June Ky announced that the Constituent Assembly to be elected would be dissolved after the Constitution had been promulgated and would not be allowed to assume an interim legislative role.

29 June US bombers launch their first attacks on petroleum, oil and lubrication (POL) installations around Hanoi and Haiphong. The attacks, which were repeated on successive days, were reported to have destroyed a substantial portion of the North's fuel handling and storage facilities. The POL strikes, which were widely regarded as a significant escalation in the war, had been the subject of some debate in Washington for months before the first attacks. The Joint Chiefs-of-Staff had been pressing for POL strikes since 1965 on the grounds that they would be far more damaging to the North Vietnamese government than attacks on infiltration routes. Defence Secretary McNamara added his support to the Joint Chiefs-of-Staff's recommendations in March and President Johnson finally gave his approval in late May. Throughout the debate, the intelligence agencies remained sceptical over the value of POL strikes, arguing that it would do little to diminish Hanoi's resolve. In the event, they were proved correct; the POL strikes, which continued throughout the summer of 1966, successfully razed Hanoi's larger storage sites, but did little to damage the smaller sites situated away from the larger cities.

7 July The Warsaw Pact countries offer troops to North Vietnam. A statement issued at the end of a meeting of the Warsaw Treaty Organization (comprising Bulgaria, Czechoslovakia, East Germany, Hungary, Poland, Romania and the Soviet Union) in Bucharest in early July declared the readiness of the member nations to send 'volunteer' forces to help North Vietnam in its 'struggle against the American aggressors'. The members also agreed to 'go on rendering [North Vietnam] ever-increasing moral and political support and every kind of assistance'.

28 August The NLF propose the formation of a broadly-based coalition government in the South. In an interview with the Australian writer and journalist Wilfred Burchett in late August, the NLF president, Nguyen Huu Tho, declared that the NLF's goal was 'a broad and democratic coalition government consisting of representatives of all social strata, nationalities, religious communities and patriotic personalities'. He said that former members of the Diem regime would be acceptable in the coalition, but ruled out the 'traitors' of the current Saigon government. Tho issued a three-point political solution for the 'South Vietnam problem': (i) the withdrawal of the troops and bases of the US and its allies; (ii) the settlement of the internal affairs of the South Vietnamese people – including reunification – without foreign interference; (iii) a 'decisive place and voice' for the NLF in any political solution.

1 September President de Gaulle appeals for a US withdrawal from Vietnam. During a four-day visit to Cambodia in early September, French President de Gaulle delivered a major speech on Vietnam before a crowd of some 250,000 in Phnom Penh. During his speech, de Gaulle strongly condemned US policy in Southeast Asia and maintained that a US withdrawal from Vietnam would enhance Washington's international influence to a far greater degree than would its continuing military commitment. The war in Vietnam had gained new strength, he said, because 'illusions regarding the use of force led to the continual reinforcement of the [US] expeditionary corps and to an ever more widespread escalation in Asia, ever closer to China, ever more provocative to the Soviet Union, incurring the ever increasing disapproval of a large number of peoples in Europe, Africa, and Latin America, and finally, ever more threatening to peace'. De Gaulle's call for US withdrawal from Vietnam was only one of a large number of international interventions in 1966 aimed at promoting peace in Indo-China.

11 September In general elections held in Cambodia, all 82 National Assembly seats are again won by candidates from Prince Sihanouk's Sangkum. However, the elections differed from those held in 1954, 1958 and 1962 in that the prince abandoned the policy of designating only one Sangkum candidate in each electoral district. This meant that the 82 seats were contested by well over 400 candidates. Although the new assembly was dominated by the Sangkum right, led by General Lon Nol, three prominent left-wingers (Khieu Samphan, Hou Yuon and Hu Nim) were elected with large majorities despite a virulent press campaign against them during the run-up to polling.

11 September A Constituent Assembly is elected in South Vietnam. Elections were held in junta-controlled areas of South Vietnam in September for a 117-member Constituent Assembly. According to government figures, 81 per cent of registered voters had cast ballots. The 117 seats were competed for by 568 candidates; 735 candidates had originally filed, but the junta's stringent screening process allowed them to ban almost anyone from competing, including those 'who work directly or indirectly for Communism and neutralism'. The draconian nature of the election law prompted Buddhist Nationalist leaders to call for a boycott of the election. The elections were also accompanied by a NLF disruption campaign; 19 people were killed on election day itself, and many more during the campaigning period.

7 October The Lao National Assembly is dissolved. The prime minister of Laos, Souvanna Phouma, arranged for the dissolution of the National Assembly in early October, less than a month after deputies had refused to approve the government's budget (the assembly had been elected in mid-1965). After the dissolution, Souvanna announced that fresh elections would be held in early 1967 and invited the Pathet Lao to field candidates.

18 October General Lon Nol is appointed as prime minister of Cambodia. In mid-October the new National Assembly elected General Lon Nol, hitherto army commander-in-chief and defence minister, as prime minister in place of Norodom Kantol. A few days after his election, the general formed a new right-wing cabinet. In a short-lived experiment aimed at countering the right-wing character of the government, Prince Sihanouk appointed a left-wing 'counter-government' or 'shadow cabinet' in late October which was authorized to criticize Lon Nol's policies and provide alternative proposals.

24/25 October President Johnson meets with the Allied leaders in Manila. At the end of a six-nation Asian tour US President Johnson attended a two-day conference in Manila with the leaders of the nations fighting as allies in Indo-China. The conference was attended by President Johnson, Premier Ky and President Thieu of South Vietnam, Ferdinand Marcos, president of the Philippines, Harold Holt, prime minister of Australia, Keith Holyoake, prime minister of New Zealand, Chung Hee Park, president of South Korea and Thanom Kittikacorn, prime minister of Thailand.

At the end of the conference a lengthy communique was issued on Vietnam, the principal points of which were as follows: (i) the Allies pledged to withdraw their forces from South Vietnam within six months on condition that 'the other side withdraws its forces to the North, ceases infiltration, and the level of violence thus subsides'; (ii) the Allies pledged to continue fighting in Vietnam for as long as was necessary, while at the same time seeking a 'just peace'; (iii) South Vietnam pledged to provide a major share of the forces needed for a 'clear and hold' action to regain territory from the NLF; (iv) South Vietnam pledged to initiate planning for a post-war economy; (v) the South pledged to produce a new Constitution by March 1967 and to hold general elections before September. The conference also issued a Declaration on Goals of Freedom, which stated: 'We, the seven nations gathered in Manila, declare our unity, our resolve, and our purpose in seeking together the goals of freedom in Vietnam and in the Asian and Pacific areas. They are: (1) To be free from aggression; (2) To conquer hunger, illiteracy and disease; (3) To build a region of security, order and progress; (4) To seek reconciliation and peace throughout Asia and the Pacific' (for text of the conference's Declaration on Peace and Progress see Appendix 20).

15 November Kong Le resigns the command of the neutralist forces in Laos. General Kong Le was the former captain who had launched the August 1960 neutralist coup in Vientiane. He turned the 8,000 troops under his command over to the prime minister, Souvanna Phouma, and went into exile in Indonesia. In a statement issued before he left for Jakarta, Kong Le claimed that he had been forced to resign the command by a group of US-backed colonels who wished to integrate fully the neutralist and rightist armies. He denied any involvement in a failed coup attempt launched in Vientiane in October by Brigadier-General Thao Ma, commander of the Royal Lao Air Force.

25 December The Salisbury report on the bombing of Nam Dinh is published. Harrison Salisbury, the assistant managing editor of the *New York Times*, visited North Vietnam in December. In a report filed from Hanoi Salisbury reported that the town of Nam Dinh, situated some 50 miles (80 kilometres) southeast of Hanoi, had been bombed repeatedly by US bombers since mid-1965, that 13 per cent of its homes had been destroyed and almost 90 civilians killed and over 400 wounded. Salisbury's dispatch set off a major debate about the air war in the US. The Defence Department conceded, on 26 December, that North Vietnamese civilians had been bombed accidentally during air strikes on military installations; however, the department insisted that there had been no change to US policy of confining air attacks strictly to military targets. However, a secret Central Intelligence Agency (CIA) study produced in January 1967 estimated that military and civilian casualties of the Rolling Thunder bombing campaign had risen from 13,000 in 1965 to as high as 24,000 in 1966, 80 per cent of whom were civilian.

While Salisbury was in Hanoi during early December the US had launched a series of heavy air raids, some within 5 miles (8 kilometres) of Hanoi city centre. According to some commentators the bombing was carried out in response to peace feelers coming out of North Vietnam. A series of indirect exchanges, code-named 'Marigold', had been under way since mid-1966 with Hanoi represented by the Polish International Control Commission (ICC) representative Janucz Lewandowski, and Washington by the Italian ambassador in Saigon, Giovanni D'Orlandi. Lewandowski, on behalf of the Hanoi leadership, had been proposing a 'political compromise' solution (as opposed to 'mutual de-escalation') and had offered to host talks in Warsaw. In early December, the US apparently agreed to attend talks in Poland, but the air assault on Hanoi prompted the North Vietnamese to halt their contact through Lewandowski.

1 9 6 7

6 February Soviet Premier Kosygin arrives in London for talks on Vietnam with Prime Minister Wilson. The talks coincided with a US bombing pause in Vietnam and both leaders attempted to piece together a formula to get the US air attacks halted permanently. Acting on President Johnson's behalf, Wilson informed Kosygin that the US would be prepared to stop the bombing of North Vietnam and stop the US troop build-up if Hanoi would subsequently halt the infiltration of its forces into South Vietnam. However, when Kosygin asked for a written version of the US offer, Johnson sent Wilson what amounted to a completely different set of proposals, under which Hanoi would have to assure Washington that troop infiltration had been stopped before a bombing halt was called. The latter version proved unacceptable to North Vietnam and the US bombing resumed on 13 February.

22 February US and South Vietnamese troops launch a major operation near the Cambodian border. It was probably the largest US/South Vietnamese army (ARVN) operation to date with some 25,000 troops taking the offensive in Tay Ninh province in an attempt to break the National Liberation Front's (NLF's) stronghold in 'War Zone C' near the Cambodian border. The offensive (Operation Junction City) was launched some six weeks after US forces had deployed the equivalent of three divisions into the so-called 'Iron Triangle' (heavily fortified forest country some 30 miles (50 kilometres) northwest of Saigon) in Operation Cedar Falls. In both operations the US/ARVN forces were frustrated by the elusiveness of the NLF guerrilla units, which more often than not simply slipped away into the jungle rather than engage with the US/ARVN force. A few major engagements did occur, and the NLF lost as many as 3,500 men during the two operations (most resulting from air strikes) against under 350 dead for the US. (See Appendix 21 for major US/Allied ground operations during 1966.)

21 March President Johnson and senior administration officials end a two-day meeting in Guam with South Vietnamese leaders. The conference was attended by (for the US) Secretary of State Rusk, Defence Secretary McNamara, Saigon Ambassador Lodge, General Westmoreland, Joint Chiefs-of-Staff Chair General Earle Wheeler and (for South Vietnam) General Thieu and Air Vice-Marshal Ky. A joint communique issued at the conclusion of the talks said that the two sides had discussed the military and political aspects of the war, South Vietnam's pacification programme and Saigon's progress towards establishing a civilian government.

1 April General Thieu promulgates a new South Vietnamese Constitution. The document had been approved by the Constituent Assembly and by the armed forces in March. The new Constitution provided for the election of a president and vice-president and for a bicameral legislature. Under an article on basic provisions, the Constitution stated that South Vietnam 'opposed Communism in any form, and every activity designed to publicize or carry out Communism was prohibited'.

2 April A left-wing peasant revolt erupts in western Cambodia. Soon after its formation in October 1967, Lon Nol's right-wing government increased pressure on the Cambodian left so that physical attacks on leftists became commonplace, whilst others were arrested. The crackdown occurred at a time when the left was successfully working to co-ordinate its country-wide underground activities. At the same time, anti-government sentiments were running high in the countryside in early 1967 as a result of the initiation of a policy which forced peasants to sell their rice crop to the state (often at a level well below market prices) to pre-empt sales to the NLF. Attacks on military units collecting the rice began in the western province of Battambang early in the year. However, on 2 April a full-scale revolt erupted in the central Battambang district of Samlaut. Bands of villagers and left-wing rebels attacked soldiers and village chiefs in Samlaut, and soon the uprising spread to other districts. Prince Sihanouk immediately charged the Cambodian Communists (dubbed by him the 'Khmers Rouges') of organizing the revolt and he dispatched paratroopers to restore order. By mid-June the prince claimed that the revolt had been crushed, although it was not until August that the unrest finally stopped.

The outbreak of the Samlaut rebellion sparked a political crisis in Phnom Penh. On 22 April Sihanouk accused a small group of left-wing deputies, including Khieu Samphan and Hou Yuon, of responsibility for the revolt; two days later Samphan and Yuon secretly fled Phnom Penh and joined Khmer Rouge fighters in the countryside. Student-led demonstrations broke out in Phnom Penh in protest at what people presumed to be Samphan and Yuon's murder. Eventually, on 30 April, Lon Nol resigned as prime minister, ostensibly to recover from injuries he had received in a recent car crash. Sihanouk himself formed an emergency government, headed by Son Sann (see biographies), which included members of the left and the right.

20 April US bombers strike at previously untouched targets around Hanoi and Haiphong. For the first time US bombers attacked two power plants within Haiphong city limits; four days later two air bases north of Hanoi were also bombed for the first time. North Vietnam claimed that the raid on Haiphong had hit the town's populated district, killing over 40 civilians and wounding another 110.

11 May U Thant issues a warning of the danger of a World War erupting out of Indo-China. At a press conference in May, the UN secretary-general, U Thant, expressed his anguish at the recent intensification of the war in Vietnam and appealed for the cessation of the US bombing of the North. He also spoke of his fears that the fighting might escalate into a confrontation between the US and China.

19 May The US defence secretary, Robert McNamara, delivers a memorandum to President Johnson which recommends a drastic break from the administrations's established policy on Vietnam. McNamara's recommendations included: a halting of the bombing of the North above the twentieth parallel; an increase in troop numbers of only 30,000 (as against 200,000 requested by General Westmoreland); and, perhaps most controversially, a scaling-down of Washington's ambitions in Vietnam to the extent that it would no longer be unthinkable to accept a coalition government in Saigon with NLF representation.

McNamara's memorandum clearly indicated to Johnson that his administration was seriously divided over future policy on Vietnam. At the outset of the Vietnam adventure, McNamara had been a staunch and hawkish advocate of bombing and troop deployment. However, by October 1966 he was advising Johnson to order a bombing cutback and prepare for a political settlement. By the time he delivered his memorandum to Johnson, the president's senior policy-makers were broadly split into two groups, one led by McNamara favouring de-escalation, and one led by Westmoreland and the Joint Chiefs-of-Staff favouring the deployment of massive military resources to win the war. Johnson opposed both accommodation and full-scale escalation, favouring instead a steady military build-up, a position that satisfied neither McNamara nor Westmoreland.

3 September General Thieu and Air Vice-Marshal Ky are elected president and vice-president of South Vietnam, respectively. General Thieu was elected to a four-year term as president of South Vietnam in an election held on 3 September. Thieu, and Prime Minister Ky, his vice-presidential running mate, received just under 35 per cent of votes cast; according to official figures, there had been a turn out of 83 per cent of registered voters (rival claims to the presidency by Thieu and Ky were resolved in Thieu's favour in late June when the Armed Forces Council effectively forced Ky to accept second place on the ticket). Of the other 10 candidates, Truong Dinh Dzu (the so-called 'peace candidate') received the strongest support (17 per cent). The NLF had launched widespread attacks in Saigon and elsewhere in South Vietnam in an effort to disrupt the elections; over 200 civilians were reportedly killed during the election campaign and on polling day itself. Opposition candidates charged on 4 September that the elections had been fraudulent and a complaint was submitted to the Constituent Assembly, which eventually validated the results in early October. A group of US observers sent by President Johnson to report on the election claimed on their return to Washington that polling had been as free and fair as circumstances permitted.

21 September The first batch of Thai troops to fight alongside South Vietnamese troops arrive in Saigon. The arrival of the 1,200 Thai combat troops brought to six the number of Allied countries which had dispatched troops to South Vietnam. As of October 1967 the number of Allied forces in South Vietnam totalled 1,251,200 and distributed nationally as follows: US 465,000, South Vietnamese (irregulars) 403,000, South Vietnamese (regulars) 327,000, South Korea 45,000, Australia 6,300, Thailand 2,500, Philippines 2,000 and New Zealand 400.

29 September President Johnson outlines new US terms for a halt in the bombing of North Vietnam. In a speech delivered in San Antonio, Texas, in late September, President Johnson made public a new US peace proposal. In the 'San Antonio formula', as it came to be known, Johnson offered to halt the bombing of North Vietnam provided that such a course of action would 'lead promptly to productive negotiations'. Unlike previous offers, Johnson did not insist on a substantial North Vietnamese de-escalation as a prerequisite for the halt, but instead he 'assumed' that Hanoi 'would not take advantage of the bombing cessation'. By the time Johnson delivered his speech, the North Vietnamese leadership had already had time to ingest the new formula. Secret negotiations based around the offer had taken place earlier in Paris, involving Henry Kissinger (see biographies), two French intermediaries and a North Vietnamese representative. However, once the formula was made public, Hanoi promptly rejected it on the grounds that it still represented a 'conditional' offer to halt the bombing.

21 October Anti-war demonstrators march on the Pentagon. A massive anti-war demonstration began in Washington on 21 October. Demonstrators congregated at Lincoln Memorial before marching to the Pentagon where they held a rally and a vigil. Many of the protesters were arrested after clashing with troops who had been called out to police the march. The Washington protest was paralleled by anti-war demonstrations in many western European countries. In London and Copenhagen, for example, police fought with demonstrators who attempted to storm the US embassies.

22 October Elections to the 137-member South Vietnamese House of Representatives take place. Over 1,100 candidates had contested the election and a turn out of 73 per cent was recorded. Candidates contested the election as individuals, so estimates of the strengths of the various groups in the House differed. *Le Monde*, for instance, estimated that Catholics and Northern refugees had won half of the seats, but other newspapers claimed that their share of the vote was much lower.

At the end of October President Thieu appointed Nguyen Van Loc, president of the Army People's Council and a close associate of Air Vice-Marshal Ky, as prime minister. Loc formed a new cabinet on 9 November which, with the exception of two new officials, was composed entirely of ministers who had served in the previous government.

21 November During a visit to the US, General Westmoreland expresses optimism on the progress of the Vietnam War. In November, President Johnson recalled General Westmoreland to the US to embark on a public relations tour to counter increasing domestic criticism of the Vietnam War. In a major address at the National Press Club, Westmoreland said that he was 'absolutely certain that whereas in 1965 the enemy was winning, today he is certainly losing'. He said that the US plan to win the war involved four distinct phases, two of which had been completed. In phase one, he explained, the US 'came to the aid of South Vietnam, prevented its collapse under the massive Communist thrust, built up our bases and began to deploy our forces'; this was completed by mid-1966. Phase two, he claimed, continued the pattern of phase one, but in addition drove the 'enemy' into sanctuaries and improved the fighting capabilities of the South Vietnamese forces. Phase three, in 1968, envisaged a reduction of US advisers in South Vietnamese training centres and continued pressure on the North to make infiltration more costly. The final phase 'will see the conclusion of our plan to weaken the enemy and strengthen our friends until we become progressively superfluous'. The South Vietnamese regime 'will prove its stability' whereas the 'Communist infrastructure will be cut up and near collapse'. 'It is difficult to conceive of a surrender' by Hanoi, Westmoreland said, 'but it is not inconceivable that the enemy will realize that he is not in a position where he can win. This is what is happening. But apparently the enemy hasn't realized it yet'.

1 9 6 8

8 January A US diplomat arrives in Cambodia for talks with Prince Sihanouk. Following indications in late 1967 that Sihanouk had adopted a more conciliatory attitude towards Washington, Chester Bowles, the US ambassador to India, paid a visit to Phnom Penh in early January as a personal representative of President Johnson. At the top of their agenda was the issue of the heavy National Liberation Front/North Vietnamese Army (NLF/NVA) presence in eastern Cambodia. Bowles apparently assured the prince that the US had no desire to launch 'hot pursuit' raids into Cambodia, but instead favoured increasing the powers of the International Control Commission (ICC) in Cambodia as a means of countering the Vietnamese presence. However, according to one commentator (Shawcross, William, *Sideshow*. London 1986. pp. 68–69.) the Bowles mission assumed a greater significance in the 1970s when the Nixon administration defended their secret bombing of Cambodia on the grounds that Sihanouk had privately indicated to Bowles that he would not object to US bombing of the NLF/NVA sanctuaries.

21 January One of the bloodiest and most protracted battles of the Vietnam War opens in mid-January at the US Marine fire base at Khe Sanh, situated 6 miles (10 kilometres) east of the Lao border and just over 12 miles (20 kilometres) south of the Demilitarized Zone (DMZ). Southwest of the base lay a special forces camp at Lang Vei, held by South Vietnamese and Montagnard irregulars. For the US and the South Vietnamese, Khe Sanh's importance rested in its close proximity to the 'Ho Chi Minh Trail' in Laos. During mid-1967 the base had been heavily stockpiled in the event of a possible push into Laos. Towards the end of 1967 US intelligence reports showed that as many as two or three reinforced NVA divisions (32,000–40,000 men) were converging on Khe Sanh. In turn, General Westmoreland (who was convinced – wrongly – that the NVA manoeuvres around Khe Sanh were part of a North Vietnamese plan to seize control of provinces immediately south of the DMZ prior to opening peace negotiations) increased marine numbers to 6,000. Westmoreland viewed the prospect of a major set-piece battle against the NVA with relish, convinced that superior US fire-power would lead inexorably to a massive defeat for Hanoi.

Early on 21 January the NVA began shelling Khe Sanh base and at the same time infantry attacks were launched on Lang Vei and on US positions in the surrounding hills. By the following day, most of the marines and South Vietnamese army (ARVN) troops had bunkered down in the base itself allowing the NVA to close in with their artillery. The US responded by launching Operation Niagara, which entailed redirecting all North Vietnamese bombing missions to NVA positions around Khe Sanh. What followed constituted one of the most concentrated bombings in the history of warfare, with an average of 300 air strikes being flown in support of Khe Sanh each day. Despite the aerial bombardment, the NVA remained in position and continued their artillery assault on the base; anti-aircraft fire inhibited the flow of supplies, but US cargo planes continued to make landings and a siege situation developed. Nine days after the NVA artillery assault had opened, the NLF opened their Tet offensive and thereby revealed the logic of the Khe Sanh siege as a strategy to divert US resources to the remote north away from the NLF's urban targets. In the US, Khe Sanh represented a turning point in the war. The daily television pictures and newspaper reports of the plight of the besieged marines aroused feelings of despair and anxiety among the public that quickly turned to anger at the politicians and their Indo-China policy. President Johnson was fixated by Khe Sanh: he had a model of the base set up in the White House and insisted on constant and detailed briefings. The prospect of Khe Sanh falling to the NVA horrified Johnson and he made the Joint Chiefs-of-Staff sign a document declaring their faith in Westmoreland's ability to retain the base. From Westmoreland he asked for an assurance that he would not be required to order the use of nuclear weapons over Khe Sanh.

The situation at Khe Sanh worsened considerably on 7 February when the NVA captured the special forces camp at Lang Vei, using tanks for the first time in the war. At the same time, Khe Sanh received the most brutal artillery barrage of the war. The North Vietnamese maintained their pressure on Khe Sanh throughout February and March, and the US meanwhile continued mass raids by B-52s on NVA positions. The NVA force was reduced to about 10,000 men in late March, and on 1 April the US First Air Cavalry Division landed some 9 miles (15 kilometres) east of the base. The relief force advanced west along Highway 9 and entered Khe Sanh unopposed on 7 April. The NVA had lost at least 10,000 men at Khe Sanh (with some units suffering 90 per cent losses), mostly as a result of the massive US bombing; under 500 marines died during the siege.

31 January NLF forces, with NVA support, launch a country-wide Tet offensive against urban South Vietnam. All southern cities and over 60 district towns were targeted for attack by at least 70,000 NLF/NVA fighters. The attack was launched during a truce which had been agreed by both sides to mark the Vietnamese New Year (Tet) celebrations. The mass movement of people travelling throughout the South prior to the Tet holiday had allowed the guerrillas to infiltrate the towns and cities with relative ease. The towns and cities where major battles erupted during the Tet offensive included Saigon and Hue (see below) and also: in the south – Bien Hoa, My Tho, Bentre, Can Tho, Vinh Long, Camau and Chau Doc; in the centre – Dalat, Nha Trang, Ban Me Thuot, Quinhon, Pleiku, Kontum and Dakto; and in the north – Khe Sanh and Lang Vei, Quang Tri, Ashau, Danang, Hoi An, Kham Duc and Quang Ngai.

Saigon: The assault on the capital took various different forms. Small commando groups carried out planned raids on selected targets such as the presidential palace, the city's radio station and the navy headquarters. The most significant raid was carried out on the US embassy by a 20-man team which managed to enter the compound and hold a section of it for six hours. Another sort of assault took place in Cholon (Saigon's Chinatown) and other working-class suburbs, where NLF guerrillas established total control of whole districts with little difficulty. On the outskirts of the city, attacks were launched on Tan Son Nhut air base (including General Westmoreland's (MACV) compound situated in base) and on the nearby South Vietnamese general staff headquarters. A nation-wide state of emergency was imposed by President Thieu on 31 January and in Saigon itself a 24-hour curfew was imposed. One of the most striking photographic images depicting the chaos in Saigon was that of police chief Brigadier-General Nguyen Ngoc Loan calmly shooting a captured NLF officer in the head. Soon after the assault, US infantry and tanks were rushed to the city and by 5 February most of the NLF/NVA troops had withdrawn to Cholon which was subjected to very heavy US bombing and strafing. From their strongholds in Cholon, the NLF/NVA launched attacks on other areas of Saigon throughout the remainder of February.

Hue: NLF/NVA troops entered Hue early on 31 January and rapidly overran every government position. A list of 'reactionaries' had been drawn up before the assault and, according to some commentators, large numbers of people on the list were summarily executed; sifting through the rubble that had been Hue in March, South Vietnamese officials claimed to have unearthed 2,500 civilian bodies buried in shallow graves. A joint attempt to recapture Hue was immediately launched by ARVN troops supported by US Marine and Air Cavalry units. The battle for the recapture of Hue lasted over three weeks and casualties were heavy on both sides. A large section of the city was reduced to ruins by heavy US bombing and, of the city's 145,000 inhabitants, over 110,000 ended up homeless.

Some commentators have claimed that the Tet offensive was unsuccessful because it failed in its stated purpose of provoking a general uprising among the urban working class in the South. At the same time, it is argued, the offensive resulted in the virtual decimation of the NLF (with as many as 45,000 casualties) and therefore ensured that the revolution passed firmly into North Vietnamese hands. Other commentators claim that the offensive was a success for the NLF and the North Vietnamese and constituted perhaps the most important event of the war. According to supporters of this theory, the offensive did fail to provoke a general uprising and NLF losses were significant, but such failures were transcended by the effects of the assault on the US public. Within the US the media reported the Tet offensive largely as a Communist success. After years of positive assessments of the war by politicians and reporters alike, the US public was stunned and depressed by the conflict and a mass reassessment of the conflict was under way.

25 February The Khmer Rouge launch a widespread guerrilla campaign. Khmer Rouge guerrilla bands seized the initiative in late February, launching a widespread campaign throughout western Cambodia's rural lands. By the end of the year the unrest had spread to well over half of the country's provinces and shootings were reported in Phnom Penh itself during the latter part of the year. During the initial thrust in February, guerrillas executed a number of government officials, seized large numbers of guns and induced as many as 10,000 peasants to leave their villages for Khmer Rouge camps in the forests. Most of the villagers returned after a few months in the forest, but the bases and communication networks they established subsequently proved invaluable.

25/26 March A meeting of 'wise men' in Washington advises Johnson against further escalation in Vietnam. President Johnson convened the meeting of his senior informal advisory group (the so-called 'wise men') to provide him with guidance on his Vietnam policy. The group included senior military figures (Generals Taylor, Ridgeway and Bradley) and high-ranking politicians and diplomats (Dean Acheson, McGeorge Bundy, George Ball, Douglas Dillon, Henry Cabot Lodge), the majority of whom had been staunch supporters of the war. However, the general advice they offered the president after their meeting was that a change of US policy on Vietnam was inevitable. A military victory was unlikely and if policy continued to be aimed towards this end then the domestic repercussions might be serious. Although some members of the group supported continued bombing, the majority called for a halt.

In the aftermath of the Tet offensive, Johnson had pondered long and hard on the future direction of his Vietnam policy. In late February he had dispatched General Earle Wheeler, the chair of the Joint Chiefs-of-Staff to Saigon to gauge General Westmoreland's views on the military situation. Wheeler's report on his return to Washington had painted a bleak picture. The NLF and the NVA were operating freely in much of the South Vietnamese countryside and it was essential, Westmoreland had told Wheeler, that the US regained the initiative through offensive action. He requested an extra 207,000 men (to raise the troop ceiling to 732,000), half to be in Vietnam by early May, the remainder by the year's end. Johnson recognized that Westmoreland's request was a turning point in the war; if he refused him, the corollary was disengagement and negotiation. Johnson gathered together a group of senior advisers under the defence secretary-elect, Clark Clifford, to review policy in the light of Westmoreland's request. The Clifford Group's initial draft opposed any further escalation on the grounds that it would provoke 'a domestic crisis of unprecedented proportions'. The Joint Chiefs-of-Staff were appalled at the group's recommendations, and a compromise was reached recommending the immediate deployment of 22,000 more troops to be followed by a weekly examination of the troop-level requirements. Following the delivery of the Clifford Group's report in early March, speculation grew in the US that Johnson was about to order a major escalation of the war. As the conjecture spread it became increasingly apparent to Johnson that approval of Westmoreland's request would be politically imprudent, particularly in an election year. In mid-March he recalled Westmoreland to Washington, and told him that he had rejected his plea for a further 207,000 men; he also informed him that he was to be promoted to army chief-of-staff and that his deputy, General Creighton Abrams, would take over as army commander in Vietnam in July. It was after his meeting with the military that Johnson, on the advice of Clark Clifford, arranged the meeting of the 'wise men'.

31 March President Johnson announces a partial end to the US bombing of North Vietnam and at the same time he announces his decision not to seek re-election. President Johnson delivered one of the most important presidential speeches of the twentieth century in late March in which he announced a partial halt to the US bombing of North Vietnam and called for a peace settlement based on the 1954 Geneva Agreements. At the same time, Johnson told the US public that he would neither seek nor accept the Democratic nomination for another term as president in the presidential elections to be held in November 1968. He said that he had concluded that he should 'not permit the Presidency to become involved in the partisan divisions that are developing in this political year'.

'Tonight,' President Johnson said, 'I have ordered our aircraft and naval vessels to make no attacks on North Vietnam, except in the area north of the demilitarized zone where the continuing enemy build-up directly threatens allied forward positions and where movements of troops and supplies are clearly related to that threat. The area in which we are stopping our attacks includes almost 98 per cent of North Vietnam's population, and most of its territory.' Johnson called upon Britain and the Soviet Union – as co-chairs of the Geneva conference – 'to do all they can to move . . . toward genuine peace in Southeast Asia'. 'Peace,' he said, 'can be based on the Geneva accords of 1954, under political conditions that permit the South Vietnamese . . . to chart their course free of any outside domination or interference'. He also called upon Ho Chi Minh 'to respond positively, and favourably, to this new step towards peace'.

3 April North Vietnam agrees to open negotiations with the US. Three days after President Johnson announced a partial halt to the bombing of North Vietnam, the Hanoi government announced its readiness to open contacts with the US 'with a view to determining with the American side the unconditional cessation of the US bombing raids and all other acts of war against the Democratic Republic of Vietnam so that talks may start'. Hanoi's acceptance of Johnson's offer to negotiate caused widespread surprise, as in the past it had insisted on the complete ending of the bombing as a condition for any negotiations.

President Johnson responded quickly and positively to the North Vietnamese statement, proposing that the talks be held in Geneva. North Vietnam rejected Geneva as a venue and proposed instead that the talks open in Phnom Penh. The two sides argued over the venue of the talks until early May when it was agreed that negotiations would be held in Paris.

30 April Lon Nol re-enters the Cambodian government. The rapidly deteriorating security situation in Cambodia induced Sihanouk to bring former Premier Lon Nol back into the government as defence minister and inspector general of the armed forces. Lon Nol had been forced to resign as premier in April 1967 as a result of his failure to fully suppress the Samlaut rebellion. Once back in the cabinet, he made quick progress through the ranks, being promoted to deputy premier in July and acting premier in December.

13 May Peace talks open between North Vietnam and the US. Talks on the ending of the bombing of North Vietnam eventually opened in Paris in mid-May. The US delegation was led by Averell Harriman, an old Vietnam hand and President Johnson's 'Ambassador at Large'; the North Vietnamese delegation was led by Xuan Thuy, a former foreign minister and head of the Communist Party's foreign relations department. The talks made little progress in the early rounds, with the US side insisting that a complete bombing halt could not be called without some form of reciprocal action by North Vietnam.

18 May A new government is formed in Saigon. Nguyen Van Loc resigned as South Vietnam's prime minister in mid-May. He was replaced by Tran Van Huong who had previously held the premiership for a short time during the period of severe political instability in late 1964 and early 1965. Tran Van Loc's government had been heavily criticized in the National Assembly for conduct of the war and its failure to win even a measure of popular support. In his first broadcast as premier in late May, Tran Van Huong included among his new government's immediate objectives the initiation of an anti-corruption campaign and the restoration of the state's authority.

31 October President Johnson announces an end to the bombing of North Vietnam. In a nation-wide television broadcast on 31 October President Johnson announced that he had ordered a complete halt to all air, naval and artillery bombardments of North Vietnam as of 8.00 a.m. on 1 November. He had made the decision, he said, in light of recent progress at the Paris talks; the US side, he claimed, had received 'confirmation of the essential understanding that we have been seeking with the North Vietnamese'. However, according to a number of commentators, Johnson's announcement of the bombing halt was a largely politically motivated act intended to boost the electoral appeal of the Democratic presidential candidate Hubert Humphrey in his contest with Republican Richard Nixon (see biographies). Humphrey was narrowly defeated on 5 November.

At the Paris talks the US had been offering to halt its bombing programme in return for an agreement by Hanoi on a number of 'understandings'. The assurances sought by the US included a pledge that North Vietnam would show a level of restraint in its military actions and would refrain from sending more troops across the DMZ. The North Vietnamese refused to give any such assurances; Hanoi's sole concession was to drop its demand that the US publicly announce that Johnson's decision to halt the bombing was a unilateral one.

After the bombing of the North ended, in early November, the US air assault on Laos was greatly intensified. The Pathet Lao issued a memorandum in January 1969 which alleged that the number of raids on Laos had risen from under 3,100 in September 1968 to over 4,700 in October and 12,700 in November. The memorandum also claimed that 137 people had been killed in a single series of raids on villages in Xieng Khouang province on 24 November.

1 9 6 9

20 January Nixon is inaugurated as US president. Richard Nixon, who had defeated Hubert Humphrey in the November 1968 presidential election, was inaugurated as the US' thirty-seventh president. Among the principal members of the new Nixon administration were Spiro Agnew as vice-president, William Rogers as the new secretary of state, Melvin Laird as secretary of defence and Henry Kissinger as the president's national security adviser.

25 January The Paris peace talks are expanded to include South Vietnamese and National Liberation Front (NLF) representatives. The first round of four-party peace talks took place in Paris, almost three months after President Johnson had announced that the talks would be extended to include representatives from the South Vietnamese government and the NLF. The US delegation was headed by former US ambassador to Saigon, Henry Cabot Lodge, who replaced 77-year-old Averell Harriman. The delegation from Hanoi continued to be led by Xuan Thuy. The South Vietnamese and NLF delegations were headed by Pham Dang Lam (head of Saigon's liaison mission at the talks) and Tran Buu Kiem (minister in the NLF Premier's Office); Kiem was accompanied by Nguyen Thi Binh, the NLF foreign minister. The talks made little progress during the first few months; the North Vietnamese and NLF delegations pressed for the replacement of the Thieu regime in Saigon by a 'Cabinet for the restoration of peace' and insisted on an unconditional US withdrawal from the South; the US and Saigon delegations concentrated on military questions and called for the 'mutual withdrawal' of forces from the South.

22 February The NLF launch a major offensive throughout the South. NLF forces, accompanied by North Vietnamese Army (NVA) regulars, launched the offensive primarily to cause a large number of US casualties to test the mettle of the new Nixon administration in its contest with the domestic anti-war movement. On the first night of the offensive, the NLF attacked over 100 targets, the majority of which were US military installations; the assault also included rocket and mortar attacks on Saigon and a number of provincial capitals and district towns. During the following month, between 20 and 65 targets were attacked every night, mainly in the provinces around Saigon, south of the Demilitarized Zone (DMZ) and in the central highlands. In the first week of the offensive, over 450 Americans were killed and after six weeks the figure had risen to 1,740. The new US administration claimed that the offensive was a breach of Hanoi's tacit 'agreement' under which President Johnson had halted the bombing of the North in late October 1968; not surprisingly, the North Vietnamese denied that any such 'agreement' existed.

18 March The US begins secretly to bomb Cambodia. President Nixon's response to the NLF's February offensive was to order the 'secret' bombing of what were thought to be key NVA positions in eastern Cambodia. 'Short duration' raids on the NVA's Cambodian bases had been requested by US military chiefs in Saigon soon after Nixon had assumed the presidency. At first Nixon stalled, heeding the advice of Kissinger and Laird and others to be wary. Eventually, in mid-March, Nixon gave his approval for a secret air strike on neutral Cambodia. However, what started as a plan to inflict quick and telling damage on key enemy bases, stretched into a 14-month-long, clandestine operation, which, when eventually revealed, left behind it a trail of corruption and deceit.

10 May The battle for 'Hamburger Hill' begins. One of the most controversial battles of the Vietnam War took place in May. Three battalions from the US 101st Airborne Division launched an operation to seize a fortified ridgeline on the edge of the A Shau Valley in mountains west of Hue, near the Lao border. One of the battalions soon engaged NVA troops entrenched on Ap Bia Hill (Hill 937), which subsequently became infamous as 'Hamburger Hill'. The US troops launched 10 assaults on the hill before it was finally captured on 20 May. The fighting was intense and casualties were high; 619 NVA and 55 US dead and a further 310

Americans injured. The hill was abandoned on 25 May and in mid-June it was reoccupied by the NVA.

In the US the battle of 'Hamburger Hill' was heavily criticized as a waste of life and energy. It proved a serious embarrassment to the Nixon administration which was desperately trying to persuade the US public that the war was being wound down and that lives were not being squandered needlessly.

14 May Nixon proposes the mutually-phased withdrawal of US and NVA troops from the South. President Nixon's first major speech on Vietnam was broadcast in mid-May. In his speech Nixon announced that he had 'ruled out attempting to impose a purely military solution on the battlefield'; he had also 'ruled out a one-sided withdrawal from Vietnam, or the acceptance in Paris of terms that would amount to a disguised defeat'. He proposed that the majority of US and North Vietnamese forces be withdrawn simultaneously from South Vietnam over a 12-month period and under international supervision. Nixon's proposal differed from earlier 'mutual withdrawal' formulas only in that it laid down a specified time-limit (12 months). The plan was quickly rejected by the NLF and the North Vietnamese.

8 June Nixon announces the first US troop withdrawal from Vietnam. During a meeting with President Thieu on Midway Island in early June, President Nixon announced that 25,000 US troops would be withdrawn from Vietnam by the end of August. Nixon's announcement signalled the activation of the policy of 'Vietnamization', under which a programme to retrain and re-equip Thieu's southern forces would serve as the vehicle for US disengagement. Melvin Laird, the US defence secretary and a master of bureaucratese, had devised the term 'Vietnamization' as an improvement on 'de-Americanization' in early 1969.

10 June The NLF forms a provisional revolutionary government. The NLF (or Viet Cong) announced in June that a Provisional Revolutionary Government of the Republic of Vietnam (PRG) had been established. According to NLF radio broadcasts, the PRG was elected at a conference convened in early June by the NLF and the Alliance of National, Democratic and Peace Forces. The government was headed by Huynh Tan Phat, a founder member of the NLF and a former head of the Viet Minh information services; other members included Nguyen Thi Binh (foreign minister), Tran Nam Trung (defence) and Tran Buu Kiem (minister in the prime minister's office). Upon its formation, the PRG adopted a 12-point programme of action, which, amongst other things, called for: the total and unconditional withdrawal of US forces from South Vietnam; the overthrow of the 'entire structure of the [Saigon] puppet administration' and its replacement by a 'really democratic and free republican regime'; and the reunification of Vietnam 'step by step, by peaceful means, through discussions and agreement between the two zones, without constraint from either side'. Cuba was the first country to recognize the PRG on 10 June; over the following few days other countries followed the Cuban lead, including North Vietnam, Cambodia, the Soviet Union and China. In Saigon, President Thieu described the formation of the PRG as a 'propaganda trick'; the US State Department commented that the new government was 'the same old wine in a new bottle'.

11 June Prince Sihanouk announces the resumption of diplomatic relations with the US after a break of four years. A month later, career diplomat Emory Swank arrived in Phnom Penh as the new US ambassador to Cambodia. Despite the prince's fresh overture to the US and his increasingly strident expressions of concern at the use of Cambodian territory by Vietnamese revolutionary forces, he continued to maintain formal friendly relations with Hanoi and the NLF. So, only two days after re-establishing relations with the US, the prince recognized the NLF's newly-established PRG.

24 June The Pathet Lao launch a successful assault north of Vientiane. The Pathet Lao, with substantial NVA support, scored a major victory against Royal Government forces in late June, capturing the strategically vital town of Muong Soui, lying to the west of the Plain of Jars and some 75 miles (120 kilometres) north of Vientiane. Moung Soui's importance rested in its position (at the junction of Route 4 – the Luang Prabang-Vientiane road – and Route 7 – which led east to the North Vietnamese port of Vinh) and in its large airfield, which was used for bombing raids on the Plain of Jars. The offensive opened on 24 June and after four days, and despite intensive US bombing, the garrison was evacuated. The Royal Government forces launched a counteroffensive in early July, but were easily driven back.

25 July At the start of a round-the-world tour President Nixon enunciates what became known as the 'Nixon Doctrine' on future US foreign interventions. He outlined the doctrine during a stop-over in Guam at the start of the tour (which included six Asian countries) at an informal news conference. During the news conference Nixon explained that, in future, he expected US allies threatened by foreign or foreign-assisted aggression to play a much greater role in their own defence. Although the statement was obviously prompted by Nixon's desire to reduce the US military commitment in Vietnam, it also reflected the radical nature of the re-evaluation of US foreign policy that was being undertaken by Kissinger and other presidential advisers. By announcing his intention to pursue a more realistic and manageable set of foreign policy goals, Nixon was in effect repudiating the idealism of 'Truman Doctrine' containment and, as such, laid to rest the basic principles of US involvement in Indo-China.

12 August Lon Nol is again appointed to the Cambodian premiership. In August, with the Vietnamese presence in Cambodia spiralling and the internal economic situation heading towards a crisis point, Prince Sihanouk appointed General Lon Nol as prime minister. Lon Nol accepted the post only on condition that he would have the right to select his own ministers and that they would report to himself and not to Sihanouk. Lon Nol's appointment of a rightist-dominated cabinet (and in particular the placing of Sisowath Sirik Matak, the prince's cousin and rival and a powerful pro-US leader of the Phnom Penh business community, as deputy premier) was a serious blow to Sihanouk's personal authority and to his neutralist policies.

23 August General Tran Thien Khiem forms a new government in Saigon. President Thieu invited General Tran Thien Khiem, the deputy premier, to form a government following the resignation of Premier Tran Van Huong. According to some reports, Khiem's appointment had been encouraged by a military faction led by Vice-President Ky. General Khiem met with little success in his attempt to broaden the government's base, as all the country's prominent politicians refused to enter his cabinet. As a result, the new government was heavily dominated by the military and the civil service. (See Appendix 22 for list of South Vietnamese premiers during the post-Diem era.)

3 September Ho Chi Minh dies. Ho Chi Minh died of a heart attack, having lived just long enough to see the first US troops pulled out of Vietnam. At the funeral ceremony in Hanoi on 8 September, Le Duan read from Ho Chi Minh's political testament, composed by Ho some four months before his death. In his testament Ho appealed for unity within the Communist Party and called upon the leadership to 'work out a good plan for economic and cultural development'. He warned that the war against 'US aggression may drag out' but urged the people to fight on until total victory. In a reference to the Sino-Soviet split, he stated that he was 'deeply ... grieved at the dissensions that are dividing the fraternal parties'. Towards the end of the testament, Ho requested that his funeral should be a simple affair 'in order not to waste the time and money of the people'.

In late September, Ton Duc Thang was appointed to replace Ho as the Democratic Republic of Vietnam (DRV) president. No one was appointed to replace Ho as chairman of the Communist Party, but the principal figures in the leadership included Le Duan, Pham Van Dong, Truong Chinh and Vo Nguyen Giap.

15 October The nation-wide anti-war 'Vietnam Moratorium' takes place in the US. The 'Vietnam Moratorium' was the biggest anti-war demonstration to date. Demonstrations were held in over 1,200 towns and cities, with the strongest support in the northeastern and west coast states. Estimates of the number taking part in the demonstration varied from over 500,000 to several million. The demonstrations were largely peaceful, middle-class affairs and the speakers included Senators McGovern and Kennedy and Coretta King.

3 November Nixon delivers his 'silent majority' speech. The success of the 'Vietnam Moratorium' unsettled President Nixon and prompted him to deliver a major speech in early November in an attempt to rally public support for his 'Vietnamization' programme. Nixon carefully outlined his plan to bring about the 'complete withdrawal of all US ground combat forces and their replacement by South Vietnamese forces on an orderly scheduled timetable'. He would not announce details of the timetable, he claimed, because flexibility was of paramount importance. However, without public support, he could not be assured of the necessary flexibility and, he warned, a US defeat in Vietnam 'would result in a collapse of confidence in American leadership, not only in Asia but throughout the world'. 'And so tonight', he declared, 'to you, the great silent majority of my fellow Americans – I ask for your support. I pledged in my campaign for the Presidency to end the war in a way that we could win the peace. I have initiated a plan of action which will enable me to keep that pledge. The more support I have from the American people, the sooner that pledge can be redeemed; for the more divided we are at home, the less likely the enemy is to negotiate at Paris.' The response to the address was overwhelmingly favourable, although some commentators questioned whether the approving telephone calls, telegrams and letters were entirely impromptu.

12 November Details of army investigations into the My Lai massacre are revealed for the first time. The anti-war sentiment in the US, already intense as a result of November's mass demonstrations, was heightened significantly when reports were published in the press of a brutal massacre of South Vietnamese civilians by US troops in early 1968. The massacre had taken place on 16 March 1968, at a hamlet called My Lai in Quang Ngai province. A platoon commanded by Lieutenant William Calley had entered the hamlet, which, according to inaccurate intelligence reports, was the headquarters of a crack NLF battalion. The US forces had instructions to burn houses and crops, kill livestock and close wells. Although the platoon met with no resistance, they embarked on an orgy of sickening violence killing hundreds of My Lai's small civilian population, including women, babies, children and old men. Some of the troops refused to participate in the massacre, and one helicopter pilot, Chief Warrant Officer Hugh Thompson, was subsequently awarded the Distinguished Flying Cross for bravely rescuing a number of wounded civilians. Estimates of the number killed at My Lai vary widely, but a subsequent investigation by the US military police concluded that close to 350 people perished.

Although reports of the atrocity were circulated by the NLF soon after it took place, the US Army launched a full, but secret, investigation only in April 1969. Charges were preferred against Lieutenant Calley in early September, and two months later details of the massacre, and of the army's investigation into it, were revealed by the US media. It was not until late the following year that Calley and others were brought to trial; in the interim, disciplinary action was brought against a number of Calley's superiors for their failure to launch an effective investigation into the massacre.

13 November A 'March Against Death' begins in Washington. Less than two weeks after President Nixon's 'silent majority' speech, over a quarter-of-a-million people took to the streets of Washington in a fresh anti-war demonstration. The so-called 'March Against Death' had been organized by a coalition of religious and political groups led by Benjamin Spock, William Coffin and Coretta King, amongst others. Demonstrators, each carrying a placard bearing the name of US soldier killed in Vietnam, marched peacefully through central Washington for some 40 hours. Meanwhile, on 15 November another huge anti-war protest was held in San Francisco.

1 9 7 0

21 February Henry Kissinger and Le Duc Tho begin their 'secret talks' aimed at achieving a settlement to the Vietnam War. Henry Kissinger, President Nixon's national security adviser, and Le Duc Tho, a senior North Vietnamese politburo member, held the first of a series of highly important meetings in a Paris suburb in late February. The meeting was held in secret at a time when the formal four-party Paris peace negotiations were in a state of deadlock. The two met secretly on seven future occasions before President Nixon revealed details of the negotiations during a major policy address in January 1972. During their first meeting Tho, emboldened by mounting domestic opposition to the war in the US reiterated Hanoi's established negotiating line, calling for a complete, unilateral withdrawal of US forces and the dismantling of the Saigon government. Kissinger pressed for the mutual withdrawal of US and North Vietnamese forces from the Republic of Vietnam (RVN), although he conceded that the North Vietnamese Army (NVA) withdrawal could be carried out 'secretly'.

18 March The 'big guns of the Cambodian right', led by Lon Nol, overthrow Prince Sihanouk. The prince had left Cambodia in January 1970 to take his annual 'liver cure' in France, planning to return via the Soviet Union and China. However, in early March, whilst Sihanouk was still receiving his medication, anti-Viet Cong riots broke out in the southeastern border lands of Cambodia, a section of the country particularly susceptible to infiltration and bombing. Within a few days the unrest had spread to Phnom Penh, where demonstrators attacked the North Vietnamese and Provisional Revolutionary Government (PRG) embassies and rampaged through the city's Vietnamese quarter. Sihanouk finally left Paris on 13 March, but instead of returning immediately to Phnom Penh, he went to Moscow. In Phnom Penh, meanwhile, Premier Lon Nol had issued an ultimatum ordering all Viet Cong and North Vietnamese troops to withdraw from Cambodian territory. Eventually, on 18 March, Sihanouk was officially overthrown. Troops and tanks took up positions outside Phnom Penh's main points during the morning, and shortly after noon the airport was closed and all contact with the outside world cut off. The National Assembly was convened and a motion withdrawing the assembly's confidence in the prince was unanimously adopted. The following day, the assembly granted Lon Nol full emergency powers and a state of emergency was declared. The US government quickly issued a statement supporting the new regime.

23 March Prince Sihanouk announces that he has formed an anti-Lon Nol resistance with the Khmers Rouges. Sihanouk was told of his deposition by Soviet Premier Aleksei Kosygin on 18 March, a short time before he left Moscow for Beijing. Once in the Chinese capital the prince began drawing up a programme of co-ordinated resistance to Lon Nol. After consultations with Zhou Enlai, Pham Van Dong and (indirectly) Pol Pot he announced the formation of a National United Front of Kampuchea (FUNK) to liberate Cambodia from the 'dictatorship and oppression' of the Lon Nol 'clique'. Khmer Rouge leaders in their Beijing offices issued a statement declaring their support for Sihanouk's proclamation. On 24 March the prince issued a communique calling on his supporters inside Cambodia to take up arms against Lon Nol. In Phnom Penh, where the coup had been greeted with some relief by the middle classes, Sihanouk's invitation was ignored; however, in the countryside there was an almost spontaneous outburst of unrest with mass demonstrations in Kompong Cham, Siem Reap and Takeo. The unrest was brutally suppressed by the army, and hundreds of peasants were killed and thousands arrested.

29 April–1 May In the largest US military operation since 1968 US and South Vietnamese forces invade Cambodia; the US/South Vietnamese army (ARVN) force remains in the country until late June, but fails in its avowed aim to destroy the Vietnamese Communist 'nerve centre'. The deposition of Sihanouk finally shattered the illusion of Cambodian neutrality, and allowed the chill wind of the Vietnam War to roam west. The prince himself had adopted a warmer attitude towards Washington during his last year in power, but his stance was positively hesitant in comparison with the rigidly pro-US orientation of the new Lon Nol regime. Within two days of Sihanouk's official removal South Vietnamese troops, accompanied by US 'Green Beret' advisers, had entered southeastern Cambodia in force. These incursions continued and, in response, the Vietnamese Communist forces migrated deeper into southern and eastern Cambodia. Lon Nol's forces were powerless to prevent the Communist manoeuvres, and took their revenge in early April by massacring hundreds of ethnic Vietnamese civilians. By the time Lon Nol made an official appeal for US military aid on 20 April, the US military command had already started preparing for a full-scale incursion into Cambodia.

The offensive started on 29 April when a 12,000-strong South Vietnamese force entered the 'Parrot's Beak' (an area of Svay Rieng province which projected into South Vietnam). On 1 May, a joint US-South Vietnamese force of some 8,000 troops launched an offensive against the salient of Kompong Cham province, known as the 'Fish Hook'. The incursion was accompanied by a protracted sequence of heavy air strikes over North Vietnam, which, according to Washington, were carried out in 'protective reaction', as reconnaissance aircraft had been fired on. Initially the invading US and South Vietnamese forces met with some resistance, but after a few days the Vietnamese Communist forces simply avoided confrontation by repositioning themselves further westward into the Cambodian interior. The troops busied themselves by destroying vast amounts of enemy equipment before eventually withdrawing in late June.

As part of his 'Vietnamization' programme Nixon had announced in mid-April that a further 150,000 US troops were to be withdrawn from Vietnam during the next 12 months. In a speech to the nation on 1 May, the president used the planned withdrawal as justification for the Cambodian incursion, claiming that the existence of Communist sanctuaries in Cambodia constituted 'an unacceptable risk' to the US troops remaining in Vietnam after the partial pull-out. In his 1980 book *The Real War* Nixon maintained, with the full benefit of hindsight, that he had ordered the invasion principally in order to bolster 'Vietnamization'. The president had also apparently been convinced that the invasion would destroy the Vietnamese Communist 'nerve centre' (COSVN). In actual fact, the assaulting forces failed to locate COSVN which had fled the 'Fish Hook' area in mid-March, travelling west and north across the Mekong. The invasion did succeed in capturing vast quantities of North Vietnamese arms and supply bunkers and, according to some commentators, it set the Vietnamese Communist offensive timetable back by as much as 18 months.

The entry of US forces into Cambodia provoked strong opposition in the US Senate. The Senate Foreign Relations Committee demanded a meeting with President Nixon within hours of his 1 May speech, the first time such a meeting had been requested since 1919. In its report issued on 4 May, the committee accused the administration of usurping Congress's constitutional authority to make wars and treaties by ordering US troops into Cambodia without congressional consent or knowledge and of conducting 'a constitutionally unauthorized Presidential war in Indo-China'.

4 May National Guardsmen kill four students at Kent State University during protests at the Cambodian invasion. The US military intervention in Cambodia provoked massive, and often violent, protest demonstrations in US universities.

The most serious incident was that at Kent State University, in Ohio, where National Guard officers opened fire on students without warning, killing four and wounding nine others. The state governor, James Rhodes, had visited the campus on 3 May (the day before the shooting) and had declared that the demonstrations, under way since 1 May, were part of a 'national revolutionary conspiracy'. However, of the four students killed, none had been taking part in the demonstrations; the only one with any strong political views had been a staunch Republican. The anger aroused among students by the Kent State shootings converted the campus protests into a nation-wide movement, so that by 8 May some 400 universities were affected. The invasion and the shootings also prompted a massive demonstration in Washington on 9 May, during which as many as 100,000 people encircled the White House and other government buildings. According to some reports, troops were secretly brought into the White House basement in order to repel a possible invasion.

5 May Sihanouk and the Khmers Rouges form a Cambodian government-in-exile based in China. In early May Prince Sihanouk announced the formation of a Beijing-based Royal Government of National Union of Kampuchea (GRUNK). The government was headed by former Cambodian Prime Minister Penn Nouth and included three Khmer Rouge leaders; Khieu Samphan, Hou Yuon and Hu Nim. The members of the government were drawn from the FUNK politburo which had been established by Sihanouk soon after his deposition. GRUNK was quickly recognized by China, North Vietnam, the PRG and North Korea.

30 June The Cooper-Church amendment prohibiting US military operations in Cambodia is passed by the US Senate. The Senate adopted by 58 votes to 37 votes the amendment to a Foreign Military Sales Bill which prohibited US military personnel operating in Cambodia after 1 July, in either combat or advisory roles, unless specifically authorized by Congress. The amendment also prohibited air activity in direct support of Cambodian forces. The Senate's approval of the amendment, sponsored by Senators John Sherman Cooper (Republican) and Frank Church (Democrat), marked the first occasion during the Vietnam War that Congress had acted to restrict the president. The amendment became law in late December, its approval having been delayed by Congressional elections in November.

17 September All four delegations attend a session of the Paris peace talks, at which the PRG submits an eight-point peace plan. Nguyen Thi Binh, leader of the PRG delegation at the Paris talks, presented the new peace plan at the mid-September session, the first attended by all four delegations during 1970. The plan was a modified version of the PRG's 10-point proposal unveiled in May 1969, differing in the following respects: (i) a period of at least nine months was proposed for a US troop withdrawal (the earlier plan had established no time limit); (ii) after the US withdrawal a cease-fire would be enforced and discussion would start on the release of POWs (the 1969 plan had made no mention of a cease-fire and had stated that a discussion of POWs would only take place at an unspecified future date); (iii) unlike the 1969 plan, the PRG declared its willingness to include members of the Saigon administration (with the exception of Thieu, Ky and Khiem) in a proposed interim government. The proposals were quickly rejected by the US and South Vietnamese delegations, the latter denouncing them as 'old, oft-repeated, absurd demands' containing 'no initiatives at all'.

7 October President Nixon issues a five-point 'standstill cease-fire' plan which receives domestic approbation but is nevertheless rejected by the North Vietnamese and the PRG. In his broadcast to the nation, Nixon called for a 'cease-fire-in-place', whereby all armed forces in Indo-China would stop fighting and remain in their present positions. Once the cease-fire was in force, he envisaged the convening of an international conference to deal with the conflicts in all three states in Indo-China. The third part of Nixon's plan called for a negotiated timetable for the complete withdrawal of US forces from Indo-China. However, he stressed that any political settlement had to protect the right of the South Vietnamese people to 'determine for themselves the kind of government they want'. The final part of his plan called for the 'immediate and unconditional release' of all POWs.

Nixon's plan was greeted positively in Washington and went some way towards mollifying the intense domestic dissent which had followed the Cambodian invasion. The plan appealed to 'doves' in the capital's political circles, many of whom initially believed that Nixon had defaulted on the principle of 'mutual withdrawal'. However, the president had simply sidestepped the issue in his speech and he later confirmed that his offer of a total US withdrawal was wholly conditional on the retreat of Communist forces from the South. This has led some commentators to suggest that Nixon's plan was little more than a domestic political ploy ahead of congressional elections due in November.

Both the PRG and North Vietnam rejected the plan. Commenting on it on 8 October, Xuan Thuy, leader of the North Vietnamese delegation at the Paris talks, said: 'Mr Nixon's bottle of peace does not contain wine but gunpowder, toxic chemical products and words in Goebbels' style.'

9 October The Khmer Republic is proclaimed and the Cambodian monarchy officially abolished, effectively completing Lon Nol's deposition of Sihanouk. The proclamation marked the end of the 1,168-year-old Cambodian monarchy; however, in a statement from Beijing Prince Sihanouk denounced the move as 'illegal and anti-constitutional, bogus, anti-popular, anti-democratic and anti-national'. The constitutional law setting up the Khmer Republic also provided that Cheng Heng would remain as head of state until the election of a new president (Heng had taken the oath of office as head of state in the aftermath of Sihanouk's deposition in March).

20 November A US team carries out an unsuccessful raid on a North Vietnamese POW compound. A small US Army and Air Force team were attempting to free US prisoners from Son Tay POW camp, situated less than 30 miles (48 kilometres) west of Hanoi. The team had landed by helicopter in the area some time before the raid, but had eventually found the camp to be empty. The raid was preceded by heavy US bombing of northern provinces, during which as many as 50 civilians died. Initially the US denied that the bombing had taken place, and claimed that North Vietnam had caused the civilian injuries by firing on a diversionary US Navy force travelling along the coast. However, the State Department admitted in late November that 'appropriate ordinance' had accompanied the Son Tay raid.

1 9 7 1

8 February South Vietnamese troops invade Laos to sever the 'Ho Chi Minh Trail' but they are eventually beaten back by North Vietnamese Army (NVA) units. In late January US and South Vietnamese forces launched their largest operation since the intervention in Cambodia in May 1970. The campaign (known by the code-name 'Lam Son 719' after a seventeenth-century battle in which the Vietnamese had defeated the Chinese) was designed to cut the 'Ho Chi Minh Trail' (see Appendix 13) and occupy and destroy NVA base areas in southern Laos.

The offensive began on 30 January, with one US unit clearing and repairing Highway 9 (running south of the Demilitarized Zone (DMZ) to the Lao frontier) and another repairing the abandoned runway at Khe Sanh. Advance parties established a fire base at Lang Vei, less than $1\frac{1}{2}$ miles (2 kilometres) from the Lao border, and further to the south artillery crews reopened a line of fire-support bases overlooking the A Shau Valley. NVA and Provisional Revolutionary Government (PRG) forces (which had discovered details of the operation from press leaks) withdrew and offered little resistance. The second part of the operation began on 8 February, with South Vietnamese army (ARVN) units alone pushing along Highway 9 into Laos (the 1970 Cooper-Church amendment prevented US ground troops and advisers from accompanying them). At first the ARVN troops made good progress in their thrust towards the town of Tchepone (the hub of the entire trail network), but on 11 February the pace of the assault decelerated. It was subsequently revealed that the reason for this was that President Thieu had covertly ordered his division commanders to halt their westerly advance once the ARVN force had taken 3,000 casualties. The hesitation proved disastrous, allowing the NVA to take the initiative. The original goal of the mission (to destroy NVA supplies and installations in two vital base areas) was effectively abandoned, and the brief entry of ARVN troops into a ruined and deserted Tchepone on 8 March did little to conceal the debacle. The withdrawal was another disaster. Most of the ARVN infantry were evacuated by air, often amid scenes of panic and under extremely difficult conditions, as the NVA anti-aircraft guns concentrated in the area inflicted heavy losses on the US helicopters carrying out the evacuation. Horrible scenes were reported of desperate men dangling from the landing skids of dangerously overcrowded helicopters. Eventually, the final batch of ARVN troops were withdrawn from Laos on 25 March. The official US report on the offensive claimed that the cumulative ARVN/US casualties totalled over 9,000, less than 1,500 of which were American. The US media challenged this figure, with some reports speculating that ARVN casualties alone were almost 10,000 (a 50 per cent casualty rate). The US report alleged that almost 20,000 NVA were killed in the offensive, a substantial figure, but one that nonetheless might well tally with the heavy accompanying US B-52 and fighter-bomber strikes.

29 March Lieutenant William Calley is found guilty of the premeditated murder of South Vietnamese civilians at My Lai in 1968. Lieutenant William Calley, the commander of the platoon responsible for the 1968 My Lai massacre, was convicted by a court martial of the premeditated murder of at least 22 South Vietnamese civilians, and was sentenced to life imprisonment. The court martial had opened in Fort Benning, Georgia, in November 1971. The verdict was greeted with outrage in the US, with many arguing that Calley had been made a scapegoat either for his superior officers or for those directing the war. Congressional indignation at the verdict, particularly among southerners, had the effect of noticeably strengthening the anti-war feeling in the country. One striking example of the change of public opinion produced by the trial was afforded by a speech made in the House on 1 April by John Flynt, a right-wing Democrat who had previously supported the war, but who now announced that it was 'wrong to compound a six-year mistake and send young men halfway round the world to fight in a war we have not the fortitude to win or end'. The national outrage over the verdict led the army, in mid-August, to reduce Calley's sentence to 20 years, making him eligible for parole within seven years. The series of trials in connection with the massacre ended on only 17 December when Colonel Oran Henderson was acquitted by a court martial of charges of dereliction of duty and of failure to investigate war crimes. Captain Ernest Medina, commander of the company responsible for the massacre, had previously been acquitted in September of charges of murder and involuntary manslaughter.

7 April President Nixon announces further troop withdrawals from Vietnam. In a broadcast on 7 April, President Nixon announced that the rate of US troop withdrawals from Vietnam was to be increased, and that accordingly 100,000 more US troops would be pulled out between May and December 1971. The withdrawals announced by Nixon represented a rate of about 14,300 a month between May and November, compared with 12,500 over the previous year. In his broadcast, Nixon stressed that his goal was 'a total American withdrawal from Vietnam' and he expressed his confidence that this would be achieved through the programme of 'Vietnamization'.

14 April The final batch of US Marines withdraw from Vietnam. The US Marines, the first US combat troops to arrive in Vietnam in March 1965, formally ended their role as a fighting force in Indo-China when a small, rearguard unit withdrew from Danang. The withdrawal reduced the strength of US forces in the northern provinces to two divisions and two brigades.

24 April A massive anti-war demonstration is held in Washington. The 200,000-strong demonstration capped a fortnight of anti-war protest throughout the country. On the day before the demonstration, some 700 Vietnam veterans, many of them disabled, had publicly thrown away their medals in Washington in protest at the war.

25 May The Steele report on drug abuse by US servicemen in Vietnam is published. A report prepared for the US House of Representatives Foreign Affairs Committee by Representative Robert Steele revealed the seriousness of the problem of drug addiction among US troops in Vietnam. The report was published only a month after Senator Mike Mansfield had drawn the attention of the Senate to the increasing number of 'fraggings' in Vietnam, whereby officers were being murdered by their own men. The Steele report estimated that as many as 41,000 servicemen, or 15 per cent of the US forces in Vietnam, were using heroin. The problem was made increasingly difficult by the alleged involvement of high-ranking government officials in South Vietnam, Laos and Thailand in the trafficking.

13 June A watershed in the history of the Vietnam War is reached when the *New York Times* begins to publish extracts from the *Pentagon Papers* – a secret official study of the origins of the Vietnam War. The study, officially titled *History of US Decision-making Process on Vietnam Policy*, but popularly known as the 'Pentagon Papers', had been commissioned in June 1967 by Defence Secretary Robert McNamara. The final report, covering the period from 1945 to the opening of the Paris peace negotiations in 1968, consisted of 47 volumes and 2.5 million words. The report had been leaked to the *New York Times* by Daniel Ellsberg, one of the authors of the study.

The study contained a mass of official information which had not been published before and parts of it conflicted with information previously supplied. Amongst other things the study showed that from 1954 the US had conducted clandestine warfare in North Vietnam; that the coup which overthrew President Diem in 1963 was carried out with the support of the US government; that the Gulf of Tongkin incidents of 1964 were provoked by South Vietnamese attacks on the North; and that intelligence reports showed that the bombing of North Vietnam had little strategic effect and had caused almost 30,000 civilian casualties in 1965–6 alone.

The Justice Department attempted to prevent the publication of the study by securing injunctions against the *New York Times*, and subsequently against other US newspapers, on the grounds that its publication endangered national security. On 30 June the newspapers were vindicated when the Supreme Court ruled that governmental restraints on the press were incompatible with the First Amendment of the US Constitution. The publication of the *Pentagon Papers* occurred at a sensitive time for the Nixon administration which was engaged in delicate negotiations with China (on the reopening of relations) and the Soviet Union (on arms limitation) and did not want to be regarded as prone to leaks. The week after the publication Nixon approved the creation of a 'plumbers' group whose principal purpose, the president later explained, was to 'stop security leaks and to investigate other sensitive security matters'. One of the group's first actions was to break into Daniel Ellsberg's psychiatrist's office in the hope of finding some disparaging material. The group's most notorious break-in occurred a year later when they entered the Democratic national committee headquarters at the Watergate complex in Washington.

1 July The PRG delegate, Nguyen Thi Binh, presents a seven-point peace plan at the Paris peace talks. In return for the establishment of a 'terminal date' for a US troop withdrawal, modalities would be drawn up for a cease-fire and the release of all US POWs. Regarding the political settlement: once the US had ceased backing 'the bellicose group headed by Nguyen Van Thieu', the PRG would enter into negotiations with a new Saigon administration to form a 'broad three-segment government' to carry out elections. The new plan was an elaboration of a North Vietnamese proposal put forward by Le Duc Tho in late June during a secret meeting with Kissinger. Coming at a time when 'peace candidate' General Duong Van ('Big') Minh was preparing to challenge Thieu in the October presidential poll, both the public and private proposals were regarded by some commentators as an apparent invitation to Washington to relax its support for Thieu ahead of the elections.

2 August A Senate report is released on Central Intelligence Agency (CIA) financing of special forces and Thai 'volunteers' in Laos. The report released by Senator Stuart Symington detailed for the first time the full extent of CIA activities in Laos. The report stated that General Vang Pao's special forces (composed in the main of some 30,000 H'mong tribesmen) constituted 'the cutting edge' of the military. They were 'trained, equipped, supported, advised and to a great extent organized by the CIA', which took care of their pay, rations and medical care. Recently, the report continued, the CIA had turned to Thai 'volunteers' to supplement the irregular forces in Laos. The 'volunteers' were transported to and from Thailand by Air America (a CIA-controlled airline).

18 August The prime minister of New Zealand (NZ), Sir Keith Holyoake, announces that all forces will be withdrawn from Vietnam by the end of 1970. Some 3,430 NZ troops had served in Vietnam between 1965 and 1971; 35 had been killed and a further 187 injured.

3 October Nguyen Van Thieu, the sole candidate, is re-elected as president of South Vietnam without opposition. According to official figures almost 90 per cent of the electorate cast their votes, of whom over 94 per cent voted in favour of Thieu. Foreign observers were, however, highly sceptical of the figures. Voting was accompanied by serious student-led rioting in the major cities and by a National Liberation Front (NLF) rocket attack in central Saigon; total casualties on the day were given as 19 killed and 51 injured.

The campaign had been set to start in late July as a three-cornered contest, with Thieu, Vice-President Nguyen Cao Ky and General Duong Van ('Big') all having announced their intention to run. Ky was disqualified from running in early August on the grounds that he had not received the necessary signed endorsements from senators or councillors (Ky alleged that he had been unable to obtain the required signatures because his supporters had been 'threatened and terrorized'). General Minh withdrew his candidacy (despite US pressure not to do so) on 20 August describing the election as 'a contemptible farce which will . . . prevent a reconciliation among the Vietnamese people'. Thieu announced in early September that he would regard the election as a vote of confidence and would resign if he received less than half the votes cast.

20 October A state of emergency is declared in Cambodia. The deterioration of the security situation (exemplified by a devastating rebel assault on Phnom Penh's oil supplies in September) and increasing inflation led the urban population and the army to become increasingly disillusioned with the government during 1971. Lon Nol responded to the simmering unrest by assuming increasingly personal political powers. On 16 October, the country's National Assembly (which had last been elected in 1966) was deprived of its legislative powers and was transformed into a 'Constituent Assembly'. Four days later, Lon Nol declared a state of emergency and announced that the government would rule by decree. A number of constitutional guarantees were restricted, including those against arbitrary arrest and imprisonment. In a radio broadcast on 20 October Lon Nol asserted that 'a fifth column' was trying to create confusion and that the government had therefore decided not to 'vainly play the game of democracy and freedom' which, he claimed, would only lead to 'complete defeat'.

1 December Lon Nol's forces are routed in a rebel counteroffensive. Lon Nol's republican forces (FANK) suffered a massive defeat during an attempt to relieve Kompong Thom, a town situated 78 miles (125 kilometres) north of Phnom Penh, which had been encircled by rebel forces since mid-1970. The operation (code-named 'Chenla II' after the sixth-century Khmer Kingdom) had started in August and after two months FANK were claiming a famous victory, having negotiated their way up Highway 6 before successfully relieving Kompong Thom. However, the republican celebrations were premature; rebel counteroffensives in October and November effectively sliced Lon Nol's forces in two, restoring the position to what it had been before the offensive began and inflicting terrible casualties on the republican side. The defeat lowered morale within the army and caused political panic in Phnom Penh, with coup rumours sweeping the city.

18 December The Pathet Lao launch a massive offensive on the Plain of Jars. A 15,000-strong force comprising Pathet Lao, North Vietnamese and left-wing neutralists launched what was their biggest offensive of the war and completely overran the Plain of Jars within four days. The Pathet Lao triumph on the Plain of Jars occurred only a few weeks after a successful offensive on the Bolovens Plateau in the far south. The loss of the Plain of Jars was attributed in part to the poor showing of General Vang Pao's CIA-financed special forces; in addition, the Communist success was also attributed to the fact that, for the first time, the North Vietnamese had deployed 130-mm field guns in Laos.

The North Vietnamese and Pathet Lao had launched similar offensives on the Plain of Jars in February of 1970 and 1971, and on both occasions they had withdrawn from the occupied territory a few months later. However, following the December offensive the Royal Government forces failed to launch a successful counteroffensive in the summer of 1972.

26 December US bombers launch the first in a series of heavy 'protective reaction' raids on North Vietnam. In late December the US Air Force carried out their heaviest and most prolonged series of air raids on North Vietnam since 1968, with over 200 aircraft taking part in 1,000 strikes over a five-day period. The raids were directed primarily against targets in Quang Binh province, which adjoined the DMZ and was a final staging post for supplies sent down the 'Ho Chi Minh Trail'. US Defence Secretary Melvin Laird claimed at a press conference on 27 December that the raids were being carried out 'primarily for the protection of American service personnel'. The North Vietnamese government stated that several inhabited areas were hit during the raids, and that heavy losses in human life had been caused. For its part, the US command admitted the loss of three planes, whilst Hanoi radio claimed that 20 had been shot down.

1 9 7 2

2 January Elections are held in government-controlled areas of Laos. Elections to the 60-member National Assembly were held in early January in the provinces controlled by the Royal Government. Representatives for Pathet Lao-controlled provinces were elected by refugees. The results of the elections reflected a growing war-weariness and general discontent over the endemic corruption in Vientiane with several members of the powerful Champassak and Sananikone families losing their seats.

25 January President Nixon outlines a fresh eight-point peace plan; the plan, which provides for Thieu's resignation as president of South Vietnam, is greeted with apprehension in the South, but is nevertheless denounced by the North. In a major policy address delivered on radio and television President Nixon announced an eight-point peace plan which included a proposal for the holding of a fresh presidential election in South Vietnam, organized by an independent body representing all political forces in the country, and held under international supervision. The proposal provided for the resignation of President Thieu one month before the election. The plan also provided for (within six months of an agreement to end hostilities): a cease-fire throughout Indo-China; the withdrawal of all US and Allied forces from South Vietnam; and the exchange of POWs. Nixon had earlier outlined the plan in a secret letter to the North Vietnamese in October 1971, only a few days after President Thieu had been re-elected in South Vietnam.

Although Nixon stated that his plan had been prepared with President Thieu's full consent, it aroused some apprehension and opposition in the South. The president of the Senate, Nguyen Van Huyen, denounced it as contrary to the South's anti-Communist Constitution. The North Vietnamese also denounced the plan. A statement issued by the Hanoi delegation to the Paris talks on 26 January said that Nixon's speech had 'testified to his perfidious manoeuvre to deceive the American electorate in this election year'.

During his broadcast President Nixon had given details for the first time of Henry Kissinger's secret Paris negotiations with Le Duc Tho which had been under way since early 1970. Defending his decision to hold secret talks with the North Vietnamese, Nixon said that 'private discussions allow both sides to talk frankly, to take positions free from the pressures of public debate'.

1 March The withdrawal of Australian troops from Vietnam is completed. The withdrawal, announced in mid-1971, entered its final phase when a troop carrier left Vung Tau carrying the last 500 soldiers. A small number of instructors and advisers remained behind.

10 March Lon Nol assumes the Cambodian presidency. During March Lon Nol moved to eliminate all potential sources of internal opposition and bestow upon himself virtually absolute powers. The process had started in October 1971 when parliament was deprived of its legislative powers and transformed into a Constituent Assembly. The assembly proceeded to draw up a draft Constitution which, whilst providing for a presidential system, also included a powerful legislature. On 10 March (the day before the assembly was set to vote on the new Constitution) Lon Nol announced that he had replaced Cheng Heng as head of state and had dissolved the assembly. Three days later he assumed the titles of president of the Republic and president of the Council of Ministers. The next day he swore himself in as the country's first president and afterwards told journalists that in future there would be no legislature, as he himself would be 'responsible for all affairs'. He appointed the veteran Khmer Serei leader Son Ngoc Thanh as prime minister on 18 March.

30 March The North Vietnamese Army (NVA) launch the largest offensive of the war in South Vietnam when after a heavy bombardment they overrun all the South Vietnamese positions immediately south of the Demilitarized Zone (DMZ). The 'Easter offensive' was subsequently extended to the southern and central fronts. The North Vietnamese employed approximately 125,000 men in 14 divisions and 26 separate regiments, supported by tanks and artillery; the National Liberation Front (NLF) played only a minor part in the offensive.

Northern Front: The NVA converged on the northern provinces in a three-pronged pincer movement; directly south from North Vietnam across the DMZ, eastward from Laos and north up from Cambodia through the A Shau Valley. South Vietnamese Army (ARVN) units in the northern provinces were thrown into confusion and were quickly routed; by 2 April, in the northern half of Quang Tri province, only the towns of Dong Ha and Quang Tri itself remained in South Vietnamese hands. Over the next few days the ARVN managed to regain some semblance of order and by 9 April a new defensive line had been established along the river Cua Viet. However, the NVA offensive resumed on 23 April, and on 1 May North Vietnamese tanks broke through the defences on the northern side of Quang Tri town, the first South Vietnamese provincial capital to fall to the enemy. Reports by correspondents described ARVN troops fleeing in panic, many throwing away their weapons and uniforms and joining in the mass southerly migration of refugees.

Central Front: The campaign on the central front began soon after the NVA had launched their northern offensive. The NVA gradually encircled Kontum, in the central highlands, and on 24 April launched a major offensive against the town, which by the end of the month was under siege. Meanwhile, NVA troops, with support from NLF forces, had taken the offensive in the second half of April in Binh Dinh and Quang Ngai provinces, situated east of Kontum. By early May the whole of the northern part of Binh Dinh had fallen, arousing serious concern in Saigon that the North Vietnamese planned to cut the South in two by occupying the whole of the central provinces.

Southern Front: The southern offensive opened on 5 April in Binh Long province (situated along the Cambodian border) with NVA and NLF attacks on Loc Ninh and An Loc. Loc Ninh fell on 7 April and the next day a strong relief force, which included an infantry division 15,000 strong transferred from the Mekong delta and one of two parachute regiments which normally guarded President Thieu, was sent to reopen Highway 13 (the An Loc–Saigon road) which was completely encircled. Nevertheless, NVA tanks and infantry broke through An Loc's outer defences on 13 April. After bitter fighting the NVA were repulsed and they began a siege, maintaining a heavy bombardment for the next three weeks without succeeding in dislodging the ARVN defenders.

16 April Hanoi and Haiphong are attacked by US bombers for the first time since 1968. The launching of the North Vietnamese offensive on 30 March prompted the US to move all four Seventh Fleet aircraft carriers into the Gulf of Tongkin and mass raids on North Vietnam by fighter-bombers followed on 6 April. The raids were the first since the bombing halt of November 1968 which were not officially described by the US as 'protective reactive'. Four days later B-52s joined in the bombing, striking as far north as Vinh (B-52s had never previously penetrated so far north). Hanoi and Haiphong were bombed on 16 April for the first time since 1968. Municipal officials in Haiphong claimed that the attack killed almost 250 civilians and injured over 500 more. The bombing of the North continued up until 8 May, but Hanoi and Haiphong were spared during this period. Protest demonstrations erupted in US universities after the Hanoi and Haiphong raids. Although most of the demonstrations were peaceful, there were scattered outbreaks of violence, the most serious occurring at Maryland University where the state governor declared a state of emergency on 20 April.

30 April A new Cambodian Constitution which extends Lon Nol's power is approved by national referendum. A referendum held in republican-controlled areas overwhelmingly approved a new Constitution which legitimized President Lon Nol's extensive powers. According to Western press reports, voters in Phnom Penh were subjected to serious intimidation by armed military police stationed at polling booths. Student-led demonstrations against the new Constitution had broken out in Phnom Penh during the weeks leading up to the referendum. The new Constitution afforded Lon Nol far greater powers than had been envisaged in a draft Constitution drawn up by the recently-abolished Constituent Assembly in March.

8 May President Nixon announces his decision to mine all North Vietnamese ports. In a national broadcast on 8 May President Nixon announced that he had ordered the mining and blockade of all North Vietnamese harbours, including Haiphong, and the maximum bombing of North Vietnamese road and rail networks. He would order an end to the bombing and the blockade once all US POWs had been released and an internationally supervised cease-fire had been set in place throughout Indo-China. Once these two conditions had been met, he said, all US troops would be withdrawn from Vietnam within four months.

Nixon said that he had ordered the action to deny the North Vietnamese the weapons and supplies needed to continue its South Vietnamese offensive. The measures were enforced immediately: in addition to Haiphong, mines were laid outside two ports to the north (Hon Gai and Cam Pha) and four to the south (Thanh Hoa, Vinh, Quang Khe and Dong Hoi). US aircraft bombed Hanoi and Haiphong on 10 May, for the first time since 16 April, and began a sustained and systematic attack on northern communications, oil supplies and industrial targets.

The decision to mine the North Vietnamese harbours was a major gamble for Nixon, coming only two weeks before he was due to travel to the Soviet Union to sign a major strategic arms agreement. The Soviet Union had 16 vessels in Haiphong harbour alone when US aircraft began dropping mines on 9 May. However, much to Hanoi's irritation, Moscow reacted with great moderation to the mining and bombing, thereby allowing Nixon to portray his decision, in the US, as a major success. The Chinese government, still revelling in Nixon's historic visit to Beijing in February, also reacted to the decision with remarkable equanimity.

4 June Lon Nol is formally elected as Cambodia's president. Lon Nol, who had assumed the presidency in March, easily defeated two other candidates – In Tam (deputy premier in the Thanh cabinet) and Keo An (dean of the law faculty at Phnom Penh University).

3 September A new 126-member National Assembly is elected in Cambodia. The elections were contested principally only by the official Social Republican Party (SRP) led by Colonel Lon Non, President Lon Nol's brother. The SRP won all the 125 seats, all but 17 of its candidates being returned unopposed. In mid-October, Hang Thun Hak, the SRP secretary-general, was appointed as the new prime minister in place of Son Ngoc Thanh who had been forced to resign.

15 September South Vietnamese forces retake Quang Tri, lost to the NVA during their March offensive. The ARVN forces opened the offensive against Quang Tri in late June, and after a fierce struggle recaptured the town in mid-September. Quang Tri had been taken by the North Vietnamese during their massive 'Easter offensive' launched at the end of March. It had been the first southern provincial capital to fall and had provided a significant propaganda coup for the North Vietnamese. The ARVN offensive to retake the town had been supported by what the *New York Times* described as 'the largest concentration of fire-power ever used in a single area in the Vietnam war, nearly all of it American'.

The ARVN forces scored other successes in the aftermath of the 'Easter offensive': the siege of An Loc was virtually raised on 12 June; NVA assaults on Kontum in May and June were repulsed, again with the assistance of heavy US bombing; and towns in the coastal province of Binh Dinh occupied by the NLF were largely recovered by ARVN in July. North Vietnamese pressure nevertheless remained intense, notably south of Danang, in Quang Ngai province, around Pleiku and in the Mekong delta.

8 October Le Duc Tho submits a draft peace agreement at the Paris talks, but the US come under increasing pressure from Thieu not to sign any agreement. At the end of five days of private talks in Paris with Henry Kissinger, Le Duc Tho placed a draft peace agreement on the table which made a number of serious concessions to the US position. In particular, the draft abandoned the North Vietnamese demands for a simultaneous settlement of military and political issues and for the resignation of President Thieu and the immediate formation of a coalition government. The draft provided for a standstill cease-fire in the South; the ending of the bombing of the North and the mining of its waters; the withdrawal of US and allied troops within 60 days; no further entry of troops or war materials into the South; and the return of all POWs. The Saigon government and the Provisional Revolutionary Government (PRG) would both continue to function, and would hold consultations on the formation of a tripartite council of national reconciliation (composed of Saigon government, PRG and ambiguous 'neutral' representatives) to supervise general elections within three months.

The North Vietnamese had shown increasing signs of a willingness to moderate their demands following the resumption of the private Kissinger-Tho talks in early August. According to some commentators, Hanoi was anxious to conclude some sort of agreement before the US presidential elections in November (as a result of which, they correctly assumed, Nixon would easily defeat George McGovern and the Democrat's policy of 'immediate and complete withdrawal' from Vietnam).

The US reacted positively to the North Vietnamese draft and after further negotiations to iron out the details President Nixon and Premier Pham Van Dong exchanged messages on 22 October agreeing that the draft would be formally signed on 31 October. Meanwhile, the US set about attempting to persuade President Thieu, who had long been implacably opposed to any deal whatsoever, of the merits of the draft treaty. Towards this end Kissinger visited Saigon from 17 to 23 October, but to little effect. On 24 October President Thieu violently denounced the proposed agreement (the details of which had still not been publicly released) and accused Kissinger of failing to see through the Communists' 'cunning plots'. In a note delivered on the same day to friendly foreign missions in Saigon, Thieu insisted that he would approve only a treaty which included a recognition by Hanoi of: the seventeenth parallel as an international boundary; the illegality of North Vietnamese troops in the South; and a recognition of the South's constitutional structures.

Thieu's rejection of the treaty prompted Hanoi to increase pressure on the US by broadcasting details of the draft and of the accompanying negotiations on 26 October. Kissinger's immediate response (delivered at a Washington press conference) attempted to perform the impossible diplomatic feat of reassuring both Hanoi and Saigon; he told the former he was convinced that 'peace is at hand' and assured the latter that there remained 'six or seven' issues still to be resolved. However, US official spokesmen in Washington stated categorically on 29 October that the agreement would not be signed by 31 October.

17 October Peace talks open between the warring parties in Laos. Following months of correspondence between Prince Souvanna Phouma (prime minister in the Royal Government) and Prince Souphanouvong (the Pathet Lao leader), and despite the fundamental differences revealed in this correspondence, peace negotiations opened in Vientiane in mid-October. The Pathet Lao delegation was led by General Phoune Sipaseuth, the government delegation by Interior Minister Pheng Phongsavan. It was agreed at the start of the talks to adopt the Pathet Lao's 1970 five-point peace proposal as a basis for discussion. The 1970 plan had proposed: a 'standstill cease-fire' and a total and unconditional ending of US bombing to be followed by a conference of all Laotian parties and the formation of a provisional coalition government.

14 November Nixon writes an uncompromising letter to Thieu on the subject of the draft peace agreement. In his letter Nixon assured Thieu that the US would press for changes in the draft agreement 'with the utmost firmness' and that if Hanoi failed to abide by the terms of the agreement 'swift and retaliatory action' would be taken. However, Nixon also warned that he did not expect to secure all the changes Thieu wanted, and hinted that a refusal by Thieu to sign a final agreement would force the US to 'consider other alternatives' (i.e. a two-party Washington-Hanoi agreement).

20 November Kissinger and Le Duc Tho resume their negotiations. The fresh round of talks between Kissinger and Tho opened in Paris, but both sides hardened their positions as the dialogue progressed. Kissinger (apparently under pressure from Nixon) placed on the table a full list of 69 changes to the draft agreement demanded by Thieu; Tho retaliated by introducing fresh demands of his own. Eventually, on 16 December Kissinger announced that the negotiations had broken down. He claimed that the talks had so far failed to reach what Nixon regarded as 'a just and fair agreement' and asserted that their failure had been caused by obstructive tactics on the part of the North Vietnamese. For their part, the North Vietnamese claimed that the talks had been sabotaged by US attempts to force substantive changes in the draft agreement.

18 December The US resumes its bombing of North Vietnam. Following Kissinger's announcement on 16 December that the peace negotiations had reached deadlock, President Nixon ordered the resumption of bombing north of the twentieth parallel (the US had halted bombing north of the twentieth parallel on 23 October in view of the progress of the peace negotiations). The bombing which followed, the most intensive of the whole war, reduced large areas of Hanoi and Haiphong to ruins, and continued until 30 December. Nearly 730 B-52 and over 1,000 fighter-bomber missions were flown and over 20,000 tons of bombs dropped. The official North Vietnamese figure for civilian deaths for the period was 1,318 in Hanoi and 305 in Haiphong, but many civilians had been evacuated into the countryside. The North Vietnamese, meanwhile, shot down 26 US aircraft, and 93 crew members were lost, a third of them captured. The bombing was finally halted on 30 December, four days after the North Vietnamese had declared their willingness to resume talks.

1 9 7 3

27 January The peace agreement ending the war in Vietnam is signed in Paris. The 'Agreement on Ending the War and Restoring Peace in Vietnam' was finally signed formally by the foreign ministers of the US, North and South Vietnam and the South Vietnamese Provisional Revolutionary Government (PRG). on 27 January (see Appendix 23). The agreement was signed at the International Conference Centre in the Avenue Kleber in Paris, where peace negotiations had been taking place since 1968. The agreement had been initialled in Paris on 23 January by Kissinger and Le Duc Tho, the two negotiators who between them had hammered out the final agreement during private talks held between 8 and 13 January.

The agreement was composed of 23 articles and provided *inter alia* for (i) a 'standstill ceasefire' from January 28; (ii) the withdrawal of all US and Allied forces from South Vietnam and the release of all US POWs within 60 days; (iii) the formation of a four-party Joint Military Commission (JMC) to enforce these provisions; the establishment of an International Commission of Control and Supervision (ICCS) (to be composed of representatives from Canada, Hungary, Indonesia and Poland); (iv) the formation by agreement between the 'two South Vietnamese parties' of a National Council of National Reconciliation and Concord, composed of 'three equal segments', to organize general elections and ensure democratic liberties; (v) the convening of an international conference on Vietnam within 30 days of the signing of the agreement; (vi) a US contribution to 'healing the wounds of war and to post-war reconstruction' in North Vietnam and throughout Indo-China. The agreement was accompanied by four protocols covering the cease-fire, the ICCS, the return of prisoners and the destruction of mines in territorial waters.

In a broadcast on 23 January President Nixon said that the agreement brought 'peace with honour in Vietnam'. In an address the next day President Thieu, who had opposed the treaty until the last moment, claimed that the agreement represented a victory for South Vietnam, but gave warning that a 'tough and dangerous' political struggle was inevitable. According to Le Duc Tho speaking in Paris on the same day, the agreement crowned '13 years of valiant struggle which the Vietnamese people have conducted against American imperialism and a group of traitors'.

28 January A cease-fire nominally comes into effect in South Vietnam, but the fighting continues. The cease-fire was largely ignored, except by the US who ceased their air operations. Each side carried on the fight, while blaming the other for violating the agreement. By early February, when the JMC and the ICCS had taken up monitoring positions in the south, the scale of the fighting declined. However, as the month progressed the fighting flared again and on 26 February the South Vietnamese delegation to the JMC accused the North Vietnamese of violating the agreement by establishing surface-to-air missile sites at Khe Sanh after the cease-fire. (See Appendix 24 for total US casualty figures in Vietnam, 1961–73, and Appendix 25 for the progression of US casualties from 1965–70.)

1 February President Nixon sends a 'secret' letter to North Vietnam on reparations. Nixon's letter to Pham Van Dong, the North Vietnamese premier, was an elaboration of Article 21 of the Paris Agreements which alluded to US post-war reconstruction aid for Hanoi. The letter, which was not revealed publicly until 1977, suggested that a Joint Economic Commission be established to ascertain Hanoi's aid requirements and established a 'preliminary' figure of $3,250 million in grant aid over five years.

10 February Kissinger arrives in Hanoi where he announces details of a planned Joint Economic Commission. Henry Kissinger paid a four-day visit to Hanoi for talks with North Vietnamese leaders including his old adversary Le Duc Tho. A communique issued at the end of the visit announced the establishment of a Joint Economic Commission to develop economic relations between the two countries, as intimated in President Nixon's secret letter to Pham Van Dong on 1 February. Talks on future economic relations between the two countries opened in Paris in mid-March, but were suspended by the US a month later in protest at alleged North Vietnamese violations of the January agreement.

12 February The first US POWs are released from Hanoi. A group of 116 servicemen flew from Hanoi to Clark Field Air Base in the Philippines. On the same day, the exchange of National Liberation Front (NLF), North Vietnamese and South Vietnamese military prisoners began. Before the exchanges began, the North Vietnamese had supplied the US with the names of 594 prisoners (562 US servicemen, 24 civilians and eight foreign civilians) and of 55 prisoners who had died in captivity. The Saigon regime was reported to hold about 26,000

POWs and the NLF about 4,000 South Vietnamese prisoners (although the Southern authorities alleged that the NLF actually held over 30,000 people). During March, disputes arose over the releases and exchanges, which in turn slowed down the US troop withdrawal process. Eventually, on 29 March the last batch of 67 US POWs were flown out of Hanoi. The exchange of civilian prisoners in South Vietnam was suspended in late July, after only three months of intermittent operation.

21 February A cease-fire agreement is signed in Laos and the US halts its bombing of the country. Less than a month after the signing of a cease-fire agreement for Vietnam in Paris, representatives of the Pathet Lao and the Royal Government met in Vientiane and signed an Agreement on the Restoration of Peace and Reconciliation in Laos. Peace negotiations had started in October 1972, but made little progress as the Royal Government refused to accept demands by the Pathet Lao that a cease-fire be accompanied by a political settlement. Fighting continued on all fronts, as both sides attempted to secure an advantageous position in the event of an agreement. After the signing of the Vietnamese settlement in January 1973, the US pressed the rightist faction within the Royal Government to conclude quickly a Lao agreement; at the same time, US bombing of Pathet Lao territory was intensified.

The military provisions of the agreement provided for: a 'standstill cease-fire' from 22 February (a condition which effectively left two-thirds of the country under Pathet Lao control); the complete and permanent cessation of all bombing and other military activities by foreign forces; the withdrawal of all foreign forces operating in Laos within 60 days from the establishment of a provisional government and the release of all POWs within the same time-frame. The provisions on political affairs called for: the establishment, within 30 days from the signing of the agreement, of a Provisional National Union Government (PGNU) composed of equal numbers of representatives of the Vientiane government (the Royal Government) and the Patriotic Forces (the Pathet Lao); the establishment of a similarly composed National Political Consultative Council (NPCC) to organize general elections; the 'neutralization' of Vientiane and Luang Prabang.

When the cease-fire came into force on 22 February the US ceased bombing operations over Laos. Sporadic fighting on the ground continued until early March, by which time reports suggested that the cease-fire was becoming increasingly effective.

26 February An international conference on Vietnam opens in Paris. As provided for under Article 19 of the January agreement, an international conference was held in Paris between 26 February and 2 March to acknowledge and approve the agreement. The conference was attended by the foreign ministers of North and South Vietnam, the PRG, the US, Britain, France, the Soviet Union, China, Canada, Hungary, Indonesia and Poland and also by the UN secretary-general, Kurt Waldheim.

17 March The presidential palace is bombed in Phnom Penh. Captain So Pothra, an air-force officer and a son-in-law of Prince Sihanouk, attempted to assassinate President Lon Nol by dropping two bombs on the presidential palace. Lon Nol was unhurt in the attack, but 47 others were killed. The attack prompted Lon

Nol to proclaim a state of emergency and arrest and detain a large number of people including members of the royal family, opposition politicians, military commanders, journalists and 55 of the country's leading astrologers, who were accused of predicting the president's downfall.

19 March Talks begin between the South Vietnamese government and the PRG. Delegations from the South Vietnamese government and the PRG (led by Nguyen Luu Vien and Nguyen Van Hieu respectively) met for their first round of political negotiations at the Chateau de la Celle-Saint-Cloud in Paris. The January agreement had provided for such talks in order that an agreement might be reached on the establishment of a National Council to arrange elections. The talks commenced in an atmosphere of acrimony that was to characterize all future rounds. From the outset, the South Vietnamese side insisted that elections would not be held until all North Vietnamese Army (NVA) personnel had returned to North Vietnam. For their part, the PRG delegation accused the South of systematic cease-fire violations.

29 March The final group of US servicemen in Vietnam leave Saigon. The 23,700 US servicemen in South Vietnam at the time of the January cease-fire were withdrawn in stages over the following 60 days. (See Appendix 26 for escalation and reduction of US troop strength in Vietnam from 1960 to 1972.) The final group of 2,501 servicemen left Saigon on 29 March. The 37,000 South Korean troops in South Vietnam, as well as the small Thai, Filipino and Chinese Kuomintang contingents, were also withdrawn during the 60 days following the cease-fire.

3 April A joint Nixon-Thieu communique charges North Vietnam with cease-fire violations. President Thieu embarked on a 15-day world tour in late March, stopping first in San Clemente, California for talks with President Nixon. The two leaders issued a joint communique on 3 April which charged North Vietnam with violating the January agreement by infiltrating men and weapons into the South and warned that continued violation would prompt 'appropriate vigorous reactions'. They also expressed grave concern that Article 20 of the agreement, calling for the withdrawal of all foreign forces from Laos and Cambodia, had not been carried out.

11 May A new 'broad-based' cabinet is formed in Cambodia in an attempt to persuade the Khmers Rouges to enter into negotiations. In the aftermath of the Paris Agreements, the US increased its pressure on the republican government to broaden its base in order to create a favourable atmosphere for negotiation with the rebel forces. However, the situation in Phnom Penh was completely chaotic and any attempt to shore up the government seemed doomed from the outset. The Khmers Rouges maintained a tourniquet on Phnom Penh, subjecting the city to an almost constant blockade and frequent bombardment. The economy was in a state of collapse, and strikes and food riots were common occurrences. Nevertheless, Lon Nol made a number of halfhearted attempts to heed the US advice: in mid-April he dismissed the Hak government, suspended the National Assembly and appointed in its place a Supreme State Council, whose members included the so-called 'opposition' figures of Sirik Matak, In Tam and Cheng Heng, all of whom had, at one time, been extremely close to Lon Nol. Eventually on 11 May In Tam was again appointed to the post of prime minister at the head of a cabinet dominated by supporters of Lon Nol.

13 June A joint communique signed by Kissinger and Le Duc Tho on the enforcement of a Vietnamese cease-fire leads to a sharp decline in the fighting. During May and June Henry Kissinger and Le Duc Tho held three rounds of talks in Paris on ways to achieve a strict implementation of the January cease-fire agreements. At the end of their third round of talks on 13 June, Kissinger and Tho initialled a joint communique containing provisions for the implementation of the January cease-fire (the document was later signed by PRG and Saigon representatives). Amongst other things the communique stipulated that a strict standstill cease-fire would be observed from 15 June and that the commanders of opposing forces in direct contact would meet to agree on measures to avert conflict. After the signing, Kissinger told a press conference that 'much of his discussion' with Tho had been concerned with 'the whole complex of issues raised by Laos and Cambodia'. Although minor violations of the cease-fire continued after the 15 June deadline set by Kissinger and Tho, there was a sharp drop in the level of fighting.

Serious breaches of the cease-fire had occurred since the signing of the January agreement, but in April particularly heavy fighting was reported. A North Vietnamese note of 16 April accused the Saigon regime of launching with US backing, 'hundreds of thousands' of operations to encroach on PRG-controlled areas. A US reply four days later rejected Hanoi's accusations and contended that it was the North Vietnamese themselves that had obstructed peace. The US claimed that over 30,000 NVA had continued moving through Laos and Cambodia into South Vietnam after the cease-fire. The constant cease-fire breaches provoked the Canadian government into withdrawing from the ICCS in late May.

15 August The US bombing of Cambodia ends. The bombing ended after Congress had earlier blocked the use of funds for the continued air war. The halt meant that all official US military operations in Indo-China had ceased. Commenting on the cessation President Nixon stated that the congressional action had undermined 'the prospects of world peace by raising doubts in the minds of both friends and adversaries concerning the resolve and capacity of the US to stand by international agreements'.

The bombing of Cambodia had developed into a major issue during 1973. The US had embarked on a massive bombing campaign over Cambodia in February, after the National United Front of Kampuchea (FUNK) had shunned an offer to enter into peace talks in the aftermath of the Paris Agreements. By August over 250,000 tons of bombs had been dropped over almost all regions of the country; the bombardment was probably successful in preventing the Khmer Rouge forces from launching an immediate, and almost certainly successful, assault on Phnom Penh. In mid-June the Senate had voted overwhelmingly to halt funds for the bombing of Indo-China, but the amendment was vetoed in late June by President Nixon who contended that the ending of the bombing of Cambodia would be 'a serious blow to America's international credibility'. A compromise was eventually worked out (and signed by Nixon on 1 July) in which the administration agreed to end the bombing in August. Anxiety in the US over the bombing had increased after a B-52 miscalculated on 6 August, dropping its entire load on the key republican stronghold of Neak Luong, killing over 130 people, mainly civilians.

The administration's embarrassment over Neak Luong was nothing compared to that which accompanied the mid-July revelations of a former air-force officer, Hal Knight. Knight, testifying before a Senate Armed Services Inquiry, revealed that US bombing attacks on Cambodia had been in progress since March 1969. For the first 14 months B-52s had carried out over 3,600 secret raids against suspected Communist sanctuaries at a time when the US government claimed to be respecting Cambodian neutrality. Official records were falsified to conceal details of the so-called 'Menu' missions from Congress. The bombings continued after the May 1970 US/South Vietnamese army (ARVN) invasion of Cambodia, and were mostly concentrated in the eastern provinces.

14 September Agreement is reached on the formation of a joint provisional government in Laos. After negotiations lasting over six months, an agreement was signed between the Royal Government and the Pathet Lao on the formation of a provisional government. The agreement provided for equal representation in: the provisional government (to be headed by a 'neutral' prime minister); the National Political Consultative Council; joint police forces to administer the 'neutralized' cities of Vientiane and Luang Prabang (each party would also be entitled to station a battalion of troops in each city); and in a Mixed Central Commission to implement the agreement.

According to the timetable laid down in the February 1973 agreements, a provisional government should have been formed before 23 March. However, negotiations started slowly and were hampered by sporadic cease-fire violations. A draft agreement was apparently agreed in principle in late July, but rightists within the government (led by Ngon Sananikone) continued to press for further concessions. The atmosphere became increasingly tense after right-wing political exiles launched an abortive military coup on 20 August and by early September negotiations were seriously deadlocked. In this situation Soviet and US diplomats in Vientiane started to apply strong pressure to secure the signing of an agreement. The agreement was formally signed in Vientiane on 14 September by Sananikone and Pheng Phongsavan for the government and Phoumi Vongvichit and General Phoune Sipaseuth for the Pathet Lao.

15 October The PRG military command issues a counterattack order. The biggest battle to date, since the cease-fire, took place in late September in Tay Ninh province when ARVN troops launched an assault on a PRG enclave. On 3 October the air force started bombing raids against NLF positions in Tay Ninh, an action which served to escalate the fighting. In a command order on 15 October the People's Liberation Armed Forces (PLAF, the PRG's regular army) authorized its main units to 'fight back at the Saigon administration [at] any place and with appropriate forms and force'. On 6 November the PLAF launch a heavy artillery bombardment against Bien Hoa air base and a month later largely destroyed the Nha Be oil storage tanks.

17 October Kissinger and Le Duc Tho are awarded the Nobel Peace Prize, but Tho refuses to accept the award. The Nobel Peace Prize had been awarded to Henry Kissinger (who had been appointed as US secretary of state in early September) and Le Duc Tho for their efforts in negotiating the Paris Agreement.

The choice of Kissinger and Tho met with widespread international criticism, chiefly on the grounds that the war in Indo-China was still raging some nine months after the signing of the agreement. In an unprecedented gesture, two of the five members of the Norwegian Nobel Prize Committee resigned in protest at the decisions. Le Duc Tho refused the prize on the grounds of Saigon and US government 'violation' of the agreement.

26 December A new Cambodian prime minister is appointed. In Tam, who had been appointed as prime minister in May, resigned from the cabinet and from the Supreme State Council on 7 December, giving as his reason lack of co-operation from some of his ministers. Lon Nol appointed the foreign minister, Long Boret, as In Tam's replacement.

1 9 7 4

4 January President Thieu declares that the war in Vietnam has restarted. In his most strongly-worded speech since the cease-fire, President Thieu declared that 'as far as the armed forces are concerned the war has begun again'. He implored his troops not to allow 'the Communists a situation in which their security is guaranteed in their zone so that they can launch harassing attacks against us'. Instead, he urged his troops to attack the areas controlled by the Provisional Revolutionary Government (PRG).

19 January A naval battle erupts between South Vietnam and China over the Paracel and Spratly Islands. A dispute between the Saigon government and China over the ownership of the Paracel and Spratly Islands (two disputed archipelagos in the South China Sea), led to a naval battle off the Paracels in mid-January, in which the South Vietnamese lost a gunboat and claimed to have sunk two Chinese warships, and resulted in the occupation of the Paracels by China. The clash was precipitated by a South Vietnamese announcement in September 1973 that it would be surveying for oil off the central Vietnamese coast, opposite the Paracels. Both the US and the Soviet Union adopted a strictly neutral attitude towards the dispute. A North Vietnamese statement on the clash commented that 'disputes handed down by history, often very complex ones' should be settled through negotiations.

19 January The South Vietnamese Constitution is amended to increase President Thieu's powers. The Saigon House and Senate approved two constitutional amendments which appeared to strengthen President Thieu's hand. The first extended the president's term from four to five years and enabled a president to serve for a maximum of three instead of two terms. The second amendment empowered the president to appoint provincial chiefs. A group of 55 opposition members denounced the amendments as 'anti-constitutional and anti-democratic' and announced that the new measures had roused them into forming a new alliance.

8 March The exchange of Vietnamese POWs under the 1973 Paris Agreement is finally completed. The exchange had been suspended in July 1973 and only resumed in February 1974, with National Liberation Front (NLF) prisoners being flown from Bien Hoa to Loc Ninh and Republic of Vietnam (RVN) prisoners from Pleiku province to Bien Hoa. An official statement released after the final exchange stated that the Saigon regime had released 26,880 military and 5,081 civilian prisoners since the cease-fire, and the PRG 5,336 military and 606 civilians. No agreement was reached on the exchange of prisoners taken since the cease-fire, nor on the fate of non-Communist political prisoners held in the South.

22 March The PRG put forward a new six-point peace proposal at the Paris talks in La Celle-Saint-Cloud. The plan proposed: a fresh cease-fire; the release of all POWs and political prisoners by 30 June; guarantees for 'democratic liberties'; the establishment of a National Council of National Reconciliation and Concord by 30 September; elections to a Constituent Assembly by 30 September 1975; the eventual merging of the armed forces. The plan was rejected by the Saigon government as 'extremely vague'. However, US officials described it as the most concrete put forward by the PRG since the 1973 cease-fire.

5 April A provisional coalition government is formed in Laos. A Provisional Government of National Union (PGNU) and a Joint National Political Council (JNPC) were finally formed, over a year after the final date laid down in the 1973 cease-fire agreement. A separate agreement on the composition of the PGNU and the JNPC had been signed in September 1973, but a right-wing attempt to secure its rejection was only narrowly defeated in early November. However, rightist influence was weakened in early 1974 by the emergence of a strong, provincial-based student movement. In February, agreement was reached on the joint administration and policing of the two 'neutral' cities of Vientiane and Luang Prabang. Prince Souphanouvong, the Pathet Lao leader, returned to a hero's welcome in Vientiane on 3 April, and two days later the 13-member provisional government (the country's third coalition) took office. Prince Souvanna Phouma remained as the 'neutral' prime minister; the five Pathet Lao representatives included Phoumi Vongvichit (deputy premier and foreign minister) and General Singkapo; the five former Royal Government members included representatives of the three great princely families (Insisiengmay, Champassak and Sananikone); two neutrals had also been appointed, chosen by agreement between the two sides. Souphanouvong had refused to enter the cabinet and instead he became president of the Luang Prabang-based policy-making JNPC.

12 April The Vietnamese peace negotiation and cease-fire machinery starts to break down. The Saigon government delegation to the La Celle-Saint-Cloud talks walked out in mid-April in protest at the Communist capture of Tong Le Chan that day, which, it was claimed, had destroyed the 1973 Paris Agreement (Tong Le Chan, a ranger base near the Cambodian border, had been under siege since February). Four days after walking out of the talks, the Saigon delegation withdrew the privileges and immunities previously granted to the PRG delegation to the Joint Military Commission (JMC); the delegation's telephone lines were cut, and its weekly press conferences and the weekly liaison flight between Saigon and Loc Ninh were cancelled. By the end of May the PRG had stopped attending meetings of the JMC and, together with the North Vietnamese delegation, had pulled out of the four-party Joint Military Team (JMT) which had been set up to search for missing military personnel. The PRG formally withdrew from the JMC on 23 June, a move which prompted the International Commission of Control and Supervision (ICCS) to suspend its activities.

17 May The battle of Ben Cat begins in the Saigon sector. From May 1974 onwards the North Vietnamese and the NLF forces in South Vietnam adopted an increasingly offensive strategy. The campaign was not a general, all-out offensive like that of spring 1972, but was rather aimed at taking a limited number of key areas. Between May and August a number of district capitals were captured in central-northern areas, but a major offensive southwest of Danang was repulsed, with both sides taking heavy casualties. One of the hardest-fought battles of the 1974 offensive opened on 17 May, when Communist forces overran South Vietnamese army (ARVN) outposts near Ben Cat (some 30 miles (50 kilometres) north of Saigon). The ARVN launched a counteroffensive and recaptured one of the outposts; attempts to retake the other two were repulsed, with the ARVN Eighteenth Division suffering heavy casualties. In mid-August, North Vietnamese Army (NVA) tanks moved south from Ben Cat, reaching the Saigon river, only 16 miles (25 kilometres) from the capital. This was the closest point to Saigon which NVA tanks had reached at any stage of the war.

24 May A new 18-point political programme is adopted in Laos. The JNPC, which had been formed in April under Prince Souphanouvong's presidency, unanimously adopted an 'Eighteen-point Programme for the Current Construction of the Fatherland' during its first session in Luang Prabang. The programme, which was eventually promulgated in late 1974, laid down a set of moderate political principles, including continuation of the monarchy, the encouragement of private enterprise and a neutral foreign policy.

1 June Thai and US military personnel withdraw from Laos. In accordance with the 1973 peace agreement, which provided for the withdrawal of all foreign military forces within 60 days after the formation of a provisional government, some 9,000 Thai 'volunteers' were flown out of Laos on 1 June. Over the next few days all US military advisers were also withdrawn. Large numbers of North Vietnamese troops remained in Laos, but they reportedly withdrew to duties concerned solely with the maintenance of the 'Ho Chi Minh Trail'.

18 June A Catholic-led anti-corruption movement is formed in South Vietnam. A conference of Catholic priests, led by Father Tran Huu Thanh, announced the formation in mid-June of the People's Anti-Corruption Movement (PACM). A declaration was adopted which declared that corruption, often carried out by 'government mafias', was 'making all the nation's constructive efforts useless'. The formation of the PACM was considered to be of great significance in that it originated among conservative Catholics, the very section of society which had formed the main basis of support for the Thieu regime. The PACM campaign intensified in early September when Father Thanh, attending a Catholic demonstration in Hue, openly charged President Thieu and his family with corruption. Father Thanh also accused Prime Minister Tran Thien Khiem of involvement in the heroin trade. A number of newspapers printed the full text of Father Thanh's so-called 'Public Indictment No. 1', and despite Thieu's denial of the charges, Catholic demonstrations increased in number and size throughout

October; a march in Saigon on 31 October ended in a two-hour battle between protesters and the police.

9 July Lon Nol proposes unconditional peace talks with the Khmers Rouges. After two weeks of talks between the republican government and the US ambassador, John Gunther Dean, President Lon Nol offered to open peace negotiations without preconditions. Earlier, the US defence secretary, James Schlesinger, had announced from Washington that the US would accept a Laotian-style coalition government (including the Khmers Rouges) in Cambodia. In his broadcast the president appealed to 'the Khmers on the other side' to enter a dialogue which, he claimed, might 'lead to a ceasefire, the withdrawal of all foreign forces from the Khmer national territory, unity and national reconciliation'. Within hours of Lon Nol's offer, Sihanouk had issued a rejection from Beijing. The prince stated that his government would 'always categorically refuse an American peace which imposes partition of our country or a coalition government with the traitors ... Peace can be realised immediately; if the US ceases to interfere in Cambodia's affairs and ceases to give military aid to the Lon Nol clique this will suffice for the Cambodian problem to be solved ipso facto'.

6 August US military aid to South Vietnam is reduced. President Nixon's 1974–5 budget proposal, presented to Congress in February 1974, had provided for $1,400 million of military assistance to the Saigon regime (an increase of $200 million over 1973–4). This sum was reduced in committee to $1,000 million and on 6 August the House approved a further reduction to $700 million (the House's action was endorsed by the Senate in late August). In proposing the reduction, the Georgian Democrat John Flynt said that it would serve as a warning to President Thieu to negotiate a political settlement.

9 August President Nixon resigns. Richard Nixon became the first president in US history to resign the presidency. His resignation followed a series of dramatic developments stemming from the Watergate affair, including the adoption by the House judiciary committee of three articles of impeachment against the president in late July. Immediately following Nixon's resignation, Vice-President Gerald Ford was sworn in as the country's new president.

18 December A meeting of the North Vietnamese politburo opens to approve a strategic plan to defeat Thieu. The North Vietnamese politburo convened in Hanoi in mid-December to formulate a two-year strategic plan to defeat the Thieu regime. The politburo had been encouraged, if not forced, to establish a precise timetable for total victory by the decay and confusion which had permeated the military in the South. Nevertheless, the plan was a conservative one and reflected the circumspection of the northern tacticians. Final victory would only be achieved after two hard years; success in 1975 was considered so unlikely that no political or economic plans for the liberated areas were drawn up.

1 9 7 5

1 January Khmer Rouge troops launch their final offensive on Phnom Penh. The elaborately-planned offensive which allowed them to quickly seize control of almost the entire length of the Mekong (from the South Vietnamese border to a point some 16 miles (25 kilometres) southeast of Phnom Penh), thereby halting supplies entering the capital. At the same time they launched a succession of attacks on the capital's outskirts, effectively impounding republican forces within the city. Over the next three months the Khmers Rouges made steady advances. The republican forces, meanwhile, experienced increasing difficulties not only along the Mekong but also by air, as the Khmers Rouges had positioned themselves so as to be able to train their 105-mm guns on Pochentong airport.

6 January The North Vietnamese Army (NVA) capture Phuoc Binh town, a victory which marks a turning point in the war. NVA forces, supported by National Liberation Front (NLF) troops, took the offensive in Phuoc Long province (situated north of Saigon near the Cambodian border) in mid-December 1974 and by the end of the month the whole province had fallen except its capital, Phuoc Binh. On 1 January the NVA opened its assault on Phuoc Binh with a massive artillery barrage and five days later the town fell. Although Phuoc Binh was not of particular strategic importance, its fall marked a turning point in the war. In Hanoi, the capture of a provincial capital (the first since Quang Tri in 1972) lent weight to the arguments being put forward by southerners, such as Tran Van Tra – who had organized the assault on Phuoc Binh – and Le Duc Tho, that total victory was achievable during 1975.

11 March The NVA capture Ban Me Thuot and begin their final offensive. With total victory in 1975 as the ultimate strategy, Hanoi deployed General Van Tien Dung and five main force divisions in the central highlands to activate the plan. The offensive began on 4 March, with a 'feint' attack on Pleiku by the NVA's 968th Division. The South Vietnamese army (ARVN) responded by redeploying elements of its 23rd Division (defending Ban Me Thuot, the capital of Dalac province) to Pleiku. On 10 March General Dung ordered the NVA 316th Division to attack Ban Me Thuot, and the next day the town fell. The ARVN 23rd Division, which had been ordered to return to Ban Me Thuot, found itself cut off on the road, whereupon the troops abandoned all their equipment and scattered into the hills. President Thieu responded to the debacle by reversing his long-held policy of not relinquishing territory to the Communists without a fight, ordering his troops to abandon Pleiku, Kontum and Quang Tri to shore up the defences around Saigon. The NVA moved into the abandoned towns and launched an attack against the northern provinces along the eastern seaboard, which effectively reduced Saigon's hold in the north to small enclaves around Hue and Danang and started a southerly trail of up to 2 million refugees. Quang Ngai and Hue both fell without a fight on 24 and 26 March, respectively. The encirclement of Danang was completed on 28 March, but ARVN troops made little attempt to defend the city. The desperation of the South Vietnamese forces to escape from the city generated some of the most harrowing scenes of the whole war. In their panic to board ships and aircraft, the troops fought one another with small arms and grenades and trampled on and shot down civilians, including women and children.

By the end of March the North Vietnamese controlled 13 provinces (compared with one at the start of the month). Nearly half of the South's army had been killed, captured, forced to retreat or had deserted and most of the major equipment items for three full divisions, including at least 200 tanks, had been lost.

1 April Lon Nol flees Phnom Penh. With the Khmer Rouge forces breaking through the republican lines on the outskirts of Phnom Penh, President Lon Nol fled, accompanied by his family and close associates. Lon Nol's name headed a list of 'seven traitors' sentenced to death by the Khmers Rouges in February. After a short stay in Indonesia, Lon Nol proceeded to Honolulu where he bought a house and settled. In accordance with the republican Constitution, the president of the Senate, Major-General Saukham Khoy, assumed the position of interim president. However, on 12 April Khoy was also helicoptered out of Phnom Penh along with John Gunther Dean, the US ambassador, and the entire US diplomatic staff.

6 April General elections take place in North Vietnam and Pham Van Dong is elected for a further term as premier. As North Vietnamese forces battled their way to Saigon in early April, the people of North Vietnam elected a new 425-member National Assembly, the fifth since 1946. The assembly convened in early June, re-electing Ton Duc Thang and Nguyen Luong Bang as president and vice-president of the Republic respectively; at the same time a new, largely unchanged Council of Ministers was approved with Pham Van Dong, premier since 1955, again at its head.

9 April As the NVA close in on Saigon the ARVN forces make their final stand at Xuan Loc. After the fall of Danang in late March, several important towns in the central provinces were abandoned without a fight, including the ports of Qui Nhon and Nha Trang on 1 April and Cam Ranh on 2 April. The NVA began moving towards Saigon, but on 9 April the South Vietnamese forces made a stand at Xuan Loc (37 miles (60 kilometres) northeast of Saigon) for the first time since the fall of Ban Me Thuot in early March. General Dung had attacked the town, effectively the last line of defence before Saigon, with three infantry divisions plus tanks and artillery, but had been repelled by the ARVN Eighteenth Division. A fierce battle ensued during which the South Vietnamese air force attacked the NVA with some potent weaponry, including 'fuel-air cluster' bombs. Eventually, after an epic stand the NVA outflanked Xuan Loc on 16 April and remnants of the ARVN Eighteenth Division finally abandoned the town five days later.

14 April Congress refuses President Ford's appeal for additional military aid to South Vietnam. In an address to both Houses of Congress on 10 April, President Ford called for the immediate allocation of $722 million in emergency military assistance and $250 million in humanitarian aid to the Saigon regime. Ford also requested Congress to authorize the deployment of US forces to assist in the evacuation of Americans and South Vietnamese from Saigon. On 14 April Ford formally sent his request to Congress in the form of three bills, but all were rejected.

17 April Victorious Khmer Rouge forces enter Phnom Penh and begin emptying the city of its war-weary population. Late on 13 April, Khmer Rouge forces occupied positions east of Pochentong, cutting off the airport from the city, and early the next morning they launched a sudden attack on the northern outskirts. The offensive became general on 15 April, when the Khmers Rouges pushed forward on all sides. By the evening of 16 April thousands of republican soldiers had abandoned the front and joined refugees fleeing from the fighting into the centre of a swollen Phnom Penh. At daybreak on 17 April the Khmers Rouges launched the final attack, and by early afternoon the republican army had formally surrendered.

The Khmer Rouge units, composed in the main of young, bedraggled soldiers, entered Phnom Penh under the leadership of independent military commanders. At first, the units were greeted by cheering crowds lining the streets, but within hours the commanders were ordering the city's entire population, numbering over 2 million, to leave for the countryside, warning that the city was about to be attacked by US agents. Neither the very old nor the very young were exempted; even the sick and wounded in the hospitals were forced to go, many of them on crutches or pushed along in their beds. On reaching their assigned destinations in one of the seven zones into which the country had been divided, the evacuees were set to work in the fields. Some evidence suggests that certain units did not fully approve of the evacuation, and carried out the order with diffidence; other sectors, possibly led by Northern Zone commanders, were emptied with ruthless efficiency. There were some reports of fighting in the city between northern troops and units from other zones, probably from the east.

21 April With the NVA on the outskirts of Saigon Thieu finally resigns the presidency. President Thieu announced his resignation in a lengthy and bitter speech to both Houses of the National Assembly. In accordance with the South Vietnamese Constitution, Vice-President Tran Van Huong, was immediately sworn in to replace Thieu. Throughout April Thieu had come under enormous internal and international pressure to step down. He had finally been compelled to do so after the fall of Xuan Loc, which had effectively opened the Saigon road to the Communists. Much of Thieu's resignation speech was taken up with accusations of US duplicity. President Nixon, he claimed, had confidentially assured him before the signing of the Paris Agreements that the US would react 'violently and immediately' to check a fresh North Vietnamese offensive and would provide 'abundant military and economic aid' to South Vietnam.

28 April 'Big' Minh takes over the Saigon presidency. President Thieu's resignation was followed by a four days' lull in the fighting and by intensified international efforts to secure a peaceful settlement. The new Huong administration in Saigon called, on 22 April, for an immediate cease-fire and the opening of negotiations without preconditions on all the problems arising from the agreements. However, the Provisional Revolutionary Government (PRG) maintained that President Huong was an integral part of the 'Thieu clique' and therefore must resign. Meanwhile, the so-called 'third force' leader, General Duong Van ('Big') Minh, with the support of French diplomats in Saigon, was lobbying for the presidency, claiming that the Communists were willing to begin negotiations with him. Huong resigned on 27 April and the South Vietnamese National Assembly handed power to 'Big' Minh. He was formally sworn in as president on 28 April, and in his inaugural speech he addressed 'our friends of the other side', calling for an immediate cease-fire and the opening of negotiations. President Minh's appeal for a cease-fire was immediately declined by the PRG, and as if to reinforce the rejection North Vietnamese fighter-bombers launched an attack on Tan Son Nhut airport.

30 April Saigon falls, the US departs and the PRG takes over control of the South. General Van Tien Dung began the final North Vietnamese assault on Saigon (the 'Ho Chi Minh Campaign') on 26 April and within two days NVA troops were in the outskirts of the capital. Tan Son Nhut airport and other parts of Saigon were subjected to a series of rocket attacks. With the city's airport virtually destroyed, US Ambassador Graham Martin (under intense pressure from Washington) ordered that the final evacuation of US and 'high-risk South Vietnamese' from Saigon be carried out by helicopter. The evacuation of Americans and Vietnamese collaborators had started in early April, but Martin remained until the very last moment, apparently convinced that a settlement might still be secured. The final evacuation began at noon on 29 April, a fleet of some 80 helicopters airlifting more than 1,000 Americans and nearly 6,000 Vietnamese out of Saigon and onto waiting US aircraft carriers. Many were evacuated from the US embassy compound itself, where wild and desperate crowds had gathered in a last-ditch attempt to escape Saigon before the Communists entered. Thousands of other South Vietnamese fled the country by sea and were picked up by the US evacuation fleet. The US operation concluded just before 8.00 a.m. on 30 April and within a few hours North Vietnamese tanks had entered the city. Exchanges of fire occurred in a few places, but in general there was little attempt at resistance. Soon after noon Colonel Bui Tin, the deputy editor of the NVA newspaper, entered the presidential palace and received the formal surrender of President Minh.

After the surrender, a Military Management Committee (MMC) chaired by Tran Van Tra took control of the city and began re-establishing order. The MMC's first communique on 1 May warned that sabotage and disturbances of public order would be severely punished, and banned, amongst other things, all 'decadent slave-culture activities of the American variety'. The process of setting up civilian revolutionary committees (with responsibility for the maintenance of order) in Saigon began shortly after the surrender, and by mid-May such committees had been formed in three-quarters of the city's boroughs. In early June the PRG, which had been recognized by at least eight countries during May, held its first cabinet meeting in Saigon.

9 May Rightist leaders start to flee from Laos. The collapse of the Thieu and Lon Nol regimes in April provided a massive encouragement to the Pathet Lao forces in neighbouring Laos; at the same time, the humiliation of Saigon and Phnom Penh dampened any faint hopes harboured by the Lao right that the US might intervene in the event of a Communist push on Vientiane. Militarily, the Pathet Lao turned the screw in April, taking control of the strategic junction of Highways 7 and 13 (some 80 miles (130 kilometres north) of the capital) from Vang Pao's special forces. The battlefield successes were accompanied by increasing political pressure, with student-led demonstrations creating an atmosphere of social unrest in the cities. Eventually, with the Pathet Lao advancing down Highway 13 towards Vientiane, panic erupted among the rightists. After a day of anti-US demonstrations in Vientiane on 9 May, Defence Minister Sisouk Na Champassak and four other rightist ministers resigned from the coalition government and fled to Thailand. General Khamouan Boupha was appointed the new defence minister and King Savang asked all troops to take orders only from the Defence

Ministry. On the same day, Vang Pao joined the exodus to Bangkok, plunging his defeated forces into confusion. Fearing reprisals, several thousand of them moved southward in order to escape across the Mekong. The virtual collapse of the right meant that one unit of the Vientiane forces after another repudiated their officers and declared their solidarity with the Pathet Lao. During the remainder of May and early June steps were taken towards unifying the army and purges started to take place within the civil service.

12 May A Cambodian gunboat seizes the US container ship *Mayaguez*. Exactly a month after the evacuation of US diplomats from Phnom Penh, a Cambodian gunboat seized the 10,000-ton US merchant ship cruising some 62 miles (100 kilometres) off the Cambodian coast. The Cambodians claimed that the *Mayaquez* was a spy ship, but the US described the seizure as 'an act of piracy' and ordered a naval task force to the area. On 14 May a force of 250 US Marines and 11 helicopters struck at Koh Tang, an island where the ship and its crew were believed to be held; in the ensuing fight with Cambodian forces dug in on the island 15 US servicemen were killed and three helicopters destroyed. However, the crew of the *Mayaquez* had in fact already been released and had been picked up on their way to Koh Tang in a fishing boat by the US destroyer *Wilson*. With the battle of Koh Tang raging, US aircraft unleashed an awesome assault on a variety of Cambodian targets including the airfield at Ream (17 Cambodian aircraft destroyed) and the country's only oil refinery. One consequence of the *Mayaguez* incident was a deterioration in Washington's relations with Thailand – the Pramoj government in Bangkok had been enraged by a unilateral US decision taken on 14 May to use Utapao (on the Gulf of Siam) as a base for the Koh Tang operation.

26 June The US closes its aid mission in Vientiane. After weeks of intense anti-US demonstrations in Vientiane and other cities and towns, the offices of the US Agency for International Development (USAID) were completely closed down in late June. The large US presence in Laos was therefore reduced to an embassy staff of less than 25 people. Commenting on the anti-US demonstrations, the *Washington Post* of 16 June declared that USAID had operated 'what amounted to a parallel government' in Laos and had been 'a handy front for the [Central Intelligence Agency] CIA'.

12 August Ieng Sary and Son Sen assume leading posts in the Cambodian Council of Ministers. The new government officially exhibited to the world after the Khmer Rouge victory was a modified version of the exiled, Sihanoukist-dominated National United Front of Kampuchea (FUNK) established in Beijing in 1970. However, most of the ministers remained in China along with Sihanouk, the new official head of state (the prince returned to Phnom Penh only in late August). In fact, the government appeared to be little more than a camouflage to mask a secretive leadership. That this leadership was also deeply divided was not, at the time, known. The first indication that a leadership struggle might be under way came in August when Ieng Sary and Son Sen were appointed to leading positions within the Council of Ministers. During the same month, Hou Youn, a minister in the original FUNK government, was probably arrested and executed.

Both Sary and Sen were associated with the Khmer Rouge faction which ultimately rose to dominance; the group, members of which had generally taken up arms against Sihanouk in the early 1960s, included Saloth Sar (Pol

Pot), Nuon Chea, Koy Thoun and the two sisters, Khieu Thirith (Sary's wife) and Khieu Ponnary (Sar's wife). Hou Youn, meanwhile, was associated with the other main faction, members of which had participated in Sihanouk's Sangkum experiment until the late 1960s; this faction included Khieu Samphan, Hu Nim, Poc Deuskoma and Tiv Ol.

23 August A 'People's revolutionary administration' is established in Vientiane. The Pathet Lao completed its takeover of the country's local administration in late August when it established a 'people's revolutionary administration' in Vientiane. The joint Royal Pathet Lao military and police forces which had been responsible for maintaining order in the city since the 1973 agreement were abolished and replaced by newly-formed workers' militia units. Luang Prabang, the country's royal capital, had passed under the control of a Pathet Lao revolutionary committee a few days before Vientiane; southern provinces had been occupied shortly after the collapse of the right in early May. Despite controlling the entire country, the Pathet Lao at this stage gave no indication that it wished to abolish formally the Souvanna coalition government in favour of a conventional Marxist model.

15 November Reunification talks open in Saigon. Southern statements on reunification issued during the summer had tended to stress that, because of the differences between the two zones, the process might take some years. Statements from the North, on the other hand, implied a preference for rapid reunification. So, a resolution adopted by the North Vietnamese National Assembly in early June stated that 'except for accidents, especially in the economic field, Vietnam must form a single political, diplomatic and economic bloc during 1976, or at the latest by the end of the following year'. Northern and southern delegations (headed by Truong China and Pham Hung – see biographies – respectively) met in Saigon in mid-November to discuss a reunification programme. The conference ended on 21 November with the issuing of a communique which stated that the first objective was national reunification 'on the state plane', and that towards this end general elections would be held to a single assembly in the first half of 1976.

2 December The Pathet Lao complete their 'peaceful revolution' with the formation of the Lao People's Democratic Republic (LPDR). A two-day national congress of people's representatives in Vientiane voted unanimously to abolish the 600-year-old monarchy and establish a LPDR, with a political system modelled closely on other Communist countries. Prince Souphanouvong was appointed as the president of the LPDR and as chair of a Supreme People's Assembly, established to draft a new Constitution. Kaysone Phomvihane, leader of the Lao Communist Party, was appointed at the head of a new government.

The Pathet Lao's decision to install a formal Communist government ahead of national elections due to take place in April 1976 largely reflected their apprehension over internal developments in November. In particular, the decision by Thailand to close the border after a mid-November clash on the Mekong precipitated events. The closure of the border not only produced great hardship in Laos (with its attendant threat of social unrest) but also emphasized the potential menace of Thai-financed resistance forces crossing the Mekong. In order to introduce a measure of stability, the Pathet Lao accelerated the inevitable process in late November – demonstrations in support of Souvanna's resignation were orchestrated; increasing numbers of high- and middle-ranking officials were dispatched for 're-education'; and, on 29 November, King Savang signed a letter of abdication.

1 9 7 6

5 January A new Constitution (the country's third following those of Sihanouk's monarchy and Lon Nol's Khmer Republic) comes into force in Cambodia. (See Appendix 27 for extracts.) The Constitution had apparently been drafted by a commission established immediately after the Khmer Rouge victory in April 1975 and had been approved by the government on 3 January.

Under the new Constitution the country was officially renamed as Democratic Kampuchea, a 'state of the people, workers, peasants and all other Kampuchean working people'. The means of production were the collective property of the state, although personal property remained in private hands. The state apparatus consisted of a People's Representative Assembly, an executive body elected by the assembly and to which it was responsible and a State Presidium chosen by the assembly. The assembly was elected by the people for a five-year term and had 250 members, representing peasants (150), other working people (50) and the armed forces (50). The Constitution afforded citizens 'full rights to a new and constantly improving material, spiritual and cultural life'. All citizens possessed the right to worship according to any religion, on condition that the religion was not 'reactionary'.

10 February A secret Sino-Cambodian military aid agreement is signed. Son Sen, the Cambodian defence minister, and Wang Shangrong, a high-ranking Chinese officer, signed a secret military agreement in Phnom Penh which provided for urgent delivery of military equipment to the poorly equipped Khmer Rouge forces. The agreement was not only a reflection of the close ideological links between Beijing and Democratic Kampuchea, but was also a demonstration of their shared perception of Vietnamese hegemony as the region's principal menace.

20 March Elections are held in Cambodia. Five hundred and fifteen candidates contested 250 seats in the elections to the newly-created People's Representative Assembly. Constituencies were organized on both an occupational and a regional basis and according to official figures, a 98 per cent turn out was recorded. Saloth Sar (Pol Pot), who at this stage was unknown to the West, was apparently one of eight people elected to represent workers in the rubber plantations. Government members elected to the assembly included Ieng Thirith, Hou Nim and Toch Phoeun, all of whom were returned as Phnom Penh factory workers' representatives.

2 April Sihanouk resigns as Cambodian head of state. Sihanouk, who had returned to Phnom Penh in only September 1975, resigned as head of state informing the government that all his wishes had been realized and that he was now enjoying 'happiness beyond my imagination'. Officially, the government conferred the title of 'Great Patriot' on the prince in recognition of his good deeds and guaranteed that he would continue to receive all his living expenses and those of his family. In actual fact, he was placed under virtual house arrest, being smuggled out of Cambodia only shortly before the fall of Phnom Penh in early 1979.

13 April A new Cambodian cabinet is appointed headed by Pol Pot. A new government structure was disclosed in Cambodia at the end of a three-day meeting of the People's Representative Assembly. Pol Pot was appointed as prime minister (in place of Pen Nouth), at the head of a government which also included as new members Yun Yat (the wife of Son Sen) and Vorn Vet. The other members included Son Sen, Hou Nim, Thiounn Thioeunn, Ieng Thirith and Toch Phoeun. It was at this point that Saloth Sar adopted the name Pol Pot, a move that caused confusion among Western 'Cambodia watchers' who were startled at what appeared to be the promotion of a complete unknown. In addition to the appointment of a new cabinet, the recently-created state presidium was also filled. Khieu Samphan was appointed president of the presidium, with So Phim and Nhim Ros as first and second vice-presidents, respectively.

Despite Pol Pot's appointment as prime minister, the new government structure was not necessarily wholly to the advantage of his clique. In particular, the elevation of So Phim and Nhim Ros to the presidium indicated that Pol Pot's position was verging on the precarious. Both Phim and Ros were influential zonal leaders with charge of their own armed forces; in addition they were both members of the previously unrepresented clique of veteran revolutionaries, associates of which had either fled to Vietnam in the early 1950s or had remained in Phnom Penh to form the Pracheachon Party. As such they represented a pro-Hanoi counterweight to Pol Pot's power base in the cabinet.

25 April Nation-wide polling takes place in North and South Vietnam to elect a new National Assembly in the run-up to formal reunification. The 492 assembly seats were contested by 604 candidates and according to official figures, just under 99 per cent of the electorate voted in the country as a whole. According to a report issued by the Provisional Revolutionary Government (PRG) in June, some 95 per cent of the former soldiers and civil servants attending 're-education courses' had their rights restored in early 1976 so that they might take part in the elections. Candidates in the South were required to be recommended by the National Liberation Front (NLF); those successfully elected in the South included Nguyen Thi Binh (PRG foreign minister), Huynh Tan Phat (PRG premier), Nguyen Huu Tho (NLF chair), Pham Hung (the southern Communist Party leader), and Vo Van Kiet (the Saigon mayor).

3 June The UN recommends a massive aid package for Vietnam. A UN report published in early June recommended that the UN secretary-general should launch a campaign to raise over $400 million for rehabilitation and reconstruction in Vietnam. The report recommended as priorities the development of the agricultural sector, including the clearing of new land and the restoration of land laid waste by defoliants, and the reconstruction of communications. The destruction and impoverishment caused by the war was detailed in the report. The infrastructure of the North had suffered terribly from the US bombing campaign with railways, roads, dams and whole towns and villages destroyed. In the South unemployment was rife and as many as 2 million people were suffering from venereal disease or drug addiction.

15 June Currency reforms are introduced in Laos. Spiralling inflation and unemployment, shortages of goods caused by Thailand's blockade of the Mekong and serious monetary confusion prompted the government to introduce the currency reforms. The two currencies in circulation (the Vientiane kip and the Lao Patriotic Front kip, the former being about one-eighth of the value of the latter) were withdrawn and a new kip introduced at an internal exchange rate of one new to 20 old kip. Externally, the new kip was effectively devalued by 70 per cent, so that the rate became fixed at 200 kip per dollar. The value of the kip in relation to the US dollar had declined dramatically during the 1970s: the free market exchange rate was approximately 600 Vientiane kips per US dollar in late 1971 but three years later this had sunk to about 1,250 per dollar and by the end of 1975 it had further declined to 5,000 per dollar; at the time of the June currency reforms the rate had fallen to 14,000 per dollar. The maximum cash exchange for each family was set at 200,000 kips and for family businesses 500,000 kips; any excess was to be deposited in the National Bank in the new currency for subsequent, controlled withdrawal.

2 July Vietnam is reunified as the Socialist Republic of Vietnam (SRV). The newly-elected National Assembly unanimously adopted a resolution proclaiming the reunification of the country under the name of the SRV. It was the first time that Vietnam had enjoyed unity since France had invaded and annexed Cochin-China in 1859. Other resolutions adopted by the assembly included the renaming of Saigon as Ho Chi Minh City and the designation of Hanoi as the capital of the SRV.

A number of appointments were also announced: Ton Duc Thang, president of North Vietnam, was appointed president of the SRV; Nguyen Huu Tho, chair of the NLF, and Nguyen Luong Bang, vice-president of North Vietnam, were both appointed as vice-presidents; Pham Van Dong, the North Vietnamese premier, was appointed as premier of the SRV. On 3 July (the final day of the assembly's 10-day session) the membership of a full new Council of Ministers was announced. Although largely composed of members of the previous North Vietnamese government, it also included six South Vietnamese: Pham Hung, Huynh Tan Phat, Vo Chi Cong, Nguyen Van Hieu, Nguyen Thi Binh and General Tran Nam Trung.

27 September As the result of a fierce power struggle within the Khmer Rouge leadership Pol Pot temporarily 'resigns' the Cambodian premiership. An official announcement by the People's Representative Assembly declared that Pol Pot had taken 'temporary leave' to improve his health and that Nuon Chea, chair of the assembly's standing committee, had been appointed as acting prime minister. Undoubtedly, the announcement was related to the ongoing power struggle within Cambodia between the Pol Pot clique and the supporters of a more pro-Vietnamese line. The struggle had become increasingly intense following Pol Pot's appointment as premier in April; some evidence suggests that his 'dismissal' was the culmination of a series of political victories for the pro-Hanoi faction. However, some commentators have claimed that Pol Pot's 'sick leave' was a well-disguised tactical manoeuvre which gave him the necessary time to formulate a strategy to purge his opponents.

Pol Pot quietly re-emerged as prime minister in late October, when his name appeared on a statement denouncing the 'Gang of Four' who had recently been deposed in China following Chairman Mao's death on 9 September. The upheavals in Beijing had undoubtedly had a major impact on the struggle in Cambodia given that a faction of the anti-Pol Pot coterie had been staunch supporters of the Cultural Revolution. Following his re-emergence, and with the full support of at least two powerful zonal military commanders (Ta Mok of the southwest and Pok of the north), Pol Pot went to war against rival pro-Hanoi zonal armies and their supporters in the central administration. Over the next two years a large number of Pol Pot's opponents were brutally executed, having first confessed their 'crimes' at the infamous State Security Interrogation Centre at Tuol Sleng secondary school in Phnom Penh. (See Appendix 28 for a list of the main victims of Pol Pot's purges.)

15 November The US vetoes Vietnam's application for UN membership. An application by the SRV for UN membership was supported by 14 of the 15 Security Council members, but was vetoed by the US. The US permanent representative at the UN, William Scranton, claimed that he had opposed the application because of Vietnam's failure to 'show satisfactory humanitarian or practical concern' over the issue of US servicemen missing in action (MIA) in Indo-China. Most of the other Security Council members expressed regret over the US position, which, they claimed, stemmed from a bilateral dispute which had little to do with the UN Charter requirements for membership.

The veto followed months of low-key contacts between Vietnam and the US. In March, Henry Kissinger had announced that the US government was in principle prepared to normalize relations with Vietnam and a series of notes were subsequently exchanged between the two governments (the North Vietnamese government prior to reunification in July). The notes were released by Vietnam in September, and they highlighted the main concerns of the two governments; for the US, the MIA issue, and for the Vietnamese, the question of the US obligation under the 1973 Paris Agreement to contribute towards post-war reconstruction.

14 December The fourth congress of the Vietnamese Communist Party opens in Hanoi. The party's long-awaited fourth congress, the first congress since 1960, was finally held five months after the formal reunification of Vietnam. The congress was a vital one with the party seeking to adjust itself towards the new goal of post-war reconstruction and socialist transformation of the South. A number of decisions were taken aimed at improving party-state relations; others were concerned with the principles of economic planning and the role of the armed forces in peacetime. The immediate economic priorities (as defined in the 1976–80 five-year plan) were the development of agriculture and light industry as a basis for the future growth of heavy industry.

At its final session on 20 December the congress formally changed the party's name from the Vietnamese Workers' Party to the Vietnamese Communist Party. A new enlarged central committee and politburo were elected. The new full politburo members were Nguyen Van Linh, Vo Chi Cong, General Chu Huy Man and Le Van Luong; three new alternate members were elected, namely Do Muoi, Vo Van Kiet and To Huu.

1 9 7 7

21 January President Carter pardons Vietnam War draft evaders. The day after his inauguration as US president, Jimmy Carter signed a proclamation granting a pardon to all Vietnam War draft evaders who had not been involved in any violent acts. The number of those known to be affected by the pardon totalled 11,300, the majority of whom had been convicted of draft evasion. Carter's proclamation fulfilled one of his election pledges and it partially superseded President Ford's 1974 proclamation establishing a conditional amnesty programme for draft evaders and military deserters.

12 March Former King Savang Vatthana of Laos is arrested and sent for 're-education'. Savang Vatthana, his son, Crown Prince Vong Savang, and other members of the royal family were arrested in Luang Prabang after apparently being implicated in anti-government guerrilla activities. After their arrest the royal family were dispatched to 're-education centres'. According to press reports in mid-1987, the ex-king and all his family died in the camps between 1978 and 1981, a claim denied by the Lao government.

Prior to his arrest the ex-king had lived in Luang Prabang holding the honorary position of supreme adviser to the president. The crown prince, meanwhile, had been a member of the Supreme People's Assembly established soon after the Communist victory in 1975.

16 March A US presidential commission arrives in Vietnam. A five-member commission appointed by President Carter to resolve the issue of US servicemen missing in action (MIA) in Indo-China visited Vietnam and Laos in March. The commission was led by Leonard Woodcock, president of the United Auto Workers' Union, and also included Senator Mike Mansfield and Congressman Sonny Montgomery. The Vietnamese delegation was led by Phan Hien, a deputy foreign minister and an accomplished negotiator. The talks began with a reiteration of the two sides' formal negotiating positions, with the Vietnamese demanding reparations as laid down in the Paris Agreements and the US calling for a 'humanitarian resolution' to both the MIA and reconstruction aid issues. However, some progress appeared to be made in later discussions. The Vietnamese authorities handed over into the custody of the commission the bodies of 12 US servicemen previously listed as MIA. The commission was also informed that an office had been opened in Hanoi to provide information on MIA issues. Hien also appeared to imply that the Vietnamese were prepared to be flexible on the form any future US aid might take, indicating that they were prepared to drop their demand for formal reparations.

18 March US restrictions are lifted on travel to Vietnam, Cambodia, Cuba and North Korea. President Carter allowed the lapse of this executive order while the Woodcock commission was still visiting Hanoi.

3–4 May Talks are held in Paris between Vietnamese and US government delegations, but the US Congress refuses to acquiesce to normalization. A mood of expectancy preceded the opening of two days of talks between US and Vietnamese government delegations in Paris. The US delegation was led by Richard Holbrooke, the assistant secretary of state for East Asian and Pacific affairs, and the Vietnamese delegation by Phan Hien. However, the raised expectations over the possible announcement of normalization plans faded as Hien doggedly pressed the US side for a commitment on reparations. The Vietnamese side raised the issue of President Nixon's 'secret' letter to Pham Van Dong (sent in February 1973, less than a week after the signature of the Paris Agreements) in which he had offered Vietnam grants to the value of $3,250 million (the text of Nixon's letter, the existence of which had been denied by the Republican administration, was eventually released by the State Department in mid-May). Holbrooke and his team attempted, unsuccessfully, to persuade the Vietnamese to drop their demands for formal reparations; Hien was assured that the US would no longer veto Vietnamese entry to the UN and that aid could be discussed after the restoration of diplomatic relations.

The situation worsened considerably when the US House of Representatives effectively intervened in the negotiations on 4 May by adopting an amendment to a State Department authorization bill providing that none of the funds authorized should be used for the purpose of 'negotiating reparations, aid or any other form of payment' to Vietnam. The previous day Henry Kissinger had also intervened, contending in a speech that any US commitments to supply aid to Vietnam were no longer binding, as North Vietnam had violated the Paris Agreement by sending its troops into the South in 1975. Despite the congressional reaction, the two delegations held another round of unsuccessful talks in Paris from 2 to 3 June, at which Hien delivered new information about 20 MIAs. It was agreed to continue the talks 'in the near future', but no date was fixed. The second round of talks sparked off a fresh reaction in Congress. Despite a personal appeal from President Carter in a letter to the speaker not to limit the ability of international banks to extend loans to Vietnam, the House of Representatives adopted, on 23 June, a foreign aid appropriations bill which *inter alia* forbade US funds to be paid 'directly or indirectly' to Vietnam, Laos or Cambodia and also repudiated Nixon's 'secret' promise of aid to Hanoi.

18 July Laos and Vietnam sign a 25-year Treaty of Friendship and Co-operation, which formalizes the 'special relationship' between the two countries. The treaty was signed at the end of a four-day visit to Laos by Le Duan and Pham Van Dong. The treaty comprised six provisions covering various forms of co-operation; however, also signed were three secret protocols covering joint defence arrangements, delineation of the Lao-Vietnamese border and Vietnamese economic aid to Laos. The timing of the treaty was significant, occurring only months after Khmer Rouge forces had launched a series of brutal attacks on Vietnamese border villages. According to some commentators Hanoi intended the treaty to act as a warning to Pol Pot, and his backers in Beijing, that Vietnam was determined at all costs to maintain its superiority in Indo-China. In Phnom Penh itself the treaty only served to confirm the ruling clique's anxieties over what they perceived to be Vietnamese plans to construct a Hanoi-led Indo-Chinese Federation.

20 September Vietnam is admitted to the UN. Vietnam became the 149th member of the UN General Assembly at the opening of its thirty-second regular session in New York. Vietnam's admission had been vetoed by the US in late 1976, but the objection had been withdrawn in May 1977 after US-Vietnamese negotiations in Paris. Speaking to the General Assembly, Nguyen Duy Trinh, the Vietnamese foreign minister, stated that his country should have been a UN member since 1945 but that it had instead been subjected, by 'imperialist aggressors', to the 'bloodiest neo-colonialist war' which history had ever known.

24 September Khmer Rouge forces launch attacks on Vietnamese border villages. The situation along the Cambodian-Vietnamese border deteriorated seriously in March 1977, with Khmer Rouge forces launching attacks into Vietnamese provinces situated, in the main, between the Mekong and the coast. The clashes were undoubtedly linked to the chaotic internal situation in Cambodia, where Pol Pot's purges were widening in scope. The scale of the fighting increased dramatically in late September, the period of Pol Pot's public emergence as leader of the Cambodian Communist Party and of his triumphant visit to China. According to Vietnamese reports (supported by US intelligence assessments) as many as four divisions of Khmer Rouge troops launched continuous attacks from 24 September onwards along the entire border of Tay Ninh province (situated on the northern side of the Parrot's Beak salient). Over 1,000 Vietnamese civilians were killed or wounded in this area between September and November; visitors to the battleground were shocked by the atrocities committed by the invading Cambodians. The Khmer Rouge, however, alleged that Vietnam was the offending party, having attacked Cambodia's eastern borderlands in September with tanks, artillery and aircraft.

27 September Pol Pot finally emerges as the Communist Party leader in Cambodia. Pol Pot delivered a five-hour speech in Phnom Penh in late September in which he publicly revealed for the first time that the Communist Party of Cambodia had controlled the country since 1975 and that he was the party general secretary. (The day after his emergence as leader of the Communist Party, Pol Pot stepped onto the international stage with a three-week visit to China and North Korea). Prior to his speech the party had been known to the Cambodian people only as Angkar (the Organization). In his speech, Pol Pot outlined his version of the party's history (a version which differed significantly from that later presented by the successors to the Khmer Rouge) and summarized the course of the war.

On the internal situation, Pol Pot confirmed that his government was pursuing a particularly radical brand of Communism based, in part, on China's 'great leap forward' of 1958. Collectivization had apparently been introduced in one stage without any previous preparation, and private land and money had been abolished. 'The collective co-operatives of the peasants,' Pol Pot said, 'have transformed the arid, impoverished Cambodian countryside of old into an increasingly beautiful countryside equipped with extensive networks of reservoirs, trenches and canals and freshened by verdant farmland. Each of these co-operatives constitutes a small collective society, which is a brand new community where all kinds of depraved cultures and social blemishes have been wiped out'. He claimed that a 'handful of reactionary elements' continued to carry out subversive activities inside Cambodia. They had to be dealt with by 'separating, educating and co-opting elements that can be won over and corrected by the people's side, neutralizing any reluctant elements so that they will not undermine the revolution, and isolating and eradicating only the smallest possible number of the elements who are cruel and who determinedly oppose the revolution'.

25 December Vietnamese forces respond to the Khmer Rouge border attacks by invading eastern Cambodia. In the aftermath of the Khmer Rouge attacks on Tay Ninh province in September, Vietnam began to formulate plans for a counteroffensive. However, firstly, Vietnam initiated a number of diplomatic manoeuvres in what appeared to be a final attempt to avoid all-out confrontation; at the same time the Vietnamese sought to determine the true extent of China's support for the Cambodian government. In early October a Vietnamese diplomatic team travelled secretly to Beijing for talks with Cambodian officials. The meeting generated little except vitriolic Khmer criticism of Vietnam's aggressive intent. In late November Le Duan paid a visit to Beijing, ostensibly to balance an earlier trip to the Soviet Union. During his visit Le Duan attempted to persuade China to reduce its support for the Pol Pot government. Le Duan failed in his task, and the speeches delivered by both sides during the visit provided evidence of the deepening Sino-Vietnamese rift and of Hanoi's increasing support for the Soviet Union. In a final attempt at mediation President Souphanouvong of Laos travelled to Phnom Penh in mid-December. Not surprisingly, Souphanouvong's championing of Indo-Chinese solidarity was greeted coolly by Pol Pot.

On 25 December, three days after Souphanouvong left Phnom Penh, a large force of Vietnamese infantry and artillery invaded Cambodia. The scale of the Vietnamese assault surprised the Cambodians and the Khmer Rouge forces were routed. A large number of Khmer Rouge were killed, others retreated in disarray leaving large tracts of eastern Cambodia under Vietnamese control. Although Pol Pot dispatched divisions under Son Sen and Ta Mok to the border in early January, the Vietnamese forces withdrew before the fresh Khmer Rouge troops arrived.

31 December Cambodia and Vietnam break off diplomatic relations. Cambodia responded to Vietnam's 25 December invasion by suspending diplomatic relations and ordering Vietnamese embassy personnel out of Phnom Penh. The Cambodian announcement finally made the dispute between the two countries public, ending months of international speculation. The breaking off of diplomatic relations was followed by the launching of an intense propaganda offensive by the Cambodians, who claimed that the invading Vietnamese forces had been 'routed shamefully'. A broadcast from Phnom Penh on 6 January alleged that almost 30,000 Vietnamese soldiers had been killed or wounded for the loss of under 500 Cambodians, a claim regarded as preposterous by most commentators.

1 9 7 8

23 March A Vietnamese crackdown on 'bourgeois traders' in the south triggers a Chinese exodus. A communique issued by the Ho Chi Minh City authorities on 23 March stated that private trade in the city would be transferred immediately to the control of 'socialist trade organisations'. The communique explained that 'bourgeois tradesmen' engaging in speculation, dealing in the black market and hoarding goods and cash, had monopolized the economy and the market, increased commodity prices and illegally enriched themselves. Although the measures were subsequently extended to the whole of South Vietnam on 31 March, the initial communique was aimed specifically at economically powerful Chinese traders in Cholon, Ho Chi Minh City's 'Chinatown'. The cautious economic policies initiated by the government in the South during 1975–7 had allowed the Cholon Chinese to gain control of a large amount of the country's industry and trade, including the vital rice trade.

The crackdown on the Cholon Chinese prompted an immediate panic response among members of the Chinese community (Hoa) in the North, thousands of whom travelled across the border into China. The initial exodus was composed mainly of industrial workers, peasants and fishermen, and not the richer southern traders. The first Chinese comment on the situation was made in late April when the government expressed concern over the exodus. Two weeks later, a Chinese note accused Vietnam of 'ostracizing, persecuting and expelling Chinese residents' and declared that a number of aid projects had been cut. By late May almost 100,000 Hoa (out of a total population of some 1.2 million) had fled to China and the tone of both sides' statements had become extremely sharp. Beijing set in motion plans to send ships to Vietnam to evacuate the 'persecuted' Chinese, but by late July the scheme had been abandoned. The flight of the southern, richer, Hoa increased dramatically during the second half of 1978 as an international traffic network in emigrants developed. According to some commentators, the Vietnamese government was heavily involved in the traffic, forcing emigrants to buy their way out.

24 May In Cambodia, Pol Pot loyalists launch a full-scale attack against Khmer Rouge dissidents in the Eastern Zone; many eastern Khmer Rouge officials, including Heng Samrin and Hun Sen, flee into Vietnam. Pol Pot's purge against 'internal reactionaries' reached its brutal climax in May when he dispatched his henchman, Son Sen, to purify the Eastern Zone. The move against the east was the culmination of an extensive sequence of provincial purges launched by Pol Pot in early 1977. The Eastern Zone represented the greatest potential threat to the Pol Pot line. It was adjacent to Vietnam and as such it had closer revolutionary links with Hanoi than the other regions of Cambodia. The zone's party secretary (and first vice-president of the state presidium), So Phim, had a considerable power base of his own and he had managed to shield his people from many of the excesses practised in other zones. However, in late May So Phim's time ran out. Troops under the command of Son Sen travelled from the centre to the east where they surrounded the party buildings in Suong. Sen's troops began executing a number of their eastern counterparts and within the week So Phim had shot himself after apparently failing in an attempt to negotiate personally a compromise with Pol Pot. Some high-ranking eastern officials, including Heng Samrin and Hun Sen (see biographies), escaped the initial killing and organized some ineffective armed resistance. By July Son Sen's troops had been joined by Ta Mok's southwestern forces and, together, they embarked on what was probably their most ruthless onslaught. Entire villages were simply hacked to death, whilst large numbers of people were forcibly deported to other zones for torture and execution. In all, as many as 100,000 people died during the eastern purge.

29 June Vietnam is admitted to the Council for Mutual Economic Assistance (Comecon). The Vietnamese balancing act with regard to the Sino-Soviet dispute tilted decidedly towards Moscow with Hanoi's formal admission to the Comecon, the Soviet bloc economic co-operation pact. Vietnam became the tenth full member, the last country to join being Cuba in 1972. Hanoi's decision to join Comecon reflected the rapidly deteriorating state of Sino-Vietnamese relations.

3 July China halts economic and technical aid to Vietnam. Following the admission of Vietnam to Comecon in late June, the Chinese government formally ended all economic and technical aid to its southern neighbour. Estimates of Chinese aid to Vietnam over the previous 20 years ranged from $10,000 million to $18,000 million. Up to 1975 it took the form mainly of war material and food supplies, whilst after the war it comprised assistance for infrastructural development, machinery and technicians. Vietnam had always received the bulk of its aid from the Soviet Union, which had been its main weapons supplier during the war; the level of Soviet aid at the time of the Chinese revocation was estimated at some $500 million a year.

6 September The Vietnamese premier, Pham Van Dong, begins a 6-week tour of the Association of Southeast Asian Nations (ASEAN) countries. Increasingly strained relations with China and Cambodia had prompted Vietnam to increase its diplomatic efforts to improve relations with the ASEAN countries. In each country – Thailand, Philippines, Indonesia, Malaysia and Singapore – he issued a pledge that Vietnam would not assist indigenous Communist guerrillas. Nevertheless, the ASEAN countries all refused Dong's offer to enter into a formal treaty of friendship with Vietnam.

27 September US-Vietnamese talks in New York almost result in a possible normalization breakthrough. US-Vietnamese talks in Paris in late 1977 had broken down after Hanoi had refused to agree to normalization without a private US aid pledge. However, during a visit to Japan in July 1978 Phan Hien, a Vietnamese deputy foreign minister, announced publicly that Vietnam was prepared to resume normalization negotiations with the US without any conditions attached. Hanoi made a number of other friendly gestures towards the US in the summer, including sending a delegation to Hawaii to discuss with US officials methods of identifying the bodies of MIAs. Therefore, both sides entered a new round of negotiations in late September in New York with high expectations of real progress. The US delegation to the talks, which were held in secret, was headed by Richard Holbrooke; his Vietnamese counterpart was Nguyen Co Thach, then a deputy foreign minister. The first round took place on 22 September and, for the US side, it proved hugely disappointing with Thach still maintaining that the US had to pay reparations. However, at a second session on 27 September the Vietnamese side yielded and agreed to normalization without preconditions. With only details remaining to be worked out, Holbrooke placed the offer before President Carter. Eventually, in mid-October, Carter, after consultations with his assistant for national security affairs, Zbigniew Brzezinksi, decided to curtail the normalization process. According to some commentators the decision was taken so as not to jeopardize Washington's relations with Beijing (the normalization of Sino-US relations was subsequently announced on 15 December). Publicly, the US informed Vietnam in late October that normalization was obstructed by the character of Vietnamese relations with Cambodia and the Soviet Union and by the worsening refugee crisis.

3 November Vietnam signs a friendship treaty with the Soviet Union. The 25-year Treaty of Friendship and Co-operation was signed during a visit to Moscow in early November by Le Duan and Pham Van Dong. Amongst other things, the treaty provided that in the event of either party becoming the object of attack they would 'immediately begin mutual consultations for the purpose of removing that threat and taking appropriate effective measures to ensure the peace and security of their countries'.

3 December A pro-Vietnamese 'United Front' is formed in eastern Cambodia. The mid-year purge of the Eastern Zone served to dispel any hopes harboured by Hanoi that the aggressively chauvinist nature of the Cambodian revolution might be altered internally. Through the application of the crudest of political tactics Pol Pot had succeeded by mid-1978 in gaining absolute control of the Cambodian revolution. This was reflected in the increasingly ultra-nationalist tone of the propaganda coming out of Phnom Penh, which was often little more than anti-Vietnamese invective. Against this background, the Vietnamese government had started to organize an anti-Pol Pot resistance movement among Cambodian refugees in September. Eventually, in early December approximately 200 of the leading survivors of the eastern purge met in a 'liberated' area of that zone to form the Kampuchean National United Front for National Salvation (KNUFNS). Led by Heng Samrin, former Khmers Rouges comprised the dominant bloc within the front's 14-member central committee. An 11-point programme was adopted, which included amongst its aims the overthrow of the 'the reactionary Pol Pot-Ieng Sary clique' and the introduction of policies 'tending towards genuine socialism'.

25 December Vietnamese and United Front forces advance into Cambodia. Some 100,000 Vietnamese troops supported by 20,000 United Front soldiers advanced swiftly into Cambodia in several directions simultaneously on 25 December. The attack was directed by General Van Tien Dung, the Vietnamese army chief-of-staff and the officer in charge of the final Communist offensive in South Vietnam in 1975. From the very beginning General Dung's experience told and Pol Pot was forced into making some major tactical errors. Deceived by early Vietnamese probes, Pol Pot concentrated half of his army in the (southern) Parrot's Beak and Fish Hook salients; Dung, however, attacked to the north and south of both salients, which enabled him to encircle the Cambodian troops and decimate them from the air. The Vietnamese troops advanced so rapidly into Cambodia that they had no time to occupy the territory which they had overrun. Nevertheless, Khmer Rouge radio continued to broadcast insanely confident battle reports, including one on 5 January 1979, which claimed that the people were 'happy and satisfied' with 'the news of the victory of our revolutionary troops'. The next day the encirclement of Phnom Penh by Vietnamese troops was virtually complete.

1 9 7 9

7 January Vietnamese forces topple Pol Pot's Khmer Rouge regime. Two weeks after the Vietnamese and United Front forces had advanced into Cambodia they entered Phnom Penh unopposed. That the city had only recently been abandoned was evident from the amount of weaponry and sensitive documentation left behind. A final flight from Pochentong had taken off on 6 January and early the next morning a train had headed west out of Phnom Penh station, carrying Ieng Sary, probably the last of the Khmer Rouge leadership to leave the city. Sihanouk had been smuggled out on 2 January. The total collapse of the regime's centre meant that the regular Khmer Rouge soldier was left with little choice but to retreat into the swamps and mountains of the Cambodian countryside. As many as 15,000 remnants soon found their way to the western provinces of Battambang, Pursat and Koh Kong, in the area between Highway 5 and the Cardamom mountains; an equal number were scattered over the rest of the country in small guerrilla bands. As many as 30,000 Khmer Rouge soldiers had been killed or injured during the retreat.

The rapid collapse of the Pol Pot government appeared to take the Vietnamese and the United Front by surprise. A front congress, called to reorganize the Communist Party, was still in progress in Kompong Cham at the time of Phnom Penh's liberation on 7 January. Nevertheless, the next day the formation of a provisional government was announced. Headed by Heng Samrin, the eight-member People's Revolutionary Council (PRC) was composed of: four Vietnamese-trained revolutionaries who had broken with Pol Pot before 1975 (Pen Sovan, Keo Chanda, Nou Beng and Mok Sakun); three members of the Khmer Rouge Eastern Zone administration who had taken up arms against Pol Pot in 1978 (Samrin, Hun Sen and Chea Sim); and one member with no previous revolutionary experience, Chan Ven.

10 January The pro-Hanoi People's Republic of Kampuchea (PRK) is founded. The PRC announced the 'dictatorial, fascist and genocidal regime of the reactionary Pol Pot-Ieng Sary clique' had been abolished and the PRK established in its place. The council reaffirmed 'its right to be the sole legitimate and legal representative in international relations, in the UN, in the non-aligned movement and in all international organisations which Kampuchea has joined'.

The new government was quickly recognized by Vietnam and Laos and by the Soviet Union and its allies. China, which had been deeply embarrassed at the ease with which the Vietnamese had toppled Pol Pot's regime, denounced the new government as a 'handful of shameless traitors and national scum'. The West also responded by roundly criticizing the Vietnamese action, and many countries, including Japan, Britain and Australia, announced the suspension of aid to Hanoi. A UN Security Council resolution calling for the withdrawal of all foreign forces from Cambodia was vetoed by the Soviet Union.

12 January The Association of Southeast Asian Nations (ASEAN) countries call for the immediate withdrawal of Vietnamese forces from Cambodia. The foreign ministers of the ASEAN countries met in Bangkok from 12 to 13 January to discuss the situation. A statement issued after the meeting deplored 'the armed intervention threatening the independence, sovereignty and territorial integrity of Cambodia' and called for the 'immediate withdrawal of all foreign troops from Cambodian territory'. However, behind the scenes, the ASEAN countries were not in complete agreement; Indonesia and Malaysia continued to regard China as the principal potential menace in Southeast Asia, whereas Thailand, isolated on the 'front line', was deeply perturbed by the Vietnamese action. Therefore, within days of the PRK's formation Sino-Thai agreement had been reached providing for the use of Thai territory to arm the Khmers Rouges.

16 February Pham Van Dong arrives in Phnom Penh. Pham Van Dong, the Vietnamese premier, paid a four-day visit to Phnom Penh to cement ties with the newly-created PRK. A 25-year Treaty of Peace, Friendship and Co-operation between the two countries was signed during the visit. The treaty stated that both countries would assist each other to strengthen their capacity to defend their independence against 'all schemes and acts of sabotage by the imperialists and international reactionary forces'. Agreements were also signed on economic and technical co-operation and on cultural, educational, medical and scientific co-operation. The Vietnamese delegation also agreed to grant Cambodia free aid in the form of food, medicine and agricultural equipment.

17 February China invades Vietnam with 80,000 troops. The invasion followed Deng Xiaoping's successful visit to the US and Japan. In Tokyo Deng told the former Japanese prime minister, Kakuei Tanaka, that Vietnam had to be 'punished severely' for invading Cambodia and that China was considering taking 'appropriate counter-action'. Chinese plans to teach Vietnam a lesson had evolved further than Tanaka perhaps realized. Since mid-January US intelligence had been monitoring a massive convergence of Chinese manpower and hardware along the Vietnamese border. During his visit to the US, Deng had informed President Carter of China's intentions. Privately, Carter had advised Deng against an invasion (thereby siding with the secretary of state, Cyrus Vance, in his long-running battle with the hawkish national security adviser, Zbigniew Brzezinski). However, the administration's mild public response to a series of frenzied anti-Soviet speeches delivered by Deng during his visit seemed to have been taken by Beijing as tacit support for the action.

The attack began at dawn on 17 February with a prolonged artillery barrage. Shortly afterwards upwards of 80,000 Chinese troops, supported by tanks and artillery, crossed into Vietnam at points along the entire length of the border. The advance took the form of six main thrusts towards the capitals of the Vietnamese provinces bordering China. The attack, relying heavily on 'human-wave' tactics, quickly lost impetus, and the Chinese numbers were boosted to some 200,000 before it was resumed. By 23 February, the Chinese had captured four of the capitals: Dong Dang, Lao Cai, Cao Bang and Ha Giang. On 27 February the Chinese launched their heaviest assault in an attempt to capture the town of Lang Son, situated on the strategic crossroads of Highway 1, leading to Hanoi, and Highway 4, between Mong Cai and Cao Bang. For the first time, the Vietnamese deployed one of their main-force divisions, the elite 308th, but Chinese infantry managed to enter the town in the evening of 2 March. Three days later, with fighting still raging in Lang Son, China announced that the Chinese forces, having 'attained the goals set for them', were withdrawing from Vietnam. However, the withdrawal was not completed until 16 March, largely because the retreating Chinese forces systematically destroyed as much of the Vietnamese infrastructure as possible before pulling out. In late March, Hanoi claimed that Chinese troops were still occupying 10 points on Vietnamese territory.

According to Vietnam, some 20,000 Chinese soldiers were killed during the invasion, and a further 40,000 were injured. For their part, China claimed that Vietnam had suffered 50,000 casualties, compared with 20,000 Chinese dead or injured. Foreign correspondents' reports agreed that the Chinese forces had performed badly against a smaller Vietnamese force, composed in the main of regional troops and local militia. The Chinese had employed outmoded tactics and obsolescent equipment against forces operating with the dual advantage of recent combat experience and intimate knowledge of the terrain. Articles in the Chinese press indirectly confirmed the military's poor performance: the *Liberation Army Daily* of 27 March said that the campaign had 'helped to clear away some erroneous ideas on the question of war'. However, despite suffering heavy losses the Chinese troops still managed to cause destruction on a massive scale to an area which had remained largely untouched by the earlier US bombing. The Chinese also drew comfort from the fact that Soviet, and to a lesser extent Indian, forces stationed along China's border remained inactive throughout the invasion.

27 March Soviet warships start using Vietnamese port facilities at Cam Ranh Bay. The arrival of a small fleet of Soviet warships in the Vietnamese port of Cam Ranh Bay was conclusive evidence that Moscow had finally emerged as Hanoi's chief patron. Cam Ranh had been developed into a major air-naval base by the US during the war in Vietnam, at a total cost in excess of $2,000 million. Situated mid-way between Vladivostok and the Indian Ocean, it was known to be of great strategic value to the Soviet Far Eastern fleet. Hence, the Soviets had been pressing for access since the US withdrawal in 1975, but the Vietnamese, wary of China's reaction, had refused. However, the Chinese invasion of northern Vietnam in February rendered Hanoi's earlier considerations redundant. So, by the mid-1980s, the Cam Ranh facilities had allowed the Soviet Union to emerge as a major naval force in Asia.

18 April Sino-Vietnamese talks begin in Hanoi but the negotiations are eventually adjourned without any progress having been made. Although both China and Vietnam expressed their willingness to negotiate on the border question in the aftermath of the Chinese invasion, talks did not begin until mid-April. At the talks, the Vietnamese proposed that both sides should establish a Demilitarized Zone (DMZ) and that border problems should be settled on the basis of respect for the borderline laid down in two nineteenth-century conventions. The Chinese side abandoned the pretence that the dispute was a territorial dispute and put forward as a basis for a settlement an eight-point statement of principles covering the whole field of Sino-Vietnamese relations; one of the points stipulated that neither side should seek hegemony in Indo-China nor station troops in other countries. The talks were adjourned in mid-May, resumed in Beijing in late June and continued until December, without any progress having been made.

21 April As many as 50,000 Cambodian refugees cross the border into Thailand. In March and April the Vietnamese forces in Cambodia launched a series of attacks aimed at driving Khmer Rouge forces further west, into the mountains of southwestern Cambodia or to the Thai border. The Vietnamese push caused a massive flow of Khmers into Thailand, a mixture of genuine civilian refugees escaping the heavy fighting and Khmer Rouge troops sheltering from the onslaught. On a single day (21 April) Western reporters watched as some 50,000 Khmers, including 8,000 soldiers, wearily trekked across the Thai border. Thai soldiers drove many back into Cambodia, where some were executed as 'deserters' by oncoming Khmer Rouge units. As the fighting subsided in late June, there were at least 250,000 Cambodians encamped along the border.

20 July A major conference on Indo-Chinese refugees opens in Geneva. The two-day conference was attended by representatives of some 65 countries and of a number of intergovernmental and non-governmental agencies and nine UN programmes and agencies. The conference had been convened by Kurt Waldheim, the UN secretary-general, in an attempt to address the crisis generated by mass emigration from Vietnam.

The flight of refugees (or 'boat people') from Vietnam by sea, which had continued at a steadily increasing rate since 1975, had become a serious international problem by early 1979. The causes of the mass emigration were both economic and political. The majority of refugees who left Vietnam during 1975–7 were middle-class southerners, more often than not with links to the Thieu regime. Many had become seriously disaffected with the new government after being transferred from urban areas to work on the land in the government's 'new economic zones'. By 1978, the middle-class emigrants were joined by an increasing number of peasants and urban workers and thousands of Hoa (ethnic Chinese). The poorer Vietnamese gave worsening food shortages and the desire to escape conscription as their reasons for leaving; the Hoa exodus, however, was caused in part by the abolition of private trade in April 1978, and in part by the growing tension between Vietnam and China. About a quarter-of-a-million northern Hoa fled across the border into China between April 1978 and mid-1979, whilst in the South thousands more escaped by sea (ironically, the refugee traffic was believed to be organized by an international syndicate of Chinese businessmen). The situation had reached crisis proportions in May and June 1979, when boat people were arriving in Southeast Asian countries at the rate of over 50,000 a month. The number of Vietnamese in Hong Kong rose from over 5,000 at the end of 1978 to 65,000 in July 1979.

At the end of the conference, Waldheim announced that the Vietnamese government had agreed to make every effort to halt illegal departures and would co-operate with the UN High Commissioner for Refugees (UNHCR) in expanding the programme for orderly departures. Waldheim also announced that he had received generous commitments in resettlement places and financial contributions; the US alone had contributed 161,000 places and $125 million for the UNHCR's Southeast Asia programme.

8 August The defection of veteran Vietnamese Communist Party member Hoang Van Hoan to China is announced. The official announcement of his arrival in Beijing stated that he had arrived 'recently' and had met Chairman Hua Guofeng and other Chinese leaders. Hoan had been dropped from the party politburo and the central committee in 1976, apparently because of his pro-Beijing stance. He had defected whilst travelling in early July from Vietnam to East Germany for medical treatment. He complained of feeling tired during a stop-over in Pakistan and asked to be allowed to wait for a later flight: he disappeared from his Karachi hotel a few days later. At a press conference in Beijing on 9 August, Hoan asserted that under Le Duan's control, Vietnam was no longer an independent country, but one 'subservient to a foreign power' (the Soviet Union). In June 1980 Hoan was sentenced to death in absentia by the Vietnamese Supreme Court for high treason.

15 August A 'people's revolutionary tribunal' opens in Phnom Penh to try Pol Pot and Ieng Sary on charges of genocide. Pol Pot and Ieng Sary were sentenced to death in absentia after a five-day trial in Phnom Penh presided over by Keo Chanda, the PRK minister of information. The indictment charged them with a long list of crimes which largely tallied with evidence earlier submitted to the UN Human Rights Commission by Western governments. According to the indictments the Khmer Rouge leaders were guilty of: initiating large-scale massacres; displacing the country's population; establishing a system of repression and coercion; conducting terrorism; abolishing all social relationships; abolishing all religious and cultural practices; maltreating children; and sabotaging the national economy.

After the trial, new evidence on Khmer Rouge atrocities continued to come to light. Macabre Nazi-like records found at the infamous Tuol Sleng prison in Phnom Penh showed that of the 14,499 people imprisoned there by the Khmers Rouges, only four had survived. On one single day (15 October 1977), a total of 418 people had been executed. In early 1987 the PRK released figures claiming that 3,314,718 people had died as a result of Khmer Rouge policies. Although this figure was in line with the PRK's past estimates, it was widely regarded as exaggerated. Official population estimates for 1984, of some 7,200,000, suggested that the death toll, above the normal death rate, had probably been under 1 million.

21 September The Khmers Rouges win the confidence of the UN General Assembly. Following a lengthy debate on Cambodian representation at the UN, the General Assembly decided on 21 September that the country should continue to be represented by the Democratic Kampuchea (Khmer Rouge) regime. The decision had been recommended by the assembly's Credentials Committee and was approved by 71 votes to 35 with 34 abstentions. Those voting in favour included China, the US and other Western countries and the ASEAN members. An Indian amendment proposing that the Cambodian seat be left empty was rejected by the assembly. A matter of weeks before the UN debate, the Khmers Rouges had released details of a new 'liberal' political programme in what was widely seen as an attempt to redress their 'genocidal' image. In mid-November the General Assembly passed an ASEAN-proposed resolution calling for 'the immediate withdrawal of all foreign forces' from Cambodia.

17 December A new Khmer Rouge government-in-exile is formed. At the end of a three-day meeting in the Cardamom mountains, the Khmers Rouges announced the formation of a new government. The principal change to the government was the appointment of Khieu Samphan as prime minister in place of Pol Pot, the latter being appointed commander-in-chief of the armed forces. The reshuffle was widely viewed as a cosmetic exercise and another blatant attempt to further the international rehabilitation of the Khmers Rouges.

1 9 8 0

7 February General Giap loses the Defence Ministry during a major reshuffle of the Vietnamese Council of Ministers. General Vo Nguyen Giap, the architect of Vietnam's military victories over France and the US, was replaced as Vietnamese defence minister in the most important government reshuffle since the death of Ho Chi Minh in 1969. Giap, who remained a deputy premier, was replaced by General Van Tien Dung, the army chief-of-staff and a politburo member since 1972. Dung had been responsible for the strategy of the final, victorious North Vietnamese offensive in South Vietnam in 1975. Other members of the 'old guard' removed in the reshuffle included the ailing Nguyen Duy Trinh, who was replaced as foreign minister by Nguyen Co Thach (see biographies), and Le Thanh Nghi, who was replaced as chairman of the State Planning Commission by Nguyen Lam. Nghi's removal was undoubtedly linked to the government's poor economic performance. The appointment of Pham Hung as interior minister in place of Tran Quoc Hoan was unofficially attributed to the security services' failure to check recent pro-Chinese activities.

20 March A decree is published providing for the reintroduction of money into the Cambodian economy. The decree, published by the Phnom Penh government, was introduced in order to encourage private enterprise, and to promote the expansion of agricultural production. Money had been abolished by the Khmer Rouge regime, with wages being paid in food rations. After the establishment of the Heng Samrin regime, trade had been conducted with Dong and Baht (Vietnamese and Thai currency), as well as with gold and rice.

30 March President Ton Duc Thang of Vietnam dies aged 91. Nguyen Huu Tho, a vice-president and a former National Liberation Front (NLF) chairman, replaced President Thang in an acting capacity on 1 April. Thang had held a number of posts in the North Vietnamese government before being elected vice-president in 1960. He succeeded President Ho Chi Minh on the latter's death in 1969.

16 April Amnesty International releases a report on 're-education camps' in Laos. The report by the London-based human rights organization claimed that thousands of members of the former administration arrested in 1975 were still detained in 're-education camps' in northern and eastern Laos. The number of political prisoners was not known, but estimates varied from 10,000 to 40,000. The report claimed that the health of some of the prisoners had seriously deteriorated because of poor diet, lack of medicines and hard labour. In most cases detainees had spent over four years in camps without receiving any family visits, and it was not unusual for a family to spend long periods without receiving any news.

17 June Thailand starts repatriating Cambodian refugees living along the Thai-Cambodian border prompting Vietnamese forces to launch a surprise attack along

142

the boundary and into Thailand. The reintroduction of a policy of 'voluntary repatriation' for Khmer refugees by Thailand was a clear demonstration of the military character of many of the refugee camps based along the Thai-Cambodian border. According to many commentators the repatriation exercise amounted to little more than a bolstering of rebel ranks ahead of the wet-season offensive. It also reflected Thai anxieties over international funding for the camps. The great majority of the 9,000 or so refugees who travelled back into Cambodia in mid-June originated from Sa Kaeo, a camp completely controlled by the Khmers Rouges. Repatriation was only nominally voluntary, the process being overseen by Khmer Rouge cadres and, when the first group reached the border, they were welcomed and led into the interior by Khmer Rouge guerrillas, clad in crisp, new Chinese uniforms.

On 23 June Vietnam retaliated over the repatriations by launching a surprise attack on refugee settlements in the area northeast of Aranyaprathet and Poipet. At one point during the fighting some 300 Vietnamese troops apparently crossed the border into Thailand, occupying three villages and setting up ambushes for Thai troops. The Vietnamese forces then proceeded to seal the border north of Aranyaprathet, halting cross-border relief operations and further repatriations. Thailand immediately lodged a protest with the UN secretary-general over the Vietnamese action and a meeting of Association of South-east Asian Nations (ASEAN) foreign ministers in Kuala Lumpur in late June unanimously denounced Hanoi's 'aggression'. The Vietnamese military action had been launched whilst Hanoi's foreign minister, Nguyen Co Thach, was in Jakarta, concluding six months of hard diplomacy aimed at breaching ASEAN's increasingly fragile unity over Cambodia. The reports of Vietnamese forces rampaging into Thailand completely undermined Thach's efforts, prompting ASEAN 'doves' and 'hawks' to close ranks.

7 July India officially recognizes the Heng Samrin regime in Cambodia. Indira Gandhi's Congress (I) government became the first, and to date only, non-Communist Asian country to recognize the Heng Samrin regime in Phnom Penh. In an address to the Indian parliament on 7 July, P. V. Narasimha Rao, India's minister of external affairs said: 'Cambodia, after all the terrible ordeals which it has had to face, needs all possible assistance from the international community if it is to develop its economy, restore its internal infrastructure and re-establish its status as a sovereign, independent, non-aligned nation.'

18 December The Vietnamese National Assembly unanimously adopts a new Constitution to replace the (1959) North Vietnamese Constitution which had been in force since reunification. The Constitution proclaimed that Vietnam was 'a state of proletarian dictatorship' and that the Communist Party was 'the only force leading the state and society'. The country was in the process of developing 'a new culture with a socialist content and a national party and people's character'. Marxism-Leninism was 'the ideological system guiding the development of Vietnamese society'. Vietnam was 'advancing directly from a society in which small-scale production predominates to socialism, bypassing the stage of capitalist development'. The central task throughout the period of transition to socialism was the industrialization of the country. Vietnamese citizens enjoyed freedom of speech, the press, assembly and association and freedom to demonstrate 'in accordance with the interests of socialism and of the people', but no one might 'misuse democratic freedoms to violate the interests of the state and of the people'. Freedom of worship was guaranteed, but religion might not be misused 'to violate state laws or policies'. The Constitution went on to define the roles of the organs of government, including the National Assembly, the Council of State, the Council of Ministers and the People's Councils. The National Assembly was the highest representative authority and the highest state authority. It had the power to draw up and amend the Constitution, make and amend laws and elect and remove members of other organs. Elected for five years, the assembly met at least twice every year. The Council of State, the Republic's collective presidency, was elected by the assembly from among its members. It performed many of the assembly's tasks when the latter was not in session. Its chairman commanded the armed forces and acted as chairman of the country's National Defence Council.

1 9 8 1

25 February The UN Food and Agriculture Organization releases a report on the food situation in Cambodia. The report warned that while the state of widespread starvation in Cambodia had been overcome, the economy remained in an extremely fragile condition. Without further international assistance, the report concluded, serious malnutrition could quickly return.

Food production in 1980 had been considerably higher than in the previous year, partly as a result of the entry of Soviet bloc know-how. Nevertheless, the yield had not been sufficient to feed the entire population. During 1981 poor weather conditions meant that the food situation again deteriorated. Flooding in the southeastern provinces and drought in the west and southwest meant that Cambodia remained dependent on relief aid during the 1982 rainy season.

26 April A new National Assembly is elected in Vietnam. The election to a 496-member National Assembly were the first to be held since the adoption in 1980 of a new Constitution and electoral law. Official Hanoi radio reported that the turn out of eligible voters had averaged 97.96 per cent nationally. A total of 614 candidates (all of whom had been approved by the Communist Party of Vietnam-(CPV-)dominated Vietnam Fatherland Front) had competed in the election. The composition of the new assembly was described as 100 workers, 92 peasants from collective farms, 49 soldiers, 121 political cadres, 110 socialist intellectuals, 15 democratic notables and representatives of religious groups and nine handicraft workers in co-operatives.

1 May The first elections since Pol Pot's overthrow take place in Cambodia. The election of a Cambodian National Assembly marked the beginning of a new phase in the political development of the People's Republic of Kampuchea (PRK) regime. Only people living in government-controlled areas were allowed to vote in the election, the first to be held since the fall of the Khmer Rouge regime. The 117 seats were contested by 148 candidates, approved by the anti-Pol Pot liberation front (KNUFNS), and according to the official returns, 99.17 per cent of the 3,417,339 electors voted.

26 May The fourth congress of the ruling Kampuchean People's Revolutionary Party (KPRP) opens in Phnom Penh. The Communist Party thereby emerged into full view for the first time since the creation of the PRK in 1979. At the congress, speeches were delivered on the contentious issue of the party's history. Pen Sovan was re-elected as party general secretary, and also elected were a 21-member central committee, an eight-member politburo and a seven-member secretariat.

27 June After the adoption of a new Constitution in Cambodia a Council of State and a Council of Ministers are elected. At its first session since the May elections the National Assembly approved a new Constitution to replace that adopted by the Khmers Rouges in January 1976. The drafting of the new Constitution had started early in 1979 and at least two versions were created before the final document was approved. The final draft had 10 chapters and 93 articles covering the political and economic system, the rights and duties of citizens and the organs of government.

Article 1 cautiously stated that the PRK was 'gradually advancing towards socialism'. The party's task was defined as 'direct leadership of the entire revolutionary task'. Foreign policy objectives included the strengthening of the bonds of 'solidarity, friendship and co-operation with Vietnam, Laos, the Soviet Union and other fraternal socialist countries' and support for 'the struggle waged by the peoples of the world over imperialism, new and old colonialism, Chinese Beijing expansionism, racism and the reactionary forces'. The Constitution declared that the national economy was under state leadership and comprised three sectors: the state-run economy, the collective economy and the family-run economy. The National Assembly was to be elected by general, direct and secret vote for a five-year term. It would meet at least twice a year and laws were to be adopted by an absolute majority and constitutional changes by a two-thirds majority. The functions of the Council of State were similar to those of the Presidium of the Supreme Soviet in the Soviet Union and the Standing Committee of the National People's Congress in China, in that it would effectively assume the duties of the National Assembly when the latter was not in session. The Council of Ministers was 'the government of the PRK; it is the organ governing society directly and which directly takes charge of economic development'.

Having approved the Constitution, the assembly elected a Council of State with Heng Samrin as its chairman (a post equivalent to head of state), Say Phoutang as its vice chairman and Chan Ven as its general secretary. A Council of Ministers was also elected to replace the People's Revolutionary Council which had governed the country since 1979. Pen Sovan, the party general secretary and defence minister, was appointed premier, thereby confirming his position as the dominant figure in the regime.

4 July A 'collective presidency' is elected in Vietnam. The recently-elected National Assembly held its first session from 25 June to 4 July, at the end of which the Council of State or 'collective presidency' was elected. The hardline veteran Truong Chinh was elected as chairman of the council; the four vice-chairmen were Nguyen Huu Tho (who had been acting president of the Republic since the death of President Ton Duc Thang in March 1980), Le Thanh Nghi, General Chu Huy Man and Xuan Thuy.

13 July A UN international conference on Cambodia opens in New York and adopts a resolution calling for the withdrawal of Vietnamese forces. The five-day conference, requested by the UN General Assembly with the aim of finding a comprehensive political settlement to the Cambodian conflict, was attended by representatives of 79 countries and observers from 25 others. Vietnam, Laos, the Soviet Union and its allies, India and some non-aligned countries refused invitations to attend. Cambodia was represented by the Khmer Rouge government; representatives from the Phnom Penh regime were not invited.

The conference adopted a resolution calling for a cease-fire, the withdrawal of foreign (i.e. Vietnamese) troops, free UN-supervised elections and the neutralization of Cambodia. The conference also tacitly accepted China's demand that the Khmers Rouges should not be disarmed, a decision described by the *New York Times* of 18 July as 'remarkable'. Not surprisingly, the Vietnamese and Phnom Penh regimes rejected the resolution out of hand. In a statement reflecting the growing tension within the rebel groups, Prince Sihanouk (who had not attended the conference) said that the resolution could only help the Khmers Rouges seize absolute power one day; the conference, he said, had 'succeeded only in pouring a bit more oil on the fire consuming my country and its people'.

4 December Pen Sovan is ousted as general secretary of the Cambodian Communist party (the KPRP) and is replaced by President Heng Samrin in a move that takes most commentators by surprise. Officials in Phnom Penh claimed that Sovan had been replaced because of illness, but some reports suggested that he had been placed under house arrest in Hanoi; his whereabouts and the reasons for his sudden downfall have never been fully explained. One theory propounded was that Sovan, a Vietnamese-trained revolutionary who had broken with Pol Pot before 1975, had been removed on the orders of the Soviet Union because of his excessive pro-Hanoi stance. Another theory was that Hanoi had removed Sovan in order to prevent him constructing a direct Phnom Penh-Moscow link. Other, less Machiavellian versions cast Sovan as the victim of an internal power struggle.

8 December Laos re-establishes diplomatic relations with France. Diplomatic relations had been severed by the government of Laos in 1978 on the grounds that Paris was pursuing a hostile policy towards it. A Lao official subsequently accused France of colluding with the Central Intelligence Agency (CIA) in plotting to overthrow the government in Vientiane. The government of Laos had also objected to the formation of a Royal Government of Free Laos by Phoui Sananikone and other exiled right-wing politicians in France in late 1978.

Relations between the two countries had improved as a result of the election of Francois Mitterrand as the (socialist) president of France in May 1981. Mitterrand and his Lao counterpart, Souphanouvong, quickly arranged for normalization talks to be held at the UN in New York.

1 9 8 2

27 March The fifth congress of the ruling Vietnamese Communist Party opens in Hanoi; leadership changes approved by delegates include the removal of Vo Nguyen Giap and Nguyen Van Linh (see biographies) from the politburo. The five-day congress was attended by over 1,000 Vietnamese delegates as well as some 30 foreign delegations. The Soviet delegation was led by Mikhail Gorbachev, then a member of the Soviet Communist Party politburo and secretariat. The party general secretary, Le Duan, delivered a largely positive political report to the congress. On the economic front, noteworthy achievements included post-war restoration and continuing efforts on foodstuffs production which had staved off famine in areas heavily affected by natural catastrophes. However, the economy continued to face severe difficulties: the root cause of the problem was that the economy was still one of small production, suffering from colonialism and 30 years of war. The party and government had also made errors in economic leadership and management. The future tasks outlined by Le Duan in his report included the completion of socialist transformation in the southern provinces. He also called for greater efforts to recruit new party members in the South. Solidarity with the Soviet Union and the two fraternal countries of Indo-China was the keystone of Vietnam's foreign policy and would be consolidated and strengthened. A striking feature of the international situation in the early 1980s, Le Duan said, was the collusion of US imperialism with Chinese expansionism. The Chinese government, he claimed, bore full responsibility for tensions in Southeast Asia and had repeatedly turned down Vietnamese proposals for the resumption of talks. Despite Chinese support for the 'Pol Pot clique', Vietnam would continue to support the Cambodian people in their efforts to liberate their country and save the Khmer nation from genocide.

A number of changes in the higher echelons of the party hierarchy were approved at the congress. Outgoing members of the politburo included General Vo Nguyen Giap, Nguyen Duy Trinh and Le Thanh Nghi, three 'old guard' Communists who had relinquished their ministerial posts in early 1980. Other outgoing members included Nguyen Van Linh (the party's future secretary-general), Le Van Luong and Tran Quoc Hoan. New members included General Le Duc Anh, architect of Vietnam's invasion of Cambodia in late 1978 and a deputy defence minister, and Nguyen Co Thach, the foreign minister, as an alternate member.

27 April A month after the Vietnamese Communist Party congress the third congress of the ruling Lao People's Revolutionary Party (LPRP) opens in Laos. The four-day congress, the first since 1972, was held in Vientiane and was attended by almost 230 delegates. A new and enlarged 49-member central committee was elected, and the central committee in turn re-elected Kaysone Phomvihane as general secretary and re-elected its politburo unchanged. In the early months of 1982 there had been some speculation that Kaysone might come under pressure at the congress to relinquish the premiership (a post he held in addition to the general secretaryship); however, in the event the congress probably served to consolidate his dominant position, with a number of his close associates being elected onto the central committee. In his political report,

Kaysone emphasized that the transition to socialism in Laos would be a gradual affair and he acknowledged that the party, in its impatience, had sometimes resorted to coercion in the past. This, he said, had had negative effects on economic and social life.

22 June A Khmer Rouge-dominated Cambodian resistance movement, the Coalition Government of Democratic Kampuchea (CGDK), is finally created. After lengthy and intricate negotiations the three rebel Cambodian factions, united only in their opposition to Vietnam's military presence in their country, reached an agreement on the formation of an exile CGDK. The agreement, signed in Kuala Lumpur, provided for Prince Sihanouk to be president of the CGDK, with Khieu Samphan of the Khmers Rouges as vice-president in charge of foreign affairs, and Son Sann (Khmer People's National Liberation Front – KPNLF) as prime minister.

Mutual distrust among the three factions had permeated the discussions, but, faced with defeat on the battlefield and under increasing pressure from the Association of Southeast Asian Nations (ASEAN) states to present a united front, antagonisms were set aside. The eventual compromise (very much an eleventh-hour affair with respect to the Khmers Rouges and the KPNLF) was also necessitated, from the Khmer Rouge standpoint, by waning international support as more and more dreadful details emerged of the outrages perpetrated by the Pol Pot government. For the KPNLF and the Sihanoukists, membership of a recognized government offered the prospect of increased access to foreign assistance, without which they would be unable to match the Chinese-armed Khmers Rouges. The Vietnamese government responded to the creation of the CGDK (which it described as 'a monster created by Chinese expansionism and US imperialism') by launching a fresh diplomatic initiative aimed at the ASEAN countries. In what appeared to be a show of contempt for the military potential of the CGDK, Vietnam announced in early July that it planned to withdraw some of its troops from Cambodia.

18 August General Phoumi Nosavan announces the formation of an anti-Communist and anti-Vietnamese 'Royal Lao Democratic Government'. General Phoumi (the former right-wing deputy premier who had fled into exile after an abortive coup attempt in 1965) made the announcement in Bangkok. He claimed that his forces had recently been co-operating with the Khmers Rouges in order to drive the Vietnamese out of Laos. Most other prominent Lao exile dissidents (including Sisouk Na Champassak and General Vang Pao) dissociated themselves from Phoumi's initiative and the general died, foiled in his aim, in late 1985.

25 October The UN General Assembly continues to accept the credentials of the Democratic Kampuchea (Khmers Rouges) government. As in previous years, the assembly Credentials Committee accepted letters of accreditation presented by the 156 UN member countries (including Democratic Kampuchea). The assembly voted by 90 votes to 29 with 26 abstentions to reject an amendment proposed by Laos under which the committee's report would have been approved 'except with regard to the credentials of Democratic Kampuchea'. The Lao amendment embodied the so-called 'empty chair' principle, whereas in previous years Vietnam had tried to secure the admission of the Phnom Penh government in place of Democratic Kampuchea.

13 November The Vietnam veterans' memorial is dedicated in Washington DC seven years after the Vietnam War ended. The dedication was made at the start of a four-day programme of events, entitled a 'national salute to Vietnam veterans'. The memorial, cut into Washington's Constitution Gardens, consisted of two walls of shiny black granite forming a wide V-shape. The names of the 57,939 US combatants who died in the war are inscribed in chronological order, starting with Major Dale Buis, killed on 8 July 1959, and ending with Lieutenant Richard Geer, who died on 15 May 1975. However, some veterans' groups complained that the monument lacked the prominence of Washington's other war memorials, and thereby reflected government and society's shame over the war.

27 November An ex-US serviceman crosses into Laos in search of servicemen missing in action (MIAs). Lieutenant Colonel James 'Bo' Gritz, a retired Green Beret special forces officer and a decorated Vietnam War veteran, led a group of US mercenaries and Lao guerrillas from Thailand into Laos for this purpose. Gritz's raiding party was ambushed and he was forced to retreat. However, he apparently organized another raid in February 1983 after which he claimed to have found some evidence that US POWs were still being held in Laos. Gritz later admitted to a US House of Representatives sub-committee that he did not in fact possess any solid evidence to prove his assumptions. The question of official US involvement in the raids arose after Gritz claimed that the Central Intelligence Agency (CIA) and the Federal Bureau of Investigation (FBI) had provided him with funding and information; both organizations denied the allegations. Reports in the US press alleged that Gritz had received some funding for his raids from the film stars Clint Eastwood and William Shatner.

1 March China outlines a five-part plan for a Cambodian settlement. According to some reports the plan had previously been submitted to the Soviet Union during bilateral talks in October 1982. The plan envisaged: (i) Hanoi making a commitment to withdraw unconditionally its forces from Cambodia; (ii) a cessation of Soviet support for Vietnamese 'aggression'; (iii) the resumption of Sino-Vietnamese normalization talks after the initiation of a withdrawal programme; (iv) the Cambodian people settling their own internal affairs after the completion of the withdrawal programme; (v) international commitments to refrain from future interference in Cambodian affairs and to respect the outcome of UN-sponsored elections.

7 March The Malaysian and Vietnamese foreign ministers hold a round of unofficial talks, prompting early, but ultimately false, speculation of a breakthrough on Cambodia. The foreign ministers of Malaysia and Vietnam, Tan Sri Haji Muhammad Ghazali bin Shafie and Nguyen Co Thach, held informal talks during the seventh Non-Aligned Summit in New Delhi held between 7 and 12 March. During the talks Tan Sri Ghazali proposed that Vietnam and Laos should meet with the Association of Southeast Asian Nations (ASEAN) countries to discuss Cambodia. The Malaysian suggestion was apparently accepted by Thach, a decision described by Tan Sri Ghazali as 'a significant breakthrough'. However, the planned meeting met with strong opposition from Thailand, which described Thach's acceptance as 'a trick'. The Thais appeared to win the day at the annual meeting of ASEAN foreign ministers in Bangkok in late March, at which the possibility of Vietnamese-ASEAN talks failed even to make the agenda.

1 April Vietnamese forces attack rebel positions along the Thai-Cambodian border. Thailand alleged that Vietnamese forces had shelled the Thai-Cambodian border during mopping-up operations around a vanquished Khmer Rouge stronghold at Pnom Chat. The exchange lasted for several hours and according to Thai sources over 30 Khmer refugees died in the barrage. Thai military officials also reported that Vietnamese soldiers had crossed into Thai territory twice during the assault. Another report said that Thai troops fought hand-to-hand battles with Vietnamese intruders on 3 April and the next day Thai fighter-bombers struck at Vietnamese positions some 25 miles (40 kilometres) north of the key border town of Aranyaprathet. For their part, the Vietnamese Foreign Ministry denied that its forces had penetrated Thai territory, but admitted that 'Vietnamese volunteer troops' had helped Cambodian regulars in attacking Khmer Rouge positions.

2 May For the first time Western journalists witness a partial withdrawal of Vietnamese troops from Cambodia. The first partial withdrawal of Vietnamese forces from Cambodia in 1982 had not been seen by journalists. According to Vietnamese and Cambodian claims as many as 10,000 soldiers were withdrawn; journalists, however, claimed to have observed only 1,000 troops at a leaving parade in Phnom Penh. The official *People's Daily* newspaper in China ridiculed the withdrawal in its 3 May edition, describing it as 'another act in a big swindle' and called for UN supervision of a complete withdrawal.

23 July Prince Sihanouk alleges that 'hundreds of thousands of Vietnamese colonists' have settled in Cambodia. Coalition Government of Democratic Kampuchea (CGDK) President Norodom Sihanouk delivered the message in a speech in Paris. There was a serious danger, the prince continued, that 'in a few years we shall have to deal with millions of Vietnamese colonists who will turn [Cambodia] into a new South Vietnam'. The Vietnamese embassy in Paris refuted Sihanouk's allegations, claiming that although some 500,000 Vietnamese had lived in Cambodia before 1970, the number who had returned after 1979 was insignificant. The embassy estimated that only 30,000 Vietnamese currently lived in Cambodia.

17 August A group of alleged coup plotters are convicted and sentenced to prison in Vietnam. Over 30 men were convicted in August of plotting a coup attempt against the Vietnamese government. The plot, which was alleged to have been hatched near Ho Chi Minh City and with the backing of China, was the first to be officially reported since reunification. Two of the plotters were sentenced to death, both reportedly former South Vietnamese soldiers and Cao Daists; the other plotters received jail sentences.

24 September Laos and Thailand establish a communication link. Laos and Thailand agreed to set up a 'hot-line' to help facilitate consultations between them and prevent possible border disputes erupting. According to Thai officials the agreement envisaged the establishment of direct communication links between Vientiane and the Thai border town of Nong Khai.

21 December A UN High Commissioner for Refugees (UNHCR) report claims that the number of 'boat people' fleeing Vietnam has declined to its lowest level. The UNHCR reported that only 30,000 Vietnamese boat people had successfully made the journey to countries of first asylum during 1983, a decrease of 10,000 over 1982. The organization attributed the fall to increased security measures in Vietnam, 'compassion fatigue' in the West and the expansion of the Orderly Departure Programme, under which some 20,000 Vietnamese were allowed to leave in 1983, compared with only 2,000 in 1979.

1 9 8 4

10 January Prince Souvanna Phouma dies in the Lao capital, Vientiane, aged 83 (see biographies). Along with his half brother Souphanouvong, Souvanna was amongst the most influential of twentieth-century Lao politicians. As leader of the so-called 'neutralists' he served as the country's prime minister for a large part of the period 1951–75. Throughout his premiership he strove to bring together the warring rightist and leftist forces battling for control of the country, but as the fighting became emeshed in the wider regional conflict during the 1960s he directed his efforts towards the task of maintaining Laos' precarious independence. Following the victory of his half brother's leftist forces in 1975 Souvanna had remained in Laos, ostensibly to serve the new regime as an 'adviser'.

27 January The Khmer Rouge attack Vietnam's main military and logistic supply centre in Cambodia. Khmer Rouge forces claimed to have struck a significant blow against their Vietnamese adversaries with a successful assault on the centre at Siem Reap which served forces on the Thai frontier. Khmer Rouge units stormed Siem Reap (situated just north of the Tonle Sap) and held it overnight, reportedly killing at least 50 Vietnamese soldiers during the attack and destroying numerous military installations. Western diplomatic sources said that while the rebel claims were usually inflated, intelligence sources in Bangkok and US military satellites had confirmed that a raid had taken place on military installations in Siem Reap's eastern outskirts. According to these reports, there appeared to have been a significant escalation in the level of rebel activities, including some instances of military co-operation between the three resistance factions.

2 April Chinese forces launch a shelling campaign against Vietnam. Tension along the Sino-Vietnamese border increased significantly during the early months of 1984. China's cross-border shelling campaign reportedly escalated into the most prolonged and serious bout of border fighting between the two countries since China's punitive invasion of Vietnam in early 1979. In the period to the end of April both sides claimed that border clashes had continued almost daily with heavy losses being inflicted on enemy troops, although neither side reported serious casualties. Vietnam alleged in early May that an offensive by three Chinese regiments against Ha Tuyen province had been repelled with more than 100 Chinese troops killed or wounded. Major clashes continued until July, culminating in a 10-hour battle on 12 July on the border of Ha Tuyen. The escalation in fighting coincided with the dry-season offensive by Vietnamese forces in Cambodia against Chinese-backed rebels; a Vietnamese Foreign Ministry statement on 4 April accused China of a 'calculated act aimed at putting pressure on Vietnam from two sides'.

7 May Chemical companies agree to establish a fund for US victims of the Agent Orange herbicide used by the US forces in Indo-China. In an out-of-court settlement, seven US chemical companies agreed to establish a US $180-million fund to compensate US Vietnam veterans claiming health damage from exposure to the herbicide Agent Orange. Veterans alleged that the chemical had produced cancers, birth defects in their children and other illnesses. The agreement was reached a matter of hours before legal proceedings on behalf of an estimated 50,000 veterans were scheduled to begin. Although they established the fund, the chemical companies continued to deny any liability in the matter. They claimed that if servicemen were injured, then the US government should be liable; under US law, however, servicemen were prevented from suing the government for war-related injuries.

During the Vietnam War approximately 44 million litres of Agent Orange (in addition to 20 million litres of Agent White and Agent Blue) were sprayed by US forces over 1.7 million hectares of cropland, forests and wooded area in South Vietnam in order to defoliate large areas of enemy operation. The US 'ecocide' in southern Vietnam has had a lasting impact on the country's agricultural development, with vast tracts of land still barren in the late 1980s. In addition, many Vietnamese women have histories of repeated miscarriages as a result of direct exposure to Agent Orange, while others have given birth to physically or mentally handicapped children.

6 June Lao troops are driven from three disputed villages by Thai forces, starting a border dispute that carries on into the late 1980s. The dispute over the sovereignty of three villages on the northern section of the Lao-Thai border (west of the Mekong) broke out in April 1984, although the entire border, which consisted of the Mekong itself for half its length, had been the scene of periodic border incidents since Communist victory in Laos in 1975. According to Bangkok, Lao forces occupied the three villages in April to prevent Thai construction of a road. On 6 June Thai forces took control of the three villages, with little apparent Lao opposition. However, in a series of radio broadcasts in late June the Lao government blamed the 'encroachment' on 'ultra-rightist reactionaries in the Thai ruling circles' and linked the episode to Chinese incursions into northern Vietnam in late April. Talks between the two sides took place in July and August, but it was not until October that Thailand withdrew its troops from the villages, maintaining a presence on high ground in the vicinity.

18 November Vietnamese troops launch the first attack of their dry-season offensive against Cambodian rebels on the Thai-Cambodian border. The 1984–5 dry-season offensive against the Cambodian rebel forces was the heaviest undertaken by the Vietnamese army and their Phnom Penh allies. By April 1985 almost all of the main rebel bases along the Thai-Cambodian border had been overrun. The opening Vietnamese thrust occurred on 18 November when some 2,000 troops stormed the Khmer People's National Liberation Front (KPNLF) camp at Nong Chan, north of Sisiphon. KPNLF forces were not driven from the camp entirely until April 1985, by which time the Vietnamese had successfully dislodged almost all rebel bases from the border area and were actively consolidating their position by mining ahead of the oncoming rainy season. Other KPNLF camps which fell after the onslaught on Nong Chan included Baksei, Sok Sann and Nong Samek in December; the group's Ampil headquarters in early January; and Sanror Changan and Dong Rak in early March. The Khmers Rouges were driven from their camps at Nam Yun and Chong Bok in early January and the next month as many as 18,000 Vietnamese troops succeeded in forcing Pol Pot's fighters out of their stronghold in the mountains of Phnom Malai. In early March the Sihanoukist base of Tatum was overrun.

1 9 8 5

14 January The Cambodian National Assembly elect Hun Sen, the country's young foreign minister, as chairman of the Council of Ministers (premier). The appointment of Hun Sen as premier capped the meteoric rise of the former Khmer Rouge unit commander. He replaced Chan Si who had died in a Moscow hospital on 31 December 1984, after three years in office.

17 June The Communist Party of Vietnam (CPV) approves a far-reaching package of economic reforms. Economic reforms introduced at the end of an eight-day party plenum were described by Hanoi radio as reflecting 'a drastic and far-reaching reorientation in our party's position and policies'. Food subsidies for state and party workers and for members of the armed forces were abolished. Economic planning by central administrative order was to be replaced by a system of pricing determined by 'socialist economic accounting and business' and of wage levels determined by productivity and by the cost of living (a new wage structure introduced three months after the plenum linked payment to efficiency and productivity).

16 August Vietnam announces a target date of 1990 for the complete withdrawal of its forces from Cambodia. Indo-Chinese foreign ministers meeting in Phnom Penh announced that it had been decided to conclude the withdrawal of Vietnamese 'volunteer' forces from Cambodia by late 1990. Vietnam had previously posited 1995 as an estimated date for the withdrawal of its soldiers from Cambodia. Hun Sen, the Cambodian Premier, told reporters at the end of the meeting that the primary reason for the withdrawal announcement had been the success of the 1984–5 dry-season offensive against rebel forces. In late August, Prince Sihanouk described the withdrawal announcement as 'pure propaganda' and claimed that by 1990 as many as 1 million Vietnamese would have been settled in Cambodia.

1 September Pol Pot 'retires' as military leader of the Khmer Rouge forces. The Khmer Rouge clandestine radio, Vonadk, announced that the Supreme Military Commission of the Khmers Rouges had been abolished and that its chairman, Pol Pot, had retired upon reaching the age of 60 to take up a position as the director of the Higher Institute for National Defence. The report stated that Pol Pot's retirement meant that Son Sen became the commander-in-chief of the Khmer Rouge forces with Khieu Samphan as Khmer Rouge president. The announcement of the change of leadership within the Khmers Rouges was welcomed by China and the Association of Southeast Asian Nations (ASEAN) countries, all of whom claimed that it removed a serious obstacle to peace talks. The Phnom Penh government and Vietnam had consistently called for the 'elimination' of the 'Pol Pot clique' as a precondition for national reconciliation. However, the leadership change was described by *Nhan Dan* (the official organ of the Vietnamese Communist Party) as a 'cheap deceitful trick' played by 'a genocidal criminal'. Hanoi's assessment appeared to be treated with some sympathy by many Western diplomats who greeted news of Pol Pot's 'retirement' with great scepticism.

12 October The Cambodian Communist Party's fifth congress opens in Phnom Penh. The four-day congress re-elected Heng Samrin as party general secretary and doubled the size of the central committee to 45 members: five new politburo and three new secretariat members were elected. During his address to the congress, Heng Samrin announced details of the country's first five-year plan (1986–90) and outlined a number of shortcomings in economic development and party organization. He also spoke at length on the country's state of 'sporadic war'.

The country's first five-year plan was to concentrate on four 'economic spearheads': food supplies, rubber, timber and aquatic products. 'Export and thrift' were the primary economic guidelines, and the existence of a mixed economy was a means of 'mitigating the weaknesses of the state-run sector' and was an 'objective reality of history'.

17 November Former Cambodian leader Lon Nol dies in exile. Lon Nol, president of Cambodia in the early 1970s and one of the country's most influential post-independence figures died in the US at the age of 72. Already prime minister from 1969, he took effective power in Cambodia by means of a coup against Prince Sihanouk in March 1970. He served as president of the Khmer Republic from March 1972 until April 1975 when he was overthrown by the Khmers Rouges.

17 March The Cambodian resistance issue their so-called 'eight-point proposal' which is subsequently codified as the group's national charter. Prince Sihanouk outlined the proposal from Beijing, a proposition that was to serve as the Coalition Government of Democratic Kampuchea's (CGDK's) diplomatic bench-mark over the following three years. In September 1986 the proposal was codified as the (CGDK's) national charter. The proposal called for the phased withdrawal of Vietnamese forces from Cambodia, with a UN-monitored cease-fire during the period of its execution. Negotiations would then be held between the Khmer factions leading to free elections and the possible formation of a quadripartite coalition comprising Phnom Penh and CGDK officials. The proposal was quickly rejected by Vietnam and Phnom Penh, the latter claiming that the object of the plan was to cover up rebel military losses.

10 July Le Duan, the general secretary of the Communist Party of Vietnam (CPV), dies at the age of 79 and is succeeded four days later by veteran Communist, Truong Chinh (see biographies). After the death of Ho Chi Minh in 1969 Le Duan had emerged as probably the most powerful member of Vietnam's 'collective leadership'. Following reunification in 1976 Le Duan was instrumental in Vietnam's pursuance of a strong pro-Soviet line.

29 October The ageing Souphanouvong is replaced as president of Laos. Souphanouvong, the 'Red Prince', resigned the presidency after suffering a stroke in September. He had been appointed president of the newly-proclaimed Lao People's Democratic Republic (LPDR) in December 1975. He was replaced, on an acting basis, by Deputy Prime Minister Phoumi Vongvichit.

13 November The fourth congress of the ruling Lao Communist Party opens. The three-day congress was held in Vientiane and was attended by over 300 delegates representing the party membership of 44,000. The general secretary, Kaysone Phomvihane, delivered a critical political report to the assembled delegates, accusing some party leaders of adopting a 'lifestyle of chieftainship' and charging others with 'laziness' and 'conservatism'. In a reference to economic reforms introduced in 1986, Kaysone claimed that the 'bureaucratically centralized ... state management system' was gradually being replaced by a 'socialist business accounting system' in which enterprises were required to make a profit and managers had freedom to set prices and salaries. Kaysone was re-elected party general secretary and five new politburo members were elected. A number of the 'old guard' on the central committee were replaced by younger provincial party leaders and military officers.

15 December The sixth congress of the ruling CPV opens and after three days leading reformist Nguyen Van Linh is elected as the new general secretary. Truong Chinh, the party general secretary since the death of Le Duan in July 1986, delivered a harshly critical political report at the start of the four-day congress in Hanoi. Truong Chinh told the assembled delegates that the Vietnamese people had lost faith in the party and government because of the poor state of the socio-economic situation. He listed a catalogue of targets which had not been met and bluntly related the devastating social impact of the party's economic mismanagement. Responsibility for the crucial mistakes, he said, rested primarily with the party central committee, politburo and secretariat and the Council of Ministers. Truong Chinh outlined some basic economic and social guidelines for the late 1980s: manpower and money would be targeted at grain and foodstuffs, consumer and export goods; the importance of the 'private capitalist economy' had to be recognized and 'bureaucratism' had to be eliminated.

On 17 December Truong Chinh and two other veteran Communist stalwarts, Pham Van Dong and Le Duc Tho, resigned all their party posts, remaining only as party 'advisers'. The following day the results of the elections to the top party posts were announced, including that of the reformist Nguyen Van Linh as the new general secretary (see biographies). The new politburo members included Major-General Mai Chi Tho, Le Duc Tho's brother and a colleague of Nguyen Van Linh during the latter's secretaryship in Ho Chi Minh City. Outgoing politburo members included General Van Tien Dung, who was removed as defence minister two months later.

1 9 8 7

5 January Serious armed clashes erupt on the Sino-Vietnamese border. Three days of heavy fighting between troops stationed on the border in Ha Tuyen province (Vietnam) and Yunnan province (China) erupted on 5 January (hostilities had broken out in the same area in October 1986). Both sides claimed that the other had instigated the battle, which, according to claims from Hanoi, resulted in the death of over 1,500 Chinese soldiers. The Chinese side claimed that 500 Vietnamese troops had been killed or wounded in the fighting and rejected Vietnamese battle-dead claims as 'sheer boasting'.

1–9 April The Communist Party of Vietnam (CPV) approves another package of economic reforms. At a plenary meeting held in Hanoi, the CPV central committee approved a wide-ranging programme of measures aimed at stimulating the struggling Vietnamese economy. Amongst other things, the plenum called for increased cash incentives for farmers and workers, an end to official intolerance of capitalist methods and a reduced reliance on central planning. Party leader Nguyen Van Linh delivered a forthright speech to the meeting, in which he said that 'never before has inflation worsened so fast, prices increased so unexpectedly, and the lives of wage earners and members of the armed forces become so much more difficult as last year [1986]'.

19 April Elections are held to the Vietnamese National Assembly. Vietnamese voters were offered the choice of 829 candidates for 496 seats in the eighth National Assembly; at the election of the seventh assembly in 1981, the seats were contested by only 614 candidates. As on previous occasions, all the candidates were approved by the Communist-dominated Vietnam Fatherland Front; however, the lists had been drawn up after public selection meetings, where contenders had faced questions and criticism. The changes to the election process were part of the widespread reforms introduced after the CPV's sixth congress held in late 1986.

3 June Amnesty International release a report detailing human rights abuses carried out by the Phnom Penh government. The international human rights organization Amnesty International claimed in its report that thousands of political prisoners had been detained without trial and tortured in Cambodia since the Heng Samrin regime had taken power in 1979. Amnesty also expressed concern over alleged acts of brutality practised by the Khmers Rouges in refugee camps under their control.

18 June Pham Hung is appointed as the new Vietnamese premier. Deputy Premier Pham Hung (74), the second-ranked politburo member and a former Viet Cong leader replaced Pham Van Dong. Dong, aged 81 and in fading health, had been premier of Vietnam since 1976 and of North Vietnam since 1955. The appointment of Hung, who was not a noted supporter of economic and political reform, was widely seen as a transitional move and was in keeping with a strong Confucian tradition of respect for seniority. Hung's appointment was ratified by the National Assembly, which also approved the appointment of Vo Chi Cong, hitherto a deputy premier, as president of the State Council ('collective presidency') in place of the veteran hardliner, Truong Chinh. Cong, a leading reformist, had been widely tipped to replace Dong as premier and his appointment to the less powerful presidency was seen as a slight setback for the party leader Nguyen Van Linh.

1 August General John Vessey, the special envoy of US President Reagan, arrives in Hanoi at the start of an important three-day visit. General Vessey, a former chief-of-staff, was the highest US official to visit Vietnam since 1977, when US President Carter had dispatched his envoy Leonard Woodcock to Hanoi. The general's visit marked a significant step towards the improvement of US-Vietnamese relations. A statement issued at the end of the visit said that 'detailed, candid and constructive talks' had taken place between Vessey and Nguyen Co Thach, the Vietnamese foreign minister. Specific measures were agreed upon to accelerate progress towards accounting for US servicemen missing in action (MIAs) in Vietnam and to address 'certain humanitarian concerns of Vietnam'. Both sides agreed that such issues 'should not be linked to broader political questions such as normalization or to economic aid'. Vessey's visit was followed by a visit to Hanoi in late August by three US medical experts, two of whom were specialists in orthopaedic rehabilitation (according to some estimates there were as many as 60,000 amputees in Vietnam as a result of the war).

13 September Former South Vietnamese officials are released from re-education camps. Close to 7,000 prisoners held in re-education camps since 1975 were released to mark Vietnam's National Day (2 September). Among those freed were Lieutenant-General Nguyen Huu Co (a former South Vietnamese vice-premier and defence minister) and nine other South Vietnamese generals.

2–4 December A meeting between Hun Sen and Norodom Sihanouk in France marks the first substantive negotiations between the opposing Cambodian factions. After years of diplomatic stalemate on the Cambodian civil war, the talks represented a breakthrough of sorts. The meeting, held at the prince's residence in Fere-en-Tardenois, France, resulted in little more than an agreement to hold further talks.

23 December A report on the state of the Vietnamese economy is delivered to the National Assembly. General Vo Van Kiet, chairman of the State Planning Commission, delivered a highly critical report on the state of the Vietnamese economy to the National Assembly in which he described the country's socio-economic situation as 'continually worsening'. General Kiet's assessment was particularly galling for the leadership given that a series of wide-ranging economic reforms had been introduced during 1987. According to the report agricultural development was torpid and whilst industrial production was increasing, quality was generally poor. General Kiet went on to say that the country's population growth rate was dangerously high, that unemployment was a growing problem and that the living conditions of the working people and the armed forces were 'very difficult' and even 'serious' in some areas.

1 9 8 8

20–21 January Further talks take place in France between Hun Sen and Norodom Sihanouk. The two leaders of the two opposing Cambodian factions met again in France a month after holding their first round of talks. After the meeting Hun Sen told reporters that he and the prince were in broad agreement on the question of the political structure of a post-settlement Cambodia. Both had agreed that a coalition quadripartite government should be created. However, disagreement had arisen over the timing of the establishment of such a government in relation to the holding of a general election: Hun Sen favoured elections followed by the formation of a government, Sihanouk the reverse.

19 February A cease-fire becomes effective after two months of heavy fighting along a disputed section of Laos' border with Thailand. The signing of a cease-fire agreement in Bangkok on 17 February by the Lao and Thai army chiefs followed three months of fighting that, on occasions, had threatened to escalate into a major conflict. Events leading up to the dispute began in May 1987 when Laos accused Thailand of massing troops in an area near the northern land border (where the western Lao province of Sayaboury met the northern Thai province of Phitsanuloke) to protect illegal logging activities. The territory under dispute covered some 31 square miles (80 square kilometres) and was made up mostly of forest-covered hills. In mid-December Thai fighter-planes bombed the area with the aim of clearing the region of Lao troops. From this point on, fighting between Lao and Thai forces began in earnest, and according to some reports as many as 700 soldiers died battling for the territory. Lao soldiers were still positioned in the disputed region when the cease-fire agreement was signed, a detail that led some commentators to suggest that the Thai forces had performed badly against their numerically weaker Lao counterparts.

10 March Vietnam's premier, Pham Hung, dies. Pham Hung, a leading 'old guard' revolutionary, died in Hanoi after a sudden heart attack (see biographies). He was replaced, in an acting capacity, on 11 March by Vice-Premier General Vo Van Kiet.

14 March The Sino-Vietnamese 'Spratly Islands dispute' re-emerges as a source of tension. Propaganda exchanges between Vietnam and China over sovereignty of the Spratly Islands escalated into fighting in mid-March with each country accusing the other of attacking its ships in the disputed archipelago. The Chinese Foreign Ministry protested to Vietnam's embassy in Beijing on 14 March, claiming that Vietnamese armed vessels had that day 'outrageously launched armed attacks on Chinese ships conducting regular surveying operations' so that the Chinese vessels had been 'forced' to fire back in defence. On the same day

158

the Vietnamese Foreign Ministry issued a statement which claimed that Chinese warships had, that morning, 'flagrantly opened fire on two Vietnamese cargo vessels', and that 'our vessels had been forced to open fire in self defence'.

16 June The Hong Kong government begins screening all incoming Vietnamese 'boat people'. An increased influx of Vietnamese boat people in the first five months of 1988 (some 5,000 more or eight times as many as in the same period of 1987) and a reduction in the rate of resettlement prompted the Hong Kong authorities to introduce a 'screening' or Refugee Determination Procedure (RDP) to differentiate 'genuine refugees' from 'economic migrants'. The former (i.e. those with a well-founded fear of persecution for political, ethnic or religious reasons) would qualify for resettlement in other countries, the latter would await repatriation to Vietnam.

22 June Do Muoi is elected by the National Assembly as the new Vietnamese premier. Do Muoi was the third-ranking politburo member (see biographies). He replaced General Vo Van Kiet, who had been appointed acting premier in March 1988 following the death of Pham Hung. Do Muoi's election as premier was particularly noteworthy in that reformist National Assembly deputies openly challenged his selection as the party central committee's sole candidate and proposed instead that Vo Van Kiet be elected to the post. In the event Do Muoi won the election, securing 64 per cent of the assembly's vote. Commentators noted, however, that 36 per cent of the deputies were therefore prepared to vote 'against' the party's wishes.

25 July The first face-to-face talks between all the Cambodian factions open in Indonesia. The first meeting between representatives of the four warring Cambodian factions was held in Indonesia between 25 and 28 July. The gathering, designated the 'Jakarta Informal Meeting' (JIM 1), was attended by Hun Sen, Prince Sihanouk, Son Sann, Khieu Samphan and representatives of certain 'interested parties', including Vietnam, Laos and the Association of Southeast Asian Nations (ASEAN) countries. Sihanouk attended the meeting in a private capacity, having resigned the Coalition Government of Democratic Kampuchea (CGDK) presidency in early July in an apparent attempt to isolate the Khmers Rouges.

At the meeting the CGDK proposed a three-stage process of Vietnamese withdrawal: during stage two, the Phnom Penh government would be dismantled and replaced by a four-party coalition headed by Sihanouk, with elections following in stage three. Phnom Penh rejected the stage two proposal, and suggested instead the creation of a Sihanouk-headed 'national reconciliation council'. Hun Sen also linked the withdrawal of Vietnamese forces from Cambodia to the cessation of Chinese military aid to the Khmers Rouges.

30 September The veteran Vietnamese Communist leader Truong Chinh dies, aged 80, following an accident in his Hanoi home (see biographies). A leading Communist for six decades, Truong Chinh represented the hardline pro-Chinese wing of the Vietnamese revolution. During the 1950s he had been the leading force behind the party's controversial land-reform movement. However, in 1956 he was removed from the party's leadership on account of the campaign's 'excesses'. He never regained his former commanding role in the party and throughout the Vietnam War and the trials of reunification he was forced to play second fiddle to the pro-Soviet Le Duan.

3 November The UN General Assembly adopts a radically revised resolution on Cambodia. It contained a number of significant revisions over earlier versions. As previously, the ASEAN-sponsored resolution called for the withdrawal of 'all foreign forces' from Cambodia. However, the new text also called for 'the creation of an interim administrating authority' to govern the country in the period between a troop withdrawal and free elections. Another change, which led some commentators to characterize the new resolution as an attack by ASEAN upon the Khmers Rouges, affirmed that there could be 'no return to universally condemned policies and practices of a recent past' in Cambodia.

1 9 8 9

19 February The second Indonesian-sponsored meeting of rival Cambodian factions opens in Jakarta, but the delegates fail to achieve a breakthrough in the search for a peaceful settlement. Diplomatic efforts to negotiate a settlement to the Cambodian conflict, which had gained impetus in January 1989 with a series of bilateral talks between the chief regional protagonists, appeared to founder in late February when the second Indonesian-sponsored meeting known as the 'Jakarta Informal Meeting' (JIM 2) of all Cambodian factions and other 'interested parties' made little progress on the key issues. Ali Alatas, the Indonesian foreign minister and JIM 2 chair, introduced a working paper at preparatory talks which attempted to strike a compromise between the opposing factions on the elections issue. The Alatas proposal allowed for both the Phnom Penh government and the Coalition Government of Democratic Kampuchea (CGDK) to continue to function while elections were held for a new Cambodian assembly. He also presented a series of options for an international control mechanism to supervise the Vietnamese troop withdrawal, the cease-fire and elections. However, opposing Cambodian officials refused to make the concessions necessary to forge any meaningful agreement. As the talks progressed to full ministerial level, it became obvious that the rival factions had actually hardened their respective positions on the two most intractable issues: the formation of a provisional quadripartite government and the composition and size of the proposed control mechanism. Despite the lack of real progress at the talks, a 'consensus statement' was issued at the close which allowed for further negotiations towards a comprehensive settlement.

2 March A group of 75 Vietnamese 'boat people' are flown from Hong Kong to Hanoi, thereby becoming the first Vietnamese refugees to return voluntarily to their country of origin. The flight to Hanoi was conducted under the auspices of the UN High Commission for Refugees (UNHCR), which had a special budget of some $360,000 set aside for transport and resettlement. Upon their arrival the refugees were informed by the Vietnamese Interior Ministry that they would not be punished but would face a stiff prison sentence if they attempted to leave the country illegally on a second occasion. All but one of the group of 75 had arrived in Hong Kong after June 1988, when the territory's policy of differentiation between 'genuine' and 'economic' refugees came into effect.

Less than two weeks after the first voluntary repatriations had taken place, the Association of Southeast Asian Nations (ASEAN) countries announced their decision to follow Hong Kong's example and begin screening genuine political refugees from those fleeing Vietnam for economic reasons; only members of the former group would be eligible for automatic resettlement in third countries.

26 March Laos holds its first national elections since Communist victory and the formation of the Lao People's Democratic Republic (LPDR) in 1975. Representatives were elected to the Supreme People's Assembly (SPA). District- and provincial-level elections had been held in June and November 1988. A total of 79 candidates (70 per cent of whom were members of the ruling Communist party) were elected for an unspecified term from a list of 121 candidates. Some 1,800,000 people (less than 50 per cent of the population) were eligible to vote, and on polling day Vientiane home service reported a high turn out.

5 April Vietnam sets a firm deadline for a full troop withdrawal from Cambodia. In a dramatic turnaround, a joint statement was issued by the three Indo-Chinese governments announcing that all Vietnamese volunteer troops would be withdrawn from Cambodia by the end of September 1989, regardless of whether or not a political solution to the conflict had been found. Vietnam had previously stipulated that its troops would return home in September only if foreign military aid to the Cambodian rebels was halted. The six ASEAN countries, along with the US and other Western nations, responded to the statement with cautious optimism. CGDK President Sihanouk, however, was dismissive, declaring that he 'diametrically rejected all decisions, conditions and agreements on Cambodia, made by Vietnam, Laos and the foreign lackey Phnom Penh regime'.

15–18 May The Cambodia issue is raised at the Sino-Soviet summit in Beijing. The feverish pace of diplomatic activity relating to Cambodia in early 1989 was largely in anticipation of the mid-May visit to China by the Soviet leader, Mikhail Gorbachev. Soviet troop withdrawals from Afghanistan and Mongolia during the first months of 1989 meant that only the Cambodian problem remained as an 'obstacle' to Sino-Soviet normalization. However, in the event, Gorbachev's visit was completely overshadowed by massive pro-democracy student demonstrations in Beijing. The protests had started in April after the death of the former reformist Communist party general secretary, Hu Yaobang, and eventually ended in early June with the Tiananmen Square massacre. Nevertheless, Cambodia was discussed by Gorbachev and Deng Xiaoping, although no new agreement was reached. Soviet Foreign Minister Shevardnadze and his Chinese counterpart, Qian Qichen, continued discussions on Cambodia, with both sides reaffirming their commitment to a joint nine-point statement issued in February, whereby the two sides had effectively agreed to disagree on the issue.

13–14 June The question of the Vietnamese 'boat people' dominates a UN conference on Indo-Chinese refugees. Ten years after the holding of the first Geneva conference on refugees, the UN secretary-general convened a second conference aimed, primarily, at finding a solution to the growing problem of the Vietnamese boat people in Hong Kong. The conference adopted by consensus a Comprehensive Action Plan (CAP) which, controversially, recognized the possibility of the compulsory repatriation of 'economic migrants' from Hong

Kong if efforts to secure their voluntary return proved unsuccessful. However, the US, Vietnam, the Soviet Union and the UN itself all expressed serious reservations about compulsory repatriation.

28 July US and Vietnamese officials sign an agreement on the resettlement of former South Vietnamese officials. After two days of talks in Hanoi between Vietnamese and US officials an agreement was reached on a plan to resettle former officials of the South Vietnamese regime in the US. Most former South Vietnamese officials underwent varying periods of 're-education' after the Vietnam War ended in 1975; over 12,500 former officials were released from 're-education camps' between September 1987 and August 1988.

30 August The month-long Paris international conference on Cambodia ends in stalemate. Months of intense diplomatic activity culminated in the convening of a 32-day international conference on Cambodia in Paris in late July. After a promising start the conference ended in stalemate, with delegates deeply divided over the issue of the inclusion of the Khmers Rouges in any future Cambodian government. Prince Sihanouk and his supporters insisted that the civil war in Cambodia would be prolonged if the Khmers Rouges were isolated. Hun Sen, and his Vietnamese supporters, maintained that the current Khmer Rouge leadership had no role to play in any future Cambodian regime. According to some commentators, Hun Sen's refusal to compromise on this central issue derived from a growing confidence on the part of Phnom Penh and Hanoi in the Cambodian government's ability to withstand a rebel onslaught after the Vietnamese withdrawal in September.

26 September Vietnam completes its troop withdrawal from Cambodia bringing to an end Hanoi's contentious 10-year commitment to its war-torn western neighbour. Prior to the withdrawal, the Vietnamese Defence Ministry announced that approximately 23,000 Vietnamese soldiers had died during fighting in Cambodia since 1979 and a further 55,000 had been wounded.

The departure of the Soviet-financed volunteer force had long been demanded by China and the West, but occurring less than a month after the collapse of the international Paris conference on Cambodia, the Vietnamese pull-out only increased the uncertainty surrounding Cambodia's future. The virtual collapse of the Paris conference meant that no international supervision mechanism had been established to verify the Vietnamese withdrawal; despite Western military assertions to the contrary, both China and Thailand issued statements after the withdrawal alleging that Vietnamese soldiers remained in Cambodia.

12 October The Lao leader ends his first visit to China in over 13 years. Kaysone Phomvihane paid an eight-day visit to China for talks with, amongst others, Deng Xiaoping and Li Peng. Kaysone had last visited China in 1976. Three years later relations between the two neighbours deteriorated when Laos sided with Vietnam in the Sino-Vietnamese conflict. Sino-Lao relations started to improve in 1986, but it was not until August 1989 that party-to-party relations were restored after a 10-year break.

22 October Khmer Rouge guerrillas score a major victory, capturing the strategic western town of Pailin less than a month after the withdrawal of Vietnamese troops from Cambodia. Pailin, situated in Battambang province close to the Thai-Cambodian border, had been under attack by the Khmers Rouges since April 1989, and by September Phnom Penh forces had lost control of most of the area around the town.

12 December The Hong Kong authorities carry out the first involuntary repatriation of Vietnamese 'boat people'. A group of 51 boat people became the first to be forcibly repatriated to Vietnam, prompting widespread international condemnation, particularly from the US government. The group, the majority of whom were women or children, were among the 7,500 boat people already screened out by the authorities as 'economic migrants'. The Vietnamese government had apparently confirmed on 11 December (the day before the operation) that an agreement on involuntary repatriation had been reached with Britain, under which Hanoi would receive over $30,000 from the Hong Kong and British governments in payment for the repatriation. However, in late January 1990, Vietnam joined with the US in opposing further involuntary repatriations, thereby paralysing British efforts to win international approval for its policy.

1 9 9 0

26 February The third Indonesian-sponsored informal meeting of the warring Cambodian factions opens in Jakarta. The meeting was primarily concerned with a new Australian peace plan which proposed a large-scale UN involvement in Cambodia. The plan was received favourably at the UN Security Council in January and February.

Despite the apparent progress at the UN, the third Jakarta informal meeting (JIM 3) ended early on 1 March after the Cambodian factions disagreed on the wording of a final communique. A major source of disagreement was Khmer Rouge objections to demands by the Phnom Penh government and Vietnamese delegation that a sentence be included in the final statement referring to the 'non-return of the genocidal policies and practices of the Pol Pot regime'.

28 March Tran Xuan Bach, a leading reformist, is expelled from the Communist Party of Vietnam (CPV) politburo at the end of an 'extremely vigorous' 15-day plenum. The plenum was reportedly one of the stormiest in the party's history. Before the plenum Bach had publicly demanded political reforms, and had only just refrained from advocating full multi-party democracy; a possibility which the plenum rejected, and in a reference to the collapse of Communism in Eastern Europe, it warned that socialism was experiencing 'a difficult period' which 'imperialists and reactionaries' sought to exploit. Economic liberalization undertaken since 1986 would be possible, it suggested only with 'political stability'.

4 June The draft text of the first Lao People's Democratic Republic (LPDR) Constitution is published. A Constitution-drafting committee had been in operation since the formation of the LPDR in 1975, but had made little progress during its first decade. The draft eventually consisted of 73 articles covering the political, legal and socio-economic system and the rights and obligations of Lao citizens. Following its publication in *Pasason*, the ruling Lao People's Revolutionary Party daily, a campaign was launched for discussion of the draft prior to its promulgation. However as of early 1991 the Supreme People's Assembly had not yet promulgated the new Constitution.

18 July US Secretary of State James Baker announces a major shift in US foreign policy towards Cambodia and Vietnam. After talks with his Soviet counterpart Eduard Shevardnadze in Paris, Baker announced that the US would no longer support the seating of the rebel Coalition Government of Democratic Kampuchea (CGDK) at the UN, unless the Khmers Rouges were removed from the coalition. Baker also announced that the US would enter into a direct dialogue with Vietnam over the issue of Cambodia and that the US might be prepared to provide humanitarian aid to the Phnom Penh government.

The Bush administration's policy change was partly designed to forestall a potential congressional rebellion over the issue. Concern in Congress over US support for the Cambodian resistance had grown during 1990 as reports indicated that a Khmer Rouge military victory was possible. Many congressmen were openly appalled at the prospect of the Khmers Rouges regaining power with the help of US overt and covert aid. At the same time, the deterioration in Sino-US relations in the aftermath of the 1989 Tiananmen Square massacre and the improvement in US-Soviet relations during 1990 had added further impetus for a US policy revision on Indo-China.

9 August A session of the Cambodian National Assembly ends in Phnom Penh after approving a recent leadership purge, including the dismissal of high-ranking officials Ung Phan, the communications minister, and Chheng Phon, the information minister. The dismissals followed an apparent power struggle in Phnom Penh in June and July during which a hardline faction led by Chea Sim, president of the National Assembly and a second-ranking member of the ruling Kampuchean People's Revolutionary Party (KPRP) politburo, had gained ground against the liberal faction associated with Premier Hun Sen.

28 August The five permanent members of the UN Security Council agree on a Cambodian peace plan. At their sixth meeting on Cambodia in 1990 they agreed for the first time on all aspects of a framework for ending the Cambodian civil war. The so-called 'P-5' plan demanded establishment of a 12-member Supreme National Council (SNC) composed of Cambodian leaders from all factions. The SNC, whilst occupying Cambodia's UN seat, would turn over most of its powers to the UN itself until the election of a new Cambodian government. The plan also called for an initial cease-fire followed by phased disarmament and for the halt of military supplies to the warring factions.

4 September A secret two-day Sino-Vietnamese summit ends in China. Discussions centred on Cambodia, the main issue blocking Sino-Vietnamese normalization. The Vietnamese delegation included Nguyen Van Linh, Do Muoi and Pham Van Dong. The Chinese side included Jiag Zemin, general secretary of the Chinese Communist Party (CCP) and Li Peng, the Chinese premier.

After the meeting relations between the two countries appeared to improve. On 16 September the Chinese government opened its southern border with Vietnam at the 'Friendship Pass' in order to allow Vietnamese athletes to travel to the Asian

Games in Beijing. General Giap crossed the 'Pass' on 18 September, to attend the Games and he arrived in Beijing the next day, the first high-ranking Vietnamese official to visit China since CPV general secretary Le Duan had visited in the late 1970s.

10 September The opposing Cambodian factions approve the 'P-5' peace plan at a meeting in Jakarta. Delegates to the fourth Jakarta informal meeting (JIM 4) accepted the UN Security Council ('P-5') framework in its entirety and committed themselves to placing it within a comprehensive political settlement at a future meeting of the Paris International Conference on Cambodia. The parties also agreed on the formation of a 12-member SNC, to embody Cambodian 'independence, sovereignty and unity' and to occupy the Cambodian UN seat during the transitional period before UN-supervised elections.

The members of the SNC were: (Phnom Penh government) Hun Sen, General Tea Banh, General Sin Song, Kong Samol, Hor Nam Hong and Chem Snguon; (Khmers Rouges) Khieu Samphan and Son Sen; (Khmer People's National Liberation Front) Son Sann and Leng Muli; (Sihanoukists) Norodom Ranaridh and Chau Sen Kosal.

17 September The ruling KPRP appoints Hor Nam Hong (hitherto minister assistant of Foreign and Judicial Affairs) Cambodian foreign minister in place of Premier Hun Sen.

19 September The first meeting of the Cambodian SNC, convened in the disused Cambodian embassy in Bangkok, breaks down after two days. The main stumbling block was the appointment of an SNC Chair. The rebel factions had wanted Prince Sihanouk as Chair and '13th member', an option that was unacceptable to the Phnom Penh government which claimed that this would provide the rebels with a 'seven to six' advantage.

The SNC eventually convened again in Paris in late December, with no agreement on the Chair arrangement. A final statement released after the talks stated that there had been 'concurrence' on the most of the fundamental points of the UN peace plan. However, a number of sticking points remained, including the Phnom Penh government's continued insistence that the plan should explicitly refer to Khmer Rouge 'genocide'.

29 September Nguyen Co Thach and US Secretary of State Baker meet in New York. The meeting came in the aftermath of the major shift in US policy towards Indo-China announced by Baker in July it constituted the highest level contact between Vietnam and the US since the end of the Vietnam War. The two sides discussed Cambodia and the issue of US personnel reported missing in action (MIA) in the Vietnam War. A US State Department official described the meeting as 'a step in the direction of normalization of relations'. Despite the improvement in US-Vietnamese relations, the US had, prior to the meeting, extended for a year an economic embargo against Vietnam. The Vietnamese were keen to see the embargo lifted in order to pave the way for a resumption of International Monetary Fund lending.

3 October General Phoune Sipaseuth meets with his US counterpart, Secretary of State Baker, at the UN in New York. The short meeting constituted the highest level contact between Laos and the US since 1975. Talks centred on the issue of some 530 US servicemen reported MIA in Laos during the Vietnam War. Phoune and Baker also discussed methods of co-operating to reduce opium cultivation and refining in Laos.

13 October Le Duc Tho, a veteran leader of the CPV, dies of cancer in Hanoi, aged 79. Tho gained international prominence for his secret negotiations with Henry Kissinger in the early 1970s which led to the signing of the 1973 Paris peace agreements. At the CPV's sixth congress in 1986 Tho formally resigned from his party posts, but he continued to play an influential role as a central committee 'adviser'.

17 October The normalization of Vietnamese-US relations is furthered with the visit to Washington of Vietnam's foreign minister, Nguyen Co Thach. Thach's visit followed his meeting with US Secretary of State Baker at the UN in New York. It marked the first official visit to the US capital by a high-ranking Vietnamese official since the end of the Vietnam War. Thach held talks with General John Vessey, President Bush's special envoy dealing with MIAs in Indo-China, and they agreed to establish a permanent US office in Hanoi to gather information about MIAs.

26 November The CPV central committee adopts a new 'Draft Platform on Socialist Construction for the Transitional Period' at the end of a plenary meeting. The document was the party's second political platform, the first having been adopted at the time of the foundation of the Indo-Chinese Communist Party (the CPV's forerunner) in 1930. The plenum also adopted a 'draft strategy for socio-economic stabilization and development up to the year 2000'. The platform and socio-economic strategy were published after the plenum for public consultation before submission to the party's seventh national congress, scheduled for mid-1991.

The platform predicted that despite the virtual collapse of the Communist system in Eastern Europe during 1989–90, 'socialism will recover its vitality, and. . . will finally score a victory'. The party had made a number of errors in the past: it had taken too much time on the initial state of the transitional period to socialism and had made 'many mistakes' in reforming prices, wages and money and in ideological and organizational tasks. But, despite such errors the leadership of the party remained the 'decisive factor for all victories of the Vietnamese revolution'. Vietnam would remain in the 'period of transition to socialism' for a further 'two or three five-year plans'. By the end of this stage, social productivity and economic efficiency will have increased at least two-fold compared to the present day.

d'Argenlieu, Georges Thierry
Born 1884 – Died 1964

D'Argenlieu served as a naval officer in World War I, but left the armed forces in 1932 and entered a Carmelite monastery. After seven years he had risen to general of the French Carmelite Order. He rejoined the French navy in 1939, escaped to England in 1940, and was subsequently appointed by de Gaulle to command the Free French Navy. At the end of the war in 1945 d'Argenlieu was appointed high commissioner for Indo-China, a post he held for just under two years. He took a rigid Gaullist vision of France's colonial future in Indo-China and acted, with great success, to frustrate any agreement between the Viet Minh and Paris. After leaving Indo-China in March 1947, d'Argenlieu re-entered the Carmelite order.

Bao Dai
Born 1913

Bao Dai was born the only son of the Emperor Khai-Dinh and at the age of nine he was sent to school in France. In 1925 Khai-Dinh died and Bao Dai returned to Hue to be crowned as the new emperor, but he soon returned to Paris to finish his education. He returned to Vietnam in 1932 with reformist intentions, but it quickly became obvious that he lacked the determination to initiate any real changes. He co-operated with the Vichy French and the Japanese during World War II, and in March 1945, upon Tokyo's orders, he abrogated Annam's French protectorate treaty and proclaimed independence. Five months later he abdicated his throne in the aftermath of the Viet Minh's August Revolution. He fled to Hong Kong in early 1946, and the following year he entered into negotiations with the French government. After two years of negotiation Bao Dai signed an agreement with President Auriol of France which provided for the creation of a State of Vietnam within the French Union. The agreement was obviously rejected by Ho Chi Minh's Democratic Republic of Vietnam (DRV) regime, but in mid-1949 Bao Dai returned to Vietnam at the head of his own French-, and US-, backed government. Following the French defeat at Dien Bien Phu and the 1954 Geneva accords, the US effectively discarded Bao Dai in favour of his prime minister, Ngo Dinh Diem. The change-over was completed in October 1955, when Diem defeated Bao Dai in a referendum and then declared a Republic with himself as president. Bao Dai, and a number of his supporters, left Vietnam for France. In 1979 he published an autobiographical work entitled *Le Dragon d'Annam*.

Do Muoi
Born 1911

Born in northern Vietnam, Do Muoi joined the Indo-Chinese Communist Party (ICP) in 1939, and, like so many other Vietnamese revolutionaries, he was imprisoned by the French in the early 1940s. After the defeat of the French in 1954 he served for a short time as party chief in Haiphong. During the 1950s and 1960s he served in the North Vietnamese government, heading the Internal Trade Ministry before taking charge of state pricing policy. He was appointed as a deputy premier in 1969 and concurrently held the construction portfolio until 1977 and the capital construction, industry, communication and transport portfolios until 1982. In 1976 he was elected as an alternate politburo member and was promoted to full membership at the party's fifth congress in 1982. He took on the premiership in July 1988, taking to the post a reputation as an economic conservative.

Duong Van Minh
Born 1916
Duong Van Minh (also known as 'Big Minh' because of his great height) entered the French army at the age of 24, was commissioned two years later and fought against the Japanese. In 1952 he transferred to the Vietnamese army and, after conducting successful campaigns against the Binh Xuyen and Hoa Hao from 1955 to 1956, he was promoted to chief of the field command in 1959. His popularity within the army and his close contacts with American circles aroused the suspicions of President Ngo Dinh Diem, and his command was abolished in 1962; he received, instead, the honorary position of military adviser to the president. The following November he led a successful coup against Diem and became chief-of-state. The new regime was a short-lived one, and Minh himself was ousted from power in January 1964, although he formally remained as chief-of-state until October. He subsequently spent some time in exile in Thailand until being permitted to return to Saigon in late 1968 by President Thieu. In 1971 he was nominated to stand against Thieu for the presidency as a 'peace candidate' but eventually withdrew in protest against alleged intimidation by the government. Minh took over the South Vietnamese presidency in late April 1975, only days before the final Communist assault on Saigon. Although he had contacts within the Communist camp, his belief that he could negotiate a final settlement proved illusory and on 30 April he surrendered to the North Vietnamese. Minh was the only senior South Vietnamese general to remain in his native land. He underwent 're-education' and was permitted to emigrate to France in 1983.

Heng Samrin
Born 1934
Samrin was born into a peasant family in Kompong Cham. He took up the revolutionary cause in the late 1950s and fled into the countryside at the time of the 1967 Samlaut rebellion. Along with his future colleague Hun Sen, Samrin received military training in the Eastern Zone during the early 1970s. After the Khmer Rouge victory in 1975, he stayed in the Eastern Zone and by 1978 he was one of the zone's highest ranking military officials. In mid-1978 Samrin fled to neighbouring Vietnam after Pol Pot's forces had set about viciously purging the Eastern Zone. The Vietnamese chose him to lead the anti-Pol Pot liberation front (KNUFNS) which was established on the Vietnam-Cambodia border in late 1978. Samrin and his supporters accompanied the Vietnamese army in its victorious assault on Phnom Penh in late 1978, and he was appointed head of the pro-Hanoi People's Republic of Kampuchea (PRK) government established in early 1979. In mid-1981 a new Constitution was adopted and Samrin became chairman of the Council of State (head of state). A few months later he replaced the ousted Pen Sovan as general secretary of the ruling Kampuchean People's Revolutionary Party (KPRP). Since the mid-1980s Samrin appears to have been partly eclipsed as Cambodia's dominant political figure by the youthful Prime

Minister Hun Sen. However, the secretive nature of Cambodian politics renders it futile to guess at the true extent of Samrin's power and of his relations with Hun Sen and other leading figures.

Ho Chi Minh
Born 19 May 1890 – Died 3 September 1969

Ho Chi Minh was born as Nguyen Sinh Cung in the central Vietnamese province of Nghe An. He received his secondary education in Hue, but in 1911 he sailed for Europe as galley boy aboard a French ship. He visited the US during World War I, but subsequently returned to France and emerged as the Vietnamese spokesman at the 1919 Versailles peace conference. In 1920 he became a founder member of the French Communist Party and two years later he attended the Comintern congress in Moscow, where he met Lenin, Trotsky and other leaders of the Russian Revolution. In 1930, having returned to the Far East, he founded the Indo-Chinese Communist Party (ICP). That year he was involved in a peasant rebellion in Vietnam and was sentenced to death in absentia by the French authorities. Little is known of his movements in the middle and late 1930s, but in 1941 he formed an ICP-dominated political unit which was later to become widely known as the Viet Minh; during World War II the Viet Minh, with US support, harried the Japanese forces throughout Indo-China. It was in this period that he formally adopted the name of Ho Chi Minh (literally, 'Ho the seeker of enlightenment').

Ho proclaimed Vietnam's independence from France in 1945, and then fought the French for nine years, finally defeating them at Dien Bien Phu in 1954. He was president of the Democratic Republic of Vietnam (DRV – North Vietnam) until his death in September 1969; he also held the post of Communist Party chairman and, for a short period in the mid-1950s, the country's premiership. Following his death in 1969, a collective leadership emerged (including Le Duan, Pham Van Dong and Vo Nguyen Giap) which successfully continued Ho's struggle to defeat the US and its South Vietnamese allies and reunite Vietnam.

Hun Sen
Born 1951

Hun Sen was born in pre-independent Cambodia and in the mid-1970s he served as a Khmer Rouge unit commander in the country's Eastern Zone administration, under the command of such figures as So Phim and Heng Samrin. Hun Sen apparently crossed the border into Vietnam months before Pol Pot launched a full-scale assault against 'internal reactionaries' in the Eastern Zone in early 1978. Consequently, he was one of the founder members of the anti-Pol Pot liberation front (KNUFNS), elements of which fought alongside the Vietnamese forces in their rout of the Khmers Rouges in early 1979.

At the tender age of 28, Hun Sen took on the demanding role of foreign minister in the new pro-Vietnamese regime founded in the wake of Pol Pot's deposition. In May 1981 his position was enhanced by election to the party politburo and secretariat. He was elected premier in early 1985 and he appears to have subsequently further consolidated his position within the government and party hierarchy. By the late 1980s Hun Sen had won widespread international recognition as an accomplished negotiator.

Ieng Sary

Born 1930

Sary was born in South Vietnam of mixed Khmer and Chinese parentage. He attended school in Phnom Penh in the early 1940s and towards the end of the decade he went to study in Paris, where he established a Marxist Circle of Khmer students, the members of which came to dominate Cambodian politics during the 1970s. It was within the circle that Sary first developed his close association with Saloth Sar (Pol Pot) and Son Sen and his future wife, Khieu Thirith. He returned to Cambodia to teach in 1957 and immediately became heavily involved in Communist activities in Phnom Penh. In 1962 his friend Saloth Sar manoeuvred himself into the post of Communist Party general secretary and Sary was elected to the politburo. The following year, both Sary and Sar left their teaching jobs in Phnom Penh and disappeared into the countryside, eventually establishing a power base in northeastern Cambodia. In 1971 Sary moved to Beijing where he quickly established Khmer Rouge authority over the Sihanouk-led Cambodian government-in-exile.

Sary was appointed deputy prime minister with responsibility for foreign affairs in the Khmer Rouge government formed in Phnom Penh in 1975. He remained loyal to Pol Pot (and, more importantly, Pol Pot remained loyal to him) during the three years or more of Khmer Rouge rule. After the toppling of the Khmer Rouge regime by Vietnam in early 1979, Sary retained his cabinet posts in the exiled government. However, he took responsibility for economy and finance in the tripartite rebel coalition, the Coalition Government of Democratic Kampuchea (CGDK) formed in 1982. Soon after their overthrow in 1979, both Sary and Pol Pot were sentenced to death in absentia by the new Cambodian government after being found guilty of numerous crimes against the Khmer people.

Johnson, Lyndon Baines

Born 27 August 1908 – Died 22 January 1973

Johnson was born in Stonewall, Texas. He took a degree and taught for a while in Houston before going to Washington in 1931 as secretary to a Texan congressman. A strong supporter of President Roosevelt's 'New Deal' he first entered the House of Representatives as a Democrat in 1937. After the Japanese attack on Pearl Harbor he entered the US Navy and was subsequently decorated for gallantry. In 1948 he was elected to the Senate as a senator for Texas, and was re-elected in 1954 and 1960. It was at the start of his third term as a senator that Johnson was chosen as John Kennedy's running-mate in the 1960 presidential elections. Kennedy narrowly defeated the Republican candidate Richard Nixon, and Johnson was sworn in as vice-president in early November. In May 1961 Johnson made an extensive tour of the Far East and Southeast Asia, after which he recommended an increase in military and economic aid to the Diem regime in South Vietnam.

In November 1963 Johnson was sworn in as US president, a matter of hours after the assassination of President Kennedy in Dallas. A year later, he was elected president, easily defeating the Republican candidate, Barry Goldwater. A few months before the election, the US Congress had passed the Tongkin Gulf Resolution which conferred extraordinary powers on Johnson to act in Southeast Asia and served as the main legal basis for US escalation of the Vietnam War. Under Johnson, US forces in Vietnam rose from less than 20,000 to over 500,000;

at the same time he initiated a programme of sustained bombing of North Vietnam in early 1965 in order to compel Hanoi into accepting a negotiated settlement. The ploy failed, domestic opposition to the war increased and in March 1968 Johnson announced that he would not be running for re-election later that year; he was replaced by Richard Nixon. Johnson died on the day before the Paris peace agreement on Vietnam was initialled by Henry Kissinger and Le Duc Tho in 1973.

Kaysone Phomvihane
Born 1920

Kaysone was born in the southern Lao province of Savannakhet, the son of a Lao mother and a Vietnamese father. In the early 1940s he entered the University of Hanoi to study law. He became involved in Viet Minh activities and in 1945 was dispatched back to Laos to liaise with Lao nationalist groups. He refused to join the Lao Issara government of 1945–6, but in 1950 he was appointed as minister of defence (and subsequently as commander-in-chief) in Souphanouvong's Pathet Lao resistance government. In March 1955 the Communist Lao People's Party (the forerunner of the Lao People's Revolutionary Party – LPRP) was founded with Kaysone as its general secretary; the following January he was appointed as vice-president of the party's front organization, the Lao Patriotic Front. Kaysone visited Vientiane in the late 1950s, but subsequently returned to Pathet Lao territory until the final stages of Communist victory in 1975. Upon his return to Vientiane, he was appointed chairman of the Council of Ministers, a post he held still in 1990. At the fourth congress of the LPRP held in late 1986 Kaysone was re-elected as party general secretary.

Khieu Samphan
Born 1932

Khieu Samphan, the son of a Cambodian judge, attended school in Phnom Penh. In the early 1950s he went to university in Paris and became a member of the Marxist Circle of radical Khmer students, led by Ieng Sary and other future members of the ruling elite. Samphan's doctoral thesis (entitled 'Cambodia's Economy and Industrial Development') was completed in 1959 and contained many of the fundamental principles of what became the Khmer Rouge government's social and economic policy. After completing his dissertation Samphan returned to Phnom Penh where he founded a left-wing journal. In 1962 he was elected to the National Assembly (one of a group of leftists enticed into Prince Sihanouk's Sangkum movement) and was appointed as secretary of state for commerce. The following year Prince Sihanouk abandoned his brief sponsorship of the intellectual left, and Samphan was forced to resign from the cabinet. Eventually, in 1967 he and other Sangkum leftists fled Phnom Penh to join the Khmers Rouges fearing a government crackdown in the aftermath of the Samlaut peasant rebellion. In 1970 he was appointed as defence minister and deputy premier in the newly-created Beijing-based revolutionary government. In the aftermath of the Khmer Rouge victory in 1975, Samphan was appointed as head of state of Democratic Kampuchea (DK). In late 1979 he replaced Pol Pot as premier of the ousted DK regime, but most commentators regarded his apparent promotion as a largely cosmetic exercise designed to boost the international appeal of the reviled Khmers Rouges. In 1982 he was appointed as vice-president with charge of foreign affairs in the Cambodian tripartite exiled coalition government.

Throughout the 1980s Samphan has constituted the public face of the highly secretive Khmers Rouges leadership.

Kissinger, Henry
Born 27 May 1923

Kissinger was born of Jewish parentage in Bavaria and at the age of 15 he and his family fled Nazi Germany for the US. He graduated from high school in New York City and entered the US Army where he served as an interrogator in counter-intelligence in Europe. He administered a district in Hesse during the first years of the post-war occupation of Germany, after which he won a US government scholarship to Harvard. Although he graduated with top honours and an award for his doctoral dissertation in 1954, he was initially denied tenure at Harvard and he took a post at the Council on Foreign Relations in New York. He established himself as a major defence specialist in 1957 with the publication of his first book, *Nuclear Weapons and Foreign Policy*, which rejected the doctrine of 'massive nuclear retaliation' in favour of a more flexible 'limited nuclear response'. This book was followed in 1961 by *The Necessity For Choice* and in 1965 by *The Troubled Partnership*, a study of the North Atlantic Treaty Organization (NATO).

During the 1960s Kissinger acted as an adviser for Nelson Rockefeller, campaigning for the New York governor in the Republican conventions of 1964 (when he lost to Barry Goldwater) and 1968 (when he lost to Richard Nixon). On the eve of the 1968 convention, Kissinger described Nixon as 'the most dangerous' of all the candidates; three months later, Kissinger accepted president-elect Nixon's offer to become his national security adviser. It was in this capacity that Kissinger conducted the secret talks in Paris with Le Duc Tho which began in 1970 and resulted ultimately in the agreement, reached in January 1973, to end the war in Vietnam. Kissinger also travelled to Moscow and Beijing for secret talks with Brezhnev and Zhou Enlai, which paved the way for Nixon's historic visits in 1972 and for the resultant detente in US relations with the Soviet Union and China. In September 1973 Nixon appointed Kissinger as secretary of state, a position he continued to hold under President Ford (he relinquished his position as national security adviser in late 1975). Kissinger was replaced as secretary of state by Cyrus Vance at the start of the Carter administration in early 1977. After leaving government Kissinger formed a highly successful consultancy firm (Kissinger Associates Inc.). He is currently one of the most popular speakers on the US lecture circuit and remains in close contact with many world leaders, meeting with, amongst others, Mikhail Gorbachev and Deng Xiaoping during 1989.

Lansdale, Edward
Born 1908

Lansdale was born in Detroit and he graduated from the University of California during the 1930s. He served with the Office of Strategic Services (OSS, the forerunner of the Central Intelligence Agency – CIA) during World War II, and afterwards he worked as an adviser for the government of the Philippines, helping to suppress the Communist-led 'Huk' rebellion and establishing his reputation as an expert in counter-guerrilla warfare. In 1954 he was posted to South Vietnam as head of a secret CIA team directed to wage 'political-psychological warfare' against the 'enemy'. He played a major role in helping his friend Ngo Dinh Diem defeat his non-Communist opponents and gain power in Saigon in 1955. The following year he was reassigned to the Pentagon where he took charge of special operations; in the early 1960s he advised the Kennedy team on the use of 'unconventional warfare resources in Southeast Asia'. Lansdale officially retired from the CIA in 1963, but he returned to Saigon two years later in a loosely-defined advisory role to US Ambassador Lodge. He returned to the US in 1968. In his novel *The Quiet American* Graham Greene depicts Lansdale as Saigon-based US official Alden Pyle.

de Lattre de Tassigny, Jean
Born 1989 – Died 1952
De Lattre was born in France in the late nineteenth century and passed out of St Cyr Military Academy in 1910. He commanded an infantry battalion during World War I and, despite serious injury, he went on to play a major role in the liberation of his homeland in World War II. It was General de Lattre who signed, on behalf of France, the German surrender in Berlin in May 1945. After the war he served as commander-in-chief of Western Union Land Forces under Field-Marshal Montgomery. In late 1950 he was appointed to the dual position of high commissioner and commander-in-chief in Indo-China at a time when the French military position, and the morale of the troops, had seriously deteriorated after recent devastating Viet Minh successes along the Sino-Vietnamese border. The arrival of de Lattre, a genuine French national hero, did much to restore morale and improve the fighting efficiency of the French forces. He introduced new military tactics which resulted in important successes against Giap's troops during 1951. De Lattre fell ill in late 1951 and returned to Paris. He died of cancer in early 1952, being notified of his promotion to marshal of France only hours before his death.

Leclerc, Jacques-Philippe
Born 1902 – Died 1947
Leclerc was born in France as the Vicomte Philippe de Hautecloque. An unknown officer at the outbreak of World War II, he became one of the war's most brilliant commanders. Initially, he operated with great success in North Africa, but in 1944 he travelled to Britain to organize the French Second Armoured Division, which landed in Normandy in early August 1944 and liberated Paris later that month. After the war, General Leclerc was appointed as commander-in-chief in Indo-China, serving under High Commissioner Admiral d'Argenlieu. Upon his arrival in Saigon in October 1945, Leclerc launched an immediate military assault on the Viet Minh, and within five months he was claiming victory in the south. It soon became obvious that any French optimism was misplaced, and Leclerc began to recognize the need for a diplomatic settlement of the conflict. In early 1947 he was replaced in Indo-China after he had refused the combined posts of commander-in-chief and high commissioner on the grounds that no French government would give him the 500,000 troops he considered necessary for a military victory. He was appointed as inspector general for North Africa and died in an air crash in Algeria in 1947.

Le Duan
Born 1907 – Died 10 July 1986
Born in the central province of Binh Tri Thien, Le Duan became politically active during the 1920s while working for the Vietnam Railway Company and in 1928 joined the Vietnamese Revolutionary Youth League. He was one of the

211 charter members of the Indo-Chinese Communist Party (ICP) founded by Ho Chi Minh in 1930. He was imprisoned by the French from 1931 to 1936 and again from 1941 to 1945. Among his cell mates were many future Communist leaders, including Pham Hung, Pham Van Dong and Truong Chinh.

Following the August Revolution of 1945 Ho assigned Le Duan to organize anti-French resistance and party organization in the south. Whilst serving in the south he was elected to the party politburo at the second congress in 1951. After Geneva and partition in 1954 he took control of all political and military activities in the Southern Zone. After Truong Chinh's removal as party secretary-general in 1957, Le Duan was summoned back to Hanoi to work within the party secretariat. Whilst in Hanoi, he began to press for North Vietnamese military intervention in the South, a policy formally adopted in early 1959 against the wishes of Truong Chinh and General Giap. Le Duan was elected general secretary at the third party congress held in 1960 and subsequently operated as Ho Chi Minh's number 2 until the latter's death in 1969. After Ho's death Le Duan gradually emerged as the most powerful figure within a government which worked under an operational code of collective leadership. His experience in the South strengthened his position within the party hierarchy after the formal reunification of Vietnam in 1976 and at the party's fourth congress held that year he was re-elected as general secretary. By 1985 Le Duan had fallen ill and early in 1986 he went to Moscow for medical treatment. Upon his return he reportedly relinquished his duties to other high-ranking (and equally elderly) figures, including Truong Chinh and Pham Van Dong. Le Duan died in 1986.

Le Duc Tho
Born 10 October 1911 – Died 13 October 1990
Le Duc Tho was born as Phan Dinh Khai in northern Vietnam. He was a founder member of the Indo-Chinese Communist Party (ICP) in 1930 and was imprisoned by the French authorities, along with other future Communist leaders, for most of the 1930s. He escaped to China in 1940 and helped found the Viet Minh the following year. He participated in the August Revolution in 1945 and the next year he accompanied Pham Van Dong to Paris for talks with the French government. In the early 1950s he was dispatched to the South, but after a few years he returned to Hanoi and to a place in the politburo. In 1960 he was appointed to the secretariat (in charge of ideology and organization), a post that he was fully occupied with until 1968 when he was nominated as a 'special adviser' to the North Vietnamese delegation at the Paris peace talks. It was in this capacity that Tho conducted secret negotiations in the early 1970s with Henry Kissinger, which eventually led to the signing of the 1973 Paris Agreement. He declined the Nobel Peace Prize offered to him for his role in negotiating the agreement. After years of diplomatic bargaining with the US, Tho travelled again to South Vietnam where he played a major role in the final military assault on Saigon. He was re-elected to the politburo and secretariat at the party's fourth and fifth congress (1976 and 1982), but at the sixth congress (1986) he formally resigned from his party posts, continuing as an 'adviser' to the central committee. According to some commentators, Tho continued to wield great influence with his 'advisory' role.

Lon Nol
Born 13 November 1913 – Died 17 November 1985
Lon Nol was born in Kampong Leav and was educated in Saigon. He began his career in the administrative services in the mid-1930s and rose quickly, becoming deputy governor of Kompong Cham in 1945. He was appointed head of the national police in 1951, and the next year he entered the army as a lieutenant-colonel, becoming chief-of-staff in 1955 and commander-in-chief in 1960. Meanwhile, he had already entered the political arena in the early 1950s as leader of his own right-wing party, Khmer Renovation, which achieved little success in the elections and was merged with Sihanouk's all-pervading Sangkum in 1955. He served as defence minister from 1959 to 1966, deputy premier from 1963 to 1966 and prime minister from 1966 to 1967. He took the premiership again in mid-1969 and less than a year later he launched a successful coup against Prince Sihanouk. After the coup, he amassed increasing amounts of personal political power and in 1972 he assumed the presidency. However great his power, he could do little to stem the Khmer Rouge onslaught and in April 1975, days before Pol Pot's forces entered Phnom Penh, he left Cambodia for exile in the US.

McNamara, Robert
Born 9 June 1916
McNamara was born in San Francisco and after graduating from the University of California he took a master's degree at the Harvard School of Business. He taught at Harvard in the early 1940s and during World War II he served in the army and the air force in Europe and Asia. He joined the Ford Company after the war and gained rapid promotion, becoming president of the company in November 1959; a month later President-elect Kennedy nominated him as secretary of defence. McNamara was perhaps the most senior US policy-maker on Indo-China under Presidents Kennedy and Johnson. His initial interpretation of the conflict was an overwhelmingly confident one: he believed that the intervention of US troops, and US military technology, would control the National Liberation Front (NLF) insurgency in the South and, in 1965, he was one of the leading supporters of the bombing policy. However, by late 1966 McNamara's position had drastically altered. He began pressing not only for a reduction in the bombing of the North, but also for a negotiated political compromise between Saigon and Hanoi. McNamara's disillusionment with the war (as evidenced by his commissioning of the study in mid-1967 which was subsequently published as the *Pentagon Papers*) opened a deep rift within the Johnson administration and served to isolate the president. McNamara resigned as defence secretary in early 1968 and was appointed as president of the World Bank, a post he held until 1981.

Mendes-France, Pierre
Born 1907 – Died 1982
Mendes-France entered the French National Assembly at the age of 25 as a Radical deputy. He was imprisoned by the Vichy authorities in 1940, but soon escaped to London and joined the Free French Air Force as a member of a bomber squadron. He represented France at the Bretton Woods conference, and after the liberation de Gaulle appointed him as minister of national economy. He resigned soon after his appointment when the government refused to accept his plans for post-war French economic recovery. From the opposition benches,

Mendes-France was one of the strongest critics of the Indo-China policies of successive administrations. He took a prominent part in the debates on Indo-China which followed the fall of Dien Bien Phu in May 1954, and in mid-June, by which time the Geneva conference on Indo-China was under way, he replaced Joseph Laniel as prime minister. He immediately pledged to achieve a cease-fire in Indo-China within one month and, towards this end, he held secret talks in Bern with the Chinese foreign minister, Zhou Enlai. The deadline imposed by Mendes-France was met and the July Geneva Agreements brought the first Indo-China War to a close. Less than a year after Geneva, Mendes-France was removed from the premiership and returned to the back benches.

Navarre, Henri
Born 1902
At the outbreak of World War II Navarre was head of the German section of French military intelligence. During the German occupation he acted as intelligence chief to the army's resistance organization in France and he subsequently took part in the invasion of Germany. He held a variety of military appointments after the war, rising to army chief-of-staff in 1952. In May of the following year he was appointed as commander-in-chief in Indo-China, and within months he began ordering the construction of a complex of supposedly impregnable fortresses at Dien Bien Phu, in northeastern Vietnam, as a lure for Viet Minh units. Navarre was confident that the overwhelming fire-power the French could concentrate against a Viet Minh assault would lead to a heavy defeat for General Giap. However, Navarre seriously underestimated the strength, determination and tactical ability of Giap's forces and in May 1954 Dien Bien Phu fell to the Viet Minh, effectively bringing France's involvement in Indo-China to a close. Navarre (who had been in Saigon during the battle for Dien Bien Phu) was quickly replaced as Indo-China commander-in-chief by General Paul Ely.

Ngo Dinh Diem
Born 1901 – Died 2 November 1963
Diem was born in Hue of a Roman Catholic family of the mandarin class. He was educated at the Hue School of Law and Administration, after which he entered the civil service and had risen to the position of provincial governor by the age of 25. In the early 1930s he entered the service of the recently-enthroned Emperor Bao Dai; he was appointed as interior minister, but soon resigned when his proposals for administrative reforms were rejected. For the next 20 years Diem lived in retirement, refusing invitations to accept office from the French, from the Japanese occupation forces and from Ho Chi Minh's Viet Minh, and in 1949 he went into voluntary exile in the US and France. After the French defeat at Dien Bien Phu, however, he accepted Bao Dai's offer of the premiership in mid-1954. The following year, Diem succeeded in crushing the armed opposition of the Cao Dai, Hoa Hao and Binh Xuyen and defied attempts by Bao Dai (who was living in France) to remove him. In October he organized a referendum which resulted in the proclamation of the South Vietnamese Republic, with himself as its president.

Diem's attempts to carry out social and economic reforms and to end corruption at first won his government a measure of popular support, but his position gradually became increasingly isolated. Unsuccessful attempts to overthrow the government by disaffected military officers took place in 1960 and 1962. In his last years, Diem's survival became increasingly dependent upon continued US support; however, his failure to compromise on the issue of overt anti-Buddhist discrimination meant that Washington (and the South Vietnamese army) began to distance themselves from Diem. Eventually, the army moved against Diem in November 1963, and both he and his brother, Ngo Dinh Nhu, were shot dead, despite having been promised safe conduct out of Vietnam by the coup leaders. The US government's 'complicity' in Diem's overthrow was documented in the *Pentagon Papers*, which claimed that the episode seriously deepened US involvement in the Vietnamese conflict.

Nguyen Cao Ky
Born 8 September 1930
Ky was born in Sontay, northern Vietnam, and after training at French military schools in Hanoi and Marrakesh took command of a squadron of the South Vietnamese air force in 1955. He was appointed as air force commander in late 1963, and he rose to political prominence a year later when he played a major role in suppressing an attempted coup. Ky was one of the leading, and by far the most flamboyant, members of the group of young officers which overthrew General Nguyen Khanh in early 1965. He assumed the premiership in June 1966 and in September of the following year he was elected as vice-president under Nguyen Van Thieu. Air Vice-Marshal Ky's relations with President Thieu deteriorated rapidly during the late 1960s and in 1971 Ky announced his intention to challenge Thieu for the presidency. However, in late 1971 Thieu was re-elected unopposed, after Ky and Duong Van Minh both withdrew from the contest claiming that it was fraudulent. Ky withdrew from politics until early 1975 when, in the face of the impending disintegration of the Saigon regime, he led calls for President Thieu's resignation. Ky was evacuated from Saigon in late April, only days after denouncing others leaving with the US as 'cowards'. He settled near Los Angeles and opened a liquor store.

Nguyen Co Thach
Born 1923
Throughout the 1980s Thach has constituted the public face of the Vietnamese government, ably representing his country in complex international negotiations on Cambodia and the 'boat people' issue. He served as one of Le Duc Tho's aides during the Paris peace negotiations and was appointed as a deputy foreign minister in the first post-reunification government. By the late 1970s Thach had unofficially taken over the role of full foreign minister from the ailing Nguyen Duy Trinh. He formally replaced Trinh in early 1980 and two years later, at the age of 59, he entered the politburo as an alternate member. At the sixth Communist Party of Vietnam (CPV) congress in December 1986 Thach was promoted to full politburo membership; two months later he was appointed deputy premier, whilst retaining charge of the Foreign Ministry.

Nguyen Van Linh
Born 1913
Born in northern Vietnam, he was arrested and imprisoned on Con Son island in the early 1930s because of his political activities. Upon his release from jail in 1936 he joined the Indo-Chinese Communist Party (ICP). The French imprisoned him again in the early 1940s, but he was freed before the 1945

'revolution' after which he established himself as one of the leading Communists in the south of the country. He remained in the South during the war against the US and was believed to have acted as Pham Hung's number two.

In 1975 he was elected party secretary in Saigon (Ho Chi Minh City) and the following year he was elected onto the politburo. Whilst secretary of Ho Chi Minh City he introduced a number of policies which provided incentives for private agricultural and industrial projects. His reformist policies were subjected to central criticism and in 1982 he was removed from the politburo (whilst retaining the secretaryship of Ho Chi Minh City). His reappointment to the politburo in 1985 was confirmed by the official party newspaper *Nhan Dan* in July 1985 and at the funeral of Le Duan a year later he was identified as a member of the secretariat. In December 1986 he was elected party general secretary, replacing the veteran Truong Chinh, who had held the post temporarily after Le Duan's death.

As general secretary Nguyen Van Linh has set an example to the impoverished Vietnamese people by adopting a particularly austere lifestyle. However, he revealed a populist streak in 1987 when he wrote a series of articles in *Nhan Dan* under the by-line 'NVL' in a column entitled 'Things which must be done immediately'. The article invariably contained a forthright attack on 'negativism', government incompetence, abuses of power and corruption and also advocated a vigorous restructuring of the economy.

Nguyen Van Thieu
Born 5 April 1923
Thieu was born in central Vietnam, the son of a small landowner. He was educated at a Catholic school in Hue and then at the city's National Military Academy. In the mid-1940s he served with the Viet Minh, but in 1948 he effectively changed sides, joining the Vietnamese National Army; by 1954 he had risen to the rank of colonel. Under Diem he served as commander of the First and the Fifth Infantry Divisions, and he personally led the latter in the coup which overthrew President Diem in 1963. Thieu was appointed chief-of-staff and commander of IV Corps in 1964, and the following February he was appointed deputy premier and defence minister in Phan Huy Quat's government. When Quat resigned in June, Lieutenant-General Thieu became the effective head of state. He was officially elected as president in 1967, and was re-elected in 1971. Thieu officiated over his country's collapse, and after the signing of the Paris Agreement in 1973 (which he opposed up to the last minute) he had little control over events. He relinquished the presidency only a few weeks before Saigon fell to the Communists in late April 1975. He was initially airlifted out of Vietnam to Taiwan, but he later settled in Britain.

Nixon, Richard Milhous
Born 9 January 1913
Nixon was born into a small farming community in southern California. He graduated from Duke University Law School in 1937 and was in legal practice until 1942 when he joined the US Navy after the US entry into World War II. He was demobilized in 1946 with the rank of lieutenant-commander and, that year, was elected to the House of Representatives for a Californian congressional district. He sat in the House for five years and gained prominence for his work on the House Committee for Un-American Activities during the Alger Hiss case. He

was elected to the Senate in 1950 and two years later was elected vice-president as running-mate of General Eisenhower. He held the vice-presidency during the eight years of Eisenhower's presidency; during his first term he fully endorsed Senator Joe McCarthy's anti-Communist 'witch hunt'.

In the 1960 presidential election Nixon was Republican candidate against John Kennedy, by whom he was narrowly defeated. He opened a legal practice in New York but, in 1962, he suffered another electoral defeat when he failed to win the Californian governorship. However, in 1968 the Republican Party again elected Nixon as their presidential candidate, and he went on to narrowly defeat Hubert Humphrey in the contest itself. The backbone of Nixon's Indo-China strategy was the policy of 'Vietnamization', whereby US troops were withdrawn and South Vietnamese troops retrained and rearmed. A few months after Nixon's re-election in 1972 the Paris Agreement on Vietnam was signed, providing for a full US withdrawal and, according to Nixon, 'peace with honour'. With the threat of impeachment hanging over him as a result of his role in the Watergate scandal, Nixon resigned the presidency in August 1974. After spending a number of years in disgrace, Nixon took on the role of US 'elder statesman' during the 1980s.

Norodom Sihanouk
Born 31 October 1922

Norodom Sihanouk, a great grandson of both King Norodom and King Sisowath, was born into the Khmer royal family in the early 1920s. In 1941, following the death of King Monivong, the French authorities placed the 18-year-old Prince Sihanouk on the Cambodian throne, disregarding in the process Monivong's son, Prince Monireth. The French appeared to have been guided by the expectation that the young and inexperienced Sihanouk would be easily manipulated. However, in the early 1950s the young king emerged as a national political leader embarking on a Royal Crusade against French rule and eventually securing his country's independence in 1953. Two years later Sihanouk formed his own political movement, Sangkum, and abdicated in favour of his father, Norodom Suramarit, so as to avoid constitutional restraints on his becoming the effective head of government. During the 1950s and 1960s Sihanouk managed to keep control of Cambodia's internal political machinery through the Sangkum; at the same time he navigated a path through the conflict in neighbouring Vietnam by maintaining a neutralist foreign policy. However, during the late 1960s, the presence of Vietnamese Communists in eastern Cambodia and the increasing potency of the internal Khmer Rouge rebellion meant that Sihanouk became dangerously vulnerable to the Cambodian right. In March 1970 he was deposed as the country's leader by a group of pro-US rightists, led by his prime minister, Lon Nol.

Following his deposition Sihanouk moved to China where he quickly established a national united front with the Khmer Rouge Communists. But, by the time the Khmer Rouge tanks entered Phnom Penh in April 1975, Sihanouk and his supporters were in no position to determine the country's future direction. Sihanouk returned to his country in late 1975, but was held as a virtual prisoner by the new rulers. He was smuggled out of the country days before Vietnamese forces entered Cambodia in late 1978 to impose a friendly regime in Phnom Penh. Over the next few years Sihanouk formed his own resistance force, the Armee Nationale Sihanoukiste (ANS), to fight Vietnamese troops in Cambodia, and in 1982 he agreed to become president of a Khmer Rouge-dominated tripartite rebel coalition, the Coalition Government of Democratic Kampuchea (CGDK). Throughout the 1980s the prince has applied his eccentric, yet considerable, diplomatic skills towards eliminating Vietnamese domination of his country and establishing a new broad-based government.

Pham Hung
Born June 1912 – Died 10 March 1988
Pham Hung was born in the southern province of Cuu Long. He was expelled from school for his involvement in radical student activities and, in 1930 became a founder member of the Indo-Chinese Communist Party (ICP). He was condemned to death by the French authorities in the following year, the sentence being commuted to life imprisonment. After being released from prison in 1945 he held a military command in the war against the French, and after the 1954 cease-fire he went to Hanoi. He was elected to the party politburo in 1957, and served for some years as a deputy premier in the North Vietnamese government. From 1967 he directed the war effort in the South as secretary of the Central Office South Vietnam (COSVN) and political commissar of the People's Liberation Armed Forces. After unification in 1976 he was appointed as a deputy premier, making him one of six southerners in the Council of Ministers. In 1980 he concurrently assumed the post of interior minister and seven years later he replaced Pham Van Dong as premier.

Pham Van Dong
Born 1 March 1906
Pham Van Dong was born in Quang Ngai province in central Vietnam, the son of a mandarin at the court of Hue. He was educated at the National Lycee in Hue and went on to study law at Hanoi University. Whilst at university in 1925, Dong helped to organize a strike and evaded arrest by fleeing to Canton, where he met Ho Chi Minh. Dong studied under Ho for a while, and then returned to Vietnam to organize Communist cells. Three years later he was arrested in Hanoi by the French and sentenced to seven years of hard labour on the prison island of Poulo Condore; one of his cell mates was Le Duc Tho. Dong was released in 1936 and he immediately resumed his revolutionary activities. Already a member of the Indo-Chinese Communist Party (ICP), he helped found the Viet Minh in 1941. Dong was appointed foreign minister in the provisional government formed after Ho's 1945 declaration of independence. In 1954 he headed the North Vietnamese delegation to the Geneva conference and the following year he was elected as prime minister, retaining charge of foreign affairs until 1963. Dong served as the North Vietnamese premier throughout the war with the US, and, in 1976, he was appointed to the same post in the government of the newly reunified Vietnam. After 32 years in the post, he was replaced in mid-1987 by Pham Hung. A few months earlier Dong had resigned from the Communist Party politburo and secretariat 'on the grounds of advanced age and failing health'. Along with other veteran leaders, he continued to serve the government and party in an advisory role.

Pol Pot
Born 19 May 1928
The most infamous of all Cambodians, Pol Pot was born as Saloth Sar in the central province of Kompong Thom. His father was a moderately wealthy

landowner and his family were connected by marriage to the royal household. He received his secondary education in Kompong Cham city and in 1949 he arrived in Paris, with a scholarship, to undertake a two-year course at the Ecole Francaise de Radioelectricite. In Paris, Saloth Sar joined a Marxist Circle of Khmer students led by his friend Ieng Sary. Sar returned to Cambodia in early 1953 (without a degree), and promptly travelled to the eastern provinces where he joined Khmer and Vietnamese Communist guerrillas in the jungle. Two years later he reappeared in Phnom Penh, where he immersed himself in left-wing activities. At the same time, he taught history in one of the city's schools and married Khieu Ponnary, the sister of Khieu Thirith, wife of Ieng Sary.

At the 1960 Communist Party congress, Tou Samouth was elected as general secretary and Saloth Sar was elected to the politburo. Two years later Samouth 'disappeared' and Sar became the party's acting general secretary. He was confirmed in the post at a special congress held early the following year, after which both he and Sary fled from Phnom Penh to northeastern Cambodia after being identified publicly as subversives by Prince Sihanouk. Sar spent much of 1965 abroad, mainly in China. During his visit to Beijing he worked closely with Deng Xiaoping (then general secretary of the Chinese Communist Party), and according to some commentators it might have been during this visit that the Khmers Rouges received Chinese support for an 'independent' (i.e. non-Vietnamese) line. By the time of the Lon Nol coup in 1970, Sar's northeastern group of Khmer Rouge guerrillas were probably the dominant element in the highly factionalized Cambodian Communist movement. The US bombing of Cambodia in the early 1970s strengthened Sar's hand in that a disproportionate number of 'moderates' died in the attacks and were replaced by new young recruits brutalized by the assault. Sar (under the name Pol Pot) was named prime minister of Democratic Kampuchea in April 1976, exactly a year after the Khmer Rouge victory in Cambodia. Except for a few months of 'sick leave' in late 1976, Pol Pot held the post until his retirement in late 1979, by which time his government had been driven out of Phnom Penh by the Vietnamese. During his premiership, he embarked on a series of massive and brutal purges to ensure that his faction of the Communist Party remained dominant. In late 1977, at the height of the purges, Pol Pot revealed for the first time that the Communist Party was controlling the country and that he was party general secretary.

After handing the premiership to Khieu Samphan in late 1979, Pol Pot remained commander of the Khmer Rouge forces until his 'retirement' in 1985. Four years later he was reported to have resigned from his last official Khmer Rouge post (as director for the Higher Institute for National Defence). Pol Pot's continued presence within the Cambodian rebel administration had long constituted a serious obstacle to a settlement of the conflict; commentators, however, reacted to the 'resignation' with a great deal of scepticism, believing that Pol Pot would continue to exercise considerable political and military influence.

Rostow, Walt
Born 7 October 1916
Born in New York, Rostow graduated from Yale and spent two years at Oxford University in the late 1930s. During World War II he served with the Office of Strategic Services (OSS) and during the remainder of the 1940s and the 1950s he taught at Oxford, Cambridge and Massachusetts Institute of Technology. In early 1961 the newly-elected President Kennedy appointed Rostow as his deputy

special assistant for national security affairs. In this capacity he visited Saigon in October 1961 with Kennedy's special military adviser, General Maxwell Taylor. Upon their return, Rostow and Taylor both recommended the immediate deployment of US troops to Vietnam in order to halt the declining fortunes of the Diem regime. Kennedy rejected the idea and Rostow was appointed as a councillor to the State Department's policy-planning council. One of the ideas developed by Rostow was the notion of quelling the southern insurgency by directly attacking their northern suppliers. In 1966 President Johnson appointed Rostow as his special assistant for national security. He soon emerged as the leading civilian backer of the hardline military bloc which was struggling for Johnson's support against Defence Secretary McNamara and other sceptics and 'doves'. With the election of Nixon in late 1968, Rostow returned to the academic world as professor of economics and history at Texas University.

Rusk, Dean
Born 9 February 1909
Rusk was born in Georgia, the son of a poor tenant farmer. He graduated from an obscure college in North Carolina and then went on to study at Oxford (on a Rhodes scholarship) and the University of California Law School. Between 1934 and 1940 he was associate professor of government at Mills College, California. During World War II he served in the army in the Burma–China theatre, rising to the rank of colonel. After the war he spent two years in the War Department in Washington, but in 1947 he was transferred to the State Department where he took charge of UN affairs. In 1950 his long association with the Vietnam conflict began when he was appointed as an assistant secretary of state for Far Eastern affairs. Even at this early stage he advocated a hardline approach towards Asian Communism, a strategy that was to remain with him throughout his career. In 1952 he left the State Department and was appointed president of the Rockefeller Foundation, a post he held for the next nine years. In 1961 President Kennedy appointed Rusk as secretary of state and he remained in the post until 1969 when he was replaced by William Rogers. Throughout his eight years as secretary of state, Rusk remained consistent in his support of a strong US military involvement in Vietnam. After leaving the government he was appointed as professor of international law at the University of Georgia.

Son Sann
Born 1911
Son Sann was educated in France. He returned to Cambodia in 1935 and worked within the (French) government service. He served as finance minister in the 'independent' government established by the French after World War II and as deputy premier in the Associated State established in 1949. Following the achievement of genuine independence in 1953, Sann held a variety of posts under Prince Sihanouk including governor of the National Bank and (in 1967) prime minister. He went into exile in Paris soon after Lon Nol took charge of the country in 1970. In 1979 he established the Khmer People's National Liberation Front (KPNLF) to co-ordinate non-Communist resistance to the newly-established pro-Vietnamese regime in Phnom Penh. By 1981 the front claimed to control 9,000 men along the Thai-Cambodian border and to have received arms from China. The next year Sann took the front into a coalition with the Sihanoukist forces and the Khmers Rouges. He was appointed prime

minister in the UN-recognized coalition, a post he continued to hold at the end of the decade.

Souphanouvong
Born 1909

'Red' Prince Souphanouvong was born into the Lao royal house of Luang Prabang, the son of Prince Boun Khong and half brother to Souvanna Phouma and Phetsarath. He was educated in Hanoi and Paris, receiving a degree in civil engineering in 1937. He returned to Indo-China in the late 1930s and spent most of the period of Japanese occupation building bridges in Vietnam. Through his Vietnamese wife, Le Thi Ky Nam, he became involved in the Vietnamese nationalist struggle and following the Japanese surrender in 1945 he and his half brothers proclaimed Laos' independence and established a provisional 'Lao Issara' government. The returning French routed the Lao Issara troops in early 1946 and Souphanouvong was wounded crossing the Mekong into exile in Thailand. He recovered and served as defence minister in the Lao Issara government in exile, which survived in Bangkok until 1949, when Souvanna Phouma led moderate members back to Vientiane. Souphanouvong, meanwhile, made his way to northwestern Vietnam, and with Viet Minh help he formed a Lao resistance government (which came to be known as the Pathet Lao) in 1950; three years later a capital was established in Sam Neua. In 1956 Souphanouvong became president of the Communist-led Lao Patriotic Front, and the next year he was appointed as minister of planning in the country's first coalition government. After the creation of a rightist regime in Vientiane in 1959 he was arrested, but managed to escape the next year. Souphanouvong returned to Vientiane again in 1962 to serve as deputy premier in another government of national union led by Souvanna Phouma. The arrangement broke down in 1963 and he returned to Sam Neua for the duration of the Lao civil war, which quickly developed into a western theatre of the Vietnamese conflict. Souphanouvong again returned to Vientiane after the 1973 peace agreement and was appointed president of a Luang Prabang-based policy-making body. He became president of the newly-formed Lao People's Democratic Republic (LPDR) in late 1975, but was forced to retire 11 years later after suffering a stroke. Nevertheless, he retained his politburo place at the Communist Party's fourth congress held in late 1986.

Souvanna Phouma
Born 1901 – Died 10 January 1984

Born in Luang Prabang Souvanna Phouma was the son of Prince Boun Khong, nephew of King Sisavang Vong, brother of Prince Phetsarath and half brother of Prince Souphanouvong. Educated in France as an engineer he worked in the Vientiane Public Works Service during the 1930s. He served as minister of public works in the Lao Issara government which governed for a brief period between Japanese surrender and French reoccupation. The French forces entered Vientiane in April 1946 and Souvanna Phouma, along with other Lao Issara ministers, fled to Thailand. By 1949 the Lao Issara movement had split and Souvanna Phouma led the more moderate members back to Vientiane, whilst Souphanouvong made his way to northwest Vietnam. In late 1951 Souvanna Phouma succeeded Phoui Sananikone as prime minister, promising to work for 'national unity'. For the next 24 years Souvanna Phouma played a central role in the affairs, and survival, of his country. As leader of the 'neutralist' faction in the three-way struggle with the Pathet Lao under Souphanouvong and the 'rightists' under Phoumi Nosavan and Boun Oum, he was prime minister for most of the period between independence in 1953 and the Pathet Lao final victory in 1975. He was appointed as an adviser to the new government, a position he continued to hold until his death in 1984.

Truong Chinh
Born 1907 – Died 30 September 1988

He was born Dang Xuan Khu in the northern province of Ha Nam Nihn and later changed his name to Truong Chinh ('long march'), after the Long March of Chinese revolutionaries in the 1930s. He was a teenage revolutionary and a founder member of the Indo-Chinese Communist Party (ICP) in 1930. Imprisoned by the French from 1931 to 1936, upon his release he soon established himself as a leading figure within the ICP and was elected as party general secretary in 1941.

After the defeat of the French in 1954 Truong Chinh helped mastermind a radical land-reform programme in the North which, by 1956, was being carried out with increasingly excessive zeal. Ho Chi Minh apparently designated Truong Chinh as the scapegoat for the programme's excesses and he was replaced as party general secretary in October 1956 by Le Duan. Although he retained his politburo place and was appointed a deputy premier in 1958, he never fully regained ground lost to Le Duan as a result of his dismissal as general secretary. In 1960 he became chairman of the National Assembly, a post he held until his election as president of the Council of State (the collective presidency) in 1981. Ironically, it was Le Duan's death in 1986 that afforded Truong Chinh the opportunity to again hold the top party post, although only for the five-month period leading up to the party's sixth congress. Along with other ageing leaders he resigned all his party posts at the December 1986 congress. In June 1987 he was replaced as president of the State Council, his last remaining official post.

Vo Nguyen Giap
Born 1912

Vo Nguyen Giap was born in Quang Binh province in central Vietnam. He was educated at a French lycee in Hue, and before he passed his Baccalaureate in 1932 he had become heavily involved in radical politics. He joined the Indo-Chinese Communist Party (ICP) in 1933, and for the six years he studied law and taught history in Hanoi. The French outlawed the ICP in 1939 and Giap and Pham Van Dong both fled to southern China; they established Communist bases on the border area, and in 1944 Giap created the first of the Vietnam Propaganda and Liberation Units, the forerunner of the North Vietnamese Army (NVA). Ho Chi Minh appointed him as interior minister in the provisional North Vietnamese government formed in Hanoi in September 1945. Over the next nine years of warfare against the French, Giap established himself as Ho's supreme military leader, and his political influence was greatly enhanced by his tactical triumph at Dien Bien Phu in 1954. During the 1960s and 1970s Giap (by now a deputy premier, defence minister and politburo member) played a major role in devising military strategies to support Hanoi's war against the US. Early on during the war, Giap pressed for a strategy which emphasized the merits of a protracted guerrilla war as opposed to a more conventional large-unit assault against the US. General

Giap's precise role in the war is difficult to gauge; towards the end of the conflict other strategists, such as Van Tien Dung, were receiving credit for NVA's battlefield successes. Following reunification in 1976 his influence declined. General Dung replaced him as defence minister in 1980 and two years later he was removed from the politburo (a post he had first been elected to in the early 1950s). He retained his post as deputy premier, but was thought to spend most of his time in retirement.

Westmoreland, William Childs
Born 26 March 1914

Westmoreland was born in South Carolina. He graduated from the US Military Academy at West Point in 1936, and during World War II he led an artillery battalion which saw action in North Africa, Normandy, the Bulge and the Remagen bridgehead. After the war his career progressed rapidly, and after a spell as an instructor at Fort Leavenworth he led an elite paratroop regiment in Korea. In 1956 he became the youngest major-general in the US Army and two years later he was given command of the 101st Airborne Division, the choice divisional command. His next assignment, in 1960, returned him to West Point as the academy's superintendent. Four years later, Westmoreland replaced General Paul D. Harkins as commander, US Military Assistance Command, Vietnam (COMUSMACV). Westmoreland advised President Johnson that South Vietnam could not survive for long without the introduction of US combat troops and in mid-1965 the build-up began. In late 1967 Westmoreland was ordered home by Johnson to reassure the increasingly agitated US public that US forces were succeeding in Vietnam; in a major address to the National Press Club, Westmoreland claimed that the war had reached the point 'where the end begins to come into view'. However, Westmoreland's optimism was largely discredited two months later when the Communist forces launched their massive Tet offensive throughout South Vietnam. After four years' service in Vietnam, Westmoreland was promoted to army chief-of-staff in mid-1968. He retired from the Army in 1972, and after a brief venture into politics, he turned to writing and lecturing.

APPENDICES

Appendix 1: French diplomatic representation in Indo-China 1940–54

Governor-Generals	Admiral Jean Decoux	July 1940
High Commissioners	Admiral Georges Thierry d'Argenlieu	September 1945
	Emile Bollaert	March 1947
	Leon Pignon	October 1948
	General Jean de Lattre de Tassigny	December 1950
	Jean Letourneau	April 1952
Commissioner-Generals	Jean Letourneau	April 1953
	Maurice Dejean	July 1953
	General Paul Ely	June 1954

Appendix 2: The Vietnamese 'sects'

Cao Dai The Cao Dai or 'High Church' sect was formed in 1919 by Ngo Van Chieu as a synthesis of Christianity, Buddhism and other religions. Amongst its 'saints' were Jesus Christ, Buddha, Joan of Arc and Victor Hugo. The sect soon turned political and after collaborating with the Japanese and later with the Viet Minh, they allied with the French in 1946, although a portion of the sect continued to support the Viet Minh. The Cao Daist army was originally armed by the Japanese but later received financial support from the French. By the mid-1950s the army, led by General Nguyen Thanh Phoung, was about 30,000 strong and controlled a large area around Tay Ninh, a region situated some 50 miles (80 kilometres) northwest of Saigon. The sect, led by 'Pope' Pham Cong Tac, claimed some 2 million adherents.

Hoa Hao The Hoa Hao, founded in the southern village of the same name in 1939 by Huynh Phu So, proclaimed a simplified version of Buddhism. As with the Cao Dai, the sect rapidly entered the political arena and built up its own private armed forces. It collaborated in turn with the Japanese and the Viet Minh, but the majority joined the French in 1947. Huynh Phu So was subsequently assassinated by the Viet Minh and the leadership passed into the hands of General Tran Van Soai, who commanded the loyalty of some 30,000 troops. General Soai controlled an area west of Saigon, extending to the Cambodian border, with a population of about 1 million.

Binh-Xuyen Anything but a religious body, the Binh-Xuyen is nevertheless usually classed as one of the three major 'sects'. It started out as a group of bandits operating from the village of Binh-Xuyen (near Saigon) which supported the Viet Minh for a while before being granted control by the French of a zone east of Saigon in 1948. By the mid-1950s its forces numbered about 15,000 men, commanded by General Le Van Hien. General Hien came to an arrangement with Bao Dai in 1954 through which Binh-Xuyen secured control of the capital's police force as well as a monopoly of the city's highly lucrative gaming houses, opium dens and brothels.

Appendix 3: French military expenditure in Indo-China, 1945–52 (million francs)

Year		Year	
1945	3,200	1949	130,000
1946	27,000	1950	201,000
1947	53,310	1951	313,000
1948	89,700	1952	435,000 (estimate)

Appendix 4: The opposing forces operating in Vietnam, late 1952

Viet Minh Over 100,000 men in the main-force units, comprising six infantry and one 'heavy' division; four independent infantry regiments; and four independent battalions. Main-force units assisted by regional forces (60,000) and guerrilla and local militia (120,000–200,000).

French Expeditionary Corps Over 200,000 men, the vast majority being part of the land force. Of this total, about 80,000 French nationals, the remainder being Foreign Legionnaires, North Africans and Indo-Chinese serving in French units.

The Associated States Over 130,000 men in the Vietnamese army, over 80,000 of whom were regulars. Only one division ready for active service as of late 1952. Militia forces organized on a local, religious or tribal basis numbered as many as 100,000 and probably constituted a more potent fighting force than the army. The Cambodian and Lao armies both had under 15,000 men each.

Appendix 5: Delegations attending the 1954 Geneva conference on Indo-China (Delegation head in parenthesis)

Democratic Republic of Vietnam (Pham Van Dong)

State of Vietnam (Nguyen Quoc Dinh)

Cambodia (Tep Phan)

Laos (Phoui Sananikone)

France (Georges Bidault)

*Soviet Union (Vyacheslav Molotov)

US (General Walter Bedell Smith)

China (Zhou Enlai)

*Great Britain (Anthony Eden)

*Co-chairs of the conference.

Appendix 6: Final declaration of the Geneva conference on the problem of restoring peace in Indo-China

(Tacitly adopted, but not signed, on 21 July 1954, by France, the Soviet Union, Great Britain, the People's Republic of China, the State of Vietnam, Laos, Cambodia and the Democratic Republic of Vietnam.)

(1) The conference takes note of the agreements ending hostilities in Cambodia, Laos, and Vietnam, and organising international control and supervision of the provisions of these agreements.

(2) The conference expressed satisfaction at the ending of hostilities in Cambodia, Laos and Vietnam. It expresses its conviction that the execution of the provisions set out in the present declaration and in the agreements on the cessation of hostilities will permit Cambodia, Laos, and Vietnam henceforth to play their part, in full independence and sovereignty, in the peaceful community of nations.

(3) The conference takes note of the declarations made by the Governments of Cambodia and Laos of their intention to adopt measures permitting all citizens to take their place in the national community, in particular by participating in the next general elections, which, in conformity with the Constitution of each of these countries, shall take place in 1955 by secret ballot and in conditions of respect for fundamental freedoms.

(4) The conference takes note of the clauses in the agreement on the cessation of hostilities in Vietnam prohibiting the introduction into Vietnam of foreign troops and military personnel, as well as of all kinds of arms and munitions. It also takes note of the declarations made by the Governments of Cambodia and Laos of their resolutions not to request foreign aid, whether in war material, personnel, or instructors, except for the purpose of the effective defence of their territory and, in the case of Laos, to the extent defined by the agreements on the cessation of hostilities in Laos.

(5) The conference takes note of the clauses in the agreement on the cessation of hostilities in Vietnam to the effect that no military base at the disposition of a foreign State may be established in the regrouping zones of the two parties, the latter having the obligation to see that the zones allotted to them shall not constitute part of any military alliance and shall not be utilized for the resumption of hostilities or in the service of an aggressive policy. The conference also takes note of the declarations of the Governments of Cambodia and Laos to the effect that they will not join in any agreement with other States if this agreement includes the obligation to participate in a military alliance not in conformity with the principles of the UN Charter or,

in the case of Laos, with the principles of the agreement on the cessation of hostilities in Laos, or, so long as their security is not threatened, the obligation to establish bases on Cambodian or Laotian territory for the military forces of foreign powers.

(6) The conference recognises that the essential purpose of the agreement relating to Vietnam is to settle military questions with a view to ending hostilities, and that the military demarcation line should not in any way be interpreted as constituting a political or territorial boundary. It expresses its conviction that the execution of the provisions set out in the present declaration and in the agreement on the cessation of hostilities creates the necessary basis for the achievement in the near future of a political settlement in Vietnam.

(7) The conference declares that, so far as Vietnam is concerned, the settlement of political problems, effected on the basis of respect for the principles of independence, unity, and territorial integrity, shall permit the Vietnamese people to enjoy the fundamental freedoms, guaranteed by democratic institutions, established as a result of free general elections by secret ballot. To ensure that sufficient progress in the restoration of peace has been made, and that all the necessary conditions obtain for free expression of the national will, general elections shall be made in July, 1956, under the supervision of an International Commission composed of representatives of the member States of the International Supervisory Commission, referred to in the agreements on the cessation of hostilities. Consultations will be held on this subject between the competent representative authorities of the two zones from July, 1955, onwards.

(8) The provisions of the agreements on the cessation of hostilities intended to ensure the protection of individuals and of property must be most strictly applied and must, in particular, allow everyone in Vietnam to decide freely in which zone he wishes to live.

(9) The competent representative authorities of the northern and southern zones of Vietnam, as well as the authorities of Laos and Cambodia, must not permit any individual or collective reprisals against persons who have collaborated in any way with one of the parties during the war, or against members of such a person's family.

(10) The conference takes note of the declaration of the French Government to the effect that it is ready to withdraw its troops from Cambodia, Laos, and Vietnam at the request of the Governments concerned and within a period which shall be fixed by agreement between the parties, except in the cases where, by agreement between the two parties, a certain number of French troops shall remain at specified points and for a specified period.

(11) The conference takes note of the declaration of the French Government to the effect that, for the settlement of all problems connected with the re-establishment and consolidation of peace in Cambodia, Laos, and Vietnam, it will proceed from the principle of respect for the independence, sovereignty, unity, and territorial integrity of Cambodia, Laos, and Vietnam.

(12) In their relations with Cambodia, Laos and Vietnam, each member of the Geneva Conference undertakes to respect the sovereignty, independence,

unity, and territorial integrity of the above-mentioned states, and to refrain from any interference in their internal affairs.

(13) The members of the conference agree to consult one another on any questions which may be referred to them by the International Supervisory Commission in order to study such measures as may prove necessary to ensure that the agreements on the cessation of hostilities in Cambodia, Laos, and Vietnam are respected.'

Appendix 7: Unilateral US Declaration at Geneva

(Issued by Walter Bedell Smith on 21 July 1954.)

The Government of the United States, being resolved to devote its efforts to the strengthening of peace in accordance with the principles and purposes of the United Nations:

Takes note of the agreements concluded at Geneva on July 20 and 21, 1954, between (a) the Franco-Laotian Command and the Command of the People's Army of Vietnam [the Viet Minh]; (b) the Royal Cambodian Command and the People's Army of Vietnam; (c) the Franco-Vietnamese Command and the Command of the People's Army of Vietnam; and of paragraphs (1) to (12) inclusive of the declaration presented to the Geneva Conference on July 21, 1954;

Declares with regard to the aforesaid agreements and paragraphs that:

(1) It will refrain from the threat or the use of force to disturb them, in accordance with Article 2 (4) of the UN Charter dealing with the obligation of members to refrain in their international relations from the threat or use of force; and

(2) It would view any renewal of aggression in violation of the aforesaid agreements with grave concern and as seriously threatening international peace and security.

In connection with the statement in the declaration concerning free elections in Vietnam, my Government wishes to make clear its position, which it has expressed in a declaration made in Washington on June 29, 1954 as follows: 'In the case of nations now divided against their will, we shall continue to seek to achieve unity through free elections, supervized by the UN, to ensure that they are conducted fairly'.

With respect to the statement made by the representative of the State of Vietnam, the United States reiterates its traditional position that peoples are entitled to determine their own future and that it will not join in an arrangement which would hinder this. Nothing in this declaration is intended to, or does, indicate any departure from this traditional position.

We share the hope that the agreements will permit Cambodia, Laos and Vietnam to play their part, in full independence and sovereignty, in the peaceful community of nations, and will enable the people of that area to determine their own future.'

Appendix 8: Declaration of Royal Government of Laos at Geneva Conference 21 July 1954

The Royal Government of Laos,
In the desire to ensure harmony and agreement among the peoples of the Kingdom,
Declares itself resolved to take the necessary measures to integrate all citizens, without discrimination, into the national community and to guarantee them the enjoyment of the rights and freedoms for which the Constitution of the Kingdom provides; Announces, furthermore, that it will promulgate measures to provide for special representation in the Royal Administration of the provinces of Phong Saly and Sam Neua during the interval between the cessation of hostilities and the general elections of the interests of nationals of Laos who did not support the Royal forces during hostilities.

Appendix 9: US aid to Laos (in millions of dollars)

Year	Military Assistance Programme	Total aid
1955	–	40.9
1956	27.4	75.7
1957	4.3	48.7
1958	5.4	36.9
1959	7.5	32.6

The vast proportion of the total aid figure was for monthly 'budget support' payments used to pay army and civil service salaries. The Military Assistance Programme figures do not include substantial Central Intelligence Agency (CIA) expenditure.

Appendix 10: The ten-point programme of the National Liberation Front (NLF)

(1) To overthrow the disguised colonial regime of the US imperialists and the dictatorial Ngo Dinh Diem administration – lackey of the US – and to form a national democratic coalition administration. 2) To bring into being a broad and progressive democracy. 3) To build an independent and sovereign economy, improve the people's living conditions. 4) To carry out land-rent reduction and advance toward the settlement of the agrarian problem so as to ensure land to the tillers. 5) To build a national and democratic education and

culture. 6) To build an army to defend the Fatherland and the people. 7) To guarantee the right of equality between nationalities, and between men and women; to protect the legitimate rights of foreign residents in Vietnam and Vietnamese living abroad. 8) To carry out a foreign policy of peace and neutrality. 9) To establish normal relations between the two zones and advance toward peaceful reunification of the Fatherland. 10) To oppose aggressive war, actively defend world peace.

Appendix 11: Representatives at 1962 Geneva conference on Laos

Laos

Quinim Pholsena (neutralist government)

Phoui Sananikone (rightist government)

Phoumi Vongvichit (Pathet Lao)

Members of International Control Commission (ICC)

Krishna Menon (India)

Howard Green (Canada)

Adam Rapacki (Poland)

Participants of 1954 Geneva conference

Lord Home (Britain)

Andrei Gromyko (Soviet Union)

Dean Rusk (US)

Maurice Couve de Murville (France)

Marshal Chen Yi (China)

Ung Van Khiem (North Vietnam)

Vu Van Mau (South Vietnam)

Prince Norodom Sihanouk (Cambodia)

Other countries bordering on Laos

Sao Hkun Hkio (Burma)

Thanat Khoman (Thailand)

Appendix 12: National Liberation Front (NLF) component members

*People's Revolutionary Party (PRP)

Radical Socialist Party

Democratic Party

Association of Workers for Liberation

Women's Union for Liberation

Union of Revolutionary People's Youth

Association of Patriotic and Democratic Journalists

Association of Writers and Artists for Liberation

Movement for the Autonomy of Tay Nguyen

Self-Defence Forces

The PRP had been founded in January 1962 as a separate southern Communist party and as the successor to the southern branch of the Lao Dong or Communist Party of Vietnam. The PRP, the NLF's overtly Communist component, adopted a leading role in the front but was itself subordinate to the Truong Vong Cuc or Central Office of South Vietnam (COSVN), which had been established in October 1961 as the direct southern arm of the Lao Dong politburo. COSVN was, in a very real sense, in charge of the entire southern struggle.

Appendix 13: The Ho Chi Minh Trail

The so-called 'Ho Chi Minh Trail' was originally developed during the early stages of the Vietnam War as a route by which South Vietnamese who had settled in the North after Geneva could return, with light arms, to join anti-government guerrillas. When President Johnson ordered the bombing of the North in 1965 and dispatched troops to Vietnam the trail came to be used by North Vietnamese forces travelling south and as the main supply route for North Vietnamese Army (NVA)/National Liberation Front (NLF) soldiers in the South. It became increasingly important to the North in 1969 when the Cambodian ruler, Prince Norodom Sihanouk, closed Sihanoukville (Kompong Som) to Chinese vessels bringing supplies for the NLF/NVA.

The 'Ho Chi Minh Trail' was not a single road, but rather a shifting network of concealed tracks. Starting in Hanoi, supplies usually entered Laos through the Mu Gia Pass, although at other times the trail would weave through the Ban Karai Pass or a road complex west of the Demilitarized Zone (DMZ). Once into Laos the supplies were channelled to a base area near Tchepone. From Tchepone (the object of a disastrous South Vietnamese invasion into Laos in 1970) the supplies were shifted to different areas depending on their eventual destination. Saravane formed a focal point for goods moving south, from another base area they were shifted eastward into South Vietnam. After the extension of the war into Cambodia the trail was extended to the west (the 'Sihanouk trail') to supply NVA/NLF forces based in eastern Cambodian sanctuaries. Most of the supplies shifted along the trail were carried in lorries, although bicycles, foot porters and animals were used. The supplies were moved mainly during the dry season, with the high point in February to April.

From the early 1960s the trail was bombed, but the attacks intensified after 1970 when B-52s started to carry out a series of massive raids. In addition defoliants were dropped to destroy the trail's natural camouflage. However, the efforts of the US to ruin the trail proved futile and it eventually proved to be a major factor in the South's defeat.

Appendix 14: The Gulf of Tongkin Resolution (7 August 1964)

To promote the Maintenance of International Peace and Security in Southeast Asia.

Whereas naval units of the Communist regime in Vietnam, in violation of the principles of the Charter of the United Nations and of international law, have deliberately and repeatedly attacked United States naval vessels lawfully present in international waters, and have thereby created a serious threat to international peace; and

Whereas these attacks are part of a deliberate and systematic campaign of aggression that the Communist regime in North Vietnam has been waging against its neighbours and the nations joined with them in the collective defence of their freedom; and

Whereas the United States is assisting peoples of Southeast Asia to protect their freedom and has no territorial, military or political ambitions in that area, but desires only that these peoples should be left in peace to work out their own destinies in their own way: Now, therefore, be it

Resolved by the Senate and House of Representatives of the United States of America in Congress assembled.

That the Congress approves and supports the determination of the President, as Commander in Chief, to take all necessary measures to repel any armed attack against the forces of the United States and to prevent further aggression.

The United States regards as vital to its national interest and to world peace the maintenance of international peace and security in Southeast Asia. Consonant with the Constitution of the United States and the Charter of the United Nations and in accordance with its obligations under the Southeast Asia Collective Defense Treaty, the United States is, therefore, prepared, as the President determines, to take all necessary steps, including the use of armed force, to assist any member or protocol state of the Southeast Asia Collective Defense Treaty requesting assistance in defence of its freedom.

This resolution shall expire when the President shall determine that the peace and security of the area is reasonably assured by international conditions created by action of the United Nations or otherwise, except that it may be terminated earlier by concurrent resolution of the Congress.

A P P E N D I C E S

Appendix 15: 1964 Casualty figures in Vietnam (MACV/US defence department figures)

	killed	wounded	missing/captured
South Vietnamese	7,000	16,700	5,000
National Liberation Front (NLF)	17,000	–	4,200
US	140	1,138	11

Appendix 16: 1964 Strength of forces in action in Vietnam

South Vietnamese	
Paramilitary/Militia	290,000
Army	240,000
National police	30,000
Air Force	10,000
Navy	8,000
Marines	7,000
NLF forces	
Full-time guerrillas	28,000–34,000
Part-time armed supporters	60,000–80,000
US forces	
Army	15,000
Air Force	6,000
Navy	1,150
Marines	850

US Defence Department figures

195

Appendix 17: Major 1965 peace manoeuvres

February (1) India, France and the Soviet Union call for a new Geneva conference on Vietnam. (2) UN Secretary-General U Thant proposes an informal conference between North and South Vietnam, the US, China, France, the Soviet Union and Britain. (3) President Tito of Yugoslavia appeals to President Johnson to open immediately negotiations with North Vietnam.

March Britain and the Soviet Union (co-chairs at Geneva) hold talks on Vietnam.

April (1) A group of Non-Aligned countries appeal for a cessation of hostilities. (2) President Johnson announces that the US is willing to hold 'unconditional discussions' towards a Vietnamese settlement. (3) North Vietnam issues its four-point position on peace talks. (4) India proposes the establishment of an Afro-Asian boundary force to police the North/South Vietnam border.

May (1) Talks are held in Paris between North Vietnamese and French diplomats. (2) A Canadian delegation visits Hanoi. (3) The US orders a six-day bombing pause.

June (1) Britain puts forward a new peace plan. (2) A Commonwealth 'peace mission' initiative fails.

July (1) Ghana launches an unsuccessful initiative. (2) The US formally calls on the UN Security Council to propose a formula.

October The Saigon government issues a four-point conditional formula for talks.

November An Italian delegation visits Hanoi.

December (1) The US orders its second bombing pause and launches a 'peace offensive'. (2) Pope Paul VI issues numerous calls for peace.

Appendix 18: Allied involvement in Vietnam

Australia In August 1965 it was announced that a further 350 troops would be dispatched and another announcement in March 1966 pledged that the total number of Australian forces in Vietnam by June would be 4,500. This increase, which included national servicemen, aroused intense controversy in Australia; nevertheless, at the end of the year a further 1,700 troops were promised. In October 1967 it was announced that an extra 2,000 men plus tanks and helicopters would be sent. In mid-1971, the Australian government declared that its forces were to be withdrawn and in March 1972 the withdrawal entered its final phase.

New Zealand The New Zealand prime minister, Keith Holyoake, announced in late May 1965 that a New Zealand artillery battery would be sent to South Vietnam to serve alongside the Australian infantry battalion in the 'Anzac' tradition. The dispatch of a second infantry company of 170 men was announced in October 1967. The withdrawal of New Zealand's small force was announced in August 1971.

South Korea Some 2,000 South Korean non-combatant troops arrived in South Vietnam in late February 1965. In July the Seoul government announced that a combat division of 15,000 troops would be sent and by September 1966 the total number of South Korean troops had risen to 40,000. This figure increased to almost 50,000 during 1967 and 1968. By early 1972, 10,000 South Korean troops had withdrawn and the government announced in September that the remainder would be pulled out between December 1972 and June 1973.

Thailand and Philippines The first Thai combat troops – a group of 2,500 – arrived in Saigon in September 1967. However, navy and air-force personnel had been operating in South Vietnam since 1965. A 2,000-strong Filipino expeditionary corps – composed in the main of engineers – had been dispatched from Manila in September 1966.

Appendix 19: USA's 1965 'Peace offensive'

Hubert Humphrey (vice-president): Visited Japan, Philippines, Taiwan and South Korea.

Averell Harriman (ambassador-at-large): Visited Poland, Yugoslavia, India, Pakistan, Iran, United Arab Republic, Thailand, Japan and Australia.

Arthur Goldberg (ambassador to the UN): Visited the Vatican, Italy, France and Britain.

Mennen Williams (assistant secretary of state for African affairs): Visited Morocco, Algeria, Tunisia, Ethiopia, Kenya, Tanzania, Uganda, Nigeria, Ghana, the Ivory Coast, Guinea, Senegal and Mali.

McGeorge Bundy (Johnson's special adviser on national security): Visited Canada.

Thomas Mann (under secretary of state for economic affairs): Visited Mexico.

Appendix 20: Declaration on peace and progress in Asia and the Pacific Manila conference, 25 October 1966

We, the leaders of the seven nations gathered in Manila:

Desiring peace and progress in the Asian-Pacific region;

Having faith in the purposes and principles of the United Nations, which call for the suppression of acts of aggression and respect for the principle of equal rights and self-determination of peoples;

Determined that aggression should not be rewarded;

Respecting the right of all peoples to choose and maintain their own forms of government;

Seeking a peaceful settlement of the war in Vietnam; and being greatly encouraged by the growing regional understanding and regional co-operation among the free nations of Asia and the Pacific;

Hereby proclaim this declaration of principles on which we base our hopes for future peace and progress in the Asian and Pacific region:

(1) Aggression must not succeed.

The peace and security of Asia and the Pacific and, indeed, of the entire world, are indivisible. The nations of the Asian and Pacific region shall enjoy their independence and sovereignty free from aggression, outside interference, or the domination of any nation. Accepting the hard-won lessons of history that successful aggression anywhere endangers the peace, we are determined to fulfil our several commitments under the UN Charter and various mutual security treaties so that aggression in the region of Asia and the Pacific shall not succeed.

(2) We must break the bonds of poverty, illiteracy, and disease.

In the region of Asia and the Pacific, there is a rich heritage of the intrinsic worth and dignity of every man. We recognize the responsibility of every nation to join in an expanding offensive against poverty, illiteracy, and disease. For these bind men to lives of hopelessness and despair; these are the roots of violence and war. It is when men know that progress is possible and is being achieved, when they are convinced that their children will lead better, fuller, richer lives, that men lift up their heads in hope and pride. Only thus can there be lasting national stability and international order.

(3) We must strengthen economic, social and cultural co-operation within the Asian and Pacific region.

Together with our other partners of Asia and the Pacific, we will develop the institutions and practice of regional co-operation. Through sustained effort we aim to build in this vast area, where almost two-thirds of humanity live, a region of security and order and progress, realizing its common destiny in the light of its own traditions and aspirations. The peoples of this region have the right as well as the primary responsibility to deal with their own problems and to shape their own future in terms of their own wisdom and experience. Economic and cultural co-operation for regional development should be open to all countries in the region, irrespective of creed or ideology, which genuinely follow a policy of peace and harmony among all nations. Nations outside the region will be welcomed as partners working for the common benefit, and their co-operation will be sought in forms consonant with the independence and dignity of the Asian and Pacific nations.

A peaceful and progressive Asia, in which nations are able to work together for the common good, will be a major factor in establishing peace and prosperity throughout the world and improving the prospects of international co-operation and a better life for all mankind.

(4) We must seek reconciliation and peace throughout Asia.

We do not threaten the sovereignty or territorial integrity of our neighbours, whatever their ideological alignment. We ask only that this be reciprocated. The quarrels and ambitions of ideology and the painful frictions arising from national fears and grievances should belong to the past. Aggression rooted in them must not succeed. We shall play our full part in creating an environment in which reconciliation becomes possible, for in the modern world men and nations have no choice but to learn to live together as brothers.

Appendix 21: Major US/Allied ground operations, 1966

Operation Crimp January: US/Allied forces pushed against National Liberation Front (NLF) strongholds in the 'Iron Triangle', 25 miles (40 kilometres) northwest of Saigon. They had little success in flushing out NLF fighters, but a major tunnel network was discovered.

Operation Masher and Double Eagle January: 20,000 US/Allied soldiers (including US First Cavalry Division) assaulted NVA Eighteenth and Ninety-Eighth and NLF First and Second regiments in Quang Ngai and Binh Dinh provinces. During the operation some 5,000 marines landed on the beaches south of Quang Ngai in the biggest amphibious operation since the Inchon operation in the Korean War. The operation failed in its aim of driving the North Vietnamese Army (NVA)/NLF northward.

Operation Utah March: US/South Vietnamese Army (ARVN) forces engaged NVA/ NLF forces at their Son Chau headquarters near Quang Ngai town. Both sides suffered heavy casualties and Son Chau was eventually taken after the entry of US Marines and ARVN paratroopers.

Operation Hawthorne June: US 101st Airborne Division battled with the NVA's Twenty-Fourth Regiment in Kontum province, central highlands. As many as 570 NVA troops were reported killed in the fighting.

Operation Nathan Hale June: US And Allied forces launched a search-and-destroy operation around the coastal city of Tuy Hoa. A major clash occurred at Dong Tri US special forces camp.

Operation Hastings July: 11,000 US Marines and ARVN troops launched a major assault on the NVA 325-B Division in Quang Tri, the South's northernmost province. According to US reports over 800 NVA were killed in the assault. The attack apparently thwarted the 325-B Division's plan to start a wet-season offensive in Quang Tri.

Operation Irving October: A US/ARVN/South Korean force attacked NVA/NLF positions in the central coastal area northwest of Quin Hon. By late October Allied forces claimed to have killed over 900 NVA/NLF troops.

Operation Attleboro November: A massive battle broke out in Tay Ninh province, astride the Cambodian border. Allied forces at the height of the fighting numbered 20,000, consisting of US First and Twenty-Fifth Infantry Divisions, the 196th Light Infantry Brigade, the 173rd Airborne Brigade and at least two ARVN battalions. They faced elements of the crack Ninth NLF Division (the 271st, 272nd and 273rd regiments) and the NVA's 101st Regiment. According to US sources, the Allies inflicted heavy casualties on the NLF/NVA, despite extremely stiff resistance, and thwarted a major assault on a US special forces camp at Suoida, near the Cambodian border.

U Minh Forest Drive December: ARVN forces launched a major drive against a NLF Mekong delta stronghold in the U Minh Forest. The drive was preceded by US saturation bombing of the area. The ARVN reported that over 100 NLF troops were killed in the drive and 18 captured.

Appendix 22: South Vietnamese premiers in the post-Diem era

Nguyen Ngo Tho	1963	Nguyen Van Loc	1967–8
Nguyen Khanh	1964	Tran Van Huong	1968–9
Nguyen Xuan Oanh	1964–5	Tran Thien Khiem	1969–75
Tran Van Huong	1964–5	Nguyen Ba Can	1975
Phan Huy Quat	1965	Vu Van Mau	1975
Nguyen Cao Ky	1965–7		

Appendix 23: Agreement on ending the war and restoring peace in Vietnam

(Signed in Paris on 27 January 1973, by the foreign ministers of the US, North and South Vietnam and the South Vietnamese Provisional Revolutionary Government.)

The parties participating in the Paris Conference on Vietnam, with a view to ending the war and restoring peace in Vietnam on the basis of respect for the Vietnamese people's fundamental national rights and the South Vietnamese people's right to self-determination, and to contributing to the consolidation of peace in Asia and the world, have agreed on the following provisions and undertake to respect and to implement them:

Chapter I. – The Vietnamese People's Fundamental National Rights.

Article 1.

The United States and all other countries respect the independence, sovereignty, unity and territorial integrity of Vietnam as recognized by the 1954 Geneva Agreements on Vietnam.

Chapter II. – Cessation of Hostilities. – Withdrawal of Troops.

Article 2.

A cease-fire shall be observed throughout South Vietnam as of 24.00 hours GMT on Jan. 27, 1973.

At the same hour, the United States will stop all its military activities against the territory of the Democratic Republic of Vietnam by ground, air and naval forces, wherever they may be based, and end the mining of the Democratic Republic of Vietnam.

The United States will remove, permanently deactivate or destroy all the mines in the territorial waters, ports, harbours, and waterways of North Vietnam as soon as this agreement goes into effect.

The complete cessation of hostilities mentioned in this article shall be durable and without limit of time.

Article 3.

The parties undertake to maintain the ceasefire and to ensure a lasting and stable peace.

As soon as the ceasefire goes into effect:
(a) The United States forces and those of the other foreign countries allied with the United States and the Republic of Vietnam shall remain in place pending the implementation of the plan of troop withdrawal. The four-party joint military commission described in Article 16 shall determine the modalities.

(b) The armed forces of the two South Vietnamese parties shall remain in place. The two-party joint military commission described in Article 17 shall determine the areas controlled by each party and the modalities of stationing.

(c) The regular forces of all services and arms and the irregular forces of the parties in South Vietnam shall stop all offensive activities against each other and shall strictly abide by the following stipulation:

All acts of force on the ground, in the air, and on the sea shall be prohibited; all hostile acts, terrorism and reprisals by both sides will be banned.

Article 4.

The United States will not continue its military involvement or intervene in the internal affairs of South Vietnam.

Article 5.

Within 60 days of the signing of this agreement, there will be a total withdrawal from South Vietnam of troops, military advisers and military personnel, including technical military personnel and military personnel associated with the pacification programmes, armaments, munitions and war material of the United States and those of the other foreign countries mentioned in Article 3 (a). Advisers from the above-mentioned countries to all paramilitary organizations and the police force will also be withdrawn within the same period of time.

Article 6.

The dismantlement of all military bases in South Vietnam of the United States and of the other foreign countries mentioned in Article 3 (a) shall be completed within 60 days of the signing of this agreement.

Article 7.

From the enforcement of the ceasefire to the formation of the Government, provided for in Article 9 (b) and 14 of this agreement, the two South Vietnamese parties shall not accept the introduction of troops, military advisers and military personnel including technical military personnel, armaments, munitions and war material into South Vietnam.

The two South Vietnamese parties shall be permitted to make periodic replacement of armaments, munitions and war material which have been destroyed, damaged, worn out or used up after the ceasefire, on the basis of piece-for-piece, of the same characteristics and properties, under the supervision of the joint military commission of the two South Vietnamese parties and of the International Commission of Control and Supervision.

Chapter III. – The Return of Captured Military Personnel and Foreign Civilians, and Captured and Detained Vietnamese Civilian Personnel.

Article 8.

(a) The return of captured military personnel and foreign civilians of the parties shall be carried out simultaneously with and completed not later than the same day as the troop withdrawal mentioned in Article 5. The parties shall exchange complete lists of the above-mentioned captured military personnel and foreign civilians on the day of the signing of this agreement.

(b) The parties shall help each other to get information about those military personnel and foreign civilians of the parties missing in action, to determine the location and take care of the graves of the dead so as to facilitate the exhumation and repatriation of the remains, and to take any such other measures as may be required to get information about those still considered missing in action.

(c) The question of the return of Vietnamese civilian personnel captured and detained in South Vietnam will be resolved by the two South Vietnamese parties on the basis of the principles of Article 21 (b) of the agreement on the cessation of hostilities in Vietnam of July 20, 1954.

The two South Vietnamese parties will do so in a spirit of national reconciliation and accord, with a view to ending hatred and enmity, in order to ease suffering and to reunite families. The two South Vietnamese parties will do their utmost to resolve this question within 90 days after the ceasefire comes into effect.

Chapter IV. – The Exercise of the South Vietnamese People's Right of Self-determination.

Article 9.

The Government of the United States of America and the Government of the Democratic Republic of Vietnam undertake to respect the following principles for the exercise of the South Vietnamese people's right to self-determination:

(a) The South Vietnamese people's right to self-determination is sacred, inalienable, and shall be respected by all countries.

(b) The South Vietnamese people shall decide themselves the political future of South Vietnam through genuinely free and democratic general elections under international supervision.

(c) Foreign countries shall not impose any political tendency or personality on the South Vietnamese people.

Article 10.

The two South Vietnamese parties undertake to respect the ceasefire and maintain peace in South Vietnam, settle all matters of contention through negotiations, and avoid all armed conflicts.

Article 11.

Immediately after the ceasefire, the two South Vietnamese parties will:

Achieve national reconciliation and concord, end hatred and enmity, prohibit all acts of reprisal and discrimination against individuals or organisations that have collaborated with one side or the other;

ensure the democratic liberties of the people: personal freedom, freedom of speech, freedom of the press, freedom of meeting, freedom of organization, freedom of belief, freedom of movement, freedom of residence, freedom of work, right to property ownership, and right to free enterprise.

Article 12.

(a) Immediately after the ceasefire, the two South Vietnamese parties shall hold consultations in a spirit of national reconciliation and concord, mutual respect and mutual non-elimination to set up a National Council of National Reconciliation and Concord of three equal segments.

The council shall operate on the principle of unanimity. After the National Council of National Reconciliation and Concord has assumed its functions, the two South Vietnamese parties will consult about the formation of councils at lower levels.

The two South Vietnamese parties shall sign an agreement on the internal matters of South Vietnam as soon as possible and do their utmost to accomplish this within 90 days after the ceasefire comes into effect, in keeping with the South Vietnamese people's aspirations for peace, independence and democracy.

(b) The National Council of National Reconciliation and Concord shall have the task of promoting the two South Vietnamese parties' implementation of this agreement, achievement of national reconciliation and concord and ensurance of democratic liberties.

The National Council of National Reconciliation and Concord will organize the free and democratic general elections provided for in Article 9 (b) and decide the procedures and modalities of these general elections.

The institutions for which the general elections are to be held will be agreed upon through consultations between the two South Vietnamese parties. The National Council of National Reconciliation and Concord will also decide the procedures and modalities of such local elections as the two South Vietnamese parties agree upon.

Article 13.

The question of Vietnamese armed forces in South Vietnam shall be settled by the two South Vietnamese parties in a spirit of national reconciliation and concord, equality and mutual respect, without foreign interference, in accordance with the post-war situation.

Among the questions to be discussed by the two South Vietnamese parties are steps to reduce their military effectiveness and to demobilize the troops being reduced. The two South Vietnamese parties will accomplish this as soon as possible.

Article 14.

South Vietnam will pursue a foreign policy of peace and independence. It will be prepared to establish relations with all countries irrespective of their political and social systems on the basis of mutual respect for independence and sovereignty, and accept economic and technical aid from any country with no political conditions attached.

The acceptance of military aid by South Vietnam in the future shall come under the authority of the Government set up after the general elections in South Vietnam provide for in article 9 (b).

Chapter V. – The Reunification of Vietnam and the Relationship between North and South Vietnam.

Article 15.

The reunification of Vietnam shall be carried out step by step through peaceful means on the basis of discussion and agreements between North and South Vietnam, without coercion or annexation by either part, and without foreign interference. The time for reunification will be agreed upon by North and South Vietnam.

Pending the reunification:

(a) The military demarcation line between the two zones at the 17th parallel is only provisional and not a political or territorial boundary, as provided for in Paragraph 6 of the final declaration of the 1954 Geneva conference.

(b) North and South Vietnam shall respect the demilitarized zone on either side of the provisional military demarcation line.

(c) North and South Vietnam shall promptly start negotiations with a view to re-establishing normal relations in various fields. Among the questions to be negotiated are the modalities of civilian movement across the provisional military demarcation line.

(d) North and South Vietnam shall not join any military alliance or military bloc and shall not allow foreign powers to maintain military bases, troops, military advisers, and military personnel on their respective territories, as stipulated in the 1954 Geneva Agreements.

Chapter VI. – The Joint Military Commission, the International Commission of Control and Supervision, and the International Conference.

Article 16.

(a) The parties participating in the Paris Conference on Vietnam shall immediately designate representatives to form a four-party joint military commission with the task of ensuring joint action by the parties in implementing the following provisions of this agreement:

The first paragraph of Article 2, Article 3 (a), Article 3 (c), Article 5, Article 6, Article 8 (a), Article 8 (b).

(b) The four-party joint military commission shall operate in accordance with the principle of consultations and unanimity. Disagreements shall be referred to the International Commission of Control and Supervision.

(c) The four-party joint military commission shall begin operating immediately after the signing of this agreement and end its activities in 60 days, after the completion of the withdrawal of United States troops and those of the other foreign countries mentioned in Article 3 (a) and the completion of the return of captured military personnel and foreign civilians of the parties.

(d) The four parties shall agree immediately on the organization, the working procedure, means of activity, and expenditure of the four-party joint military commission.

Article 17.

(a) The two South Vietnamese parties shall immediately designate representatives to form a two-party joint military commission with the task of ensuring joint action by the two South Vietnamese parties in implementing the following provisions of this agreement: the first paragraph of Article 2, Article 3 (b), Article 3 (c), Article 7, Article 8 (c), Article 13.

(b) Disagreements shall be referred to the International Commission of Control and Supervision.

(c) After the signing of this agreement, the two-party joint military commission shall agree immediately on the measures and organization aimed at enforcing the ceasefire and preserving peace in South Vietnam.

Article 18.

(a) After the signing of this agreement, an International Commission of Control and Supervision shall be established immediately.

(b) Until the international conference provided for in Article 19 makes definitive arrangements, the International Commission of Control and Supervision will report to the four parties on matters concerning the control and supervision of the implementation of the following provisions of this agreement: the first paragraph of Article 2, Article 3 (a), Article 3 (c), Article 5, Article 6, Article 8 (a).

The International Commission of Control and Supervision shall form control teams for carrying out its tasks. The four parties shall agree immediately on the location and operation of these teams. The parties will facilitate their operation.

(c) Until the international conference makes definitive arrangements, the International Commission of Control and Supervision will report to the two South Vietnamese parties on matters concerning the control and supervision of the implementation of the following provisions of this agreement: the first paragraph of Article 2, Article 3 (b), Article 3 (c), Article 7, Article 8 (c), Article 9 (b), Article 13.

The International Commission of Control and Supervision shall form control teams for carrying out its tasks. The two South Vietnamese parties will facilitate their operations.

(d) The International Commission of Control and Supervision shall be composed of representatives of four countries: Canada, Hungary, Indonesia and Poland. The chairmanship of this commission will rotate among the members for specific periods to be determined by the commission.

(e) The International Commission of Control and Supervision shall carry out its tasks in accordance with the principle of respect for the sovereignty of South Vietnam.

(f) The International Commission of Control and Supervision shall operate in accordance with the principle of consultations and unanimity.

(g) The International Commission of Control and Supervision shall begin operating when a ceasefire comes into force in Vietnam. as regards the provisions in Article 18 (b) concerning the four parties, the International Commission of Control and Supervision shall end its activities when the commission's tasks of control and supervision regarding these provisions have been fulfilled.

As regards the provisions in Article 18 (c) concerning the two South Vietnamese parties, the International Commission of Control and Supervision shall end its activities on the request of the Government formed after the general elections in South Vietnam provided for in Article 9 (b).

(h) The four parties shall agree immediately on the organization, means of activity, and expenditures of the International Commission of Control and Supervision. The relationship between the International Commission and the international conference will be agreed upon by the International Commission and the international conference.

Article 19.

The parties agree on the convening of an international conference within 30 days of the signing of this agreement to acknowledge the signed agreements;

to guarantee the ending of the war, the maintenance of peace in Vietnam, the respect of the Vietnamese people's fundamental national rights, and the South Vietnamese people's right to self-determination; and to contribute to and guarantee peace in Indo-China.

The United States and the Democratic Republic of Vietnam, on behalf of the parties participating in the Paris Conference on Vietnam, will propose to the following parties that they participate in this international conference: the People's Republic of China, the Republic of France, the Union of Soviet Socialist Republics, the United Kingdom, the four countries of the International Commission of Control and Supervision, and the Secretary-General of the United Nations, together with the parties participating in the Paris Conference on Vietnam.

Chapter VII. – Regarding Cambodia and Laos.

Article 20.

(a) The parties participating in the Paris Conference on Vietnam shall strictly respect the 1954 Geneva Agreements on Cambodia and the 1962 Geneva Agreements on Laos, which recognized the Cambodian and the Laos people's fundamental national rights, i.e. the independence, sovereignty, unity and territorial integrity of these countries. The parties shall respect the neutrality of Cambodia and Laos.

The parties participating in the Paris Conference on Vietnam undertake to refrain from using the territory of Cambodia and the territory of Laos to encroach on the sovereignty and security of one another and of other countries.

(b) Foreign countries shall put an end to all military activities in Cambodia and Laos, totally withdraw from and refrain from reintroducing into these two countries troops, military advisers and military personnel, armaments, munitions and war material.

(c) The internal affairs of Cambodia and Laos shall be settled by the people of each of these countries without foreign interference.

(d) The problems existing between the Indo-Chinese countries shall be settled by the Indo-Chinese parties on the basis of respect for each other's independence, sovereignty and territorial integrity and non-interference in each other's internal affairs.

Chapter VIII. – The Relationship between the United States and the Democratic Republic of Vietnam.

Article 21.

The United States anticipates that this agreement will usher in an era of reconciliation with the Democratic Republic of Vietnam as with all the peoples of Indo-China. In pursuance of its traditional policy, the United States will contribute to healing the wounds of war and to post-war reconstruction of the Democratic Republic of Vietnam and throughout Indo-China.

APPENDICES

Article 22.

The ending of the war, the restoration of peace in Vietnam, and the strict implementation of this agreement will create conditions for establishing a new, equal and mutually beneficial relationship between the United States and the Democratic Republic of Vietnam on the basis of respect for each other's independence and sovereignty, and non-interference in each other's internal affairs. At the same time, this will ensure stable peace in Vietnam and contribute to the preservation of lasting peace in Indo-China and Southeast Asia.

Chapter IX. – Other Provisions.

Article 23.

This agreement shall enter into force upon signature by plenipotentiary representatives of the parties participating in the Paris Conference on Vietnam. All the parties concerned shall strictly implement this agreement and its protocols.

Appendix 24: Total US casualty figures in Vietnam, 1961–73

Killed in action	45,941
Non-combat deaths	10,298
Wounded in action	300,635
Missing or captured	1,811

Appendix 25: US casualty progression in Vietnam, 1965–70

	Troop numbers (year end)	Killed (to date)	Wounded (to date)
1965	184,300	1,363	7,645
1966	385,300	6,644	37,738
1967	485,300	16,021	99,762
1968	536,100	30,160	192,850
1969	474,000	40,200	262,796
1970	335,800	44,241	293,529

Appendix 26: US military personnel strength in Vietnam, 1960–72

Escalation		Reduction under 'Vietnamization'	
900	Dec. 1960	474,000	Dec. 1969
3,200	Dec. 1961	335,800	Dec. 1970
11,300	Dec. 1962	184,000	Dec. 1971
16,300	Dec. 1963	139,000	Feb. 1972
23,300	Dec. 1964	69,000	May 1972
184,300	Dec. 1965	39,000	Sept. 1972
385,300	Dec. 1966	27,000	Dec. 1972
485,300	Dec. 1967		
536,100	Dec. 1968		
542,400	Jan. 1969		

Appendix 27: The Constitution of Democratic Kampuchea 5 January 1976 (extracts)

The sacred and fundamental aspirations of the people, workers, peasants and other labourers as well as those of the fighters and cadres of the Kampuchean Revolutionary Army.

Whereas a significant role has been played by the people, especially the workers, poor peasants, lower-middle-class peasants and other strata of urban and rural working people, who account for more than 95 per cent of the entire Kampuchea nation, who assumed the heaviest responsibility in waging the war for the liberation of the nation and the people, made the greatest sacrifices in terms of life, property and commitment, served the front line unremittingly, and unhesitatingly sacrificed their children and husbands by the thousands for the battle at the front line;

Whereas great sacrifices have been borne by the three categories of the Kampuchea Revolutionary Army who fought valiantly, day and night, in the dry and rainy season, underwent all kinds of hardship and misery, shortages of food, medicine, clothing, ammunition and other commodities in the great war for the liberation of the nation and the people;

Whereas the entire Kampuchea people and the entire Kampuchea Revolutionary Army desire an independent, unified, peaceful, neutral, non-aligned. sovereign Kampuchea enjoying territorial integrity, a national society informed by genuine happiness, equality, justice and democracy, without rich or poor and without exploiters or exploited, a society in which all live harmoniously in great national solidarity and join forces to do manual work together and increase production for the construction and defence of the country;

And whereas the resolution of the Special National Congress held on 25, 26, and 27 April 1975 solemnly proclaimed recognition and respect for the above desires of the entire people and the entire Kampuchea Revolutionary Army, the Constitution of Kampuchea stipulates as follows:

CHAPTER ONE
The State
Article 1

The State of Kampuchea is an independent, unified, peaceful, neutral, non-aligned, sovereign and democratic State enjoying territorial integrity.

The State of Kampuchea is a State of the people, workers, peasants, and all other Kampuchea working people.

CHAPTER TWO
The Economy
Article 2

All important means of production are the collective property of the people's state and the common property of the people's communities.
Property for everyday use remains in private hands.

CHAPTER THREE
Culture
Article 3

The culture of Democratic Kampuchea is of a national, popular, forward-looking and healthful character such as will serve the task of defending and building Kampuchea into an ever more prosperous country.
This new culture is absolutely opposed to the corrupt, reactionary culture of the different oppressive classes of colonialism in Kampuchea.

CHAPTER NINE
The Rights and Duties of the Individual
Article 12

Every citizen of Kampuchea is fully entitled to a constantly improving material, spiritual and cultural life. Every citizen of Kampuchea is guaranteed a living.
All workers are the masters of their factories.
All peasants are the masters of their rice-paddies and fields.
All other working people have the right to work.
There is absolutely no unemployment in Democratic Kampuchea.

Article 13

There must be complete equality among all Kampuchean people in an equal, just, democratic, harmonious and happy society within the great national union for defending and building the country.

CHAPTER FIFTEEN
Worship and Religion
Article 20

Every citizen of Kampuchea has the right to worship according to any religion and the right not to worship according to any religion.
All reactionary religions which are detrimental to Democratic Kampuchea and the Kampuchean people are strictly forbidden.

Appendix 28: Principal victims of Pol Pot's purges

Name	Position	Date of execution
Non Suon	agriculture minister	Nov. 1976
Koy Thuon	commerce minister	Jan. 1977
Touch Phoeun	public works minister	Jan. 1977
Sua Doeum	trade minister	Feb. 1977
Hou Nim	information and propaganda minister	April 1977
Nhim Ros	vice-president of state presidium	March 1978
So Phim	vice-president of state presidium	May 1978 ('suicide')
Phuong	rubber plantations minister	June 1978
Mey Prang	communications minister	Nov. 1978
Cheng An	industry minister	Nov. 1978
Vorn Vet	deputy premier	Nov. 1978 ('suicide')

Angkar 'The organisation'; the term by which the secretive ruling Cambodian Communist Party was known under Pol Pot's rule.

Annam The French protectorate of central Vietnam; known to the Vietnamese as Trung-Bo.

ANS Armee Nationale Sihanoukiste; one of the two non-Communist elements of the Coalition Government of Democratic Kampuchea.

ARVN Army of the Republic of Vietnam; the South Vietnamese army.

ASEAN Association of Southeast Asian Nations; currently comprising Brunei, Indonesia, Malaysia, the Philippines, Singapore and Thailand.

B-52 The main US delivery vehicle for conventional bombs in Indo–China.

Binh-Xuyen Saigon-based gangsters driven out of the city by Diem in 1955.

Cao Dai A Vietnamese sect founded in 1919 as a synthesis of Christianity, Buddhism and other religions; centred around the South Vietnamese province of Tay Ninh.

CGDK Coalition Government of Democratic Kampuchea; founded in 1982 as a diplomatic vehicle for the discordant Cambodian rebels.

Cholon Chinese quarter of Ho Chi Minh City.

CIA US Central Intelligence Agency.

Cochin-China Southern Vietnam, ceded to the French in 1873; known to the Vietnamese as Nam-Bo.

Comecon Council for Mutual Economic Assistance; Soviet bloc economic community.

COSVN Central Office for South Vietnam; the Communist Party of Vietnam's southern branch which controlled political and military operations in the South.

CPK Communist Party of Kampuchea; usually refers to the Pol Pot-led faction of the Khmer Communist movement.

CPV Communist Party of Vietnam; the post-1976 party name.

DK Democratic Kampuchea; Cambodia's official name under Pol Pot, 1976–9.

DMZ Demilitarized Zone along the seventeenth parallel dividing South and North Vietnam.

Dong The Vietnamese currency.

DRV Democratic Republic of Vietnam; proclaimed by Ho Chi Minh in 1945.

FANK French acronym for Lon Nol's republican forces.

FUNK French acronym for National United Front of Kampuchea; post-1970 coalition between Sihanouk and the Khmers Rouges.

GRUNK French acronym for the Beijing-based Royal Government of National Union of Kampuchea formed by Sihanouk and the Khmers Rouges in 1970.

H'mong Northern Lao tribe which provided the backbone of US-financed right-wing forces in Laos; also known (derogatively) as the Meo.

Hoa Hao Militant Vietnamese sect centred in the Mekong delta.

ICP Indo-Chinese Communist Party; formed by Ho Chi Minh in 1930 and formally dissolved in late 1945.

ICSC International Commission of Supervision and Control.

JIM Jakarta Informal Meeting; the mechanism by which the warring Khmer parties gathered for talks after 1988.

JMC Joint Military Commission.

Kampuchean Krom Khmer term for southernmost section of Vietnam, occupied by the Vietnamese in the eighteenth century.

Khmer Dominant ethnic group in Cambodia.

Khmer Republic The name by which Cambodia was known under Lon Nol's rule.

Khmers Rouges Term coined by Sihanouk for the Cambodian Communists which came to power in 1975; after 1982, the Communist and militarily-dominant element of the Coalition Government of Democratic Kampuchea.

Kip The Lao currency.

KNUFNS Kampuchean National United Front for National Salvation.

KPNLF Khmer People's National Liberation Front; one of the two non-Communist components of the Coalition Government of Democratic Kampuchea.

KPRP Kampuchean People's Revolutionary Party; usually refers to the post-1979 anti-Pol Pot faction of the Cambodian Communist movement.

Lao Dong Vietnamese Workers' Party; the name of the Vietnamese Communist Party from 1951 to 1976.

LPDR Lao People's Democratic Republic; formed in 1975 after the Pathet Lao's final victory.

LPRP Lao People's Revolutionary Party; the ruling Communist Party in Laos.

MAAG US Military Assistance Advisory Group; first American military advisers posted to Indo-China in 1950.

MACV US Military Assistance Command, Vietnam; superseded MAAG in 1962.

MIA Missing In Action.

Montagnards Indigenous mountain people of Vietnam.

NLF National Liberation Front for South Vietnam; created in 1960 and dubbed the 'Viet Cong' (Vietnamese Communists) by the US and South Vietnamese regimes.

NPCC National Political Consultative Council; Souphanouvong-led body formed in Laos after the 1973 agreement.

NVA North Vietnamese Army.

OSS Office of Strategic Services; forerunner to the CIA.

Pathet Lao Literally 'land of the Lao'; used by commentators to refer to the Lao Communist movement in general.

PGNU Provisional Government of National Union; the formal name of the 'third coalition' in Laos (1974–5).

Pracheachon Left-wing Citizen's Group which operated in Cambodia in the 1950s and early 1960s.

PRG Provisional Revolutionary Government of South Vietnam; proclaimed in 1969 by the National Liberation Front and other southern groups.

PRK People's Republic of Kampuchea; the pro-Vietnamese government formed in 1979 after the toppling of the Pol Pot government.

PRP People's Republican Party.

Riel Cambodian currency.

RLA Royal Lao Army.

RLG Royal Lao Government.

RVN Republic of Vietnam (South Vietnam).

Sangkum Sangkum Reastr Niyum (Popular Socialist Community); Sihanoukist political movement, 1955–70.

SEATO South-east Asia Treaty Organization; established in 1955 and formally dissolved 22 years later; its members were Australia, France, New Zealand, Pakistan, the Philippines, Thailand, Britain and the US.

SMM Saigon Military Mission.

SPA Supreme People's Assembly; created in Laos after the 1975 revolution.

SRV Socialist Republic of Vietnam; the name given to the newly unified Vietnamese state in 1976.

Tet Vietnamese lunar new year holiday period.

Tongkin The French protectorate of northern Vietnam; known to the Vietnamese as Bac-Bo.

UNHCR United Nations High Commissioner for Refugees.

USAID US Agency for International Development.

Viet Cong Derogatory US/South Vietnamese term for the National Liberation Front.

Viet Minh Viet Nam Doc Lap Dong Minh Hoi (Vietnamese Independence League); created as a Communist-led national front organization in 1941.

Vietnamization Nixon's programme for US withdrawal 'with honour' from Vietnam.

B I B L I O G R A P H Y

Cambodia

Barron, John and Paul, Anthony, *Peace with Horror: The Untold Story of Communist Genocide in Cambodia* (Hodder and Stoughton, London 1977).

Becker, Elizabeth, *When the War was Over* (Simon and Schuster, New York, 1987).

Chandler, David P., *A History of Cambodia* (Westview Press, Boulder, Colorado, 1984).

Chandler, David P. and Kiernan, Ben, *Revolution and its Aftermath in Kampuchea* (Yale University Press, New Haven, 1983).

Chandler, David P., Kiernan, Ben and Boua, Chanthou, *Pol Pot Plans the Future: Confidential Leadership Documents from Democratic Kampuchea* (Yale University Press, New Haven, 1988).

Etcheson, Craig, *The Rise and Demise of Democratic Kampuchea* (Westview Press, Boulder, Colorado, 1984).

Kiernan, Ben, *How Pol Pot Came to Power* (Verso, London, 1984).

Kiernan, Ben and Boua, Chanthou, eds. *Peasants and Politics in Kampuchea 1941–1981* (Zed Press, London, 1982).

Kiljunen, Kimmo, ed. *Kampuchea: Decade of the Genocide* (Zed Press, London, 1984).

Kirk, Donald, *Wider War: The Struggle for Cambodia, Thailand and Laos* (Praeger, New York, 1971).

Leifer, Michael, *Cambodia: The Search for Security* (Pall Mall Press, London, 1967).

May, Someth, *Cambodian Witness* (Faber and Faber, London, 1986).

Mysliwiec, Eva, *Punishing the Poor: the international isolation of Kampuchea* (Oxfam, Oxford, 1988).

Osborne, Milton, *Politics and Power in Cambodia* (Camberwell, Victoria, 1973).

Osborne, Milton, *Before Kampuchea, Preludes to Tragedy* (Allen and Unwin, London, 1979).

Picq, Laurence, *Beyond the Horizon: Five Years with the Khmer Rouge* (St. Martin's Press, New York, 1989).

Ponchaud, Francois, *Cambodia Year Zero* (Penguin, London, 1976).

Shawcross, William, *Quality of Mercy: Cambodia, Holocaust and Modern Conscience* (Deutsch, London, 1984).

Shawcross, William, *Sideshow: Kissinger, Nixon and the Destruction of Cambodia* (Hogarth Press, London, 1986).

Sihanouk, Norodom, *My War with the CIA* (Penguin, London, 1973).

Sihanouk, Norodom, *War and Hope: the Case for Cambodia* (Sidgewick and Jackson, London, 1980).

Stuart-Fox, Martin and Ung, Bunhaeng, *The Murderous Revolution* (Tamarind Press, Bangkok, 1986).

Vickery, Michael, *Cambodia 1975–1982* (South End Press, Boston, 1984).

Vickery, Michael, *Kampuchea: Politics, Economics and Society* (Frances Pinter, London, 1986).

Wright, Martin, ed. *Cambodia: A Matter of Survival* (Longman, Harlow, 1989).

Yathay, Pin, *Stay Alive, My Son* (Bloomsbury, London, 1987).

Laos

Adams, Nina and McCoy, Alfred W., eds. *Laos: War and Revolution* (Harper and Row, New York, 1970).

Brown, MacAlister and Zasloff, Joseph J., *Apprentice Revolutionaries: The Communist Movement in Laos, 1930–1985* (Hoover Institution Press, Stanford, 1985).

Dommen, Arthur, *Conflict in Laos: the Politics of Neutralization* (Pall Mall Press, London, 1964).

Fall, Bernard, *Anatomy of a Crisis: The Laotian Crisis of 1960–61* (Doubleday, New York, 1969).

Hannah, Norman B., *The Key to Failure: Laos and the Vietnam War* (Madison Books, New York, 1989).

Langer, Paul F. and Zasloff, Joseph J., *North Vietnam and the Pathet Lao: Partners in the Struggle for Laos* (Harvard University Press, Cambridge, Massachusetts, 1970).

Le Bar, F.M. and Suddard, A., *Laos, its People, its Society, its Culture* (HRAF Press, New Haven, 1960).

McCoy, A.W., *The Politics of Heroin in Southeast Asia* (Harper and Row, New York, 1972).

Phomvihane, Kaysone, *Revolution in Laos* (Progress Publishers, Moscow, 1981).

Ratnam, Perala, *Laos and the Superpowers* (Tulsi Publishing House, New Delhi, 1980).

Stuart-Fox, Martin, *Contemporary Laos: Studies in the Politics and Society of the Lao People's Democratic Republic* (St. Martin's Press, New York, 1982).

Stuart-Fox, Martin, *Laos: Politics, Economics and Society* (Frances Pinter, London, 1986).

Toyce, Hugh, *Laos* (Oxford University Press, London, 1968).

Zasloff, Joseph J., *The Pathet Lao: Leadership and Organisation* (Heath, Lexington, 1973).

Vietnam

Archer, Robert, *Vietnam: The Habit of War* (CIIR, London, 1983).

Beresford, Melanie, *Vietnam: Politics, Economics and Society* (Pinter Publishers, London, 1988).

Boettcher, T.D., *Vietnam: the Valour and the Sorrow* (Little, Brown and Co., Boston, 1986).

Braestrup, P., ed. *Vietnam as History: Ten Years after the Paris Peace Accords* (University Press of America, Washington, 1986).

Butler, D. *The Fall of Saigon* (Simon and Schuster, New York, 1986).

Buttinger, Joseph, *The Smaller Dragon: A Political History of Vietnam* (Praeger New York, 1958).

Buttinger, Joseph, *Vietnam: A Dragon Embattled*, 2 vols. (Praeger, New York, 1967).

Cameron, A.W., *Vietnam Crisis, a Documentary History (1940–56)* (Cornell University Press, New York, 1971).

Davidson, Lieutenant-General (retd) Phillip B., *Vietnam At War: The History 1946–1975* (Sidgwick and Jackson, London, 1988).

Del Vechio, John M., *The 13th Valley* (Sphere Books, London, 1983).

Eisen, Arlene, *Woman and Revolution in Vietnam* (Zed Books, London, 1985).

Facts On File, *South Vietnam: US-Communist Confrontation in Southeast Asia*, 7 vols. (Facts On File, New York 1966–73).

Fall, Bernard, *The Two Vietnams: A Political And Military Analysis* (Pall Mall Press, London, 1963).

Fall, Bernard, *Hell in a Very Small Place: The Siege of Dien Bien Phu* (J.B. Lippincott, Philadelphia, 1967).

Fenn, Charles, *Ho Chi Minh: a biographical introduction* (Studio Vista, London, 1973).

Fenton, James, *All The Wrong Places* (Penguin, London, 1990).

Fforde, Adam, *The Limits of National Liberation: Economic Management and the Reunification of the Democratic Republic of Vietnam* (Croom Helm, London, 1984).

Fitzgerald, Frances, *Fire In The Lake: The Vietnamese and the Americans in Vietman* (Macmillan, London, 1972).

Freeman, James A., *Hearts of Sorrow: Vietnamese-American Lives*. (Stanford University Press, California, 1989).

Gardner, Lloyd, *Approaching Vietnam: From World War II through Dienbienphu* (Norton, New York, 1989).

Gelb, L.H. and Betts, R.K., *The Irony of Vietnam* (Brookings Institute, Washington, 1979).

Hackworth, Colonel (retd) David H. and Sherman, Julie, *About Face: The Odyssey Of An American Warrior* (Touchstone, New York, 1989).

Herr, Michael, *Dispatches* (Picador, London, 1979).

Herring, G.C.,*America's Longest War: The United States and Vietnam 1950–1975* (Wiley, New York, 1979).

Higgins, Hugh, *Vietnam* (Heinemann Educational Books, London, 1982).

Hodgkin, T., *Vietnam, the Revolutionary Path* (Macmillan, London, 1981).

Kahin, George McTurnan and Lewis, John W., *The United States In Vietnam* (Dial Press, New York, 1967).

Kahin, George McTurnan, *Intervention: How America Became Involved in Vietnam* (Alfred Knopf, New York,

Karnow, Stanley, *Vietnam: A History* (Penguin, London, 1984).

Kolko, Gabriel, *Vietnam: Anatomy of War 1940–1975* (Unwin, London, 1987).

Landsdale, E.G., *In the Midst of Wars: An American Mission to Southeast Asia* (Harper and Row, New York, 1972).

Le Duan, *This Nation and Socialism Are One: Selected Writings of Le Duan* (Vanguard Books, Chicago, 1976).

McAlister, J.T., *Vietnam: The Origins of Revolution* (Allen Lane, London, 1970).

Maclear, Michael, *Vietnam: The Ten Thousand Day War* (Thames Methuen/Mandarin, London, 1981).

Mangold, Tom and Penycate, John T., *The Tunnels of Cuchi* (Hodder and Stoughton, Sevenoaks, 1985).

Marr, David, 'Vietnam: Harnessing the Whirlwind' (essay in Jeffrey, Robin,*Asia: the Winning of Independence* (Macmillan, London, 1981).

Nguyen Van Canh, *Vietnam Under Communism, 1975–1982* (Hoover Institution Press, Stanford, 1983).

Nixon, Richard M., *No More Vietnams* (Arbor House, New York, 1985).

O'Brien, Tim, *If I Die In A Combat Zone* (Delacorte Press, New York, 1973).

The Pentagon Papers: The Defence Department History of US Decision-Making on Vietnam, ('Senator Gravel Edition') (Beacon Press, Boston, 1971).

Pike, Douglas, *Viet Cong, the Organization and Techniques of the National Liberation Front of South Vietnam* (MIT Press, Cambridge, Massachusetts, 1966).

Pike, Douglas, *PAVN: People's Army of Vietnam* (Presido Press, Novato, 1986).

Pilger, John, *The Last Day* (Syndication International, London, 1975).

Porter, Gareth, ed. *Vietnam: The Definitive Documentation of Human Decisions* (Earl M. Coleman Enterprises, New York, 1979).

Porter, Gareth, ed. *Vietnam: A History In Documents* (Meridian, New York, 1981).

Race, J., *War Comes to Long An: Revolutionary Conflict in a Vietnamese Province* (University of California, Berkeley, 1972).

Salisbury, Harrison, *Vietnam Reconsidered* (Harper and Row, New York, 1985).

Sheehan, Neil,*A Bright Shining Lie: John Paul Vann and America in Vietnam* (Jonathan Cape, London, 1989).

Short, Anthony, *The Origins of the Vietnam War* (Longman, Harlow, 1989).

Smith, Ralph B., *Vietnam and the West* (Heinemann, London, 1968).

Smith, Ralph B., *An International History of the Vietnam War.* Vol. 1: *Revolution Versus Containment, 1955–61* (St. Martin's Press, London, 1983).

Snepp, Frank, *Decent Interval, an Insider's Account of Saigon's Indecent End* (Random House, New York, 1978).

Stevens, Robert Warren, *Vain Hopes, Grim Realities: The Economic Consequences of the Vietnam War* (New Viewpoints, New York, 1976).

Truong Nhu Tong, *Journal of a Viet Cong* (Cape, London, 1986).

Tuchman, Barbara W., *The March of Folly: From Troy to Vietnam* (Abacus, London, 1985).

Turley, W.S., *The Second Indo-China War: A Short Political and Military History* (Westview Press, Boulder, 1986).

Turner, Robert F., *Vietnamese Communism: Its Origins and Development* (Hoover Institution Press, Stanford, 1975).

Vo Nguyen Giap, *People's War, People's Army* (Praeger, New York, 1962).

B I B L I O G R A P H Y

Vo Nguyen Giap, *Unforgettable Days* (Foreign Language Publishing House, Hanoi, 1978).

Willenson, K., *The Bad War: An Oral History of the Vietnam War* (New American Library, New York, 1985).

Williams, William, Appleman, McCormick, Gardner, Lloyd and LaFeber, Suzanne, *America In Vietnam: A Documentary History* (Norton, New York, 1989).

Wright, Stephen, *Meditations In Green* (Abacus, London, 1985).

Southeast Asia and Indo-China

Burchett, Wilfred, *The China-Cambodia-Vietnam, Triangle* (Zed Press, London, 1981).

Cable, James, *The Geneva Conference of 1954 on Indo-China* (Macmillan, London, 1986).

Chanda, Nayan, *Brother Enemy: The War After The War* (Collier Books, New York, 1986).

Coedes, George, *The Making of South East Asia* (translated by H.M. Wright) (University of California Press, Los Angeles, 1966).

Evans, Grant and Rowley, Kelvin, *Red Brotherhood at War* (Verso, London, 1984).

Hall, D.G.E., *A History of South East Asia* (Fourth Edition) (Macmillan, London, 1981).

Joint Committee on Foreign Affairs and Defence *Power in Indo-China since 1975* (Australian Government Publishing Service, Canberra, 1981).

Keys, Charles F., *The Golden Peninsula: Culture and Adaptation in Mainland Southeast Asia* (Collier Macmillan, London, 1977).

O'Ballance, Edgar, *The Indo-China War 1945–54: A Study in Guerrilla Warfare* (Faber and Faber, London, 1964).

Pandey, B.N., *South and Southeast East Asia 1945–79: Problems and Policies* (Macmillan, London, 1980).

Poole, Peter A., *Eight Presidents and Indo-China* (Robert E. Krieger Publishing, New York, 1978).

Scholl-Latour, Peter, *Death in the Ricefields: Thirty Years of War in Indo-China* (Orbis Publishing, London, 1981).

Segal, Gerald, ed. *Political and Economic Encyclopedia of the Pacific* (Longman, Harlow, 1989).

Selected Journals

Asian Survey (Berkeley).

Bulletin of Concerned Asia Scholars (Colorado).

Economist (London).

Facts On File Weekly World News Digest (New York).

Far Eastern Economic Review (Hong Kong).

Far Eastern Economic Review Yearbook (Hong Kong).

Indo-China News (Cambridge, USA).

Journal of Southeast Asian Studies (Singapore).

Keesing's Record of World Events (Cambridge, UK).

CHINA

Cao Bang
Lao Cai
Lang Son
Dien Bien Phu
Hanoi
BURMA
Haiphong
Sam Neua
Gulf of
Tongkin
Luang Prabang
Sayaboury
L A O S
Vientiane
Nong Khai
Savannakhet
Da Nang
THAILAND
Pakse
V I E T N A M
Ampil
Aranyapratet
Battambang
Siem Reap
Qui Nhon
Pleiku
Stung
Treng
Pailin
Tonle
Sap
Mekong River
Samlaut
Kratie
Pursat
Snoul
CAMBODIA
SOUTH CHINA SEA
Gulf of
Siam
Phnom Penh
Cam Ranh
Takeo
Svay
Rieng
Tay Ninh
Kompong
Som
Kampot
Ho Chi Minh City
Can Tho

Miles
0   50   100   150
0   100   200   300
Kilometres

Indo-China (Vietnam, Laos, Cambodia)

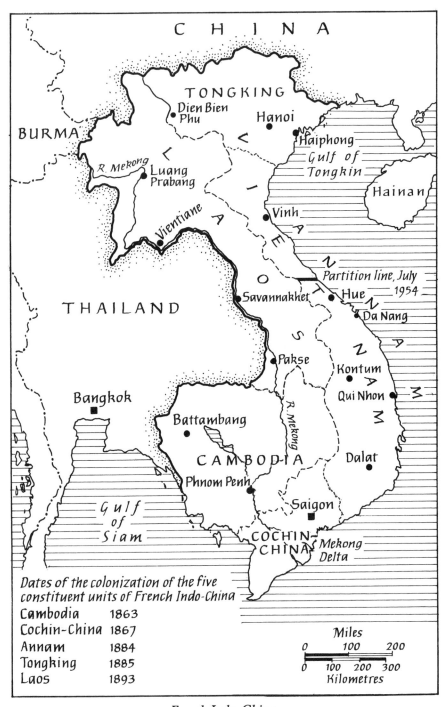

C H I N A

TONGKING

Dien Bien
Phu
Hanoi

BURMA

Haiphong
Gulf of
Tongkin

Hainan

R. Mekong
Luang
Prabang

Vinh

Vientiane

Partition line, July
1954

Savannakhet
Hue

THAILAND

Da Nang

Pakse

Kontum

Qui Nhon

Bangkok

Battambang

R. Mekong

Dalat

CAMBODIA

Phnom Penh

Saigon

Gulf
of
Siam

COCHIN-
CHINA
Mekong
Delta

Dates of the colonization of the five
constituent units of French Indo-China

Cambodia	1863
Cochin-China	1867
Annam	1884
Tongking	1885
Laos	1893

Miles
0   100   200
0   100   200   300
Kilometres

French Indo-China

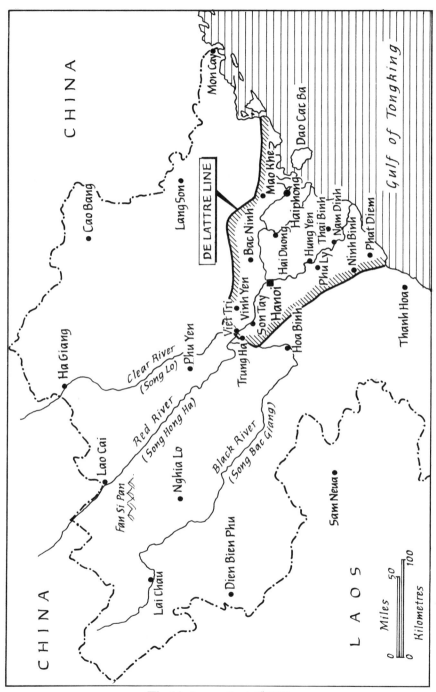

The 'de Lattre line' (1952)

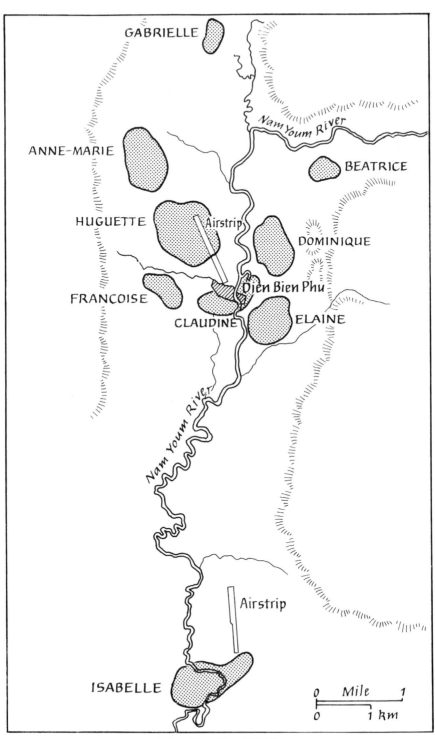

GABRIELLE

ANNE-MARIE

HUGUETTE   Airstrip

BEATRICE

DOMINIQUE

Nam Youm River

Dien Bien Phu

FRANCOISE

CLAUDINE   ELAINE

Nam Youm River

Airstrip

ISABELLE

0   Mile   1

0   1 km

Dien Bien Phu (1954)

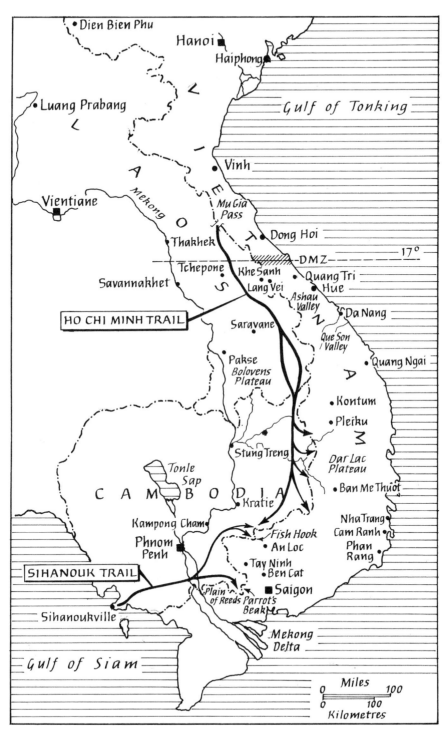

The 'Ho Chi Minh' and 'Sihanouk' trails

The Tet offensive (1968)

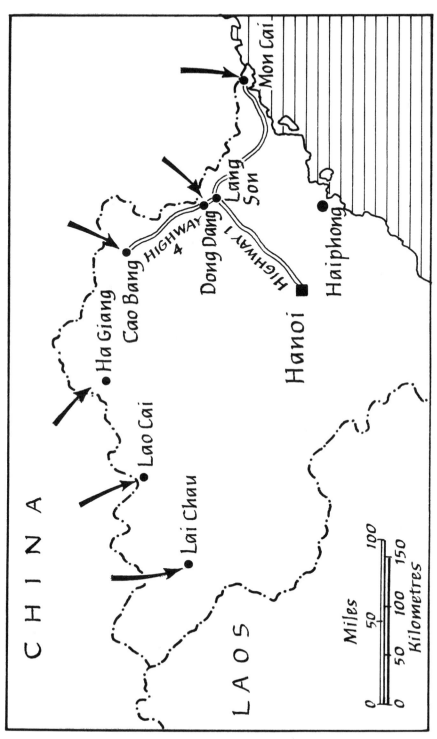

China's 'punitive' invasion of Vietnam (1979)

INDEX